W9-CFA-951

DISCARDED

Nashville
Public Library
Foundation

*This book
made possible
through generous gifts
to the
Nashville Public Library
Foundation Book Fund*

DECIPHERING CYBERSPACE

For Janice, my kindred spirit and companion who makes it all possible

DECIPHERING

CYBERSPACE

MAKING THE MOST OF
DIGITAL COMMUNICATION TECHNOLOGY

LEONARD SHYLES
VILLANOVA UNIVERSITY

SAGE Publications
International Educational and Professional Publisher
Thousand Oaks ▪ London ▪ New Delhi

Copyright © 2003 by Sage Publications, Inc.

All rights reserved. No part of this book may be reproduced or utilized in any form or by any means, electronic or mechanical, including photocopying, recording, or by any information storage and retrieval system, without permission in writing from the publisher.

For information:

Sage Publications, Inc.
2455 Teller Road
Thousand Oaks, California 91320
E-mail: order@sagepub.com

Sage Publications Ltd.
6 Bonhill Street
London EC2A 4PU
United Kingdom

Sage Publications India Pvt. Ltd.
M-32 Market
Greater Kailash I
New Delhi 110 048 India

Printed in the United States of America

Library of Congress Cataloging-in-Publication Data

Deciphering cyberspace : making the most of digital communication technology / Leonard Shyles, editor.
    p. cm.
Includes bibliographical references and index.
  ISBN 0-7619-2219-9 (cloth) -- ISBN 0-7619-2220-2 (pbk.)
  1. Telecommunication--History. 2. Cyberspace. 3. Information society. I. Shyles, Leonard, 1948-
  TK5102.2 .D43 2002
  303.48´33--dc21

                                        2002006992

02 03 04 05 10 9 8 7 6 5 4 3 2 1

Acquiring Editor:	Margaret H. Seawell
Editorial Assistant:	Alicia Carter
Production Editor:	Claudia A. Hoffman
Copy Editor:	Kate Peterson
Indexer:	Molly Hall
Cover Designer:	Ravi Balasuriya

CONTENTS

ACKNOWLEDGMENTS

I thank Villanova University for providing the atmosphere necessary for scholarly research to proceed. In particular, I wish to thank Father Kail Ellis, Dean of the College of Arts and Sciences, for supporting this project with his advice and guidance. I also thank the Department of Communication and especially my Chair, Terry Nance, for her support.

I thank my sponsoring editor at Sage Publications, Margaret Seawell, for her unyielding faith and advocacy for this project. Margaret is a writer's dream who inspires her authors to strive for the best. Thanks also go to Alicia Carter, editorial assistant at Sage, for shepherding the project to speedy completion with a sure hand.

I thank all the contributors, both authors and interviewees, who have made this book a great single volume on a complex topic: Mark Banschick, Josepha Silman Banschick, Dan Birenbaum, Charles Ehlin, Marvin Kane, Keith Lee, Janessa Light, JoAnn Magdoff, Rick Marx, Leigh Maxwell, Thomas McCain, Katherine Neikirk, Judy Pearson, Jeffrey Rubin, and Michael Young. All clearly and concisely contributed important insights on a breathtaking constellation of issues. I am truly blessed to have been able to work with such a great group.

I am fortunate to have done this project with such fine people, ethical actors whose word is their bond, who are great at what they do, and who are willing and able to share their expertise with the world. I consider them to be not just colleagues, but friends.

— Leonard Shyles

INTRODUCTION

This collection of new chapters by media experts, social psychologists, and legal scholars explores the current digital telecommunication revolution, of which the Internet is but a current manifestation. It is especially intended for upper-level undergraduates and graduate students studying mass communication, telecommunications, and digital media. The book presents a brief, clear, conceptual view of digital communication technology, assessing its nature and impact on individuals, institutions, and society on the threshold of the new millennium. To bring greater depth and perspective to a broad and diverse field, *Deciphering Cyberspace* also features interviews with industry engineers and leading practitioners.

This book is written with one main goal: to demystify digital communication technology. We present in simple language a three-element model that makes the subject of digital communication accessible. By examining digital media from the perspectives of *technology*, *markets*, and *policy*, we present a clear yet comprehensive view of the nature and impact of cyberspace.

Deciphering Cyberspace explains the physical nature of digital communication systems; the book also describes social, psychological, and legal aspects of digital media and telecommunication networks. Knowing how such systems work and what their impact is from multiple perspectives has the practical benefit of enabling you to make informed choices about which systems can best serve your individual and organizational needs. A guiding principle of the book, therefore, is that a sound conceptual grasp of the nature of digital media can help you keep connected in our increasingly mediated world.

In addition to mass media students, other audiences for this book include administrators and corporate executives wanting to know how digital systems can improve their business, novices considering adopting systems for work and play who want to learn more about how to assess a system before buying one, and those concerned about forfeiting their privacy to a new device who want to know how at risk they are for various abuses and what legal remedies are available to counter them. Still other audiences include parents wishing to protect their children from exposure to objectionable content.

■ TECHNOLOGY

Deciphering Cyberspace begins from the premise that all communication systems are composed of physical elements that enable them to function; therefore, to assess their capabilities, it is essential to understand the *technical* properties of such systems. Understanding the physical nature of digital media is critical in deciding which systems are best suited to your needs. Knowing how systems work rather than merely being able to operate a particular device that may become outdated in a year or two enables you to function more effectively in the new media environment. For this reason, the book explains the physical principles that govern the functioning of *all* digital communication systems, not merely those currently in use.

For example, music audiences can now download music from the Internet instead of using CDs, a prospect that did not even exist when digital CDs began replacing analog tape as the standard storage medium for music. However, to understand which systems are best for a given function, it is necessary to understand how their technical characteristics (storage capacity, signal quality, transmission, retrieval, dissemination capabilities, etc.) compare with one another. Knowing how systems work and their technical characteristics, and not just the procedures for operating a particular piece of equipment, is a central focus of the book.

The first three chapters, by Shyles, provide a comprehensive explanation of the physical nature of digital media. Chapter 1, "Radio and Television Broadcasting," explains how sounds, images, and other forms of electronic communication are converted into radio energy to be transmitted through space at the speed of light. The technologies used to accomplish this have undergone continuous development and refinement since 1900, but the principles on which they are based have remained a constant since the inception of broadcasting, and remain as critical to today's digital information technologies as they were to the transmission of Morse code via wireless telegraphy more than a century ago. It is therefore essential to understand broadcasting in order to know how current digital media work, for without radio energy, much of today's commerce in messages (i.e., cell phone conversations, digital video, and satellite communication) would be impossible.

Chapter 2, "Computers in Communication: Concepts and Application," explains from both conceptual and physical perspectives how computers enable users to create (*encode*), store, manipulate, and display (*decode*) electronically any kind of information, including data, text, images, and sound. First, on a conceptual level, the chapter explains the nature of binary code, and how any kind of information may be transformed into binary code, the only information format the modern digital computer can understand. Then, on a physical level, the chapter explains how integrated circuits, composed of millions of transistors acting as electronic switches, capture and store the code used to represent voice, text, and video information.

Chapter 3, "Sending Messages Across the Network," explains how digital information is transmitted, making message sharing among distant users possible. A central topic is *bandwidth*, or the capacity of a channel to move information from one place to another in a given period of time. Currently, the main conduit for such traffic is the public switched telephone network (PSTN), largely accessed through modems, including wire and cable technologies, and those using radio energy for wireless transmissions. Without the PSTN and similar (private) networks, e-mail and the Internet as we know them could not exist, leaving computer users isolated from one another.

The chapter covers technologies that transfer messages through wire and cable (copper, coaxial, and fiber optic), and through wireless facilities (terrestrial microwave and satellite transmitters). All are currently used in telephony and in broadcasting for voice, image, and data transmission. Rounding out the chapter are short descriptions of how telecommunication networks provide access to users through switching and signaling architectures, and how digitalization, packet switching, multiplexing, and signal compression all increase network capacity, enabling more efficient use of available bandwidth.

MARKETS ■

To succeed, new technologies that offer superior features to those already in use must appeal to potential users. They must come to be perceived as offering significant advantages over what they replace, and at an acceptable level of risk. As has been noted elsewhere:

> An engineer's opinion of a new device is secondary, perhaps even irrelevant, to whether the item will succeed in the marketplace. Doubters of this view need only recall past media inventions that offered improved programming but failed as consumer products: eight-track tape, quadraphonic stereo, and video laser disks, for example. Therefore, the most powerful computer, or any other program package or communication device, is not the one with the greatest fidelity, storage capacity, or speed of delivery, but *the one that people will use*. (Shyles, 1997, p. 6)

As stated, technical superiority alone cannot guarantee the success of new systems. In addition to possessing superior technical features over what they are intended to replace, new devices must also come to be perceived by various publics as able to meet their needs or fulfill their desires, and at a reasonable cost. Therefore, ergonomic, cognitive, affective, and emotional factors; social and economic factors; cultural and ethical norms; issues of taste; and compatibility with established values all affect the adoption of new innovations and the appeal of new products.

It is difficult to predict what impact perceptions will have on the adoption of a particular innovation by a social group, even after a device becomes available. To reduce risk, a new product may be developed in accordance with a research program designed to tap the wishes of the public for hints about the most promising directions to pursue. However, even in successful cases, devices may come to be used in ways never considered by the inventor or the marketing campaign; users often surprise designers by employing products in novel ways. For example, rap artists scratch vinyl records with phonograph needles to produce percussion effects for their music; new age architects use old tires filled with sand to build homes in the great Southwest that are remarkably efficient at withstanding heat. In these cases, products are clearly used in innovative ways unintended by their inventors.

It should be stated clearly at the outset that *Deciphering Cyberspace* does not use the term *markets* the way marketing professionals do. Whereas *marketing* refers more narrowly to research on a proposed product designed to build brand name awareness, or to test new products in order to develop promotions and advertising campaigns for them, this book uses the term *markets* more expansively. In this book, *markets* refer to the functions, uses, and gratifications of telecommunication systems for users on social, psychological, and practical levels. Digital media systems may be viewed in terms of the purposes to which they are put, as well as their social, psychological, and practical effects. Marketing professionals may therefore be interested in these chapters for the insight they provide about why users adopt some products and how they use them.

For example, in Chapter 4, "Children in Cyberspace," authors Mark R. Banschick and Josepha Silman Banschick offer an insightful and sweeping panorama of the impact of digital media on one of its largest and most devoted market segments: young people. Firmly grounded in the psychological theories of Piaget, Freud, Dewey, and Erikson, and working from the perspective of decades of clinical practice in child psychiatry, the authors advance a theory of *amplification* to account for unprecedented extremes made possible by the Internet, extremes that offer both benefits and risks to children and that increase the potential for good and productive work as well as for inappropriate and immoral endeavors. Say the authors: "The freedom and anonymity [of the Internet] offer a vast world of experimentation that can be liberating but can also promote unhealthiness." They explain how, on the one hand, the Internet helps shy users connect to others online, leading to a widening of the repertoire of social intercourse, while empowering pedophiles to exploit victims via chat rooms without even leaving home.

The chapter addresses three crucial aspects of child development affected by the Internet: intellectual growth and education, social influence, and identity and value formation, in the contexts of commercialism, intimacy, peer pressure, blurring generational boundaries, violence, independence and rebellion, work and play, social roles, and sexual and moral development. The chapter makes a much-needed contribution to theory on the effects of digital media on children by assessing the impact of the Internet on the social, psychological, cognitive, and emotional life of young people. It offers readers a perspective useful for understanding the impact of the Internet on one of its largest, most important, and involved audiences.

Chapter 5, "Social and Psychological Uses of the Internet," further explores the social and psychological functions of cyberspace. Authors JoAnn Magdoff and Jeffrey B. Rubin use their experience as psychotherapists (and several case studies) to explore ways the Internet affects our sense of mind, body, and self. They describe how different age groups use digital systems differently, and how users' worldviews condition such use. They describe how insinuating computers into the social world alters the cadence of human interaction, increasing social commerce and the achievement of desired goals among actors, sometimes in unforeseen ways. They use several case studies as a backdrop to articulate the concept of *emergence*, when "disparate units, people, ideas, and bits of code connect and link in unexpected ways that suddenly trigger many more . . . connections" that may have been wholly unanticipated. According to the authors, emergence affords users "the means to leap to novel levels of interaction" offering "unprecedented possibilities for the transformation of the self."

Two additional chapters on markets deal with the adoption and use of instructional technologies (IT), the first from the standpoint of teachers and students, and the second from an administrative perspective. For people operating in networked environments, including corporate, government, and nonprofit organizations, these chapters offer a wealth of insight and information about how organizations and individuals will likely be affected by the introduction of digital media.

In Chapter 6, "Connected Learning in the Information Age," authors Thomas A. McCain and Leigh Maxwell argue that new and emerging digital media are transforming education as no prior media innovation has done before. With pointed awareness, they warn of the importance of avoiding the hyperbole so often associated with past communication technologies that were once heralded with hope and promise, only to fail to win wide acceptance in the classroom. As an object lesson, they quote Thomas Edison's 1922 vision for the movies: "The motion picture is destined to revolutionize our educational system and in a few years it will supplant . . . the use of textbooks." They argue that the digital network is a true innovation, unlike previous candidates; their reasoning is the substance of their chapter.

They describe how digital media are already changing the very definition of such terms as *teacher*, *student*, *education*, and *learning*. In addition, the infrastructures being transformed by tools that make connected learning possible comprise all the elements of our educational institutions, including the physical trappings traditionally associated with schools (classrooms, books and journals, etc.) and the roles of individuals who work and study there.

The authors argue that the new arrangements created by digital telecommunication are increasing possibilities for education and a myriad of other human enterprises while reducing the space, time, and effort required for such pursuits. Among the features of the new media not available in past innovations, and that account for their success, are their two-way nature and their flexibility in providing both synchronous and asynchronous rapid access for multiple users in distant locations, qualities that afford users unprecedented interactive capacity, feedback, convenience, and efficiency. In addition, users can now access a wide range of applications covering a broad scope of subject matter, capabilities that all bode well for the future of digital media in distance learning, inside and outside of the traditional classroom. The impact of such media on organizational culture and their effect on traditional educational practices (lecturing vs. dialogue, conducting research, assessing knowledge claims) are also addressed, with fascinating implications for the future.

In Chapter 7, "Adopting Instructional Technologies," author Judy C. Pearson draws from her administrative experience to offer guidance to future supervisors faced with the challenge of adopting IT. Her advice and expertise are invaluable to corporate executives, nonprofit organization officers, and government agency managers.

Pearson presents a brief history of IT, including a description of the capabilities of digital systems currently available. She presents a rationale for the attraction of IT organizations to systems, outlining the potential for IT to control costs and improve efficiency in providing instruction to the work force. Pearson also considers the advantages of IT adoption in promoting democratization, leveling the playing field for users of diverse backgrounds. She also presents major criticisms.

Pearson is sensitive to both intended and unintended effects of IT adoption in the workplace. She advises maximizing workplace morale when IT systems are adopted, and she warns of the danger of failing to deal effectively with morale issues in securing successful integration of systems after capital investments have been made. Pearson is knowledgeable about and sensitive to IT's differential fit into different work environments, and the danger of yielding to political pressure in adopting systems that may not be suitable for a given setting. To achieve IT's promise, Pearson offers a clear set of principles based on her experience as an administrator useful to all charged with the job of adopting IT systems.

POLICY ■

The law can significantly affect the development and application of new technologies. Even in the most progressive, laissez-faire business environment, legislators must often regulate the way technology operates. Policy goals may include ensuring fair and equitable distribution of the benefits of new products to promote the general welfare and stimulate robust commerce in the marketplace. Of course, special interests may try to shape regulation solely for their benefit or profit. However, ideally, laws are enacted to maximize advantages for all interested parties.

For example, in the early days of radio, broadcasters who generally opposed government intervention requested federal controls when unregulated use of the airwaves led to chaos. Station owners had been increasing transmitter power to reach listeners at the expense of other broadcasters in the same area, a practice that resulted in jamming neighbor stations using the same frequencies. The bedlam that followed destroyed the system for all users. As a result, broadcasters requested federal regulation to restore the system.

In 1927, Congress created the Federal Radio Commission (FRC) to solve the problem. The FRC regulated the hours of operation for all radio stations and placed a ceiling on transmitter power. Thus, stations could once again reach their audiences, and broadcasting blossomed into a prodigiously profitable operation. In this case, regulation was viewed as clearly good for business.

Since that time, policy has not been restricted only to laws governing the physical nature of radio energy. The government has also enacted rules concerning military, economic, social, and cultural issues. For example, federal regulations created the Emergency Broadcast Service, placed limits on the number of stations that a single party could own (limits that have been relaxed over the years), made rules regarding advertising, and passed laws dealing with obscenity and indecency.

From the above, it is clear that the federal government has had a long history of regulating telecommunication interests. The Communications Act of 1934, creating the Federal Communications Commission (FCC), and the Telecommunications Act of 1996, opening competition among media and telecommunication interests, are two more recent examples of efforts by the federal government to shape the way media may serve the convenience, interest, and necessity of U.S. citizens. Thus, to decipher cyberspace, it is of critical importance to understand the relationship of law, regulation, and policy to technology development.

In Chapter 8, "Law and Regulation, Part I: Individual Interests," authors Keith Lee and Janessa Light grapple with the interpretation and application of existing mass media law regarding individual rights in light of digital technology development. The struggle to mold the existing regulatory structure to the Internet shows clearly that traditional legal principles do not always fit the new realities, sometimes requiring the creation of new laws.

Say the authors: "In this ever-shifting legal landscape of cyberspace, it is important for Internet users to be aware of their personal rights and remedies as they communicate over this new medium." The authors then embark on an analysis of freedom of expression in the application of the First Amendment to the Internet, including a discussion of indecent speech, the use of filters, and the case of child pornography. Discussion then moves to the topics of privacy, with specific reference to employee privacy in the workplace, the misappropriation of identity and identity theft, the use of *cookies*, and anonymous speech. They conclude with an exploration of the legal ramifications of intellectual property, specifically focusing on copyright violations in *linking* and *framing*, and copyright issues related to music and video piracy.

In Chapter 9, "Law and Regulation, Part II: Business Interests," authors Janessa Light and Katherine Neikirk tackle the topic of how the courts extend existing business regulation to fit the new digital technology manifested by the Internet. What are the legal issues companies and consumers should be aware of in transacting business over the Internet? How do the courts apply legal principles developed over centuries to digital systems that have only begun to emerge over the past decade?

As the authors make clear, this is not the first time that traditional legal principles have been applied to a new technology—the law has managed to deal with radio and television, technologies that the Founding Fathers never imagined. Light and Neikirk discuss the rights and remedies concerning a person's business interests in cyberspace, including trademarks in domain names, registration of domain names (including discussion of an area of the law called *cybersquatting*), and using trade names for navigation via *metatags* and *ad keying*. They discuss the Internet's impact on the field of personal jurisdiction and examine defamation law on the Internet with respect to liability, collection of damages for defamation, and defenses.

An objective of both of these chapters was to link explicitly, wherever possible, the legal principles used for judgments about cyberspace to the rationales used in prior cases concerning earlier media systems. By so doing, it is hoped that readers, lawyers and nonlawyers alike, will get a clearer picture of how some legal judgments are made and how regulatory frameworks develop.

THE INTERVIEWS ■

Five people contributed interviews for this book. They were chosen to offer their insights and perceptions from the perspectives of e-commerce and technology. Two are electronics engineers. Another, a computer programmer, is a mainframe expert. The remaining two are both working in e-commerce; one is a Web designer for other businesses; the other is a contributing editor to a dot.com company.

Each interview provides a unique view of how technology, markets, and policy interact to shape the business side of the digital telecommunication revolution. For readers interested in knowing more about the work-world across the digital landscape, these interviews will deepen your understanding of what it's like to be on the front lines.

To decipher cyberspace, it is necessary to understand the nexus of activity between technology, markets, and policy and how these forces interact to shape digital telecommunication. By presenting its subject matter from this perspective, *Deciphering Cyberspace* provides understanding of how digital media operate and what their effects are on individuals, organizations, and society. It makes the world of digital communication accessible, enabling you to make more rational, optimal, practical judgments about what it can do for you.

PART I

TECHNOLOGY

CHAPTER 1

RADIO AND TELEVISION BROADCASTING

Leonard Shyles

The Industrial Revolution in the mid-19th century moved America from an agrarian to an industrial economy. That historic shift affected all aspects of life. Inventions such as the steam engine, electric light, telephone, and automobile profoundly influenced the way we live and work, travel and socialize, make love and war, and otherwise entertain ourselves in public and private.

We now stand on the threshold of the 21st century, which brings with it a shift as profound as that of the Industrial Revolution—a *New Revolution* propels us from an industrial to an information age. One central and celebrated innovation responsible for this change is the computer, which has been affecting modern life in a myriad of ways as it transforms even those devices responsible for the last transition from an agrarian to an industrial world.

However, computers are not solely responsible. Long before computers became common to home and workplace, the telegraph, telephone, radio, television, and communication satellites, among other media marvels, put

AUTHOR'S NOTE: Portions of this chapter are reprinted with permission from *Video Production Handbook*, by Leonard Shyles, 1997, Boston: Houghton Mifflin.

people instantly in touch with one another around the globe. Working together, these devices make global communication possible; in combination, they enable us to encode, transmit, store, retrieve, and display information in the forms of data, text, live-action images, and high-fidelity sounds, often in real time, thereby enriching communication. In contrast, the computer by itself is little more than a data storage, retrieval, and processing device, utterly incapable of providing the communication functions we have come to expect from our media systems and networks.

This chapter explains the development and function of traditional broadcasting systems that have enabled us to communicate instantly across continents for more than a century. When these systems are linked with computers, the resulting infrastructure makes the Internet, e-mail, and streaming video possible. A spate of additional communication, information, and entertainment services as yet unimagined is not far behind.

But to understand what lies ahead, it is essential to understand how traditional broadcasting works, as well as computers and the telecommunication systems that form the backbone of our telephone network, including cellular and mobile services. I also discuss how broadcasting and digital technologies connect through the telecommunication network and ancillary systems to make the world of digital media possible.

■ BROADCASTING IN AMERICA

The desire to communicate from afar is part of human nature. Long before radio and television enabled us to broadcast sounds and images instantly around the globe, we invented less powerful means to send messages to distant places. For example, we invented the megaphone, which extends the reach of the human voice, but not greatly. Other methods of communicating long-distance have included beacons, semaphore flags, drums, smoke signals, and telegraphy.

What these systems share is that they all rely on prior agreements (or *codes*) between senders and receivers about what various signals will mean. For example, anyone who does not know the sounds or letters associated with flag positions in semaphore will not get the message even if the flags can be clearly seen. It is the code or pattern of intelligence conveyed by the flags, not the view of the flags themselves (the physical carrier), that makes it possible to convey messages. In short, clear reception of the carrier is a necessary but not a sufficient condition for successful transmission of meaning.

Successful communication relies on both unimpeded reception of a message's physical component and accurate decoding of the pattern of information (or *intelligence*) it contains. Of course, it is still possible to misinterpret messages after they are received, but cultural issues of meaning are not even considered until an encoded message is received and decoded.

The Significance of Code

How is intelligence carried in a message system? A common feature of communication is the need to *vary* some aspect of a signal in order to encode information. A pattern of some kind must be crafted into some physical form for a message to be generated, stored, transmitted, received, and consumed. And all patterns require some form of variation or change.

For example, the newspaper business uses paper and ink as physical means for carrying writing. These materials are part of the infrastructure of the newspaper business, along with delivery trucks, the postal system, cameras to shoot photos that appear in their pages, and so forth.

But the physical substances are not the message. In the newspaper, it is the language carried by the paper via writing that constitutes messages, not the paper and ink, which are mere carriers, able to store scribbles and gibberish as well as messages.

Similarly, the film and video industries use thin ribbons of celluloid treated with silver nitrate and/or Mylar coated with magnetic oxide to serve as carriers. These materials are but a few of the substances that form the infrastructures of these businesses, along with sets, props, lights, and so on. But again, the physical materials must be encoded with patterns corresponding to light and sound to convey meaning. Mylar and celluloid are mere carriers.

In summary, the symbolic content contained in a message is not the same as the substances used to carry it; rather, messages are in the variations or patterns carried by the physical materials delivered to receivers. As stated, a message's physical components are necessary but insufficient for communicating meanings between senders and receivers.

On a simpler level, consider again communication using semaphore flags. If the sender of semaphore flag signals fails to move the flags (no encoding), no message is sent even if the flags can be clearly seen. Similarly, in Morse code, if the telegrapher were to send nothing but dots at regular intervals, there would be no information to decode, since there is nothing in Morse code associated with an endless series of dots. In the technical language of radio and television broadcasting, the term for creating a pattern through variation is modulation. The term *modulation* is synonymous for imposing a pattern, change, or variation on a carrier.

Among the most pervasive, rapid, and successful systems ever developed for communicating at a distance are radio and television broadcasting. To explain the process of sending audio/visual messages via broadcasting, I first describe the physical nature of radio energy, which makes broadcasting possible, and then describe how audio signals and televised scenes are encoded, transmitted, received, and decoded. After describing traditional terrestrial broadcasting, I focus on significant developments over the past half century that have extended its reach and range, including satellite broadcasting and cable television, both of which have advanced traditional broadcasting without changing its analog nature. I also describe the more recent transition from analog to digital broadcasting, which will make possible an eventual shift to high-definition television. Beyond improved picture quality, the move from analog to digital platforms in video transmission promises a cornucopia of new video services that will increase television's potential for both producers and consumers.

■ THE BASICS OF ELECTROMAGNETIC RADIATION

Among the physical phenomena that make broadcasting possible is the propagation of radio waves, or electromagnetic radiation, through space. At the simplest level, rotating a loop of copper wire in a magnetic field generates radio energy. Such rotation induces an electric current in the wire. As the wire passes through each full rotation, the intensity and direction of the flow of electrons varies in an orderly manner called a sine wave (see Figure 1.1). Figure 1.1 indicates that sine waves produced by continuous rotation feature several characteristics, which, we will see later, are also present in sound and light waves. These include frequency (the number of cycles per second, or cps), period (the time it takes for one cycle to occur), amplitude (the magnitude of voltage at its greatest intensity), wavelength (the length of one cycle in meters), and phase (the difference between the same points on different waves). In a vacuum, radio waves travel at the speed of light, about 186,000 miles per second, or 300,000,000 meters per second.

Propagating Radio Waves

In 1819, the Danish scientist Hans Oersted, while experimenting with electrical effects of magnetic fields, discovered that magnetism and electricity were related. By 1831, Michael Faraday had discovered induction, the ability of an electric current in a wire to create a similar current in a nearby wire without physical contact between them. Based on Faraday's discovery, Joseph Henry developed the first efficient electromagnet.

In 1837, Samuel F. B. Morse used Henry's discoveries about electromagnets to patent a long-distance telegraph system using electrical signals to encode messages. This method was a significant improvement over optical telegraphy

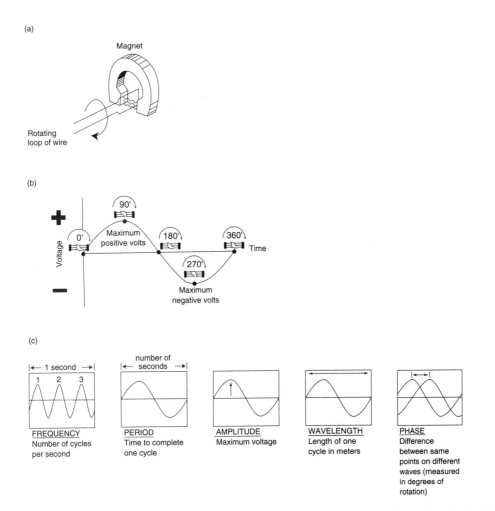

Figure 1.1   The basic sine wave of radio energy. (a) The wave is produced by a loop of wire rotating in a magnetic field. (b) One cycle of a sine wave, as the loop goes through a full (360 degrees) rotation. (c) Properties of a sine wave.

systems in use at the time, which depended on telescopes and clear weather to send messages. Morse's electrical telegraphy system was more powerful and reliable than the optical systems then in use. It worked under more varied weather conditions and could send messages farther, more quickly, and more reliably than its predecessors.

As electrical telegraphy developed, it was observed that some "leakage" of electricity from telegraph wires appeared to magnetize some nearby metallic objects. This phenomenon was explained in 1865 by the English physicist

James Clerk Maxwell, who presented evidence that electrical impulses emitted from wires traveled through space in a manner similar in form and speed to light waves. Maxwell called them electromagnetic waves.

Thomas Edison tried to capitalize on this leakage phenomenon to send telegrams to people aboard moving trains. Unfortunately, the waves sent into the atmosphere by the telegraph wires were a chaotic mixture of signals leaking from other wires in the area, making the patterned dots and dashes from any particular message unintelligible.

The problem of how to separate electromagnetic waves from one another was solved by the German scientist Heinrich Hertz. In 1887, Hertz demonstrated that an electromagnetic wave using an oscillating circuit could be propagated and detected amid other waves. An oscillating circuit produces an electric current that changes direction at a stable frequency. An example of an oscillating circuit (albeit a relatively slow one compared to radio frequencies) is that found in a typical American household electrical outlet, which supplies alternating current (AC) at 60 cycles per second. In honor of Hertz's discovery, the unit called a hertz (abbreviated Hz) was adopted in the 1960s as a synonym for "cycles per second."

It was soon confirmed that a radio wave, when propagated at a stable frequency, does not mix with waves of other frequencies. In 1895, the Italian scientist Guglielmo Marconi sent the first wireless telegraph message. These early wireless messages were in the form of Morse code, using the simplest modulation technique, namely, an interrupted continuous wave (ICW). In this method of radio modulation, a continuous, alternating current, made up of a succession of identical sine waves, is broken into a series of pulses corresponding to the dots and dashes of Morse code. This is done simply by opening and closing a circuit for relatively short or long periods in order to turn the radio wave on or off. Thus, radio energy was used for the first time as the physical material to carry a pattern of intelligence to encode information.

Although ICW is still widely used, it is limited in that it does not vary enough to carry sounds, such as music or speech. Eventually, advances in digital technology would make it possible to store enough pulses of information in binary code (patterns of 0s and 1s) to render sounds and/or images on CDs, videodiscs, and computers. In Marconi's day, however, further advances were needed to permit broadcasting of audio signals.

Converting Sound Into Electrical Energy

Alexander Graham Bell made possible the advance from Morse code to the sending of an electrical replica of the human voice (voice modulation). In 1876, Bell invented the telephone, which makes a current of electricity vary with changing sound waves generated by the human voice. The telephone transmits a pattern of electricity that faithfully matches a pattern of sound waves made by speech. How does this happen?

A telephone mouthpiece uses a microphone to convert sound waves (vibrations in the air) into a matching pattern of electric current. To do this, sound waves created by the voice are directed onto a thin metal diaphragm, which vibrates according to a pattern of sound waves imposed on it.

A metal diaphragm (typically a thin disk of aluminum) forms the top of a cylinder containing carbon particles that can conduct electricity. When sound waves enter the mouthpiece, they cause the aluminum to vibrate so that the carbon particles are rapidly squeezed and loosened. When electricity flows through the cylinder, the current increases and decreases as the carbon particles are squeezed and released. Loud sounds cause sound waves to press hard on the diaphragm, compressing the carbon particles tightly, making it easier for electric current to flow, thus increasing the amount of electricity passing through the circuit. When the sound is low, less pressure is exerted on the carbon particles, allowing them to remain more loosely packed and making it harder for current to pass, resulting in a smaller current.

In this way, the current passing through the circuit matches the pattern of sound waves striking the diaphragm. If it is a close match, an accurate replica, we call it high fidelity (*fidelity* means faithfulness to the original). This process of changing (modulating) sound waves into patterns of electricity is termed transduction, and the telephone is therefore a transducer.

At the receiving end, how is the electrical pattern transformed back into sound (demodulated)? The telephone is equipped with an earpiece that has a diaphragm that can freely vibrate in and out. In the center of the diaphragm is a coil of wire acting as an electromagnet. A permanent magnet surrounds the electromagnet, supplying a force against which the electromagnet pulls. As the incoming current varies in strength, so does the magnetic force of the electromagnet. Magnetic forces surrounding the diaphragm cause it to vibrate at the same rate, vibrating the surrounding air. The sound waves generated by this motion create a replica of the original sound. Figure 1.2 diagrams this process.

The encoding and decoding processes in microphones and loudspeakers work essentially the same way as in the telephone. Standard radio and television microphones, though, are sensitive to a fuller range of the audio spectrum and therefore have higher fidelity than those found in telephones. Likewise, radio and television speakers have more power and fidelity than telephone earpieces.

Modulating Radio Waves With Amplified Audio Signals

The telephone makes it possible to project an electrical version of the human voice through long distances over wires, and then to recover a replica

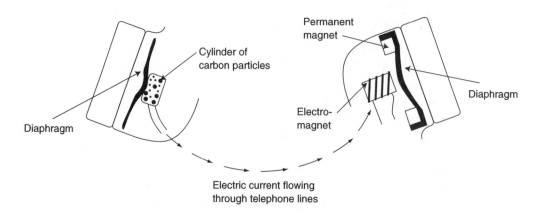

Mouthpiece (transmitter)   **Earpiece (receiver)**

Figure 1.2   Operation of the telephone, a simple transducer. Sound entering the mouthpiece vibrates a metal diaphragm atop a cylinder of carbon particles through which an electric current is passing. This vibration produces a pattern of electric current that replicates the pattern of the sound waves. At the receiver end, the incoming current creates variations in the strength of the earpiece's electromagnet, which causes the receiver diaphragm to vibrate, reproducing the original sound.

of the original sound from the transmitted electricity. It soon became possible to modulate radio waves in a similar way without wires. This change resulted from the work of two electrical engineers, England's Sir John Ambrose Fleming and America's Lee De Forest.

Attenuation and Amplification

Sound waves, like radio waves, naturally dissipate as they move farther away from their source. As distance increases, the strength of a wave decreases. This phenomenon is called attenuation. To picture this process, imagine the effect of dropping a stone into a pond of still water. The stone causes circular waves of water to move away from the point where it hits, and as the waves move outward, they weaken. At some distance, the original disturbance decreases (attenuates) to such a degree that the water remains undisturbed by the original splash.

In Fleming's day, it was already well known that electron motion produces current in a closed circuit. In the language of electrical theory, Fleming

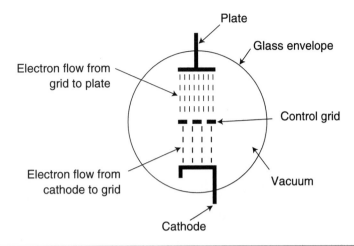

Figure 1.3   A triode vacuum tube solved the problem of amplifying radio signals. Small voltage changes on the control grid modify the electrical flow from the cathode to the plate.

knew that a voltage applied to a metal wire conducts electrons. What Fleming discovered, however, was that an electrode inside an evacuated heated filament lamp (a glass vacuum tube) could also conduct an electric current. Fleming noticed a one-directional current between the heated filament (called the cathode) and the positive electrode (known as an anode or plate). Because it contained two elements, Fleming called the device a diode.

De Forest extended Fleming's work by interposing a thin metal open-meshed grid between the heated filament and the anode. When a separate voltage was fed to the grid, De Forest could control the magnitude of electricity flowing from the cathode to the plate. With a grid, De Forest obtained a large voltage change at the plate from just a small voltage change on the grid. Thus, by introducing a third element to Fleming's diode, De Forest's triode made it possible to amplify weak radio signals received from distant radio transmitters. Figure 1.3 diagrams the triode vacuum tube, the original heart of radio amplifiers. Since the 1950s, successive generations of solid-state technologies (transistors, semiconductors, integrated circuits, and microprocessors) have replaced vacuum tubes, but the principles of amplification are the same in both tube and solid-state technologies.

Modulating the Carrier

By feeding an electrical signal converted from sound waves to the grid of a triode, relatively weak audio signals could be amplified enough to be used

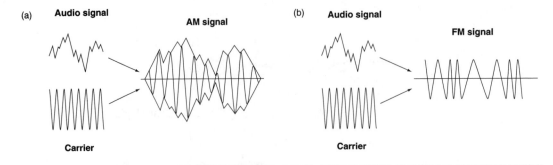

Figure 1.4 AM and FM signals. (a) In AM transmission, the audio signal modulates (varies) the amplitude of the carrier wave. (b) In FM transmission, the audio signal modulates the frequency of the carrier wave.

for radio transmissions. However, before sound waves could be transmitted to distant points without wires, the amplified audio signal had to be superimposed onto a radio frequency (RF) carrier. This is because sound waves are pressure waves and do not propagate across space at the speed of light like electromagnetic radio waves.

The RF carrier is created with an oscillator, an electronic circuit that produces a sine wave at a specific frequency. The RF carrier may then be modulated or made to vary by an audio signal (voice or other information) superimposed on it. In other words, the pattern imposed on the RF carrier is sound, converted into an electrical signal, supplied by a microphone or some other audio source (e.g., a CD or cassette tape).

The two most common techniques of modulating a radio wave are amplitude and frequency modulation. When an audio signal modulates the amplitude of a carrier, the process is called amplitude modulation (AM). When the audio signal modulates the frequency of a carrier, the process is called frequency modulation (FM). In AM radio, the carrier consists of a sine wave whose amplitude is made to copy the variations of an audio source. In FM radio, it is the frequency of the carrier wave that is changed by an audio source. Figure 1.4 illustrates these two common types of voice modulation in radio broadcasting.

As it turns out, FM modulation is superior to AM because it produces better fidelity with much higher noise immunity. For example, auto ignition noises and high-tension lines can cause hum and static on AM signals because those disturbances can adversely affect the amplitude of the received carrier. By contrast, FM signals are generally not affected by impulse noise from the atmosphere and human-made sources.

Transmitting the Carrier

Audio signals imposed on RF carriers may be further amplified. Finally, they are fed from a transmitter to an antenna for propagation. In standard AM transmission, the range of frequencies used for radio carriers is between 535 and 1705 kilohertz (abbreviated kHz, meaning thousands of hertz). Each channel is allocated a frequency range (or bandwidth) of 9 kHz to operate in. This means there is enough space in the radio spectrum allocated for 130 AM radio channels in any given area.

Roughly speaking, radio waves propagate in all directions unless they are intentionally altered from this pattern. The effective coverage area can radiate for miles surrounding the transmitting antenna, making it possible for millions of radio sets in a coverage area to receive a signal. However, because radio signals attenuate as distance increases, they must be amplified at the receiver to make them strong enough to drive a speaker.

Demodulating the Carrier

The function of a radio receiver is to tune into a particular frequency from among those available, detect the modulated carrier operating at that frequency, and remove the audio signal from the carrier. This part of the process is known as demodulation. The isolated audio signal is then amplified and directed to a speaker so that the original audio information can be heard. A block diagram of the demodulation process is presented in Figure 1.5.

FROM RADIO TO TELEVISION TRANSMISSION ■

So far, we have provided a basic model of how audio information is transmitted via radio energy to distant points and then recovered. But how does radio energy broadcast motion images? Some preliminary facts set the stage for an explanation of the process of video transmission.

Channel Space

In using radio energy to transmit sound plus full-motion images, a greater portion of the radio spectrum (bandwidth) is needed than for sound alone. This is because there is a lot more information present in motion images plus audio than in audio alone. The need for greater bandwidth to transmit greater amounts of information is analogous to a fire department using larger diameter hoses than those used by homeowners in their gardens to deliver a greater amount of water per given unit of time.

(a)

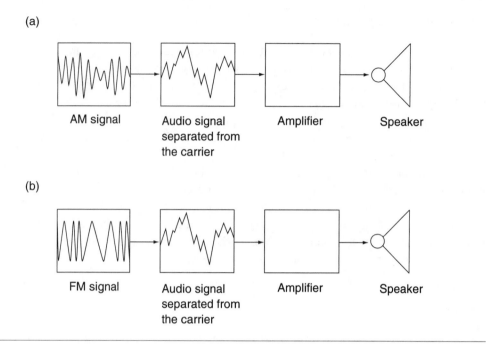

(b)

Figure 1.5   Demodulation of (a) AM signals and (b) FM signals.

To accommodate television's need for greater bandwidth, whereas American broadcasting allocates 9 kHz per channel for standard AM radio, television bandwidth is more than 660 times larger, or 6 MHz (6000 kHz) per video channel. This means that one television channel contains enough bandwidth to accommodate more than 600 AM radio stations.

Determining how much radio spectrum would be allocated for each television station was done after a great deal of technical debate and testing by the National Television System Committee (NTSC). The NTSC's first objective was to suggest technical standards that would permit an acceptable level of picture quality or resolution. With enough resolution, the video image would be clear, convincing, and aesthetically pleasing. However, the NTSC also wanted to conserve spectrum space, using no more than necessary for each channel assignment.

The NTSC rightly viewed the radio spectrum as a limited natural resource, which it continues to be today, even though technological developments have increased its usable range. In spite of these increases, the race for bandwidth by new technologies (satellites, cellular and mobile telephones, digital applications, etc.) is unrelenting, and this continues to make it essential to allocate its use wisely.

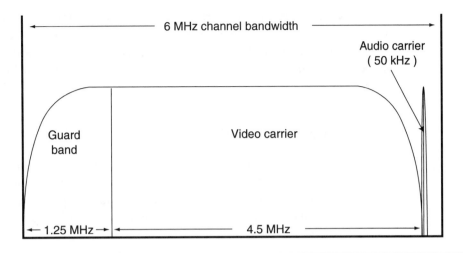

Figure 1.6 Audio and video portions of a standard 6-MHz television channel.

The job of the NTSC was tricky, because any increase in image detail requires a commensurate increase in bandwidth for each channel. Unfortunately, every increase in channel bandwidth reduces the total number of channels in a given portion of the spectrum.

As it turned out, the standard bandwidth for each television channel, adopted in 1941, was allocated to be 6 MHz. This allowed 4.5 MHz for the AM-modulated video signal, a complex video waveform (explained later) including synchronization, scanning, blanking, and eventually, color information. The remaining 1.5 MHz provided a guard band or buffer between adjacent channels operating in the same geographic area, to reduce interference, and space for transmitting the FM-modulated audio portion of the television signal. Figure 1.6 diagrams these original features of the television channel.

Over time, ancillary signals have been embedded into existing television channels to provide supplementary services (e.g., closed-captioning for the hearing impaired). In addition, further portions of the radio spectrum have been allocated to accommodate satellite transmissions, digital video, and a spate of data, text, and interactive services.

It is interesting to note that amplitude modulation is used for the video portion and frequency modulation for the audio portion of the television signal. This is because FM is less subject to noise and interference than AM, making it less subject to static, and therefore more suitable for audio reception. Furthermore, AM is better suited for video transmission because it exhibits fewer problems caused by multipath reception of the signal, which occurs when the same signal, because of reflections from obstacles such as buildings and bridges, reaches a receiving antenna from more than one path. Because the distance traveled by multipath signals is usually different, different parts of the signal arrive at the antenna at the same time. For AM signals, this causes less severe interference at the television receiver than would occur if the signals were FM.

Converting Light Into Electrical Energy

Just as telephone and radio technologies harness natural qualities of electricity and electromagnetic radiation to transmit voice-modulated audio signals, television relies on natural phenomena of photoelectric effects, including photo-conductivity and photo-emissive effect, to convert light into, and back from, electrical energy.

Photo-Conductivity

To change light into electricity, video depends on photo-conductivity, which occurs when light on some metals increases the flow of electricity in those metals. One of the earliest examples of photo-conductivity was observed in 1873 with the metal selenium. When selenium was used in an electrical circuit, the current through it increased during exposure to light. Unfortunately for video applications, selenium responds too slowly to light to be useful for replicating natural motions. But luckily, cesium silver and other silver-based materials are excellent for such applications.

Photo-Emissive Effect

In the photo-emissive effect, discovered by Hertz in 1887, visible light results from some materials' exposure to energy that may not be visible to the eye. Sources of such energy include streams of electrical energy or photons of higher-than-visible light energy, such as ultraviolet rays or X-rays. The photo-emissive effect is similar to that seen in radium dials once used to make watch faces glow in the dark.

In the picture tube of a television receiver, the inside of the screen is coated with fluorescent material. When a stream of electrons strikes the screen, it glows because of the photo-emissive effect. As the stream of electrons is made stronger, the portion of the screen struck by the electron stream glows more brightly. When the stream is made weaker, the glow decreases. If the stream can be modulated in accordance with the darker and brighter portions of a scene focused by the lens of a television camera, that scene can be rendered on the screen. If the re-creation process can be done quickly enough, then smooth motion can be rendered convincingly.

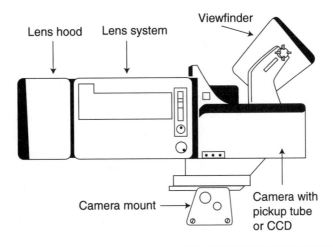

Figure 1.7   The most basic parts of a video camera.

In monochrome (black-and-white) television receivers, the fluorescent material needs only to be able to glow with a range of brightness roughly proportional to the intensity of the stream of electrons hitting it; color is of no consequence—only brightness variations are important. However, in color television, materials that glow with different colors when streams of electrons hit them must be used. To understand this process, let us begin with the major components of the monochrome television system.

Monochrome Video

Television cameras (Figure 1.7) use a lens system to focus light from a scene into a pickup tube or, in microprocessor systems, a charge-coupled device (CCD). The pickup tube or CCD is the place where light reflected from a scene is converted into an electrical signal. The output is then amplified and fed to external circuits for recording, routing to closed-circuit locations, broadcast from a transmitter, or transmission via cable or satellite to some distant point.

Within a studio complex featuring more than one camera, each camera is connected to a camera-control unit (CCU). The CCU enables a technician to adjust and match camera operation for all cameras to eliminate jarring differences in how they render the same scene. In a television studio, camera operators can immediately view the video signal routed to the viewfinder of each camera.

The Basics of Scanning

Transmitting all the details of a given picture simultaneously over the same circuit would lead to a chaotic mixing of signals in a single output, resulting in an unintelligible product similar to what jig-saw puzzles tend to look like when they are dumped from their boxes. Such visual chaos is analogous to what Edison faced when he tried to send intermixed wireless telegraph signals to receivers aboard moving trains.

To maintain the fidelity of the original image seen by the camera when it is received by a television set, small areas of the picture are converted into discrete magnitudes of electric current matching the brightness information present in each portion, and then each is sent out in order. This is done so each picture element (pixel) can be received and converted into light without being confused with any others.

In theory, we could create a separate circuit for each area of the screen and then send all of the information at once. But such a method is impractical because it would require hundreds of thousands of separate circuits for just one video channel of NTSC video (one for each pixel). Instead, a scanning method is used to transmit the brightness information for each pixel in turn. Scanning makes it possible to use just one circuit per channel.

The original monochrome video system converted picture information into electrical signals by focusing light onto a mosaic of pixels, each composed of an individual cesium silver globule. In such a system, when a scene to be televised was focused on the mosaic, electrons became stored in each pixel in magnitudes roughly proportional to the intensity of light focused on each one. Stored electrons were then instantly attracted by an anode in the camera tube, leaving the mosaic with a copy of the original scene in the form of varying amounts of electrical charge.

In American broadcasting, the mosaic is currently composed of 525 horizontal lines, containing about 211,000 pixels. An electron gun is used to scan each line from left to right, top to bottom, in an orderly fashion. As the electron beam passes each pixel, it replaces electrons lost to the anode, enabling the video signal to exist in an external circuit. This signal is then coupled to video amplifiers for immediate transmission.

Interlaced Scanning

The human visual system detects flicker, a source of severe eye fatigue, below about 45 image presentations per second. To defeat flicker problems, the film industry has adopted a standard film speed of 24 frames per second, each illuminated twice, for a rate of 48 presentations of picture information per second. For television, a system called interlaced scanning is used to avoid flicker problems (Figure 1.8).

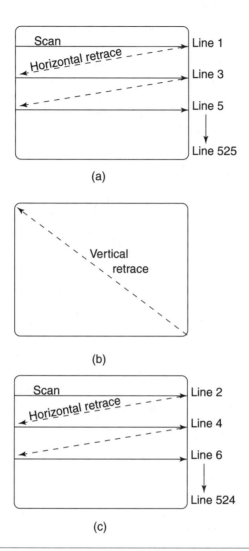

Figure 1.8   Interlaced scanning. (a) The electron beam scans the odd-numbered lines of the screen. (b) The beam then retraces vertically to the top left starting point. (c) Finally, the beam scans the even-numbered lines, completing the total 525-line frame.

Interlaced scanning takes advantage of persistence of vision or the tendency for an image to persist for a short period of time after a stimulus is no longer physically present to our eyes. In interlaced scanning, instead of having 525 successive sweeps of the screen, two separate scans of 262.5 lines are used. An electron beam alternately scans the odd numbered lines of the 525, and then the even numbered lines, thus creating the illusion of covering the entire field twice. This arrangement defeats the flicker problem, resulting for practical purposes in the appearance of smooth motion.

Each successive scan of 262.5 lines is called a field. Because line frequency (normal wall current, or AC power) in the United States is 60 Hz, it is convenient to scan each field in 1/60 of a second. As a result, 60 fields per second are televised, a rate fast enough to eliminate flicker. Each complete scan of all 525 lines, or two successive fields, is called a frame. Thus, 30 frames per second are televised.

Electromagnet coils surrounding a fixed cathode ray tube (CRT) inside the camera control the scan of the electron beam across each line. As the gun projects a stream of electrons at the tube face, varying magnetic forces generated within the coils bend it along its path. In this way, the camera performs its work without using any mechanical parts. This makes the scanning process extremely reliable.

Each time the beam finishes a line, it returns to the extreme left position, but shifted downward to the next odd or even line, to begin scanning again. This move back is called horizontal retrace. When the beam finishes scanning the last line, it returns to the top left position to begin the entire process over again. This move back is called vertical retrace. During each retrace, the electron beam is turned off in order to eliminate spurious illuminations. The signal to turn off the electron beam is called the blanking signal. The vertical blanking interval (VBI) and retrace signals, along with the synchronization information needed to keep the receiver precisely in step with the transmitter, are embedded in the overall television signal.

In reality, the VBI reduces picture detail, such that only 483 lines of the 525 transmitted are ultimately delivered with viewable picture information. However, it is during the VBI and in some other parts of the video signal that additional text and information services (e.g., closed-captioning) have found a home since the NTSC established technical standards for American television.

Receiver Operation

A television set receives video, audio, and all ancillary signals needed to replicate the original televised scene and audio information. It has a loudspeaker, a phosphor-coated picture tube, an electron gun, circuits for synchronization and scanning purposes, and currently, with increasing frequency, additional equipment for receiving specialized services (i.e., set-top boxes, translators, converters).

Regardless of tube size, the standard *aspect ratio* of tube height to width is three units by four units, respectively. As with the television camera, the neck of the picture tube is fitted with magnetic deflection coils that control the direction of an electron beam. The beam scans horizontal paths across the picture tube's phosphor coating.

When a television signal is received, the sound component (transmitted as FM) is routed to circuits where it is demodulated and sent to a loud-speaker. The video or AM portion of the signal is routed to the picture tube, where it directs the electron beam to emit electrons in amounts roughly in proportion to the brightness levels of the original scene. As the electron beam sweeps across the face of the picture tube, its varying intensities cause variations in the brightness of the phosphors, replicating the original scene.

To synchronize the video signal so that pixels can be reassembled without mixing them up, deflection coils around the neck of the picture tube are fed horizontal and vertical sync pulses from the original video signal. These pulses control the deflection of the electron beam across the screen, thus keeping the receiver in step with the original signal.

Color Transmission and Reception

Color television broadcasting began after the monochrome system was already in place and millions of black-and-white sets were in use. This made it desirable to find a color system compatible with monochrome technology (hence economic and marketing constraints were at work on even the most basic engineering decisions from the beginning). To make color television compatible with monochrome transmission, color information was added to the monochrome signal without changing the 6-MHz bandwidth set aside for each TV channel. In addition, both black-and-white and color receivers were made capable of receiving both monochrome and color signals. This meant transmission had to be virtually identical for both monochrome and color systems.

Chrominance, Luminance, and Saturation

To transmit chrominance (color or hue) information, the color camera's optical system separates the light entering it into three primary colors: red, blue, and green. It is a fortunate characteristic of human vision that virtually any color can be reproduced from these additive primary colors. Furthermore, any colored light can be specified with only two additional qualities: luminance or brightness, and saturation or vividness. Saturation can be thought of as the degree to which a color is free from impurities, such as dilution by white light. Low-saturation colors are paler, whereas highly saturated colors are more pure and vivid.

In early color cameras, light was broken into its primary color components using filters and a set of dichroic mirrors. A dichroic mirror passes light at one wavelength while reflecting light at other wavelengths. Today, most color cameras use a prism block called a beam splitter to break light into its primary colors.

Once the light has been split, the separate light beams are directed into three separate pickup tubes for processing into video signals. When a CCD microprocessor is used, a silicon lattice absorbs different wavelengths of light at different depths in order to distinguish colors. In either case, the patterns of electrical voltage generated in an external circuit match the levels of the original pattern of light received by the camera.

Some cameras use a single imaging element with a filter to separate incoming light into its component values. Others use filters to separate light into only two colors, and additional microprocessors to assign values to the third color needed to reproduce the colors the camera is seeing.

In color cameras, video signals from the three pickup tubes or the CCD are combined to produce a signal containing all of the picture information to be transmitted. Signals are combined using a phase-shifting technique so that they can be transmitted in one video channel and then retrieved without confusion. The overall signal contains the audio and picture information as well as blanking and synchronization pulses, and so on. This colorplexed video signal modulates the video carrier for transmission to receivers.

Black-and-white television sets treat the color portion of the video signal as if it were part of the intended monochrome transmission. To avoid degraded reception, the scanning motions are used to mask the chrominance signal. This way, any pixels brightened by interference during one line scan are made to darken by an equal amount on the next line scan. The net effect of chrominance signal interference over successive scans is thus virtually eliminated.

The tube in the color receiver contains three electron guns that project separate beams, which deflect simultaneously in the standard interlaced scanning pattern over the face of the picture tube. One of the guns projects the red color signal, one projects blue, and the third projects green.

The screen of the receiver is coated with phosphor dots that glow either red, blue, or green when struck by a stream of electrons. The phosphors are uniformly distributed over the face of the picture tube, arranged in adjacent groups of three dots that form tiny triangles, each containing a phosphor dot for each color. The dots are so small that a single one cannot be distinguished by the viewer's eye. The color of any one triangle is the additive function of the varying intensities with which each dot in the triangle is made to glow by the strength of the electron beam hitting it. Virtually any color may be rendered with this method. If electrons from all three guns strike their respective dots in a triangle with the right intensity, the color of that triangle will appear white. If no electrons strike a trio of dots in a triangle, the color of that triangle will be black. In this way, black and white images are possible on a color receiver.

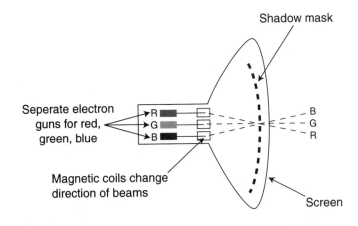

Figure 1.9   Diagram of the television receiver, showing how the shadow mask keeps the separate electron beams targeted at the proper points on the screen.

To ensure that the electron beams from the red, blue, and green guns hit only phosphor dots that glow red, blue, and green, respectively, a metal plate called a shadow mask is inserted close to the phosphor coating between the electron guns and screen (Figure 1.9). The plate is pierced with more than 200,000 holes and is positioned so that it masks two of the dots in each triangle from being hit by unwanted electrons. In this way, the electron beams are confined to the phosphor dots of the proper color.

Signal Transmission

Television signals may be propagated over the air from terrestrial antennas for distribution within local television markets, or they may be distributed across the country via telephone long lines using coaxial or fiber-optic cables. When such facilities are not available, convenient, or cost-effective, microwave relay links may be used to distribute television programs.

Sometimes microwave delivery is not feasible due to distance, power, terrain, or other limitations; in such cases video transmissions can be sent using satellite[1] uplinks. Since the mid-1980s, satellites have significantly extended the reach of television through the use of transponders, or orbiting microwave receiving/transmitting stations, to send live or taped video signals from the field to reception points over roughly a third of the earth's surface.

To use a satellite, a terrestrial transmitter (uplink) is aimed at a preassigned transponder aboard a satellite traveling in a geosynchronous orbit 22,300 miles above the earth's surface. A satellite's orbit is geosynchronous when the satellite stays above the same spot on the earth's surface throughout its orbit. The advantage of a geosynchronous orbit is that once a connection between a ground station and a transponder is made, no further adjustment is needed to maintain constant communication between them.

Aboard the satellite, microwave radio signals received by the transponder are converted to another frequency to avoid interference or jamming problems and then sent back to earth. Because signals from orbiting satellites come from more than 22,000 miles away, the coverage pattern, or footprint, as it is called, blankets about a third of the earth's surface. Because the coverage pattern from a satellite is so great, satellite communication is termed distance insensitive.

A virtually unlimited energy supply for the transmission systems aboard satellites is provided by solar cells. But not all satellite functions are powered this way. For example, over time, satellites tend to drift slightly from their geosynchronous positions. To correct for drift, periodic radio communication is used to tell on-board computers to fire some fine-adjust rockets. However, the rockets are powered by a finite supply of fuel, not by solar power. Hence, eventually the fuel runs out. When this happens, the satellite can become useless, and must be retrieved and refueled, or replaced. Even with this limitation, however, satellites can provide reliable service for decades.

■ THE EXPANDED VIDEO SYSTEM

Since the 1960s, the development and growth of microwave, cable, and satellite technologies have made live transmission and reception possible from almost any location on earth. The camcorder and desktop editor have put production capability into the hands of the audience. Videotape and recorders now enable receivers to store programs for later use, and permit audiences the luxury of watching programs repeatedly and at their convenience. Special effects and digital graphics machines permit virtually endless enhancement and manipulation of video images. High-quality audio and multiple speaker configurations offer stereo and surround sound for consumers' home entertainment systems. Interactive systems are enabling users to engage in dialogue with program providers and with one another. Projection and big-screen video have begun influencing the thinking of homebuilders to include entertainment theater space as a selling point in new homes. Even the remote control has changed the way we watch television, as well as influencing the way programmers think about how to capture and hold our attention.

Clearly, since the advent of television, technical innovation has made it more engaging than it was in its infancy. Yet the core of the system serving

American households in the 21st century still uses radio energy to transmit analog signals with the same technical standards instituted in the 1940s.

However, the picture is changing right before our eyes. We are witnessing a profound transition to a new set of technical standards featuring a shift from analog to digital platforms that will engender new forms of mediated communication services based on a convergence of television, telecommunication, and computer technologies.

What evolves will deliver an explosion of interactive information and entertainment services as yet unimagined to American households and beyond. The new system will make it possible for us to communicate with one another as never before, even originating our own programming if we wish. The age of interactive digital television (DTV) is upon us. What are some of the implications of this change?

The Adoption of a Digital Television Standard

On December 24, 1996, the Federal Communications Commission (FCC) announced[2] its decision to adopt a digital television standard for a free, universally available digital broadcast television service for America. Originally, the main goal of developing an advanced television system was to provide America with higher-quality video images, known as high-definition television (HDTV). However, rapid development of digital technologies has expanded the objectives of public interest groups, computer and television manufacturers, telecommunication providers, cable and satellite interests, filmmakers, broadcasters, and others interested in enhanced audio/video services.

Beyond HDTV, the dawning of the digital age now implies expanded applications to include movies on demand, telephone and computer data delivery, interactive programming, distance learning, paging systems, home shopping and e-commerce applications, and so on. Ironically, with all the possibilities created by the development of DTV, some experts have begun questioning whether HDTV will even be a part of the new system.

Understanding the public policy and economic interests behind DTV development is key to understanding the technical configuration of the new system. Among the goals of the FCC was to adopt a "world leading digital broadcast television technology" that would

1. put more video program choices into the hands of American consumers,

2. provide better-quality audio and video than that which is presently available with the current NTSC system,

3. provide innovative services due to data transmission capability, and

4. offer compatibility (interoperability) between video and computer technology to spur innovation and competition.

To achieve these goals, the FCC began inquiries in 1987 into the potential for advanced television (ATV) services. At that time, industry research teams suggested more than 20 systems. In February 1993, after determining that any system to be adopted would be fully digital, four such systems were considered. All were believed capable of becoming better with further development.

In May 1993, seven companies and institutions representing the four remaining systems formed a "grand alliance"[3] to develop a "best of the best" single system to present to the FCC for approval. Over the next two and a half years, a final digital system was developed, tested, documented, and recommended to the FCC. In December 1996, the system was approved.

The Advanced Television System Committee (ATSC), comprised of a 54-member group including television workers, television and film producers, trade associations, television and equipment manufacturers, and segments of the academic community, has endorsed the newly adopted DTV system as "the best digital broadcast television system in the world." The ATSC has characterized the system as having unmatched flexibility and ability to incorporate future improvements. However, some industry parties have voiced objections about having the government impose the standard. Some questioned whether it might be better to allow market forces to dictate standards rather than have the government intervene. Some suggested having the government issue standards only for spectrum allocation, transmission, and reception, to avoid interference problems, but to leave all other conditions (e.g., frame rates, number of scanning lines, aspect ratio of the screen) open.

Ultimately, the FCC decided that letting market forces determine standards would lead to the development of incompatible systems that would be too costly to consumers who might have to invest in several different receivers to gain access to different programs. Incompatible systems might also require the use of set-top boxes, translation devices, and other interface hardware and software that might slow down encoding, transmission, and decoding of data streams, thus degrading the efficiency of the entire system. In addition, the FCC reasoned that a government-mandated standard would be the best way to guarantee universal access to broadcasting services for all Americans. The FCC viewed broadcasting as unique, free, and available to nearly every American who relies on it as a primary source of information and entertainment. Because of these characteristics, the FCC reasoned that the goals of certainty and reliability take on a special significance and strengthen the case for adoption of a government-imposed DTV standard. Finally, the FCC reasoned that allowing different standards to develop might make the conversion process from the current analog system to a fully digital service more difficult. For these reasons, letting the market drive the selection of a standard was rejected.

To make the DTV standard as industry friendly as possible, the FCC invited standards to be developed by industry parties. In this way, it was believed the DTV system that developed would better reflect industry needs. For this reason, the standard is called "voluntary."

Characteristics of the New Standard

Like the NTSC television format, the new DTV standard calls for each television channel to occupy a 6-MHz bandwidth. To fit the more complex digital signal demands of DTV (at times with many times the picture resolution of the current NTSC format) into the same space used for current analog signals, digital compression techniques (described in more detail in the chapter on computers) are used. However, unlike the NTSC format that uses only interlaced scanning of 525 lines at 30 frames per second on a screen three units high by four units wide, DTV remains relatively flexible on these dimensions.

For example, to promote compatibility (interoperability) with other services including rerunning archives of NTSC programs, newer telecommunication and computer-based media, and film formats, the DTV standard can broadcast and receive both interlace-scanned programs and those produced in a new noninterlaced scanning format called progressive scanning. In progressive scanning, each line is scanned in order, with no skipping, at a maximum rate of 60 frames per second (double the current NTSC frame rate).

The new system will also accommodate the current NTSC horizontal line format as well as a newer format. Currently, the NTSC format is fixed at 525 lines of pixels distributed in a rectangular arrangement. In this design, the distance between pixels is greater horizontally than vertically. However, in the new system, a maximum of 1,080 horizontal lines of pixels will be featured in a square arrangement; that is, pixels will be equally spaced in horizontal and vertical directions. As a result, new receivers will be compatible with both NTSC format programs as well as many computer displays.

Furthermore, two new line formats are planned in the DTV standard, including one with 720 lines per frame and one with 1,080 lines per frame in a 16:9 aspect ratio of width to height. The 16:9 aspect ratio and square pixel arrangement mean that when 720 horizontal lines are being scanned (not counting those lost to blanking and retrace), 1,280 vertical lines of pixels are used, for a total of 921,600 pixels potentially contributing to the overall video image. Similarly, when 1,080 horizontal lines are used, 1,920 vertical lines of pixels are used, for a total of 2,073,600 pixels potentially contributing to the overall image. These numbers are five to ten times greater than those associated with the NTSC format, and help convey the added picture resolution that will be available from the new system. Several frame rates are also planned including 24, 30, and 60 frames per second, making DTV more compatible with film, NTSC video, and computers.

Finally, the 16:9 aspect ratio provided by DTV is more compatible with the format used in many films produced throughout the world and with flexible letter-boxing capability; presenting programs produced in aspect ratios different from the 16:9 format becomes easy. Letterboxing is a technique used to preserve the original aspect ratio of a film by blacking out portions of the screen, usually at the top and bottom. Film content is not cut from the frame. With letterboxing, the complete frame is transmitted, and no parts of the picture are left out.

In addition to these characteristics, new system capabilities include the following:

1. Layering of video and audio signals that enables multiplexing and transport of different programs simultaneously over the same channel. For example, layering makes it possible to broadcast two HDTV programs at the same time, or "multicast" (transmit multiple data streams) of several standard definition television (SDTV) programs at a visual quality better than that currently available. Current estimates claim that more than five such programs or dozens of CD-quality audio signals can be multicast simultaneously.

2. RF transmission.

3. Rapid delivery of large amounts of data (e.g., the contents of the daily newspaper could be sent in less than two seconds).

4. Capability for interactive transmission of educational materials.

5. Provision for universal closed-captioning for the deaf.

With all of these developments, it appears that DTV will continue to expand the power, pervasiveness, and influence of television. As new configurations continue to become available, it will become increasingly important for message makers and consumers to understand how new devices may be used to reach and influence audiences, and how audiences will use them for their own ends.

■ CONCLUSIONS

Satellite communication, cellular telephones, and microwave links carrying faxes, e-mails, and computer databases all depend on wireless transmission of modulated radio signals to connect distant users. Without these infrastructures, millions now on the wireless network would be isolated from one another. As long as we use radio energy to send data representing sounds and images across space at the speed of light, it will be necessary to know how broadcasting works in order to have a full understanding of digital telecommunication. Understanding how broadcasting systems operate is one of the essentials.

NOTES ■

1. Since the 1960s, satellite technology has increasingly supplemented our telecommunications network. The appendix contains a spectrum allocation chart and lists some parts of the radio spectrum allocated for various satellite services.

2. See Federal Communications Commission Fourth Report and Order, *Advanced Television Systems and Their Impact Upon the Existing Television Broadcast Service*; M. M. Docket No. 87-268 (December 24, 1996). This document was originally retrieved from the World Wide Web at www.fcc.gov.

3. The members were AT&T, General Instrument Corporation, Massachusetts Institute of Technology, Philips Electronics North America Corporation, Thomson Consumer Electronics, the David Sarnoff Research Center, and Zenith Electronics Corporation.

CYBERINTERVIEW

Michael Young

On May 26, 2001, I spoke with Michael Young, chief technology officer, president, and founder of Young Design Inc. of McLean, Virginia, now referred to as YDI (on the Web at ydi.com). Young, trained as an electronics engineer, came to the world of cyberspace and e-commerce with more than two decades of experience in radio engineering. His expertise in digital telecommunication is in both hardware and software design of wireless Internet technology for industrial applications. As the entrepreneur-owner of YDI, he is a corporate manager as well as technical wizard of new custom-designed systems for his clients. His insights are therefore from the perspectives of both business and technology.

Shyles: Please relate to my readers a short bio. You were born and raised where?

Young: Staten Island, New York. I went to school at Monsignor Farrell High School, in Staten Island, then to Polytechnic Institute of Brooklyn where I got my degree in electrical engineering in 1973. In 1975, I got my master's degree in radio and television broadcasting from Brooklyn College, where I was an intern for two years. Then I was in the Army for almost four years, in the Signal Corps, stationed in the Pentagon working for the U.S. Army Audio-Visual activity.

S: And you've always been a radio hobbyist.

Y: Yes and a ham radio operator since my sophomore year of high school.

S: Briefly, what got you interested in radio?

Y: My grandfather influenced me. He was my champion. He was interested in radio and had a short-wave radio receiver and he saw my interest. I remember him taking me to the local electronics store and he bought me an AM radio kit. I put it together. I think I was in third grade. He was a retired insurance salesman. In the 1920s, he was involved with radio when it first came out. He would tell me stories, like one about that big prizefight with Jack Dempsey in the 1920s. His father listened to the radio and heard who had won the fight. It was over after the first round. So my great-grandfather went to the barbershop and said, "Oh how do you like that knock-out in the first round?" And everybody in the barbershop asked, "How do you know that? The fight is just starting. We won't know till tomorrow when the papers come out." And he answered, "Oh my son has this thing called radio and they broadcast the fight and I know it already." I would go over to his house and we would build things together. So my grandfather was the one that sort of nudged me along. And by the time I was in seventh grade, I got involved with walkie-talkies and CB radio, talking without wires. I thought that was really it! I remember being in seventh grade, opening up an old tape recorder, sitting it on the workbench, and looking inside. I didn't know what it all was, but I saw wires, electronic components, and glowing tubes. Now I know they were capacitors and resistors and other things. I remember looking at all of the wires and connections and thinking, "How does that work? All those electrons running around and out comes this sound that I recorded!" I was fascinated by it and I made it my business to learn all about it and I did. That was the mid-1960s.

S: Bring us up to date from when you left the Army.

Y: While on active duty in the Signal Corps, I was a producer/director for the U.S. Army Audio-Visual activity in the Pentagon. I kept my hands in electronics by working on projects at home, building amateur radio repeater stations. I didn't do anything professionally until I got out of the Army and I met up with a fellow ham operator. We started a business back in Staten Island called Buttonwood Communication. In 1979, we applied our amateur radio-telephone technology using walkie-talkies with small headsets to allow brokers on the trading floor of the New York Stock Exchange to place orders or take orders from upstairs without having to go back to their booth. They could be in the middle of the trading crowd, and be phone-connected to their office while still on the trading floor. Such an application was unheard of back in 1980. Cordless phones and cell phones didn't even exist. But I had this technology since the early 1970s because we were doing it on amateur radio. Nobody even had cell phones back then, but my ham buddies and I all had phone connections in our cars.

S: So you were using ham radio frequencies at the Stock Exchange?

Y: No. We were using commercial two-way radio frequencies at the Stock Exchange. I had developed a method of using those frequencies on the trading floor by focusing the signal and using weak power.

S: . . . with a directional antenna?

Y: Several actually, carefully placed to cover the three trading floors of the exchange. As a matter of fact, we applied for and got a patent on that technology. We deployed an eight-unit system. It worked great. But when we went and gave the Stock Exchange the price tag, they said that it would be too expensive and that was the end of it.

S: So, from a technical standpoint, did your system operate such that if there were X number of traders on the floor, then you had to have X number of transmitters and X number of antennas?

Y: No. We had a multichannel base station antenna system that shared antennas. It could support many channels.

S: So that really is like cellular phone.

Y: Yeah, but it wasn't cellular because cellular reuses the frequencies over and over again. In our system, a broker would be on one channel and operate on it from anywhere on the trading floor. But we could only use a few hundred channels due to Federal Communications Commission (FCC) rules.

S: There was a regulatory limit on the technology.

Y: Yes. The fact that we only had a few hundred channels was a regulatory imposition. If we needed more channels than that, I would not have known what to do. We'd have had to petition the commission for more spectrum somewhere.

S: As a businessman, do you feel the regulatory environment influencing your business decisions and what technologies you decide to build?

Y: Absolutely. Regulatory policy ultimately determines what equipment gets made and what frequency it operates on. In addition to spectrum assignment issues, transmitter power, occupied bandwidths, and many other technical parameters are controlled by regulations. We are significantly constrained by regulation. In fact, in a strong sense, the market is driven by regulations. Regulations say, "You can do this," and once a regulation is put in place, then we see how we can make equipment to sell. Today, spectrum space available for wireless communication drives the industry. When new technologies come out, the manufacturers pound on the FCC to release or reallocate spectrum. And sometimes technology and industry interests drive policy. A good example of that is the personal communication service (PCS) band, which is where cellular telephones operate. When spread-spectrum technologies came out, industry pressured the FCC to break some more radio frequencies loose. They demonstrated that spread-spectrum techniques could get better range than the 800-MHz analog systems without needing external car antennas. The result was the 1.6- to 1.8-GHz PCS band. These frequencies weren't originally allocated for that. But the technology made it possible for people to carry much smaller devices. Now you can buy cell phones at the local convenience stores.

S: That's a good example. How about a case where the technology is feasible, you get compliance from the law, and you still have a failure?

Y: Yes, the IVDS spectrum on 218 MHz is a good example. IVDS stands for interactive video data service. Several years ago, a start-up company out in Herndon, Virginia, wanted some VHF spectrum that didn't require a line-of-sight to offer a two-way interactive TV. They wanted to use radio channels to send signals from a set-top box back to a base site to allow interactive video for users, including keyboard strokes or mouse clicks. This was not high-speed data, just low-speed text. So they lobbied the FCC, and the commission found some VHF frequency spectrum that wasn't really being used: 218 to 219 MHz. They pressured the FCC for authorization to use it for the IVDS. Another company wanted to use it primarily for the link from the set-top box back to the base. Data to the box would come to the set-top box using the vertical blanking interval on a TV channel. From a technical perspective, everything worked, yet IVDS was an abysmal failure. And my company lost lots of money because of it. Sometimes the technology would work like a charm (as in my wireless equipment), but for marketing, business reasons, mismanagement, price, or other issues, the project fails. Not one, but two IVDS companies went out of business before they paid all their bills, and wound up owing us a lot of money. That's one reason technology development is such a struggle. Interactive television is a recent example of a feasible technology that failed in the marketplace. Is there any interactive TV out there?

S: I don't see it.

Y: And the promise of IVDS was interactive video without cable. All you needed was a broadcast antenna or rabbit ears, and you could have an interactive TV.

S: Sounds perfect.

Y: You would think so. The investors did.

S: And it's on the old broadcasting model of over-the-air television.

Y: Right. It needs no cable.

S: But you have to buy a set-top box.

Y: Yes. And there's the rub. Someone has to make that investment. And it turns out that in order to get the set-top box to do everything you need it to do, it is cost-prohibitive at a few hundred dollars per box. And nobody wants to spend that kind of money on a TV set-top box. In 1996, we made a transmitter that fit in an interactive set-top box that used an IVDS radio channel to talk back to the central base site, and it worked. What was lacking was the content and programming to induce consumers to want to have it. Why buy it? The only reason is to see desirable programming not available with other techniques. And there's the rub. That's a marketing issue; that, plus the price of the equipment.

S: In other words, without programming there is nothing there to induce a purchase.

Y: That's correct.

S: So the old adage "Build it and they will come" is not always true.

Y: Right. But sometimes it is. For example, PCS is a hot market. People want cell phones, and it's a wildly successful product, with millions of subscribers.

S: Because people want to call home from the beach, airport, or wherever without having to use a pay phone.

Y: That's correct. It's a convenience issue. The cellular companies took a big risk to put a multi-billion-dollar infrastructure in place. But once it was set up, consumers came; they came in droves. Now cell phone companies are beginning to give cell phones away virtually for free because they know the payback could be a hundred times their cost for it in subscriber fees.

S: As an engineer, what distinguishes the way the world works today in media systems from the way the world was 20 years ago?

Y: You could say it in one word: *bandwidth*. Bandwidth is a measure of a medium's ability to transmit information (virtually all digital these days) from one point to another in a given amount of time. In other words, bandwidth is the amount of information, usually in the form of data in bits per second, a channel can pass. The bandwidth infrastructure as it is today simply did not exist 20 years ago in 1980. when almost everything was analog: two-way radios, phone lines, long-distance microwave links, TV and radio signals. By contrast, today, with development of high-speed digital networks, we now can deliver lots of data. So it is the flexible use of bandwidth that is making the difference. For example, 20 years ago, the fastest dial-up modem was only 300 bps (bits per second). This was fine for just typing keystrokes. Forget about graphics. Then things began to change. By 1984, dial-up modem speeds were up to 2,400 bps. At that time, I was a consultant for a modem manufacturer when they released their first 2,400-bps modem, and I remember asking the marketing director: "Will people be willing to pay over $1,000 for this modem? Do they really need all this speed?" Then modem speeds made quantum leaps about every 18 months from 9,600 to 14.4k to 28.8k to the current V90 standard of 56 kbps. But current FCC regulations prohibit dial-up connections faster than about 50 kbps. So while the modem could talk at 56 kbps, firmware in the device keeps the actual connection rate in the low 50 kbps.

S: Another example of regulation holding back technology.

Y: Correct. If the FCC ever eases this restriction, you will be able to upgrade your modem to true 56 kbps. But these are still analog signals. Today we can deliver much higher bandwidths digitally. The PC in my home receives Internet data at 500 kbps using DSL (a digital subscriber line). What has happened is that companies have taken old phone lines built in the 19th century, namely, twisted-pair copper wire designed for voice, and figured a way, by using special digital signal processing chips, to use those wires to carry more and different types of digital data, without changing the wires in the streets. So with DSL we can get several hundred kbps on existing wires without altering the existing phone lines by using a DSL modem at the client end and a DSL modem at the telcos' (telephone companies') central offices, which is easy to do compared to running new cable. Cable TV has become another means to deliver high-speed digital signals. When the cable industry began, some had the vision of doing two-way cable, but they didn't implement it. It was too expensive. However, new cable TV systems deployed today need to be two-way from the start. That is now mandated by regulations.

S: You mean two-way signals on the same cable?

Y: Yes, using different frequency bands for the up and down links.

S: There are some technologies that require a wire in one direction and a separate conduit the other way.

Y: That's correct. An example of this is digital T-1 lines. They have one pair of wires for transmission and one line for reception.

S: And the amplifiers have to go in one direction.

Y: Right. They are equipped with one-way amps, called repeaters, on each line. But cable TV systems have only one coax cable (or a pair of cables for dual-cable systems) since they originally were intended for one-way broadcast of TV channels. To make it two-way on the same cable they have to take all the one-way amplifiers and replace them with more expensive amplifiers to split the bands up, with low-frequency bands going in one direction to the head-end and high-frequency bands going to the customers. This needs to be done to make it a full duplex system on a signal cable. Since those amplifiers are all over the cable system, it is an expensive proposition to install or replace them.

S: What about T-1 lines for telecommunication?

Y: T-1 lines came out in the 1960s for point-to-point links. Each carries 24 digitized voice channels plus control signals. Since they are digital and a large T-1 infrastructure was in place, they were adopted to carry Internet and other data. But we digress. Let's focus again on the digital dimension of the changes of the last 20 years. Unlike the analog era, we have progressed to a stage where we can now use the bandwidth of one 6-MHz TV channel to send information of various kinds at a rate of 20 megabits per second.

S: Which equals three digitized analog TV signals.

Y: Correct. Truth be told, 6 MHz of the radio spectrum allocated for each analog television channel is wasteful today. From the perspective of digital platforms, this turns out to be an extremely inefficient use of those 6 MHz. It was great in 1950, but not so good in 2000. Nowadays, with digital capability, we have the technology to make better use of that bandwidth. Back in the 1950s, vacuum tubes were commonplace, so we couldn't digitize, compress, pack data, and employ sophisticated modulation techniques on our signals. In fact, from the beginning of broadcasting up through the 1980s virtually everything was analog, and bandwidth was an inflexible channel space that was allocated for distinct purposes with no versatility—essentially each channel was dedicated to one function. But now we have a highly varied multi-media Internet connection with pictures, graphics, music files, and high-speed downline and high-speed upline communication capability.

S: Yes, but anyone who uses the Internet on even rare occasions knows that streaming video is nowhere near the quality of an analog 6-MHz conventional television signal even in the year 2001.

Y: That is correct. And the reason for that is limited bandwidth. In order to deliver a good video picture you need to dedicate about 2 megabits per second of digital data flowing in your direction.

S: When are people going to have that?

Y: Probably not until that "final mile" infrastructure is upgraded to handle it. This will occur with the proliferation of fiber-optic cables especially when they finally reach the average household. But that is a decade or two away at least. Right now the only access for small businesses and consumers are

- Dial-up modems at about 50 kbps.
- DSL lines at 300 kbps to 800 kbps typically.
- Cable TV modems at around 500 kbps.
- Pricey satellite links.
- MMDS (multichannel multipoint distribution service) in certain select cities. This is the 2.5G-Hz-licensed band. MCI/Sprint own 80% of these licenses. Speeds up to 1 Mbps are possible over such channels.
- License-free spread spectrum on the 2.4-GHz band. Data rates in excess of 3 Mbps are possible here.

As far as high-speed Internet access in the United States, there are about 4.7 million cable Internet users, 2.2 million DSL subscribers,

100,000 satellite subscribers, and maybe 50,000 Internet customers currently using the license-free bands. Larger businesses typically demand dedicated bandwidth and usually get a T-1 or fractional T-1 line from their building to the phone company's central office. From there it gets switched to an ISP (Internet service provider), which could also be the same phone company. There are also DS3 lines that are 45 Mbps and fiber-optic OC3 lines that are 155 Mbps. Typically, only larger ISPs and huge companies get fiber-optic cables. They need it and they can afford it. My company, YDI, is filling that gap in the meantime with a higher-speed alternative. We sell equipment that offers high-speed wireless Internet access in license-free radio frequencies, specifically in the 2.4- and 5.8-GHz bands. Typical client speeds with burstable data can be up to 3 or 4 Mbps with affordable equipment. Point-to-point microwave links with more expensive equipment will soon offer 100-Mbps full-duplex links—all on license-free bands. Our typical customer is a local or regional ISP looking to offer high-speed Internet service but who cannot (or will not) use DSL through the local phone company's phone lines. The systems we provide will enable such customers to offer broadband Internet access without the need to use the telephone lines that are owned and controlled by the local phone company. The key to this successful development is that they can operate through the use of spread-spectrum radios. When used with our pole-mounted amplifiers, long ranges (up to 30 miles) can be achieved. The only rub is there must be unobstructed line-of-sight between the base and remote antennas. No trees. No buildings. The antennas must see each other. While this is a significant limitation, especially in areas with tall trees, it is still a positive development. We tell our ISP customers (who we call WISPs for wireless ISP) to look at the areas they can cover and forget about those blocked by obstacles, at least when they start. Later on, they can look at setting up other base stations to start filling in the coverage areas. We call these base stations WIPOPs. That stands for wireless Internet points of presence. Spread-spectrum method is extremely complicated, but they've got it down to a science now, using low-cost DSP (digital signal processing) chips that do all the complicated coding and decoding. These didn't exist 20 years ago. When DSP chips came out in the mid-1980s, they cost several hundred dollars. Now you get them for a few bucks and they're more powerful and draw less power than they once did.

S: How many transistors are on such a chip?

Y: Typically millions.

S: Will that kind of method of handling signals be used for the Internet in your view?

Y: The DSP chips I am talking about generally deal with modulating and demodulating signals on the physical level with many potential applications. The Internet is its own animal all by itself which must be considered apart from everything else. You can't categorize it because it's a series of routers linked to high-speed connectors that nobody owns. The most amazing thing about it is that it's more ubiquitous and decentralized than the airwaves. For example, in Washington, D.C., I can say WJLA is assigned channel 7 and can operate on this chunk of airwaves in this area. But the Internet doesn't fit into any prior model. People have put up Internet routers everywhere. They get high-speed data connections to those routers and just blindly pass traffic that fits the protocol without any filtering and there's no regulation on it. Nobody owns it and it's worldwide. It's the spider that creeps everywhere.

S: So who sets up the routers around here?

Y: All Internet service providers have routers connected to the Internet. These routers connect to super routers at nearby metropolitan area exchanges. These exchanges (called MAEs) have very big pipes (meaning very high capacity data connections) to the other MAEs. Remote areas of the world that are not connected by fiber or cable get Internet access through satellite links. They relay data back through the MAEs.

S: You've been an engineer for over 25 years. Could you have predicted the emergence of the Internet?

Y: No one could have. Originally, its purpose was to form a network of computers that could share information. The U.S. government set up a protocol for sending information back and forth, including e-mail, without having to make a phone call; it would be always online. The infrastructure grew from there. But it was not until the late 1980s that long-distance data networks began to surpass the data rate. Then in the 1990s, fiber-optic technology really took off, with no regulation really governing it. But optical fiber has yet to be installed in that "final mile" connection from local exchange offices to households. You still need your local phone or cable company to give you some kind of data connection, unless, of course, your local ISP was using a satellite or a license-free wireless solution. But nobody controls what goes on the Net. The access service provider does not control what you type on your keyboard. Neither does your typical ISP.

S: Whom are you paying when you buy your Internet connection?

Y: You pay the ISP and the local phone company or cable provider if you are using their cables. They, in turn, purchase Internet bandwidth from wholesale Internet providers such as UUNet, Qwest,

Sprint, MCI, and so on. And these guys have the "big pipe" backbone connecting super routers together.

S: Didn't AT&T and the Bell System have a monopoly on all these long-distance connections?

Y: Yes, until the early 1970s when MCI came out with its plan for an alternative long-distance connection. They went to the FCC and said, "We want to set up microwave radio stations point-to-point between New York and Washington for phone traffic." AT&T fought hard to disallow it. And they lost. So MCI set up its own backbone parallel to AT&T's long-lines and that opened the door. AT&T's fears were realized. Soon everybody began setting up microwave stations.

S: Like Sprint.

Y: Sprint, MCI, and many others. Prior to MCI, the Bell System had had a monopoly on virtually all telephone services. It had convinced the FCC that other systems and equipment would degrade the system. It was the Carter phone decision in the late 1960s that effectively ended AT&T's monopoly. A guy named Carter wanted to add an acoustic coupler and modem to transmit data over a standard telephone handset. It would have allowed two-way radio equipment to connect with the telephone network for telephone conversations. But back then nothing could go on a phone line unless it was an AT&T product developed by Bell Labs. That was the law. But Carter said, "I want to use a machine that *I* make." But the Bell System objected—the Bell System claimed it would degrade the quality of the service. Now it's true that if you put junk equipment on the line it could cause interference. For example, if your audio levels are too high it could cross into your neighbor's lines and cause trouble. That was just one of the issues. Putting extra voltage on the lines could damage central office equipment and so forth. If you didn't have sufficient isolation between the plug in the wall and the phone line, it could short and have high voltage going on the phone line, and so on.

S: So they had a valid criticism.

Y: They absolutely did, but their premise was that AT&T was the only company smart enough to install equipment.

S: And that's not a valid premise.

Y: Of course it's not valid, and the FCC became convinced of that. So an intelligent compromise was reached. The FCC set up specific technical guidelines for equipment to be connected to the phone system that Bell Labs could approve and that all manufacturers could comply with. This was the birth of FCC Part 68. It set the parameters and test requirements that must be satisfied and approved by an FCC-certified independent testing lab. If you look on the label on the bottom of every phone you should see the Part 68 Certification. The Carter phone case opened the floodgates for all of the telephones, cordless phones, and answering machines that everybody now has. Combined with MCI's long-line success and market share, AT&T share started to dwindle. And today they are only one of several big players in the telecom field. In 1980, only forward-looking technologists would have been able to predict all the fiber-optic cable stretched everywhere. Back then, fiber-optic technology was in its infancy. The trick was getting long fiber-optic cables runs without the need for repeaters everywhere. Curiously enough, a lot of fiber-optic cables are buried along railroad tracks. That's because they go everywhere, are controlled access, meaning the public doesn't have access to them, and the right of way is clear. Crews can bury cable several feet under the ground and not have to worry about anyone coming along and digging it up because train tracks are a guarded infrastructure. I think it will only be a matter of time before fiber-optic cable gets routed locally to businesses and consumers.

S: The consumer household, the hundreds of millions of households in America, the final mile.

Y: Right. And when we get that virtual infinite bandwidth using fiber to these locations, there will be yet another shift in our lifestyles. The way the transistor from the 1950s changed our quality of life and how the Internet today changes how we do things, this near unlimited broadband will move us to even the next level, whatever that may be.

S: When will we get natural motion on the Internet?

Y: When you get to about a megabit per second the staccato starts to disappear. At 2 megabits per second, it's almost full motion. Three or 4 megabits will simulate broadcast-quality video.

S: Is that done through compression techniques?

Y: Yes. They take a video image, digitize it, and compress the data. Then they decompress it at the receiving end, like MP3 music files.

S: So when the "big pipe" gets to the home, we can get Internet video.

Y: Something like that. But it may not come through the network we now call the "Internet." Once that infrastructure is in place, that's when you're going to see the convergence of TV, Internet, data, and telephones. It may take 20 years or more, but we will see it in our lifetime, barring a global disaster.

S: New topic. What are you personally working on right now in your company?

Y: Low-cost customer premise equipment (CPE) for our license-free 2.4-GHz systems.

S: So how do you know what to make? Do you meet with your WISP customers?

Y: All the time. We offer workshops and training about our license-free equipment and technologies. Then I listen to what they need, and after a while it becomes clear to me what product is needed. It's an incremental thing. We start out with a product, and get feedback from our customers as to what the next generation of this product should be. It's not like you wake up one day and have the complete solution. After all, it took Ford 50 years to come up with the first Lincoln Continental.

S: Many other technology companies like Cisco, Lucent, and 3Com are struggling. Is your company doing well?

Y: Yes. In fact, we are growing every year. We provide our ISP customers a wireless means to offer high-speed Internet service without the involvement of the local phone company. To a man, they all despise the local phone company and hate working with them. In the past, they have needed to rely on them since they had to use their infrastructure (i.e., their wires) to get service to customers, be it DSL, T-1 lines, or dial-up phone lines. ISPs had to pay the phone company recurring charges to use those lines. Needless to say, this cost is passed on to the customer. In this capacity, the local phone company (or the DSL provider in this area) is the access service providers. They were a step in the system that had to be dealt with to be in business. But it gets worse. The local phone companies also offer Internet access themselves. They are competitors to local ISPs and who also own the infrastructure that ISPs need. And independent ISPs have found the telcos less than eager to cooperate because these telcos earn much more revenue from offering Internet service on their lines than by just leasing the lines to the local ISP. They schedule installations out for months, provide low-priority technical support, and so on. So when our wireless high-speed alternatives became available, independents were all over it. This is why my company has been growing at 200%-400% every year since 1998, despite the drop in tech stocks in mid-2000 and early 2001.

S: Do these ISPs know anything about radio?

Y: In many cases, they know very little, if anything, about wireless data. We offer training class and lots of application drawings on our Web site (www.ydi.com). Our technical sales staff helps them by suggesting designs. But it is up to them to get the radio gear professionally installed and tested. We have affiliations with installation companies should they need help in this area.

S: You say your equipment is in the license-free radio bands. Why not the licensed band?

Y: We decided not to play in the licensed-band arena, like the licensed PCS, MMDS band, and others because to do so you have to spend tens of millions of dollars to get licenses for these frequencies. You must bid on them and compete with big players to do that. And we're too small for that. But in the license-free bands, we can design a radio system, get it certified for a license-free operation, and sell it. You could buy the equipment yourself, set a WIPOP up somewhere, and offer wireless Internet connectivity to your neighborhood immediately.

S: So you're providing broadband wireless Internet access capabilities to ISPs that don't want to go through the phone company?

Y: Exactly.

S: What's wrong with you providing Internet service directly to customers?

Y: We don't want to be an Internet service provider. We are equipment providers. That's our business. Mack Truck is not a shipping company. They sell their products (trucks) to shipping companies who use them to transport goods. Our ISP customers use our products to transport data. And there are thousands of Internet service providers worldwide.

S: So now the ISP has 100% control of the ISP and doesn't have to rely on the local telco.

Y: Correct.

S: What if the equipment breaks down?

Y: Well, if the equipment breaks, they are responsible to do first-level troubleshooting. Remember: 100% control also means 100% responsibility.

S: OK, but if something goes wrong with the piece of equipment what do they do?

Y: They send it back to us and we repair or replace it.

S: So do you have many returns?

Y: No, because this equipment is low power, highly reliable, and solid state. About one third of the returns have nothing wrong with them. Another third is damaged by the customer and only the last third actually has a hardware failure.

S: How is business for your ISP customers?

Y: Booming and growing! The market we're in is exploding, because ISPs are discovering this technology every week. Most are making money with our wireless technology. Those that aren't making money aren't successful because of business reasons or did not deploy the wireless network properly. In most cases, they did not do a business plan or get professional technical advice and tried to do it all on their own with limited knowledge.

S: Let's move to a close. In your view, what should the reader know most about deciphering cyberspace in the future?

Y: To have a full understanding of the way things will be, you should understand the technologies that will give us near unlimited bandwidth. Pay attention to the new technologies that provide high bandwidth in the future. You will see fiber-optic networks proliferate like cable TV and Ethernet have in the past two decades. Routers and switchers will move data through them optically, not electronically, at unheard of speeds. But all these tethered technologies will not satisfy all the need for more bandwidth. We need it wirelessly as well. And the third-generation (3G) cell systems, MMDS, and license-free bands will not be enough. The solution might be found in a brand-new wireless technology on the horizon called ultra wideband (UWB). This technology brings speed spectrum to a new level. It is one that spreads a high-speed data signal across many gigahertz of bandwidth. By doing that, the actual RF energy on any given frequency is virtually immeasurable. Thus, it can be overlaid on top of all the existing radios currently in service on those bands without interfering with them. Likewise, a UWB receiver can pick up signals from its companion transmitter without any interference from the existing radios. And if that were not exciting enough, UWB does not need clear line-of-sight like other microwave radios. It will, to a degree, penetrate steel-reinforced concrete walls. In the fall of 2000, the FCC authorized UWB transmitters to be tested in the 1-GHz to 6-GHz band. But we must take a wait-and-see approach. If all the hype turns out to be true, then UWB could do to the wireless data industry in the 21st century what the transistor did to the electronics industry in the mid-20th century. Then we will have our "Bandwidth Utopia": virtual infinite bandwidth brought to fixed locations via fiber optics and to mobile users via UWB. And the world will be a different place because of this.

S: By then, your business will have changed and you will have moved on.

Y: By that time, maybe I'll have made my fortune, retired, and let the technology go where it will go.

S: That's a wonderful place to end. Thank you very much.

CHAPTER 2

COMPUTERS IN COMMUNICATION

Concepts and Application

Leonard Shyles

Electronic communication has been greatly enhanced by the integration of computers into older broadcasting and telecommunication systems. Both e-mail and the Internet are popular applications that rely on computers and these earlier technologies for transmitting messages between users. When messages are sent successfully, the older systems on which they depend are largely invisible to users, who may employ a desktop, laptop, handheld PC (personal computer), or older mainframe terminal to encode and receive messages.

Yet many who communicate through these media do not know how text, voice, and images are captured and transmitted. One advantage of knowing how the process works is that it can help you select products best suited to the applications needed for business and pleasure. Another is that understanding the capabilities and limitations of various systems leads to more realistic expectations and less frustration concerning their performance.

The purpose of this chapter is to explain from both conceptual and physical perspectives how computers enable users to create (*encode*) and display (*decode*) electronic communication. In computers, the main substance acted on by electrical signals for coding and storing information is silicon, a natural occurring element comprising 28% of the earth's crust, the world's most plentiful element after oxygen. When treated with other materials, silicon can be used to encode, store, and manipulate any kind of information, including text, images, and sound. To explain how computers make this possible, I first describe how binary code may be used to represent any kind of information.

■ THE LANGUAGE OF BINARY CODE

The idea of transforming information into binary code is not new. It predates the modern digital computer by centuries. Simply put, binary code uses just two symbols to record information. But how can just two symbols capture the endless complexity of audiovisual messages?

As mentioned in the last chapter, it is essential to *vary* some aspect of a signal for it to carry a message. Some variation or change is required to impose a pattern of intelligence on any medium. And it is the pattern of intelligence, not the medium itself, that contains messages. Without some variation (or *modulation*) of a signal, no message is possible.

To illustrate, imagine once again a Morse code telegrapher sending an endless series of dots at regular intervals. In this case, no message is sent because there is nothing to differentiate one part of the signal from another. Electrical impulses may be received perfectly clearly, but no message is carried in such a transmission beyond indicating that someone or something has begun opening and closing a Morse code key at regular intervals. In Morse code, there is simply no meaning associated with an endless series of dots; hence, no message is transmitted. What is missing is some change or variation in the signal that enables a pattern of intelligence to be encoded and then interpreted.

To allow some variation to occur, Morse code uses the simplest possible format: two symbols, the dot and the dash. Actually, to be accurate, when sent via telegraph wires, as has been done since the mid-1800s, Morse code does not use literal "dots" and "dashes." The symbols are actually short and long electrical impulses in varying sequences corresponding to specific letters of the alphabet through prior agreement (*code*). But regardless of whether the symbols are dots and dashes, long and short electrical impulses, circles and squares, zeros and ones, or any other pair of arbitrary symbols, the main point is that some signal modulation is needed to encode messages, and a minimum of two symbols is required to provide it; one is not enough.

Around 1900, telegraphers began using Morse code to communicate to distant places without wires (*wireless telegraphy* is what such transmissions were called) by propagating patterns of radio energy in long and short bursts separated by moments of no transmission. This version of Morse code, as mentioned in the last chapter, was called ICW, for interrupted continuous wave transmission. Long before Morse code, African bush tribes sent messages in similar fashion using combinations of high- and low-pitched sounds via signal drums.

In summary, the important thing about all these communication systems is that *two symbols are the minimum needed for imposing a pattern of intelligence on a medium*. Using two symbols to carry intelligence in a message system illustrates the power of binary code.

A Brief History of Binary Code

Long before binary code became a central element in the development of digital computers and mass communication systems, it was used for expressing and assessing concepts (e.g., codemaking, logical analysis) and for practical applications (e.g., controlling a variety of machines, including music boxes, player pianos, and weaving looms).

For example, as early as the 16th century, Francis Bacon (1561-1626) used binary code consisting of the letters *a* and *b* in varying combinations to convey secret messages.[1] Later, Joseph-Marie Jacquard (1752-1834) used punched cards for controlling the operation of looms. And later still, English logician George Boole (1815-1864) developed a system of logical analysis (called a *propositional calculus*) using the two conditions of "true" and "false" based on the functions "and," "or," and "not," to clarify arguments and spot faulty reasoning. Thanks to the work of Claude Shannon (1916-2001) beginning in the 1930s, Boole's propositional logic, which provided the conceptual foundation, was adopted as the basis for developing the electrical circuits in the public switched telephone network (PSTN), and later for designing the circuitry of modern digital computers.

The key feature across all these examples is the use of two and only two conditions for reaching outcomes. In Bacon's secret code, each letter of the alphabet is represented by the letters *a* and *b* in a unique combination, similar to the way Morse code uses dots and dashes. In the Jacquard loom, preselected regions of cards have either punched holes or unpunched areas, which control the movement of needles in weaving machines. And in Boole's algebra, the terms "true" and "false" are assigned to statements according to logical rules to obtain valid inferences in predictable ways. In each case, only two conditions are used to express an idea or accomplish some goal (e.g., communicate in code, weave designs into fabric, decide the validity of arguments).

Decimal	Binary
1	1
2	10
3	11
4	100
5	101
6	110
7	111
8	1000
9	1001
10	1010
16	10000
32	100000
64	1000000
100	1100100
256	100000000
	Etc.

Figure 2.1   A sample of decimal numbers with their binary equivalents in each row.

The Binary Number System

Beyond these functions, binary code can also be used to express any numerical value and to perform mathematical calculations. These aspects of binary code are extraordinarily important, because they make it possible for any type and amount of information to be rendered into numerical code using only zeros and ones, including text, images, and sound. And as we will see later, such a system is particularly well suited to the electronic circuitry of modern digital computers, because it is easy to express two alternative conditions electrically using an array of switches that can be turned on and off.

The binary number system is named such because it uses only two symbols (0s and 1s) to represent any number, and although it is limited to just two, it is completely versatile. For example, decimal numbers (so called because they use ten symbols, from 0 through 9) may be expressed in binary form as shown in Figure 2.1.

Notice that when the supply of digits runs out, decimal numbers move one place to the left, where they are used all over again in a new column at an increased power of ten. In binary, the same practice is followed, but with one difference: When the numbers move over, they increase in value by powers of only two. So, as Figure 2.1 shows, the number 10 in the decimal system is expressed as 1010 in binary, where the digit "0" on the far right tells us there are no *ones*, the digit next to it tells us there is one *two*, the next no *fours*, and the last on the far left, one *eight*, for a total of $10_{decimal}$, and so on.

As mentioned, it should be clear that as places move from right to left in the decimal system, digit values increase tenfold (i.e., place values go from *ones* to *tens* to *hundreds* to *thousands*, etc.), whereas when places move in the binary system, values increase by powers of only two (i.e., from *ones* to *twos* to *fours* to *eights*, etc.). Nevertheless, using binary code, notice that it is possible to represent any number.

The ability to represent any numerical value using only zeros and ones is critically important, because if any number can be represented by a unique string of zeros and ones, then it is clearly possible to code all 26 letters of the alphabet, including upper- and lowercase, punctuation marks, and so on, through the same means. And if all this can be rendered in binary code, then by extension it is possible to use binary code to express any thought that can be put into language.

However, notice also that binary code is a difficult one for human beings to use because long strings of repeating zeros and ones can quickly become hard on our perceptual systems, as the binary number representing the number $256_{decimal}$ illustrates (see Figure 2.1). But whereas binary numbers may be difficult for human beings to process, it is just the opposite for computers, which are highly compatible with a two-state system of variation, mainly because electrical impulses may easily be turned on and off with the flick of a switch, just like a lightbulb. In fact, machines in general (not just computers and calculators) are excellent at dealing with two-state systems, especially where repetitive work is required. And in such applications, binary code finds a natural home.

Perhaps one of the oldest and most famous examples of the use of binary code to perform practical work is Jacquard's loom, developed in France in the early 19th century. Many consider it the starting point of digitally[2] controlled machines.

In weaving looms, a warp thread is either lifted or not lifted (thus the binary quality) when a shuttle passes through to produce a woven fabric with a particular design. In the early days of the textile industry, this process had been controlled by a laborer who monitored the warp threads and lifted them at the appropriate moment to create the desired design, clearly a job featuring a degree of exactitude perhaps exceeded only by its drudgery and boredom.

By the 1720s, a mechanical method had been developed to increase speed and accuracy and to reduce monotony for human operators. For example, in 1725, a cylinder wrapped with a sheet of perforated paper was used to control the action of a set of needles pulling thread. Then, in the early 1800s, a significant innovation occurred. According to one account, Jacquard was asked to fix some looms that were in disrepair. He replaced the cylinder and perforated paper with prism-shaped forms fitted with punched cards featuring different perforation patterns. Now a worker could quickly produce fabrics with a variety of designs on the same loom simply by changing cards. This change made Jacquard's loom the first *programmable* weaving machine; it revolutionized the weaving industry and is still in operation today.

■ THE MOVE TOWARD MACHINE CALCULATION

The goal of reducing drudgery was not limited to the work world; mathematical calculation has its own brand of tedium associated with it. Using mechanical means to reduce computational labor for astronomers, navigators, census takers, and tax officials motivated many inventors to try to develop calculating machines that could reduce the toilsome grind of computing while increasing speed and accuracy.

Among them was the great German philosopher scientist Gottfried Wilhelm Leibniz (1646-1716). Leibniz sought to reduce the endless computing chores for his associate, astronomer Christian Huygens, commenting that "it is unworthy of excellent men to lose hours like slaves in the labor of calculation, which could safely be relegated to anyone if machines were used." In 1673, Leibniz created a mechanical calculator that used a hand crank to drive a stepped wheel to speed up calculation. In this arrangement, a wheel was moved for each computation, thus allowing the user to calculate mechanically simply by entering the correct numbers. The Leibniz calculator was based on the decimal system.

Later, to further the pursuit of mathematical accuracy, British inventor Charles Babbage (1791-1871) designed a programmable calculating machine. In 1822, Babbage published a paper describing a device called a *difference engine* that could compute scientific tables. It had toothed wheels on shafts turned by a crank. As he saw it (apparently in agreement with Leibniz), the machine was created to eliminate the "intolerable labor and fatiguing monotony [of mathematical calculation representing the] lowest occupation of the human intellect." A working prototype of his invention that proved its feasibility was produced that year, a six-digit calculator, also based on the decimal system.

By 1833, Babbage had developed plans for a more versatile calculating machine called an *analytical engine*. Based on the decimal system, it was designed to solve a wider range of problems than its predecessor by using a set of instructions on punched cards. The punch-card format, inspired by the success of the Jacquard loom, was the binary feature of Babbage's invention— regions on each card had either a hole or an unpunched area to program information into the machine.

It was touted by Babbage as "a machine of the most general nature," the first general-purpose programmable computer. It featured a "mill" and a "store," components analogous to the central processing unit (CPU) and memory component of today's computers, respectively. Babbage's invention was to be composed of cogs and wheels. The store was designed to hold as many as 148 decimal numbers. As each computation was completed, the result was to be moved from the mill to the store where it could either await further use or be printed out.

Babbage's ideas were clearly influenced by the programmable nature of Jacquard's loom. But producing an actual prototype of his machine proved impractical. Judging from the drawings and plans that still exist, it would have been the size of a locomotive; it was to have been operated by steam. Unfortunately, its mechanical structure was too intricate to produce a reliable copy, and it was never built.

However, in 1890, Babbage's idea of using punched cards for computing did find use in a statistical tabulating machine. American inventor Herman Hollerith (1860-1929), the son of German immigrants, built a functioning machine for data processing applications for the 1890 U.S. census.

Hollerith's cards were roughly the size of dollar bills. Each had 12 rows, with 20 locations for entering information on age, sex, marital status, and so on. Census takers transferred data from forms to cards by punching out the appropriate hole for each data point. The cards were then placed onto rows of pins. Two hundred and forty pins were available for use on each card. When a pin was aligned with a hole, it would poke through and dip into a small cup of mercury, completing an electrical circuit, causing a decimal counter to advance one place. Thus, the presence or absence of a hole in each designated area on a card, and not the numbering system, constituted the binary nature of Hollerith's machine. In this way, Hollerith was able to conduct a full analysis of the data for the U.S. census in a fraction of the time it took to conduct the 1880 census.

Hollerith's invention was heralded a great success. He claimed the title of "first statistical engineer" and formed the Tabulating Machine Company, selling his invention to railroads and governments, including czarist Russia. In 1924, Hollerith's company became IBM Corporation.

Among the advantages Hollerith had that Babbage lacked were access to electricity and finer production capabilities in machine tooling and mechanical engineering. By contrast, Babbage, unfortunately ahead of his time, was active in the pre-electrical era. More unfortunate, the practical expression of his ideas was limited by contemporary construction standards. The mechanical objects commonly available in 1820 England included watches, clocks, guns, and pumps; in industry, there were looms, lathes, presses, mills, and turbines. But none of these inventions was even remotely on the level of intricacy required for his difference engine, which needed to be built to much finer tolerances and technical standards than were possible at the time. Babbage's device had hundreds of components; all needed to be machined to impossible specifications, or his invention would break down. Furthermore, because the gears comprising the counting mechanism were designed for the decimal system, a great deal of complexity was demanded. The only binary quality of his machine was that it used punched cards featuring the presence or absence of holes to control its action, just like the Jacquard loom.

It would take the insights of German inventor Konrad Zuse (1910-1995) to determine that using binary numbers would reduce mechanical complexity to manageable levels, making complicated mechanical calculation both reliable and efficient. Zuse's insights came just in time. America at the turn of the 20th century had begun drowning in a flood of data. The population was increasing; immigration was at an all-time high. The need to analyze scientific data and gather information for policy decisions in both industry and government had grown to new heights; big business was awash in paperwork. For example, it was becoming clear that if all the calculating needed for the 1900 census were to be done by hand, it would take more than ten years to complete. Thus, America's computing needs had reached a crisis point. If necessity is the mother of invention, the perfection of machine calculating was now inevitable.

By the 1890s, the calculator had finally become a viable business aid. Production of finely tooled gears and axles made reliable calculating machines possible on a wide scale. The Tabulating Machine Company had been leasing machines to paying clients; now companies that had use for such devices wanted their own and could afford to buy them.

The latest ones were designed for addition, and little more; a few were rigged to perform multiplication. But performing just these calculations was enough to make them successful products. Key-operated and spring-driven interfaces were developed to facilitate data entry. Built-in printers were soon added for more readable display. By 1913, the Burroughs Adding Machine Company had 2,500 employees and $8 million in sales (Augarten, 1984, p. 82).

But machines that could perform simple arithmetic could not solve more intricate problems. Across the sciences, the need was growing to develop more sophisticated calculators that could help engineers solve complex equations. For example, in architecture, it was necessary to determine the integrity of static structures, including computing the amount of stress buildings could reasonably be expected to withstand without collapsing. Equations that could accurately account for the weight, elasticity, and strength of various building materials were becoming increasingly complex.[3]

Demand also increased for solving differential equations for predicting the trajectory of moving objects affected by gravity, water currents, and so forth. Rocket science was an especially important field; in theoretical physics, understanding more about light and heat was key. Predicting the behavior of such phenomena required solving complex equations demanding months of computing by teams of engineers. Developing machines (called *differential analyzers*) that could provide solutions to such problems became extremely important.

The first differential analyzers were analog devices that used electric motors attached to shafts linked together with gears of different sizes to represent the variables of interest. But rearranging shafts and machine parts to represent new data took days to set up. By the 1940s, vacuum tubes had replaced some parts of these early devices, but they remained analog in nature, and as a result, limited in their accuracy.

During the 1930s, six equations were the practical limit for engineers to solve using an adding machine, paper and pencil, and/or a chalkboard. If the number of equations were doubled, there was an eightfold increase in the number of calculations required. At this level of complexity, a team of engineers would need months to compute a solution. And as complexity increased, accuracy decreased. Such grinding toil was dreaded by most mathematicians.

In this environment, Konrad Zuse, a young mechanical engineering student in college in Berlin, devised a way around the calculation glut. He made three prescient decisions that changed the way calculating would be done forever. According to Augarten (1984), Zuse developed

> a universal calculator that could solve *any* equation equipped with an arithmetic unit (or central processing unit) for performing the computations; a memory for storing the numbers; a control unit for supervising the flow of numbers and instructions within the machine; a so-called program unit for reading instructions . . . from punched tape; and an output unit for displaying the results.
>
> Second, Zuse decided to use binary, rather than decimal, math. . . . The . . . economy of the binary system meant that the calculator's components could be as simple as on/off switches.
>
> Finally, Zuse devised a simple set of operating rules to govern the machine's . . . operations [which were] . . . a restatement of the basic axioms of *Boolean algebra*. (p. 89)

Harnessing Boolean Logic for Machine Calculation

As has already been demonstrated, in addition to using binary numbers to represent any numerical value, binary code can also represent words, as the dot-dash sequences of Morse code illustrate. Thus, binary code can serve as an all-purpose language using the simplest form of signal modulation to represent and manipulate both numerical and verbal concepts with unprecedented efficiency and reliability.

By adapting binary code to a system of properly rigged electrical circuits, it becomes possible to perform complex mathematical calculations and a variety of linguistic manipulations by machine. But just what is entailed in the phrase "properly rigged" that enables the leap from conceptual foundations to the practical application of such ideas in a stand-alone machine?

■ CONCEPTUAL FOUNDATIONS

In 1832, British mathematician George Boole applied binary code to his study of symbolic logic; his goal, grandiose as it may seem, was to devise a universal language. In 1847, Boole published an article titled "The Mathematical Analysis of Logic"; in 1854, he published "An Investigation of the Laws of Thought." These two essays revolutionized the science of logic. In them, Boole had devised a system of symbols and rules that could be applied to statements, making it possible to evaluate the truth-value of arguments constructed from them.

In Boole's system, three basic constructs (called *logic gates* or *operators*) are all that are needed to perform logical analysis and mathematical calculation with symbols and numbers, respectively. The three gates in Boolean algebra are called AND, OR, and NOT. Boole's gates are binary in nature because they categorize statements as either true or false. (Of course, the names given to the two binary conditions are completely arbitrary and can be anything—including true/false, dot/dash, yes/no, open/closed, zero/one, or even "ish" and "kabibble.")

Let's illustrate the way Boole's system of logical analysis works, demonstrating its binary nature with a concrete example. Imagine a trip to the bakery to purchase a cake. To keep things simple, let's limit our discussion to cakes that are either chocolate (*C*) or vanilla (*V*). Let's also specify the number of layers—*T* for cakes with two layers, *H* for three layers, and *S* for seven-layer cakes. Finally, let's specify the type of icing the cakes have—let *B* signify cakes with butter icing, and *N* for those that are butter free. Thus, in summary, we have three classifications we can choose from: *cake flavor* (of which there are two categories—chocolate and vanilla), *number of layers* (of which there are three categories—two layer, three layer, and seven layer), and *type of icing* (of which there are two categories—butter icing and butter free).

Now let's apply Boole's binary logic to combine and differentiate these concepts. For greater clarity, let's also illustrate it using Venn diagrams. In Boolean notation, we indicate the union of two categories (i.e., we combine every object from one class with everything from another) with a plus sign, +. So *T* + *H* refers to all two- and three-layer cakes (see Figure 2.2). Furthermore, we indicate the intersection of two groups with a multiplication sign, ×. This sign tells us to capture all members or objects that are in both of two groups. So *V* × *T* refers to "all vanilla two-layered cakes" (see Figure 2.3).[4]

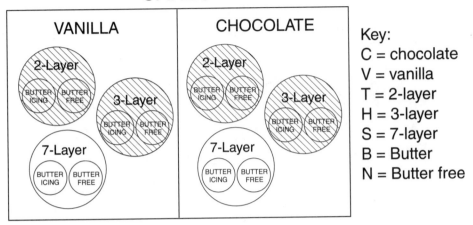

Figure 2.2   Venn diagram of cakes available at the bakery.

NOTE: This Venn diagram illustrates the Boolean notation expressing the *union of two classes*; in this case, the union of all two- and three-layer cakes, $T + H$ (or $T \cup H$). Union combines everything in one class with everything in another.

In Boolean algebra, note that the laws of normal arithmetic apply, including the commutative, associative, and distributive laws. For example, in conventional arithmetic, the *commutative* law, which applies to both addition and multiplication, states that we can add or multiply two numbers in any order and still get the same right answer. The commutative law for addition is symbolized this way:

$$A + B = B + A \text{ (i.e., } 2 + 3 = 3 + 2).$$

Ans.: 5

The Boolean equivalent of this would be capturing all two-layer cakes and combining them with all three-layer cakes, or vice versa; either way, we wind up with the same result (i.e., put simply, this says, "the union $T + H$ is the same as $H + T$").

Similarly, the commutative law for multiplication says:

$$A \times B = B \times A \text{ (i.e., } 2 \times 3 = 3 \times 2).$$

Ans.: 6

CAKES

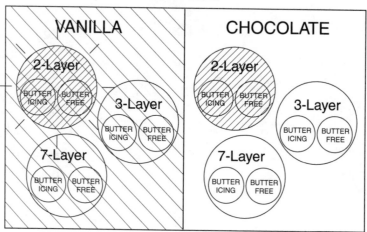

Figure 2.3   Venn diagram of cakes available at the bakery.

NOTE: This Venn diagram illustrates the Boolean notation expressing the *intersection of two classes*; in this case, the intersection of all vanilla and two-layer cakes, $V \times T$ (or $V \cap T$). Intersection captures all members that are in both of two classes. (Intersection required two treatments to arrive at a final result [only the double cross-hatched area qualifies.])

The Boolean equivalent of this, for example, would be capturing all cakes that are both vanilla and two layers (i.e., "the intersection of $V \times T = T \times V$"). (Note: The commutative law does not apply to subtraction and division.)

Furthermore, addition and multiplication are also *associative*. This means that we can add or multiply numbers in a different order and still get the same right answer. The associative law for addition is symbolized this way:

$$A + (B + C) = (A + B) + C \text{ (i.e., } 2 + (3 + 4) = (2 + 3) + 4).$$

Ans.: 9

From the above, the Boolean equivalents of this should be obvious. Similarly, the associative law for multiplication says:

$$A \times (B \times C) = (A \times B) \times C \text{ (i.e., } 2 \times (3 \times 4) = (2 \times 3) \times 4).$$

Ans.: 24

This law also has a Boolean equivalent; just substitute cake letters and follow the above equation.

Finally, multiplication is *distributive* over addition. This means we can multiply the sum of two numbers by a third number or we can multiply each separately by the third number and then add the products together to get the same right answer. The distributive law is symbolized this way:

$$A \times (B + C) = (A \times B) + (A \times C) \text{ (i.e., } 2 \times (3 + 4) = (2 \times 3) + (2 \times 4).$$

Ans.: 14

The above also holds in Boolean algebra.

All these laws apply to Boolean algebra, except that in Boolean logic, they refer not to numbers but to classes, and this is what makes Boolean algebra so powerful: It does not relate only to numbers but to concepts, understood in terms of classes of objects.

Boole's rules constitute what has come to be known as *set theory*. And the application of Boole's logic to *sets* of objects rather than to objects themselves is easily seen using Venn diagrams, as the above figures show. Venn diagrams graphically show how Boole's system operates, and how it may be used to assess validity and spot faulty reasoning.

However, there is one Boolean function that differentiates it from normal algebra. In Boolean algebra, as mentioned above, the commutative, associative, and distributive laws all apply. But unlike conventional math, in Boole's system, the "+" function is distributive over the "×" operator. This is not so for conventional algebra. See for yourself. In normal algebra:

$$A + (B \times C) \ne (A + B) \times (A + C).$$

Substituting: $2 + (3 \times 4) \ne (2 + 3) \times (2 + 4)$ (i.e., $14 \ne 30$).

But in Boolean logical notation,

$$A + (B \times C) = (A + B) \times (A + C)$$

is valid. To see that it is, let's test it. What does this equation say in terms of our bakery example? To illustrate, we change terms as follows:

$$S + (H \times V) = (S + H) \times (S + V).$$

The left side of the equation tells us to capture all seven-layer cakes and all three-layer vanilla cakes (see Figure 2.4). The right side tells us to capture all seven- and three-layer cakes, then to capture all seven-layer and all other vanilla cakes, and then keep only those that are handled twice. The result should be that what is captured through this two-step process should be the same as what was captured from the process indicated by the left half of the equation (see Figure 2.5). Compare Figures 2.4 and 2.5 and notice that both processes yield the same result.

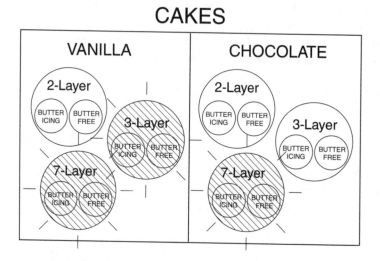

Figure 2.4   Venn diagram of cakes available at the bakery.

NOTE: This Venn diagram illustrates the Boolean notation for $S + (H \times V)$ or $S \cup (H \cap V)$. This notation says to capture all seven-layer cakes and all three-layer vanilla cakes, as shown.

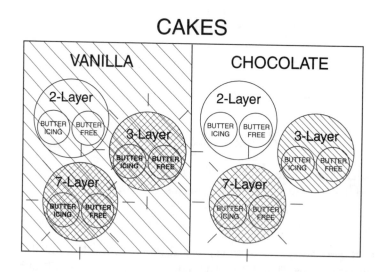

Figure 2.5   Venn diagram of cakes available at the bakery.

NOTE: This Venn diagram illustrates Boolean notation for $(S + H) \times (S + V)$ or $(S \cup H) \cap (S \cup V)$. This notation says to capture all seven- and three-layer cakes, then all seven-layer and all other vanilla cakes, and to retain only those that are handled twice. The result matches that of Figure 2.4, illustrating that that the "+" function is distributive over the "×" operator, unlike conventional algebra.

As this exercise demonstrates, union takes one treatment to get to the final event, while intersection requires two treatments to get to the same outcome. In ordinary language, the above Boolean equation says that the union of seven-layer cakes and three-layer vanilla cakes is equal to what is in common between seven-layer and three-layer cakes, and seven-layer vanilla cakes—awkwardly stated but true.

FROM THEORY TO PRACTICE ∎

As early as 1867, American pragmatist philosopher C. S. Peirce began popularizing Boole's system of logical analysis in the United States. Over a period of 20 years, Peirce refined and extended Boole's work and came to realize that Boole's system of logic could be easily adapted to electrical switching circuits—an electric current, Peirce reasoned, could be either on or off. So, for example, using Boole's NOT gate, cakes could be described as either chocolate or not chocolate, vanilla or not vanilla, and so on. Furthermore, with Boole's AND gate, one could capture the intersection of two classes with binary logic using yes/no (or, in the case of electrical circuits, on/off) choices. And with Boole's OR gate, simple binary operations could also be used to capture the concept of the union of two classes. In short, Peirce realized that it was easy to rig an electrical circuit with an array of switches that could serve as perfect analogues for each of Boole's logic gates.

This realization was potentially a powerful leap from theory to practice, a move that should make any pragmatist proud. However, applying Boolean logic to the world of electrical switching came to full fruition not through the efforts of pragmatist Peirce but through the work of math theorist and engineer Claude Shannon, who, in 1936, bridged the gap between theory and practice as a student at Massachusetts Institute of Technology, while maintaining a mechanical differential analyzer designed to predict the influence of gravity on airplanes.

Shannon adapted electrical switching circuits to parallel Boolean logic, thus paving the way for computers to process statements in logical and predictable ways. To demonstrate how this was done, we first illustrate how Boole's three fundamental logic gates, AND, OR, and NOT, operate using the simple binary conditions TRUE and FALSE to characterize statements alone and in combination with one another. Notice that each logic gate is rigged to produce just one result, determined purely on the basis of the information presented to it.

For example, a simple AND gate (see Figure 2.6) is fed information about the truth-value of two statements; that is, each statement is characterized in advance as either true or false. The AND gate takes this information and produces a result (either TRUE or FALSE) depending on the status (or "truth value") of the two pieces of information it has received.

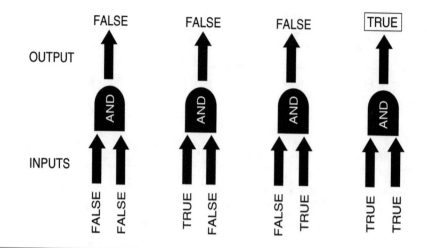

Figure 2.6 Diagram of an AND gate, depicting two inputs, both of which must be true to yield a true output. In all other cases, a false output results. A maximum of four different conditions can exist for AND gates with two inputs.

In an AND gate, a true result is produced only if the two incoming statements are both characterized as true. In all other cases, a false outcome results. In other words, AND gates deliver a TRUE output only if both of its inputs are true, and a FALSE output in all other cases.

By contrast, OR gates deliver a TRUE output if *any* of the incoming information is true. The only time an OR gate yields a FALSE result is when both pieces of incoming information are characterized as FALSE (see Figure 2.7).

Finally, NOT gates simply reverse the truth-value of the incoming information; that is, if an incoming signal is TRUE, it produces a FALSE output, and if the incoming signal is FALSE, it produces a TRUE output (see Figure 2.8).

To show how Boolean logic may be used to process statements, let's go back to the bakery. You walk in and say to the clerk, "I'd like any seven-layer or two-layer chocolate cake with butter icing; or any vanilla cake with butter icing and any number of layers but seven; or any three-layer cake."

The Boolean expression for this set of conditions looks like this:

$$(C \times B \times (S + T)) + (V \times B \times (1 - S)) + H.^5$$

Let's substitute the words AND and OR for the notions of intersection and union, respectively, to make the above expression more like ordinary language. The union of two classes takes in items from the first class *or* the second class (the plus sign, +, refers to union and is indicated by the term OR). The

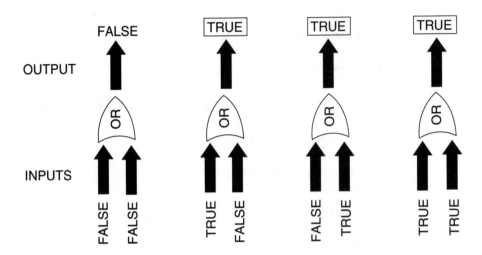

Figure 2.7 Diagram of an OR gate depicting two inputs, either of which may be true to yield a true output. In only one case does a false output result: when both inputs are false. All four possible conditions are shown for an OR gate with two inputs.

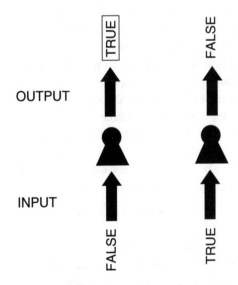

Figure 2.8 Diagram of a NOT gate depicting the two conditions that can exist for a single input. A NOT gate accepts just a single input, which it inverts.

intersection of two classes includes items from *both* of two classes (the multiplication sign, ×, refers to intersection and is indicated by the term AND). Finally, the term NOT may be substituted for every occurrence of a 1 followed by a minus sign, indicating the universe of all objects under discussion minus a particular subset.

Changing signs to words yields the following equivalent statement:

$$(C \text{ AND } B \text{ AND } (S \text{ OR } T)) \text{ OR } (V \text{ AND } B \text{ AND } (\text{NOT } S)) \text{ OR } H.$$

This means you are willing to purchase a cake from one of three classes. You want either

a chocolate cake with butter icing that has either seven or two layers

OR

a vanilla cake with butter icing that has any number of layers but seven

OR

any three-layer cake.

Now, let's assume the clerk places on the counter a two-layer chocolate cake with butter-free icing. Does this fit your criteria? Obviously, if the first two choices require a butter icing, the clerk's choice fails in the first two cases; the cake also fails to match the third criterion, which requires that the cake have three layers. So that cake fails.

But how would a Boolean test determine whether the cake is one you would buy? That is, how can we use binary logic to process the information to determine that the cake the clerk has offered (a two-layer chocolate cake with butter-free icing) is unacceptable?

Let's substitute the letters **T** for true, for each criterion under consideration satisfied by the cake on the counter, and **F** for false, for each criterion that the cake on the counter fails to satisfy. Again, here is the formula you have specified for what you have ordered:

$$(C \times B \times (S + T)) + (V \times B \times (1 - S)) + H.$$

Comparing what we have ordered with what is on the counter, and substituting the letters **T** for those qualities that match what we want and **F** for those that do not, yields the following:

$$(\mathbf{T} \times \mathbf{F} \times (\mathbf{F} + \mathbf{T})) + (\mathbf{F} \times \mathbf{F} \times (\mathbf{T}^6 - \mathbf{F})) + \mathbf{F}.$$

Now let's reduce the above expression to its simplest form using the rules of algebra already reviewed. If the result is a **T**, then the cake is one you

AND	F	T
F	F	F
T	F	T*

Figure 2.9   Truth table displaying all possible conditions for the *intersection* of two classes (symbolized by "×" corresponding to a Boolean AND gate).

*The output is true only when both inputs are true.

would buy; if an **F**, no sale. Remember an AND gate describes the intersection of two classes, yielding a true outcome if and only if both terms (*operands*) around the multiplication sign are true; in all other cases, AND gates yield a "false."

There are four possible conditions for the intersection of two classes, and only one of the four yields a true result. For example, given two classes, say "A" and "B," then both A and B can be true, or A can be false when B is true, or A can be true when B is false, or both can be false. There are no other possibilities. Figure 2.9 displays all possible sets of conditions (all combinations) associated with AND gates in the form of a truth table.

By contrast, OR gates (the *union* of two classes designated by the + symbol) yield a true result when at least one operand around the + sign is true; OR gates produce false results if and only if both operands are false.

There are four possible combinations for the union of two classes, and in three of the four a true outcome results. For example, given two classes, say "A" and "B," then both A and B can be true, or A can be false when B is true, or A can be true when B is false, or both can be false. Figure 2.10 displays these four possible combinations associated with an OR gate and shows that only in the last case is there a false outcome. The truth table associated with the OR gate is shown in Figure 2.10.

Finally, a NOT gate acts as a simple inverter, which, unlike the others, accepts only one input, and reverses its truth-value. The truth table associated with a NOT gate looks like that displayed in Figure 2.11.

Using these three truth tables, we compute the result of our Boolean test to determine whether or not to buy the cake on the counter. Here is the expression we must reduce:

$$(T \times F \times (F + T)) + (F \times F \times (T - F)) + F.$$

OR	F	T
F	F*	T
T	T	T

Figure 2.10 Truth table displaying the four possible conditions for the *union* of two classes (symbolized by "+" corresponding to a Boolean OR gate).

*The output is false only when both inputs are false.

T	F
F	T

Figure 2.11 Truth table displaying the two possible conditions for the *inversion* of the truth-value of a class (symbolized by "–" corresponding to a Boolean NOT gate).

The first expression (after getting rid of the double parentheses) reduces to

$$\mathbf{T} \times \mathbf{F} \times \mathbf{T}$$

(where the **F + T** reduces to **T** in compliance with OR gates that make the entire expression true when either of the alternatives is true).

Similarly, the next one reduces to

$$\mathbf{F} \times \mathbf{F} \times \mathbf{T}$$

(where the "subtraction" from the universe of a false operator does no harm to the true remainder). And the last item standing alone in the expression remains as it is, namely, false.

According to the truth table for AND gates, since both operators on either side of an intersection symbol must be true for the entire expression to be true, we are left with three false outcomes; therefore, the entire expression is ruled false, something we knew all along.

Let's imagine that the clerk now places a single-layer vanilla sheet cake with butter icing on the counter. Will you buy it? Let's plug in the truth-values using the criteria you originally set down, which were as follows:

$$(C \times B \times (S + T)) + (V \times B \times (1 - S)) + H.$$

The sheet cake, which is only one layer, is designated as a "none of the above" choice when it comes to the number of layers. Plugging in the truth-values, here's what we get:

$$(\mathbf{F} \times \mathbf{T} \times (\mathbf{F} + \mathbf{F})) + (\mathbf{T} \times \mathbf{T} \times (\mathbf{T} - \mathbf{F})) + \mathbf{F}.$$

As before, the first expression (after getting rid of the double parentheses) reduces to

$$\mathbf{F} \times \mathbf{T} \times \mathbf{F}.$$

Similarly, the next one reduces to

$$\mathbf{T} \times \mathbf{T} \times \mathbf{T}.$$

And again, the last item standing alone in the expression remains as it is, namely, false.

Reducing further, we get $\mathbf{F} + \mathbf{T} + \mathbf{F}$, which finally reduces to $\mathbf{T}$, since only one operand must be true to make the entire expression true; you buy the cake.

We can now explain how Boole's rules of set theory, outlined above, may be applied to the practical world of electrical switching circuits to see how the same logical processes may be mirrored by properly rigged machines.

Application to Electrical Circuits

Thanks to the work of Claude Shannon, Boole's thoughtful analyses found practical application in the switching circuits used to process signals in telephone networks and, later, modern digital computers. In 1938, Shannon published his groundbreaking article, "A Symbolic Analysis of Relay and Switching Circuits." In it he said:

> Any circuit [may be] . . . represented by a set of equations, the terms of the equations corresponding to the various relays and switches in the circuit. A calculus is developed for manipulating these equations by simple mathematical processes, most of which are similar to ordinary algebraic algorisms. *The calculus is shown to be exactly analogous to the calculus of propositions used in the symbolic study of logic* [emphasis added]. . . . By this method it is always possible to find the simplest circuit containing only series and parallel connections, and in some cases the simplest circuit containing any type of connection. (p. 1)

A few paragraphs later, Shannon credits Boole as the theorist who provided the conceptual foundation on which Shannon based his practical work,

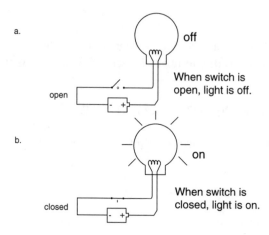

a.

off

When switch is
open, light is off.

open

b.

on

When switch is
closed, light is on.

closed

Figure 2.12   A simple series circuit with one terminal.

noting "the equivalence of this calculus with certain elementary parts of the calculus of propositions. The algebra of logic originated by George Boole is a symbolic method of investigating logical relationships" (p. 2).

Shannon's research demonstrates how Boole's logic gates may be realized in series and parallel electrical circuits. Begin with the simplest circuit, featuring one electrical source (i.e., a battery), one load (i.e., a lightbulb), and one switch, arranged in series with one another as depicted in Figure 2.12. As shown, when the switch is open (see Figure 2.12a), there is no flow of electricity through the circuit and the lightbulb is off; conversely, when the switch is closed (see Figure 2.12b), electricity flows through the circuit, and the lightbulb is on.

Next consider circuits featuring two switches connected in series (Figure 2.13), or in parallel (Figure 2.14). The first mimics Boole's AND logic gate; the second his OR gate. Successful outcomes (unimpeded flow of electricity) occur in direct correlation with the truth tables associated with these gates.

Shannon asserted six postulates (paraphrased below) to coincide with the two-terminal series and parallel[7] circuits that mimic Boole's logic gates:

1. A closed circuit in parallel with a closed circuit is a closed circuit (see Figure 2.14, part d)

2. An open circuit in series with an open circuit is an open circuit (see Figure 2.13, part a)

3. An open circuit in series with a closed circuit in either order is an open circuit (see Figure 2.13, parts b and c)

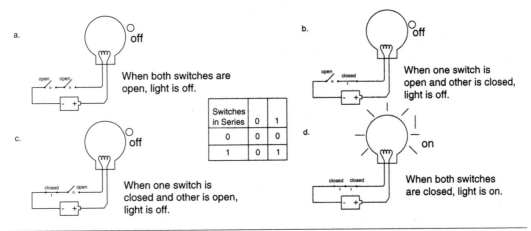

Figure 2.13   Electrical circuit with two switches connected in series mimics Boole's AND logic gate because both must be closed to result in the lightbulb going on to complete the circuit.

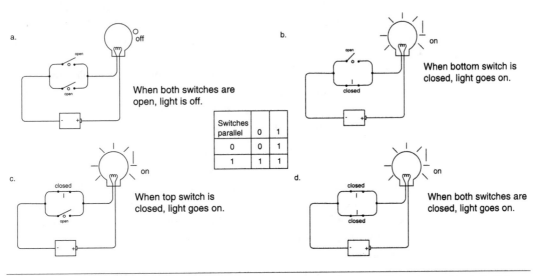

Figure 2.14   Electrical circuit with two switches connected in parallel mimics Boole's OR logic gate because only one must be closed to result in the lightbulb going on to complete the circuit.

4. A closed circuit in parallel with an open circuit in either order is a closed circuit (see Figure 2.14, parts b and c)

5. A closed circuit in series with a closed circuit is a closed circuit (see Figure 2.13, part d)

6. An open circuit in parallel with an open circuit is an open circuit (see Figure 2.14, part a)

These circuits, as mentioned, simulate Boole's logic gates and their associated truth tables; the series circuit is analogous to the AND gate, where both switches must be closed in order to get the lightbulb to light. And the parallel circuit is analogous to the OR gate, which results in a lit lightbulb when either switch (or both) are closed. Thus, if we equate "true" with the unimpeded flow of electricity (resulting in lit lightbulbs), and "false" with no flow, we have captured logical analysis and externalized it in a stand-alone machine. As Petzold (1999) puts it, this "unite[s] the algebra of George Boole with electrical circuitry and . . . make[s] possible the design and construction of computers that work with binary numbers" (p. 95).

In adapting Boole's logical calculus to the world of electrical circuitry, notice a change in nomenclature: We substitute a 1 for true outcomes and a 0 for false outcomes. This change is consistent with the language of binary numbers, allowing us to express all logical operations in the form of *bi*nary digi*ts* (or *bits* as they have come to be called in the computer industry). In summary, switches wired in series perform the equivalent of Boolean AND operations, and switches wired in parallel perform the equivalent of Boolean OR operations.

Let's array a set of switches to mimic our bakery example, illustrating how any set of statements may be represented by a properly rigged electrical circuit, no matter how complex (see Figure 2.15). Here again is the formula representing the criteria you will accept in a cake:

$$(C \times B \times (S + T)) + (V \times B \times (1 - S)) + H.$$

Remember that two switches wired in series mimic a logical AND gate (represented by the symbol $\times$) and two wired in parallel mimic Boole's logical OR gate (represented by the symbol $+$). We can then represent the vanilla sheet cake option with an electrical circuit as shown in Figure 2.15. Notice that there is an alternative that satisfies our prespecified set of conditions (and completes the circuit resulting in a lit lightbulb): It is the vanilla sheet cake with butter icing (a sheet cake satisfies the condition of being any number of layers except seven). Thus, electrical circuits may be rigged according to Boolean principles to select acceptable propositions from among a set of candidate propositions.

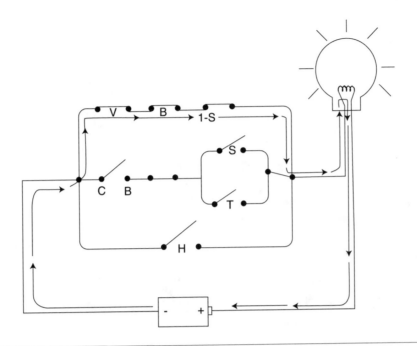

Figure 2.15 Wiring diagram mimics the conditions for the purchase of a vanilla cake with butter icing and any number of layers except seven.

NOTE: Arrow shows flow of electricity through completed circuit (see Figure 2.2 for key).

There are two theoretical principles of interest in this example: first is the notion that information can be processed as a series of yes-no choices in terms of binary digits (0s and 1s), and second, that such information can be simulated in an electrical circuit. These are Shannon's central ideas, the former based squarely on Boole's logical calculus.

But how can these ideas be used to get a machine to solve complex equations? Developing such applications took the work of several researchers in addition to Shannon. Among them were John Atanasoff, physics professor at Iowa State College, and George Stibitz, researcher at Bell Telephone Laboratories. Like Konrad Zuse, these thinkers decided to use binary rather than decimal numbers to simplify the job of rigging machines to do math.

Using relay switches, batteries, and flashlight bulbs, Stibitz, in the late 1930s, built a device that could perform binary addition. His *binary adder*, as it came to be called (see Figure 2.16), consisted of an array of Boolean AND, OR, and NOT gates arranged in a cascade format. To this day, the binary adder is a basic component of all digital computers, and depending on

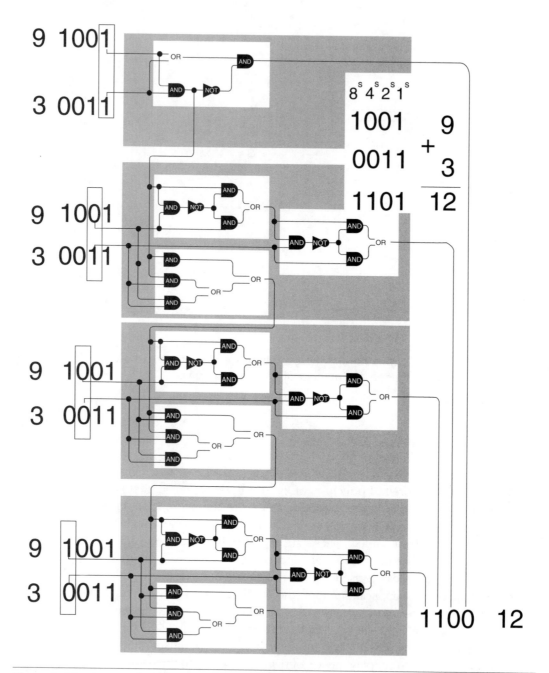

Figure 2.16 A cascade of binary adders arranged to perform addition, in this case 9 + 3 = 12 (decimal).

how binary adders are arranged, they can be used to perform complex mathematical operations beyond simple addition.

Of course, the more complex the mathematical operation, the greater is the number of switches required to provide the capacity to handle the task. This is especially true when each bit of manipulation is done using binary rather than decimal numbers (i.e., as Figure 2.16 indicates, adding 9 and 3 in decimal requires fewer steps than doing so in binary). Nevertheless, as far as building the machinery is concerned, it is simpler to do the job using the binary format, even though it takes more steps to get the job done.

It wasn't until 1940 that Stibitz managed to expand the basic principles of the binary adder to get a machine to perform subtraction, multiplication, and division using what he and his associate at Bell Labs, Samuel Williams, called a *complex number calculator*. Stibitz and company connected this new device to several Teletype machines, and to the amazement of all observers, for the first time in the United States, successfully demonstrated remote-controlled electromechanical computation.

Coincidentally, similar developments were taking shape in Germany, when, in 1939, Zuse independently built a calculating machine based on the binary number system using lightbulbs, relays, a keyboard, and then, later, 35-mm film with punched holes for entering instructions.

As fate would have it, the start of World War II precipitated intense, independent computer technology development programs on both sides of the Atlantic. The varied and numerous military programs included developing massive data processing capability for full-scale mobilization, fast computing for solving complex equations to improve the accuracy of weapons (e.g., calculating ballistics trajectories), and code breaking. All these needs spurred rapid development of alternative technologies (e.g., the development of transistors using semiconductors) designed to perform computing operations more quickly, at lower cost, and with greater efficiency and reliability than those that came before. These developments will be covered shortly.

For now, however, I skip ahead in time to introduce several applications based on the theories discussed so far. The purpose for the skip is to illustrate how binary code can be used to encode text and audiovisual information. I focus first on the encoding of alphanumeric characters because so much content is available in textual form (i.e., Web sites, newspapers, magazines, books). Then I present an example of digital voice coding to illustrate how sound is rendered into binary code, and an example of digital image coding. The last section of this chapter then leaps back in time to describe the hardware that makes it possible for mainframes, PCs, laptops, and handheld devices to encode, store, retrieve, and display so many different types of information.

■ ASCII: WHY 1 (A SINGLE STANDARD) IS A BEAUTIFUL NUMBER IN THE COMPUTER INDUSTRY

At any given moment, a binary digit (bit) has the capacity to store only one of two pieces of information, expressed as a zero or a one, a choice between two alternatives. To increase capacity, more bits are needed. So, for example, if you want to record the flavor of a cake as either chocolate or vanilla, one bit is all you need: a *0* could stand for *chocolate*, a *1* for *vanilla*.

But to characterize the cake further, say in terms of both flavor (chocolate or vanilla) and type of icing (i.e., butter vs. butter free), two bits of code are required. That's because four states or conditions are now in play, and that is the number that can be accommodated with two bits of code: The first bit can be 0 while the second bit is 0 (say, a chocolate cake with butter icing); or the first bit can be a 1 while the second bit is 0 (vanilla with butter icing); or the first bit can be 0 while the second bit is 1 (chocolate/butter free); or both can be 1s (vanilla/butter free).

In like manner, if three bits are used, eight conditions can be accommodated; in other words, the capacity to characterize a unique combination of conditions jumps to eight with three bits of code, as shown in the eight rows of Figure 2.17 (perhaps the column on the far left designates sugar vs. sugar free). Notice the trend. The number of unique possibilities or sets of conditions that can be characterized as the number of bits increases is equal to 2^n, where n is the number of bits. So, if there are three bits in use, the number of unique conditions that can be handled (the *capacity* of three bits) is 2^3 or 8. With four bits, 16 unique conditions can be captured, and so on.

The Implications of This Trend for Accommodating Text

The relationship between the number of bits of binary code and the capacity to code information is critical for capturing text, since there are many graphical characters that must be displayed, including 26 letters in the English alphabet (52 if you count upper- and lowercase), ten digits, and a variety of punctuation marks (commas, periods, dollar signs, etc.). In addition, a number of control commands are needed to provide the syntax to control the layout of the graphical content, including spacing between words and sentences, tab and backspace commands, carriage returns, line feed, and so forth.

Clearly, four bits of code are not enough to handle all the possibilities that text demands, since more than 16 characters are included in just one case of the alphabet alone. The question is, how many bits should be set aside for alphanumeric text?

0	0	0
0	0	1
0	1	0
0	1	1
1	0	0
1	0	1
1	1	0
1	1	1

Figure 2.17 Eight unique combinations are possible with three bits of code.

In 1967, this question was answered in the United States when the American Standard Code for Information Interchange, or ASCII (rhymes with "gas key") was developed. It calls for a seven-bit code standard for alphanumeric characters. With seven bits available, it is possible to manipulate 128 unique items of information, which is a large enough capacity to accommodate all the letters of the alphabet (both upper- and lowercase), all ten digits, punctuation marks, and various control commands for spacing, tabs, line feed, and such.

By using ASCII code, computers can exchange textual information without translation (a huge advantage). The first 32 ASCII bits are reserved for syntax functions such as backspace and carriage return, which control screen displays and printers. The rest are used for displaying visible characters (except the first and last of these which are used for space and delete functions).

As mentioned, adopting a single standard makes it easy for computers to exchange textual information. Without such standardization, a translation interface of some sort would be necessary for text to be successfully traded between computers using different systems, soon leading to chaos, or isolation. Under a worst-case scenario, trading documents between different systems would be prohibitively expensive because a new translation device would be needed each time. That is why the heading of this section calls 1 a beautiful number in the computer industry: An agreed-on standard simplifies the sharing of information among computers. Of course, there are advantages to developing unique architectures, especially in cases where it is desirable to limit access to keep sensitive information private and secure (medical records, crime histories, etc.).

These scenarios highlight a key technology issue at the heart of the infamous Microsoft antitrust lawsuit, namely, that by developing software that uses the same platform, greater compatibility, access, and commerce (meaning ease of trading materials between users) accrues to all—how egalitarian. Of course, the technology aspect is not the only one that carries weight in the worlds of business and regulation (profit margins and customer satisfaction are some of the nontechnical considerations), and that is as it should be, because monopolistic practices, even when dressed in egalitarian language, can still be deleterious to our economic health.

At the time ASCII was developed, computer memory was very costly, but it was obvious that a six-bit code lacked the capacity to handle the volume of alphanumeric text. So a seven-bit architecture was adopted. As it turns out, however, almost all computer systems today are based on an eight-bit architecture (each eight-bit chunk is called a *byte*); that is, information is stored in chunks of eight-bit bytes, even ASCII code. To accommodate the eight-bit byte format, ASCII code, entrenched in a seven-bit format, sets the first digit on the far left to zero to serve as nothing more than a place holder, or it may be pressed into service as a quality control device called a *parity check*, where the computer can be programmed to recognize that if the eighth bit is ever a 1, it knows that something is wrong with the way the data are being framed.[8]

For ASCII-coded documents, it is possible to determine the amount of computer memory required for a given portion of text. For example, an 8½-by-11-inch manuscript page typed using Times New Roman 12-point type with 1-inch margins, having 16 characters per inch, 6½-inch-long lines, and 23 lines per page, uses 2,392 bytes of computer memory.

■ CAPTURING SOUND WITH BINARY CODE

ASCII code is great for coding text, but not for sound and pictures. How is binary code used to capture sound? It is clear from the first chapter that sound is an analog phenomenon; that is, it is a continuous stream of information, usually made up of waves of compressed air that cause the diaphragm or other generating element of a microphone or your eardrums to vibrate sympathetically, enabling a faithful reproduction of the original sound to be produced so that the message contained in it may be transmitted and received successfully. In analog recording, physical sound vibrations

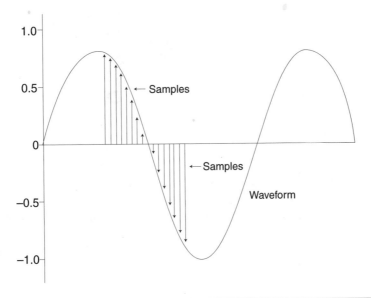

Figure 2.18   Illustration of the sampling phase of the analog-to-digital conversion.

are converted into a pattern of electricity matching the original stimulus; this process, called *transduction*, converts the continuous fluctuations of sound waves into a corresponding pattern of electricity.

By contrast, in digital recording, or in the conversion of the voice, say, for cellular telephone transmission, binary numbers are used to represent the varying fluctuations of electricity generated by sound waves through a process of *sampling* and *quantization*. To do this, the pattern of electricity matching sound signals is converted into a digital data stream using an *analog-to-digital converter*. How does this happen?

In the sampling phase of the analog-to-digital conversion, a circuit captures instants of the audio waveform at rapid intervals on the order of thousands of times per second (see Figure 2.18). Each unit captured (each sample) is then converted to a number according to its amplitude at that particular moment. The number associated with each sample is then stored in binary form. Figure 2.18 illustrates this part of the analog-to-digital conversion process.

After the sound is sampled, another circuit takes each sampled value and quantizes it—that is, each unit is then assigned a value of amplitude nearest the one that has been captured from an array of available choices. Thus, each sample is represented by the nearest allowable level of voltage the circuit is programmed to assign (see Figure 2.19). Any actual value seen to lie between two quantization steps is assigned the value closest to it.

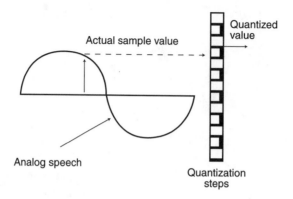

Figure 2.19 Illustration of the quantization phase of the analog-to-digital conversion.

In the cell phone industry, analog-to-digital converters must use sampling rates and a number of quantization steps great enough to ensure serviceable voice quality, but not so great that the capacity of the bandwidth granted by the Federal Communications Commission for such use renders service unprofitable.

To pitch the technology so as to maintain voice quality without squandering spectrum, a formula called a *Nyquist theorem* is used. The Nyquist theorem says that to maintain acceptable voice quality, an audio waveform should be sampled at "twice the highest frequency in the waveform" (Webb, 1998, p. 104). While the sound spectrum for human hearing is known to be from about 15 Hz to 15,000 or 20,000 Hz (15 to 20 kHz), the commonly used portion of the spectrum for plain old telephone service (POTS) is only about 4 kHz. Hence, a sampling rate of 8,000 (8 kHz) is deemed sufficient. An internationally agreed-on standard for voice coding is therefore 8 kHz.

To make the best use of the available spectrum, several additional voice-coding techniques are used to reduce the amount of information sent (covered in the next chapter). All are designed to reduce the amount of bandwidth required to transmit an acceptable signal, thus increasing further the utility of the spectrum.

In the case of compact disc (CD) recordings, where fidelity is of paramount importance, and transmission and bandwidth issues are not a concern, a greater number of samples quantized more finely are used. In both cases, once samples have been quantized, each bit of audio information is placed into a sequence called a pulse train consisting of zeros and ones representing on-off electrical signals, which are, at the receiving end, converted back into discrete voltage values closely resembling the original signal. This is done through the use of a digital-to-analog converter. It is this signal that is finally fed to either the earpiece of a telephone or to amplifiers connected to the speakers of a stereo system.

CAPTURING IMAGES ■

Digital image capture for both still and motion visuals is similar to the method just described for CDs, but with a much larger data capacity. In the case of images, the analog information (i.e., light focused by a camera lens on a scene of interest) is converted into an electrical signal that is then coded as a digital data stream. To accomplish this, a charge-coupled device (CCD) is the transducer instead of a microphone or telephone mouthpiece.

A digital camera lens focuses light onto a CCD panel consisting of several hundred thousand tiny light-sensitive diodes called *pixels*. Each pixel measures the amount of light hitting it, translating the brighter stimuli into higher electrical charges and the darker stimuli into lower electrical charges. In this way, a mosaic of light intensities renders the original scene, creating a faithful black-and-white image of it.

To add color to the picture, a beam splitter is used to separate the light entering the camera into varying levels of red, green, and blue light (see Chapter 1 for more on this aspect of the imaging process). In some digital cameras (called three-chip cameras), a separate chip is used for each of these colors, from which the full color spectrum is reconstructed through an overlay process.

In cameras using only one chip, selected pixels are fitted with permanent color filters. In such cameras, a computer determines what the true color of the light is arriving at each pixel by interpolating information from the surrounding area. This method results in less accurate rendering of the scene to be captured, but saves significant expense by requiring only one chip.

Digital video cameras work essentially the same way as digital still cameras, but with an additional sensor layer behind the image panel, allowing each image to be transferred to the second layer so that the first layer can refresh itself in order to capture additional images in rapid succession. This process happens many times per second, creating the illusion of motion.

Finally, the analog visual images are digitized essentially the same way as sound, through a process of sampling, quantizing, and coding. In the sampling stage, a number of selected instants of the analog signal (measured in MHz rather than kHz) are captured. Then each is assigned a quantized value from among an array of choices. Then, the values are coded into binary number equivalents composed of sequences of zeros and ones. In recovering the information to make it viewable again, a reversal of this process is accomplished through a digital-to-analog conversion.

■ STANDARD COMPUTER ARCHITECTURE: ALU, CCU, MEMORY, INPUT, AND OUTPUT

Once created, binary code representing content of whatever kind must be accessed properly for the content to be kept intact. If data are processed incorrectly, if sequences are apprehended out of order, or if parts of units are chunked with parts of adjacent units rather than with the ones they were originally framed with, the pattern of intelligence could be confounded, resulting in a mishmash of incomprehensible output. To avoid this problem, rules of syntax must be imposed on the data to make it interpretable; that is, the code representing the content must be viewed as an object to be captured or framed properly to keep it intact.

To process code successfully, computer architecture contains several components that are necessarily segregated from one another. In 1945, Hungarian mathematician John von Neumann described the basic architecture of the modern computer. His concept of computer architecture featured five components: a central arithmetic logic unit (ALU) to carry out mathematical calculations, a central control unit (CCU) to integrate operations, a memory to record data and hold permanent instructions about how to process it, a component for entering data (an *input* component), and an *output* component for displaying data to make content accessible to users (see Figure 2.20).

Input components include such devices as the keyboard and computer mouse, but those are not the only ones. Others include pressure-sensitive touch screens like those seen in restaurants, and plastic pens used to enter data on handheld PCs. Common output components include RGB video monitors and CRT computer screens, printers, audio speakers, telephone receivers, and headphones, among others.

The von Neumann architecture is still in use today. In addition, von Neumann specified that each of the computer's operations be performed in sequence one at a time (an imposition of temporal order to guard further against confusion). To do this, a clock chip is used to sequence operations.

Input and Output Components as Sensors and Effectors

When using ASCII code to type a document, the input device is usually a keyboard; the output device may be a printer or a screen display of some sort (i.e., a cathode ray tube monitor or CRT). Other items can serve as input and output devices. Furthermore, the computer's output can be fed back into the computer, creating a feedback loop that can initiate changes in conditions in the surrounding environment, similar to the way a thermostat connected to a room air conditioner controls the temperature in the room.

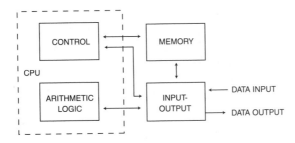

Figure 2.20 A general block diagram of a digital computer.

In the case of a simple thermostat, two metals located in close proximity expand when the room heats up, closing an electrical circuit, causing the air conditioner to turn on. When the room cools, the metals contract, opening the circuit, causing the air conditioner to turn off. In this way, the temperature in the room is controlled without human intervention. Computer systems may be rigged similarly to control more complicated and varied sets of conditions. They exhibit what has come to be called artificial intelligence (AI).

In such systems, binary code can store information designed to interact with sensors (e.g., temperature gauges) in the environment through an array of preset instructions. The computer's output may be linked to effectors in the environment (e.g., an air conditioner) that can cause changes that may in turn be recorded by sensors that can once again influence the effectors. Such *feedback loops*, as these systems are called, routinely alter a machine's relationship to the environment with a wide variety of practical benefits.

A dramatic use of computer feedback loops to alter conditions in the environment and accomplish goals may be seen in the military aviation setting. For example, Air Force pilots stress the desirability of using computer software to perform tasks that are beyond human response time that can save a pilot's life. Consider the flight of some high-performance jet fighters that would be impossible without AI software programmed to monitor and adjust the surface of the aircraft's forward-swept wings. In this case, sensors feed information to an onboard computer to adjust the warp of the airfoil to maintain the stability of the aircraft while in flight. Sensors permit thousands of algorithmic operations to trigger effectors to continually adjust the jet's wings during flight, a job clearly unsuited to a pilot's capability (no person possesses the vigilance, endurance, motor coordination, and quickness required to perform this task).

In the same setting, sensors and effectors conjoined with AI software are programmed to monitor pilots' decisions to initiate radical flight maneuvers, which, if followed, could overstress the wings of the aircraft to the point of structural failure. When such a maneuver is requested, AI software intervenes to reduce the severity of the request in order to preserve the integrity of the airframe, thereby preserving the survivability of the aircraft and the crew. It should also be noted that if such a radical maneuver could also result in the blackout of the pilot, then the same AI software that overrides the pilot's request in order to avert the destruction of the airframe can also be credited with the additional feature of guarding against a pilot's loss of consciousness, an event which could . . . result in . . . [destruction of the] aircraft perhaps killing the crew. (Shyles, 1990, p. 4)

Sensors working in tandem with binary code abound in less dramatic settings to monitor test equipment and perform measurements. Common examples include bicycle odometers, medical thermometers, and blood pressure gauges. In the bicycle computer, a magnet mounted on a spoke of the front wheel sweeps past a sensor fixed to the front fork of the bike each time the wheel revolves, closing a circuit and relaying information to a microprocessor that computes speed, distance, and even pedal cadence. The desired output is then displayed on a read-out on the handlebars.

In the automotive setting, sensors take information from the environment that is then fed through microprocessors programmed to effect safety procedures if certain measurements exceed predetermined parameters. An antilock braking system (ABS) illustrates just such an arrangement. In cars equipped with ABS, sensors in the brakes are designed to detect wheel-lock; when it occurs, effectors override the operator's foot pressure, releasing the brakes just enough to avoid skidding. Similarly, thermostats in the passenger compartment equipped with sensors and effectors connected to the air conditioner and/or heater work with microprocessors to maintain compartment temperature within a preselected range.

These examples show how computers can be connected to sensors and effectors to control functions in response to one or more environmental conditions they are rigged to monitor. They show how computer code can be used in tandem with machines to control conditions in the environment based on information received from the outside world, making it possible to automate a virtually endless variety of processes and devices without human intervention.

But what is happening *inside* the computer to process at superhuman speeds the information it can take from the sensors and effectors connected to it? To answer this we go back to the points in history when electromechanical relays gave way to vacuum tube technology, which in turn gave way to transistors, leading to the development of the microprocessors that drive the modern digital computer.

Figure 2.21 The Mark I computer.

SOURCE: IBM.

MODERN COMPUTERS ■

The Mark I

Had Charles Babbage been born just two generations later, he might have lived to see the world's first working analytical engine. The automatic sequence calculator, also called the Mark I, was switched on for the first time at Harvard University in 1943, in the midst of World War II. Over 50 feet long and 8 feet high, it contained more than 750,000 parts connected with 500 miles of wire, and used 420 switches set by hand to enter decimal values for computation (see Figure 2.21).

The impetus behind the Mark I's development came from the U.S. Navy, among other interested parties. The Navy needed a faster and more accurate way to calculate missile trajectories than the trial-and-error methods then in use. There was also a need to develop faster computing methods for deciphering secret-coded enemy messages. As Rowland (1997) tells it:

> Britain was . . . embarked on a desperate program to construct a fully electronic digital computer. Having broken the German cipher system at Bletchley Park, there was still an urgent need to speed the process of computation. . . . Banks of super-secret electromechanical machines, themselves far in advance of anything . . . ever heard of, were falling behind the flow of available information. Important messages were being decoded too late to be of use. (p. 238)

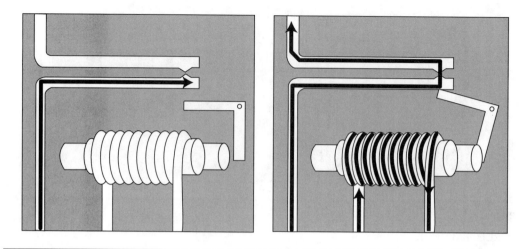

Figure 2.22   The electromechanical relay switch.

NOTE: In the electromechanical relay switch, when the switch is open, no current flows. But when current is passed through the coil, a magnetic field attracts the pivot causing two contact points to close the circuit, letting the current flow.

Although the Mark I successfully speeded up the calculation process, in truth it was obsolete even before it was finished being built, first, because it used the decimal system, which complicated the programming process. Second, it used electromechanical relays to operate the switches, which made it significantly slower than a fully electrical machine would be.

In the 1940s, electromechanical relays (Figure 2.22) were widely used in the telephone industry for switching telephone calls. Each relay consisted of a copper coil wrapped around an iron bar, which, when energized with an electric current, created a magnetic field that attracted one end of a nearby metal pivot. The opposite end of the pivot would then swing, pressing two contact points together. This action closed a circuit, allowing current to flow to another part of the telephone network, where the same process could be repeated or until a call reached its destination. More than 3,000 relays were used in the Mark I. In operation, the clicking of the machine, according to one observer, resembled the sound of a roomful of ladies knitting.

The Mark I could add or subtract numbers up to 23 digits long in 3/10 of a second; it could multiply them in 3 seconds. Yet these performance characteristics, although unprecedented at the time, were slow compared to what was possible with a fully electronic machine using vacuum tubes in place of relays. In spite of its limitations, the Mark I continued in service for 16 years.

From Relays to Vacuum Tube Technology

A fully electronic version of the Mark I called the electronic numerical integrator and computer (ENIAC) was soon developed. However, it was not completed until after the war ended. Nevertheless, it was the fastest computer in existence when it finally entered service.

ENIAC, standing 18 feet high and more than 80 feet long, was twice the size of the Mark I, and contained more than 17,000 vacuum tubes functioning as switches to conduct its calculations. It weighed 30 tons, and took up 1,800 square feet of floor space. It could perform 38 nine-digit divisions in under a second, and required teams of technicians to program and maintain it.

Programming ENIAC involved changing hundreds of patch cords on a panel resembling a telephone switchboard—a tedious job at best. To make matters worse, occasionally the cleaning staff would accidentally knock a plug out of the board and would stick it back into a random hole to avoid detection, frustrating to the utmost ENIAC's engineering staff (Rowland, 1997, p. 239).

The use of vacuum tubes represented a breakthrough in computer development. Tubes enabled switching capability based on purely electrical technology, giving rise to the first high-speed computing machine. But with more than 17,000 tubes, and their inherent tendency to overheat and blow out, their sheer number virtually guaranteed frequent breakdowns.[9] Yet even with these shortcomings, the transition from relays to vacuum tubes increased computing speed a thousandfold.

From a practical perspective, tube failure was not ENIAC's worst problem—the worst problem was its inability to change instructions. It could compute only with the numbers presented to it by its current configuration of patch cords. This meant that for the machine to work on a new problem, a technician had to physically reroute its wiring, a job that could take hours or days to complete. In modern-day language, ENIAC's "programs" were all hard-wired.

In response to this shortcoming, ENIAC's engineering team, headed by John W. Mauchly and J. Presper Eckert of the University of Pennsylvania's Moore School of Engineering, began designing EDVAC, the electronic discrete variable automatic computer. EDVAC was to include programming capability using mercury-filled tubes that could store instructions electronically. In addition, EDVAC was to use binary rather than decimal code, thereby reducing the number of tubes required to process information.

The Moore School engineers' stored-program idea sparked competition among computer scientists, leading to the 1949 development of EDSAC, the electronic delay storage automatic calculator, by British scientist Maurice Wilkes from Cambridge University. Ultimately, EDSAC and not ENIAC became the first working computer that could successfully store and retrieve programs, thus eliminating a major practical shortcoming of machine calculation. This breakthrough meant that a single machine could now quickly process code representing different kinds of information.

Wilkes's trumping of the Moore School team with EDSAC did not deter Mauchly and Eckert from continuing their development efforts. In 1950, they unveiled UNIVAC, or universal automatic computer, the first stored-program computer designed for commercial applications. UNIVAC was unique in that it stored instructions on magnetic tape instead of punch cards.

Based on Mauchly and Eckert's design, the Remington Rand Company delivered its version of UNIVAC to the U.S. Census Bureau in 1951. It was ten times faster than ENIAC, using only 5,000 vacuum tubes in a space 14 feet long, 9 feet tall, and about 7 feet wide. Over the next few years, 46 UNIVACs were sold for commercial use.

From Tubes to Transistors

The advance from electromechanical relays to vacuum tubes for switching computer circuits on and off resulted in a thousandfold increase in signal processing speed, a leap made possible because vacuum tubes have no moving parts—all action was electronic. As mentioned in Chapter 1, triode vacuum tubes feature a cathode that emits electrons, an anode (or *plate*) that attracts electrons, and a grid to control the flow. Depending on the conditions presented to it, the triode can act as an amplifier or a switch—that is, depending on the voltage supplied to the grid, the flow of electrons from the cathode to the anode can be made much larger or can be completely shut off. If properly tweaked, triodes can also act as rectifiers, turning alternating current into direct current. The ability of the triode vacuum tube to perform all these functions made it a versatile electronics tool, especially in broadcasting, telecommunication industries, and computer technology.

But vacuum tubes were not perfect. They were large, hot, electricity hogs, and unreliable—they quickly burned out. When thousands of them were crammed in a box, the temperature inside could soon exceed 120 degrees F. Such conditions required too much maintenance. Something better was needed. Something cooler. More reliable. Smaller. Less piggish.

By the late 1940s, alternative technology was already being sought to replace vacuum tubes in the communication industries. Physicists' study of atomic structure revealed that electrical conductivity was related to a substance's outer orbital electrons. It was well known that some materials were excellent conductors (most metals) and some were quite poor (e.g., rubber, plastic, ceramic, and materials used for wire insulation).

But other materials that behaved in a way that was somewhere in between conductors and insulators were not so well understood. These *semiconductors*, as they were called, were composed of elements that acted like insulators when in a pure state, but when treated with atoms from other elements (when *doped* with impurities), they acted like conductors. These elements included germanium and silicon. Dopants included phosphorous and boron.

Among the companies most interested in developing semiconductor technology were AT&T and Bell Laboratories. Their main goal was to find replacement technology for the vacuum tube, the workhorse used for amplification and switching in the telephone network. In addition, the military had intense interest in what came to be called solid-state electronics for their defense and nascent space programs—smaller, lighter, more reliable computer technology offered a more promising future for both sectors.

From a physical perspective, it was discovered that the atoms of a semiconductor are arranged in a crystal lattice that conducts electricity very poorly when in a pure state. But when treated with impurities from other elements, in some cases, the impurity sets up bonding that results in the presence of an extra electron, giving the material a negative charge. In other cases, the presence of impurities results in "holes," places where an electron might be if it were available, giving the material a net positive charge.

In these states, the theory was that semiconductors could conduct an electric current, performing the exact same work as vacuum tubes, but without the heat and with far less electricity consumption. In addition, semiconductors, it was theorized, should be able to conduct electric current in either direction, depending on whether they were negatively or positively charged. In practical terms, the ability to use semiconductors as replacements for vacuum tubes would depend on how successfully they could be doped with impurities.

In research supported by Bell Labs's solid-state physics activity, led by William Shockley, extremely small amounts of germanium soldered to a metal base were used with fine gold foil wires to test the amplifying capabilities of the new technology. In December 1947, Shockley's team applied an audio signal to one of the gold wires acting as an *emitter* (the equivalent of the vacuum tube's cathode), resulting in an amplification of the signal received 2/1000 of an inch away at the other gold wire acting as a *collector* (equivalent to the vacuum tube's anode or plate). The output signal was 50 times larger than the input signal. The semiconductor amplifier had passed its first test.

By 1951, after three more years of research, Shockley's team had produced the first reliable solid-state junction *transistor* (called so because depending on the conditions presented to it, it acted as either a *trans*mitter or a re*sistor* of electric current).[10] It consisted of a three-layer germanium structure, with the bottom and top layers serving as emitter and collector, respectively, and the middle layer serving as the base (Figure 2.23). At the junctions between emitter and base, and base and collector, an exchange of

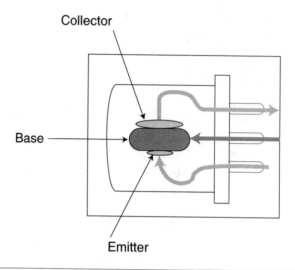

Figure 2.23 Illustration of the first solid-state junction transistor.

electrons occurred. Depending on the level of exchange, a depletion area could be created on either side of the junctions, which could impede the flow of current. But when enough current was applied, the depletion area diminished, and current flowed. In this way, a very small amount of voltage made the transistor act as a switch or an amplifier to a main signal current.

Transistors could do everything vacuum tubes could do but without any of the tube's shortcomings—no overheating, no breakable glass or filaments, no overconsumption of electricity. Transistors were everything vacuum tubes were not—they were small, cool, light, and reliable. Their tiny size meant their electric signals had to travel only a small distance to reach their destinations; that meant a great increase in data processing speed and efficiency.

By the mid-1950s, junction transistors made of silicon (the main ingredient of beach sand) made their debut, reducing costs significantly. Since then, the manufacture of silicon crystals has improved, as have doping techniques, leading to further reductions in prices for solid-state electronics.

From Transistors to Integrated Circuits

The trend toward miniaturization put pressure on manufacturers to find ways of connecting transistors without soldering wires by hand. The components had become too small for that kind of treatment. In addition, hand wiring was destined to keep prices high, and too often resulted in wires coming loose.

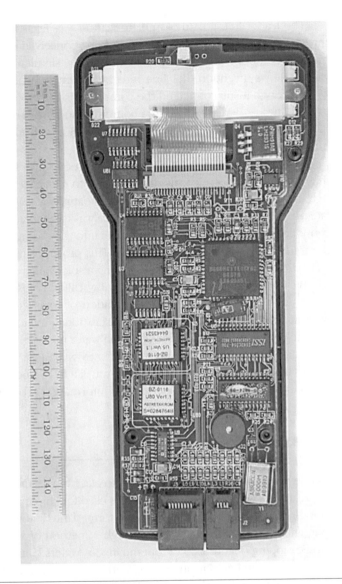

Figure 2.24   An integrated circuit.

SOURCE: Meade's Autostar. Reprinted with permission from John F. Amsbaugh and Richard Seymour, Seattle, WA.

Manufacturers also wanted to develop ways of mass-producing transistors. Rather than making them one at a time, companies began etching them into large silicon wafers using a photoengraving process. Soon entire sets of transistors consisting of amplifiers, resistors, and capacitors, were being produced together on a single substrate of semiconductor material (Figure 2.24).

The leader in the field of miniaturization was Texas Instruments, which, through the efforts of its employee Jack Kilby, conceived of a plan to produce multiple components of semiconductor material simultaneously on the same wafer. Kilby's invention, the first integrated circuit (IC), made its debut in 1959. Though it still connected the components with wire soldered by hand, its viability was demonstrated in a computer built from more than 500 such ICs for the Air Force that took up less than 1/150th the space required by the machine it replaced.

Around the same time, Robert Noyce, director of research and development for Fairchild Semiconductor, was able to capitalize on a breakthrough in transistor manufacturing that used thin coatings of silicon dioxide to insulate the transistor's junctions. Noyce's idea was to eliminate the need for conventional wires by etching a layer of metal into the coating at the junctions of the transistors where wire was needed. This process eliminated the need to affix wires to the transistors by hand using a soldering iron and microscope.

By 1962, mass production of ICs (now called *chips*) was in full swing. Since that time, the size of each generation of transistor has decreased as their number on a single chip has increased. Today, millions of transistors are routinely installed on substrates of silicon wafer no larger than a baby's pinky fingernail (Figure 2.25). It is no wonder they work faster than ever; electric signals from switch to switch need only travel a few hundred thousandths of an inch to open or close a logic gate for information processing.

■ CHIP MANUFACTURING

Precise production techniques are used to place hundreds or thousands of ICs onto a silicon wafer. The silicon substrate used for chip manufacture is refined from ordinary sand, which is melted and formed into ingots (cylinders two feet long and six inches in diameter) through a method of accretion resembling candle dipping (Figure 2.26). From the ingots, wafers ½ mm thick are cut by a diamond saw and fired in an oven to sterilize and polish them. Each wafer will make several hundred chips, each of which may contain millions of transistors. All the work is done in a sterile facility called a *clean room* designed to filter out all unwanted debris, including the minutest dust particles.

Each wafer is then treated with an insulating layer of silicon dioxide in an oxidation furnace and coated with a light-sensitive plastic called photo-resist. A photo-mask containing the pattern of a circuit design printed on glass using a process called electron beam lithography is then positioned over the treated silicon wafer. The wafer is then exposed to ultraviolet light, hardening the photo-resist layer in the areas not shielded by the mask. Then acids are used to remove the unexposed photo-resist, leaving parts of the silicon wafer bare.

1982: 286 Microprocessor
The 286, also known as the 80286, was the first Intel processor that could run all the software written for its predecessor. This software compatibility remains a hallmark of Intel's family of microprocessors. Within 6 years of it release, there were an estimated 15 million 286-based personal computers installed around the world.

1985: Intel386™ Microprocessor
The Intel386™ microprocessor featured 275,000 transistors--more than 100 times as many as the original 4004. It was a 32-bit chip and was "multi tasking," meaning it could run multiple programs at the same time.

1995: Pentium® Pro Processor
Released in the fall of 1995 the Pentium® Pro processor is designed to fuel 32-bit server and workstation applications, enabling fast computer-aided design, mechanical engineering, and scientific computation. Each Pentium® Pro processor is packaged together with a second speed-enhancing cache memory chip. The powerful Pentium® Pro processor boasts 5.5 million transistors.

1997: Pentium® II Processor
The 7.5 million-transistor Pentium® II processor incorporates Intel MMX™ technology, which is designed specifically to process video, audio and graphics data efficiently. It was introduced in innovative Single Edge Contact (S.E.C) Cartridge that also incorporated a high-speed cache memory chip. With this chip, PC users can capture, edit, and share digital photos with friends and family via the Internet; edit and add text, music, or between-scene transitions to home movies; and, with a video phone, send video over standard phone lines and the Internet.

2000: Pentium® 4 Processor
Users of Pentium® 4 processor-based PCs can create professional-quality movies; deliver TV-like video via the Internet; communicate with real-time video and voice; render 3D graphics in real time; quickly encode music for MP3 players; and simultaneously run several multimedia applications while connected to the Internet. The processor debuted with 42 million transistors and circuit lines of 0.18 microns. Intel's first microprocessor, the 4004, ran at 108 kilohertz (108,000 hertz), compared to the Pentium® 4 processor's initial speed of 1.5 gigahertz (1.5 billion hertz). If automobile speed had increased similarly over the same period, you could now drive from San Francisco to New York in about 13 seconds.

Figure 2.25   Some generations of integrated circuits (microprocessors) provided by the Intel Corporation since 1982.

SOURCE: Intel's Web site, courtesy of Intel Corporation: http://www.intel.com/intel/intelis/museum/exhibit/hist_micro/hof/hof_main.htm

Figure 2.26 A fresh ingot of silicon before being cut into wafers with a diamond saw.

SOURCE: WallStraits.com

The exposed portions of the silicon are then bombarded by dopants in a process called ion implantation to form the components for each chip. After the components are installed, aluminum connections are made between them, using additional layers of silicon dioxide for insulation. The aluminum is also installed via an evaporation process using a similar masking technique to control where the connections will be. Depending on how complex the chip is, the process just described may be repeated many times.

When production is complete, each chip is tested with electrical probes to make sure it works as planned. Those that do not are junked (about 70% fail at this point). The rest are sliced from the wafer into individual chips; then machines weld wires to the connectors. A plastic casing is put on each chip, and the wires are bent down (Figure 2.27). Finally, the chips are again tested. Defective chips are again discarded. The remainder is shipped.

Although chip manufacture is roughly the same for all ICs, the doping and connection patterns differ widely, leading to different types of chips with very different purposes. For example, some chips are *memory* chips, designed to store information. One specific kind of memory chip called a ROM (read-only memory) chip acts as a permanent store for binary code— that is, the transistor switches are set to react to electricity flowing through them the same way each time electricity flows through them. It is like a file cabinet that simply holds the information (programs) inside.

Another type of chip is called a RAM (random-access memory) chip. RAM chips allow new information to be encoded and then deleted when no longer needed. RAM chips allow transistor switches to create different patterns of electric signals to flow, representing different types of information.

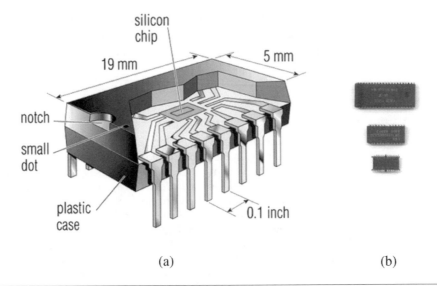

(a)   (b)

Figure 2.27   Some images of integrated circuits encased in plastic with wire connectors. (a) A diagram of an integrated circuit showing the inside. (b) Microchips.

SOURCE: (a) Advanced Micro Devices Inc. (b) Western Electric.

Yet another critically important type of chip is that which performs calculations and makes logical decisions that control a computer's activities in different parts of the machine. This chip is called the CPU (central processing unit) chip.[11] Another is a clock chip that uses a quartz crystal to time operations so that all instructions are carried out one at a time in proper sequence. Together the various chips coordinate and execute computer operations to ensure that the information processing proceeds as planned.

CONCLUSIONS ■

The modern digital computer, through the use of binary code and silicon chip technology, has made it possible for individuals to *encode* a wide variety of textual and audiovisual messages that were once produced only by publishing houses, recording companies, and television studios. It is a critical element of our communication system that enables us to transform into digital code the audiovisual and text-based messages we use for work and play. But the ability to make and *transmit* such messages is not the result of computers alone. Rather, it is the integration of computers with broadcasting and telecommunication infrastructures that permits message sharing among users. Without the PSTN and broadcasting technologies, e-mail and the

Internet would not exist. The purpose of the next chapter is to explain how computer data are integrated with these older technologies to provide transmission capability, to make communication among distant users possible.

■ NOTES

1. Although the term *code* often implies secrecy among users, it does not always carry that meaning. In this book, the term connotes a prior agreement among users as to what different symbols will mean, as in Morse code, which, for example, designates a dot as the symbol for *e*, a dot followed by a dash as the symbol for *a*, and a dash as the symbol for *t*, making the word *eat* appear as ". .＿ ＿".

2. The term *digital* refers to the representation of information by the use of discrete or discontinuous signals. Computers are digital machines because they code all information into sequences of 0s and 1s. The opposite of digital coding is *analog*, where information is represented in continuous values, as in a clock featuring hands that move continuously around the face. Analog clocks display all times of the day, whereas digital clocks can display only a finite number of times (i.e., tenths of a second). In general, human beings experience the world in analog fashion. For example, our visual systems allow us to perceive smooth and unlimited gradations of color and shape. However, analog information can be rendered into digital form, as in a picture composed of discrete dots that appears smooth from a distance. In addition to being digital, computers are also binary, because they use only two digits, 0 and 1, as opposed to more than two discrete choices, to represent data.

3. For example, construction on the Empire State Building began on January 22, 1930, on a 79,000-square-foot site, and reached a height of 1,454 feet. The building was completed in a little over a year. Few buildings exceed its dimensions even today. It has 102 stories, and weighs 365,000 tons. It used 200,000 cubic feet of limestone, and 60,000 tons of steel in its frame. This enormous construction is a testament to the efficacy of engineering and architectural prowess that required accurate computing of highly complex equations facilitated by the calculating machines developed during the early 1900s.

4. Boole introduced his own symbols for signifying various operations with classes to avoid confusion with standard algebra. For the union of two classes, instead of a +, Boole used the symbol ∪. For the intersection of two classes, instead of a ×, he used the symbol ∩.

5. Adapted from Petzold (1999, pp. 92-95).

6. Here we substitute the symbol **T** for the 1 because we are happy with any cake that is not seven layers. The 1 stands for the entire universe of cakes, so the $1 - S$ therefore includes all cakes that are not seven layers.

7. In the language of electrical theory, a *series* circuit is one in which there is one and only one path for current to flow; by contrast, a *parallel* circuit is one in which there are one or more points where the current divides and follows more than one path.

8. In reality, ASCII is not completely universal. It is widely used, but it is not unique. For example, some Asian nations use a double-byte character set (DBCS) to accommodate the thousands of ideographs used in China, Japan, and Korea. Translation issues abound in these cases. To deal with the problems associated with incompatibilities across the various systems in use, several computer firms developed

Unicode, a 16-bit alternative to ASCII, designed to accommodate all languages. Every character in Unicode requires two bytes. This means Unicode has a 65,536-character capacity, which seems robust enough to handle the load. Of course, Unicode doubles ASCII's memory requirements, but in today's world, that increase does not pose much of a problem.

9. For example, with 17,000 tubes operating at a frequency of 100,000 pulses per second, there were 1.7 billion chances each second of sustaining a system failure.

10. In 1956, Shockley and his team members John Bardeen and Walter Brattain shared the Nobel Prize in physics for their development of the transistor.

11. For a more detailed treatment of how memory and other types of computer chips work, written in delightfully plain language, see Davies and Wharton (1983).

CYBERINTERVIEW

Dan Birenbaum

On January 11, 2001, I interviewed freelance contractor Dan Birenbaum, a veteran computer programmer working as a mainframe expert for the last 20 years. For the last several years, he has been in the *legacy* area, which means upgrading computer facilities for private corporations that need to make a transition, often from mainframe storage to PC platforms, without losing any data. In the two years preceding this interview, Dan worked on making the Y2K transition as seamless as possible. Dan's views of the field come from a wide variety of experiences working on the inside for more than a dozen major corporations.

Shyles: What is your current job title?

Birenbaum: Programmer, systems analyst, designer, jack-of-all-trades for over 20 years.

S: When you were in school learning a field, were you studying computers?

B: No, I came to work in this field as a result of economic circumstances. I was looking toward a professorship in political science. My college degree was actually in philosophy. Then I got a master's in political science in 1977 from the New School for Social Research in New York.

S: Do you work in New York City?

B: On occasion. Right now I'm doing a project in New Jersey for a company that handles stock transactions. I'm transforming its computer system from one older technology to a less old one to prepare it to become newer still. And all of my work has to be invisible to users while I'm doing it. No one can see any differences based on what I am doing, even while they are reviewing reports or screens or any other output.

S: This is mainframe work?

B: Yes.

S: That's your specialty?

B: Yes it is.

S: How did you get from political science into being a mainframe specialist?

B: I took a nine-week, intensive course in the late 1970s when push came to shove and it was time to make a buck. I went for an intensive course, got a certificate in computer programming. I had never written a program before in my life and I had to write six of them in nine weeks, using punch cards. I wrote three in Cobol, and three in Assembler, and I came out with a resume and then looked for a job. I got a job as a trainee programmer, and kept that for about a year. Then, in a different company I got a job as a junior programmer, got promoted, got another job after that. I soon found that switching jobs was the best way to make more money and gain broader experience. It was much faster than to stay within a corporation and wait for promotions. For at least 80% of the 20 years I have been an independent consultant, a subcontractor, a hired gun, a job shopper, a job hopper, depending on the terminology. I got a very wide exposure to different standards in the industry; more than I would have had I stayed in one place.

S: Do you like it that way?

B: Yes. That way, I'm able to get involved, do the job, and stay out of most of the politics.

S: How would you characterize "the politics"?

B: The politics has to do with how a project is shaped down to the task level, what the corporate culture is like, what the personality of the management is like, what the reporting standards, if any, are, that is to say project tracking, assignments, responsibility for blame if things go wrong, the assignment of praise. As far as the different places I've worked, they include companies that handle shipping, finance, brokerage, leasing, retail, manufacturing, television broadcasting, and electricity supply.

S: What were you doing with the Y2K issue a year ago?

B: For the Y2K issue, I was working for an overseas electronics manufacturer, with very large interests in the United States. I was hired to go through thousands of their programs (not by myself, of course; there were bunches of us doing this), trying to find anything that had to do with dates and date calculations. We needed to see to it that the year 2000, which ends in 00, would not be confused with the year 1900, or any other ending in 00. The problem arose because decades ago many programs were written using only the last two digits of the year in order to save computer memory, which had been a great consideration. Only the decade and the last digit of the year was used. In other words, if it was 1996, only 96 would have been used and the 19 was omitted. So, in the year 2000, it became necessary to make it clear to all the programs that you had the new century as part of that date, and not the year 1900 any more. The possibility of confusing the year 2000 with 1900 could be a problem in programs that, let's say, are responsible for calculating interest, especially where the period of time is calculated by subtracting one date from another that includes the year. That's just one simple case. And it's incredible how often date-sensitive information comes into play. Late charges, for example, or pay periods, billing periods, interest calculation. It's amazing how many calculations use a date range or scheduling factor.

S: Like government checks for social security.

B: I did a project at a utility company where they were charged a fee when electricity was transmitted over the lines of a different company. Computing charges, including interest if they missed the cutoff payment date, all needed to be monitored. This "wheeling" of electricity with its fees and potential interest charges was only one part of the project. The Y2K issue made it clear that dates and times are always the fourth dimension. You always have your data, which is to say the quantity of whatever it is you are tracking or measuring whether it is nuts and bolts or options or shares or kilowatts—you are always tracking the quantity, and quantities have various attributes associated with them. So you need to specify the who, what, where, and when about the information you have collected. But when you get to the "when" part of it, you enter that fourth dimension, which is the time factor, the date. Very often there are dates associated with other pieces of data. So, all over people were faced with the possibility of their systems not failing so much as calculating erroneously, and the more subtle the error, the more insidious it would be, and the more dangerous it would be because the more errors the company committed, the less credibility the company would have. Ultimately, the fear was that a Y2K debacle would spell less profitability, or worse, for the business, the government, or any computer system-using entity because it would result in an inability to calculate who owed whom what and when.

S: It seems the Y2K problem was successfully solved.

B: We had a smashing success because so much time and budget were devoted to it. Basically, the fear was so great that companies and governments were willing to throw large sums of money at it. Of course, there are some who say, "Well the problem was overrated." But at the time no one wanted to bet that the problem was minor, so spending money became easier.

S: Do you have a sense of how much?

B: That's a problem. As Carl Sagan used to say, "billions and billions." Probably even beyond. Among other approaches, we used automated technology which enabled us to take large volumes of programs and scan them for dates, tracing every place that that date's information was used. Almost any address in a computer's memory can store numeric data, and a programming language can reference it by name. This means that date information can flow into a myriad of places in the system. So it was like taking ten cups of water and pouring water from one into the next, into the next, into the next, while in a dark room and you have to find all of the cups and make sure that all the water is going from one cup to another without missing a drop and without missing a cup, and if you don't do that your system fails, or produces erroneous results. The automated technology we used could find the ten cups and enable you to install the correction in one shot; that is, it would apply the same fix to all of your programs so it would be universal and seamless. Then testing procedures could be instituted, and that is where things are made and broken. So these automated technologies for the Y2K fixes definitely made our work easier and probably saved a great many proverbial rear ends. There are still latent Y2K bugs out there. Not too many, but I understand that a couple weeks ago a Norwegian railway had a glitch because of the turnover to 2001.

S: The transition to Y2K seems to have gone smoothly. But it must be hard for companies built on mainframe databases to keep up with new developments.

B: I've seen tremendous change. When I took my course we didn't have terminals or screens to look at. Everything was done through punch cards. You'd punch holes in the cards and a stack of cards would be a program. Another stack would be your data. Then you'd feed them in and you'd get paper reports—hard copies. Today, it's a totally different world. Now conceptually it is not so different from what we had before. What's come today is in its deepest conception a lot like what it was decades ago. But the amount and types of information are greater. The Internet gives us the ability to be anywhere around the world instantly to dig into all kinds of information. It's tremendous. Research that took hours to do when I was in graduate school now takes minutes. The e-mail communication aspect is really great.

S: Yes, and that depends on the telecommunication network, not just the computer. A computer in and of itself is not enough to explain e-mail.

B: No, they must be networked. But even in old computer mainframe arrangements, there are telecommunication components to it. It has communication channels, switches, terminals. Even the mainframe itself could have a front-end computer and a back-end computer, segregated for different kinds of processing. In the mainframe jargon, the connectivity is part of what is known as standard network architecture. Today, in the legacy world of the mainframe computer, programs are being run on a 24/7 basis, so you can no longer have your online time where you look at your screens during the day and you run your batch cycle at night. You have to be able to run your online function anytime because there could be people in different parts of the world accessing it, usually through the Web. And your nightly batch cycle therefore is no longer a batch cycle. It's bursts and packets that run in small pieces of time throughout the day and night. So the entire design concept has changed to accommodate the new demands, and that's what a lot of my work is these days—taking apart long cycles, and making them more efficient, making them run faster, finding different ways of combining the data, of doing updates and extracts, so that you don't interfere with the user. That's a radical change from what's been in the mainframe world all of this time. This is one impact of the World Wide Web on the "legacy systems" world. Old application systems fit a batch world. But, as soon as you had terminals and screens, you could look up something in real time or near real time. And as soon as you had that, you usually could not do massive updating of files while they were in use because accessing both data for reports and the screens at the same time could result in one user locking another out, sort of like having two football players diving for the ball at the same time. Only one of them is going to get it. And the other is effectively locked out. This is how it was with the online world and the batch world, and basically the line of demarcation was the nighttime—the night belonged to the batch runs and the daytime belonged to the online activity, which could involve updating or retrieval of information. Of course, over time, ingenious solutions were devised to create parallel files and databases. The trick then became proper synchronization of the data in multiple repositories. Now there are no longer nighttime and daytime functions; everything needs to be able to function all the time. So now the whole trick is how to run the batch cycle and anything else, like database reorganizations that might have to run for several hours, and break it into segments that can run during the day or that can run anytime without interfering with the rest of the business.

S: Where are things headed?

B: Faster and more is the usual thing. We will also have to start regulating for information overload. There is a thing called wall-to-wall data, and most people don't handle wall-to-wall data very well. Computers do, but people don't.

S: What does that mean?

B: It means tell me everything about X or Y. Describe every aspect and relationship that holds between two or more variables. Computers do this very well, even when it's not necessary. So it's the responsibility of business analysts to prioritize in order to select the important variables and leave out the irrelevant ones. In too many places the computer and the "systems" have been allowed to shape the business or operation more than the business has shaped the use of the tool, the computer. This is like letting the tail wag the dog. There exists a continual tug-of-war between the purposes the computer is supposed to serve and the serving of the computerized system.

S: Well now that's a philosophical point. How do you see things developing? What trends do you see for the use of computers for work and play?

B: In terms of work and developing systems, in the future, we will design systems that allow users to be anywhere in the world. The concept of an office per se is becoming obsolete. Sure analysts still have to meet (either in person or through some virtual contact) to get the concept of what needs to be done. But as they translate it for those who will design and implement the system, the analysts, tech writers, and programmers can be anywhere in the world. Much of the Y2K work was farmed out via satellite to places on the other side of the globe, the fixes were applied, and the systems were returned to their host addresses. If done well, if everyone understands what they were supposed to do, then things can get done properly. I think three conditions need to be met before shifting into full work-from-anywhere mode: first, the ability of telecommunications to handle human nuances better; second, the need for hierarchical management, that is to say visible overt control, must diminish; and third, the capacity of energy must go even higher in rapid bursts to alter the existing work paradigm. This is a bit more extensive than the shift from suits and ties to casual Friday.

S: So do you like the term *cyberspace*, metaphorically speaking, or dislike it because the notion of space and time is so different?

B: My first reaction is that I like it. It's a positive thing. It's extra dimensions. However, it can be confusing.

S: It seems misleading to me to talk about virtual space or cyberspace because you are not in a nether space. You're in a chair in your home or office.

B: Yes, but the database you are interacting with can be productively thought of as being in something we call cyberspace. When I create or modify a program or system, part of my job is to see to it that it does the job for which it was created. I run the program and see what comes out the other end. What does it look like, what is presented on the screen? Are we getting unexpected results, wrong results? Quality assurance is part of the process. You must test the work as part of the method. If you put something in without testing, it's like building a rocket, putting somebody in the capsule, and saying, "OK, let's launch it." You don't do that. While it is not often a life-and-death situation, it's a bad outcome if it doesn't work or if it works wrong. So when I work on a project, I think of data as residing in cyberspace, not users. I often think of the data residing in a pinball machine. And I have the control of a program with a very high number of flippers on it. Every condition that you put into the program is going to perturb the system in a different way and generate a different outcome. You have to see what those different outcomes are. And you have to test for the most likely, and you have to test for some strange situations also. And that's where cyberspace is for me. I am not in cyberspace; the data are.

S: You'd have to know what you are willing to call a correct answer before you run to say whether you have matched it.

B: Exactly. To determine whether the thing functioned properly, we look at the throughput. We trace the data through from the start to the end to make sure things don't bomb out or seem strange at the end.

S: So let's say your corporate clients hire you. Do you meet with them at the beginning of the process to determine how they define success?

B: Yes. The first thing that's necessary is to find out "what's this business about?" What goals or milestones can we agree on?

S: What is the team meeting like the first time? Is there any commonality across the meetings that you've seen?

B: It depends on what phase of the project I've come into. If it's at the very beginning, then you really have to start with a very high level of description of the business, and if the business has been around for a while, and many that I've been involved with have been, you read a ton of literature to acquaint you. You're basically paid to be a detective, paid to get into the innards of the thing because without doing that you can't fulfill a purpose of proper automation. And that's true for financial institutions, retail institutions, leasing companies, manufacturing, automotive, stock trading, consulting firms, and a government.

S: And you are usually called to upgrade their computer systems?

B: Upgrade standards and systems, design systems, or help a company that had half of its operations scattered on different computer systems, sometimes with vendors. But sometimes it's only a matter of rewriting some programs or job control language in order to enhance efficiency or add functionality. Right now, I'm making a completely transparent changeover from an older file structure to a database structure.

S: How did they find you?

B: Part of it is kind of like an "old boy" network because those of us who are in the legacy world in the mainframe world deal with certain kinds of databases and software. Legacy work refers to application systems that were written on mainframes and have existed for years or decades, as opposed to personal computers or any of the more recent technologies. By now, even some of the "client server" systems built on PC networks are considered part of the legacy world if they can't interface with the Internet or the Web. Much critical data live in that legacy world. So now all of the Web and Internet technology not only have to interface with that world, they represent additional layers on the cake. So we do something called data mining, which means we dig into old databases and extract the rules of operation as well as data for that business. Then we pull out history and make it possible to cross-reference it with what's new.

S: Are the manuals still available?

B: [Amid snickers] There are, but documentation is always the poor cousin, and must be thought of as suspect. Personally, I never trust it. And anybody who's worth his salt doesn't.

S: Do you write documentation of your work?

B: I try to embed comments. Usually the management budgets too little time and money to do it properly. The same is true for the implementation stage, which should have the documentation coordinated with it and not come after the fact. The best that I've ever seen is documentation written by those who've done the design. They use pieces of the programming system to create documentation.

S: And how often does that happen?

B: Exactly once in all of my career. However, I have seen enough bits and pieces of other systems to realize that it does happen at other times. But no documentation is the equal of the programs so people that come in to fix or maintain a system get the best information from working the programs and seeing where they take them. Documentation can be good at specifying the possible values of a given field. In order to solve a problem, the only way you'll solve it is to go into the program itself, and go into the data files themselves and try your best to figure out what it's doing.

S: Let's shift gears for a moment. How do you feel about giving your credit card information online? Are you mistrustful or worried about your security and privacy?

B: Personally, I am a bit paranoid, because unless you have a sealed computer in a sealed room and you do a strip search of whoever's using it, going in and out, there's always going to be a potential for data leakage. And the more connectivity there is, the greater the potential for data leakage. But despite my paranoia, the desire for convenience has won out. And that's where I figure that noncomputer mechanisms such as insurance and law enforcement will step in to combat hackers or other destruction that may take place.

S: Cyberterrorism lurks in the back of your comment, right?

B: Absolutely. Cyberterrorism is real, it exists. There are laboratories, companies, and government organizations that devote their time to creating viruses and capturing every known virus so that they can write defenses against them. It's as if you had a battle going on between the locksmiths and the lock pickers. It's constant. And cryptography and encryption play a great role in this. We have already seen the coupling of a political war and a cyberwar where a Pakistani hacker group took down the foreign ministry Web site of Israel. There have been others. So there have been real attacks and counterattacks going on. A book called *Information Warfare* (Schwartau, 1996) documents cases of economic blackmail through cyberspace. All of the potential for security leaks, errors, and information deviation that would exist within a corporation now can be foisted on the public because of the Internet and its interconnectivity.

S: Along this line, do you think it is a good idea for the U.S. government to have access to databases via what is being called a Clipper Chip to combat vandalism by cyberthieves?

B: The Clipper Chip allows the government to go into anybody's system and decrypt what he or she had written for the sake of security. The justification is as an antiterrorist capability. And there is some value to it. I can't completely dismiss it. However, the question is whether or not that would be used judiciously; who's going to monitor its usage?

S: So it comes down to the ethics of the user.

B: Exactly, as in everything else. It's not the technology, it's the people who stand behind the technology. If you have complete faith in them, then there's no problem. Of course, we must remember what Lord Acton said, "Power corrupts and absolute power corrupts absolutely." And the trouble with computers, particularly now that we have the Internet, is that people can develop a sense of omniscience and omnipotence. They can sit in their remote corner of the world and go into your computer and your files and basically alter them, delete them, or simply suck information out of them, and you may not even know that they are there. If you don't have your own defensive software, firewalls, radar, in effect, seeing who's pinging. I mean the whole side to the Internet with cookies and with the embedding of information and codes into what are other people's programs by outside companies onto your machine is common practice. So, in effect, you have everything intertwined already. And to have a government agency step into this without publicly debated legislation, I think, is some very dangerous ground. Cyberspace needs to be defended exactly the same way real space would be. The freedoms that we know, freedom of the press, freedom of religion, need to be defended equally in the world of cyberspace as they would be in the conventional world.

S: So as of January 2001, when we are speaking, what advice would you give to folks to protect a highly connective system like the Internet?

B: Just as I wouldn't walk around a dangerous neighborhood flashing a lot of jewelry, a lot of wealth, I would advise Internet users not advertise what they've got, unless you want the business or you want to attract people. Limit the amount of personal, private information that you keep on your machine. Ideally, don't keep any there. Keep track of every place that you've communicated with. When you get your bills or anything else look for the patterns and the statistics on it and see that it's really you, and it's really your transactions that are coming through there. Several of the larger banks have already gotten pattern recognition software in place so that, for example, if I go on vacation and am suddenly charged from someplace else, a letter or a phone call comes and they ask about its authenticity. One of the consequences is that individuals now have to be more conscious of their own patterns and have to look at the record of their spending money or whatever they're dealing with in terms of information to see that they are not getting any extra charges or any strange queries. Ultimately, it's a commonsense kind of a thing. Every convenience has its downside. The disadvantage of the Internet's convenience is the loss of privacy and possibly security. And because this is a truly international medium, it's much more difficult to control than it might be if it were restricted to just something going on within the borders of the United States.

S: Switching gears again, what skills enable you to do the jobs that you've been hired for?

B: Some say that musicians, mathematicians, and logicians make good programmers. And I have two out of three on that one: logic and music. It's the ability to see how pieces fit together. To put it another way, you've got something that you're starting out with and something you want to end up with. Somehow you have to create a middle to transform it. Another skill is to be able to synthesize, to translate what technical and nontechnical people are saying about their business or about their function. And then you have to come up with a model that resembles something that they're doing, and you have to let psychology into this as well, and you have to sometimes be able to see around corners that other people don't even know are there yet in order to get to the result. This is all like an iceberg. You see very little on the top, and then there's this vast world underneath.

S: It sounds to me like you like what you do.

B: I've been exposed to a lot of interesting, bright people. At times I've also felt that computers are fast idiots that are programmed by slow idiots. I've seen waves of people from overseas come in, which I think has really kept businesses going at the level that they needed to be. The Russian immigration, for example, brought a lot of people who were well trained in the techniques, using older technology, and they were doing things in much more efficient ways than a lot of Americans. That sustained quite a bit of American business for a while through the 1970s, 1980s. Another wave came from East Asia, which has also supplemented the work force, and a wave from

South Asia, mainly India and Pakistan. So these three waves provided enough human resources as it's called. People have provided enough skill to keep these very large systems going because what may have started out as a single idea, or a cluster of ideas, over decades has expanded and expanded and expanded to the point that you have things running now that no one person is completely familiar with. No one has a picture of the entire database in his head and how it interacts. No one, given whatever documentation there is, understands certain critical synchronization points. In other words, when you create a particular file, when you create a particular cluster of information, or a database record, or whatever the entity is, first of all there's a rediscovery process of how it works, and that's critical to being able to get it to work properly in the 24/7 world.

S: What's in most demand these days?

B: Web designers are very hot. There is always some new language coming in. People able to design Web sites, and interfaces to them, who are knowledgeable about getting applications up that fit the business needs in a short time are hot right now. Jobs for programmers are very much in demand these days. However, there is also a demand for people who can manage teams and projects. When you have people in more senior managerial positions who are able to pull a team together and to direct it and coordinate it, that is in demand, and that is where a great deal of money is.

S: Does a company ever hire you and ask you to do something and you come back to them and say, "This is impossible"?

B: Yes, that has happened; however, one or two things have to go along with that: I make a recommendation for an alternative solution, which is not going to be outlandish in terms of time or money, or I say, "What you want is impossible," and I am prepared to walk away from the whole thing.

S: What makes it impossible? They don't have enough transistors on their chip?

B: Basically. Sometimes the speed of the machine, or the speed of a rewrite access, which is still a physical thing going to a specific part of a hard drive, will not permit more than a certain amount of information in a certain amount of time, no matter what you do. This problem can exist in the mainframe. For example, with large databases, older databases, once they have a certain volume of records on them they become inefficient because they're looking to put the records wherever there's room. They're filling it in and so you have internal pointers to send the data from point A to point B to C to D. Now the applications program doesn't know about that, it doesn't have to. That's happening inside the software, the database software, let's say. And the more chaining that you have the more reads you have to have, the more access you have to have, the more lookups, the longer things take. So the way around that, naturally, is to take it and reorganize it, compress it. But what's the problem with that? It takes time to collapse it. So suddenly the amount of time it takes to collapse it, to reorganize your data, is longer than the time that you have available to you on the cycle. Unfortunately, a lot of places have let the problem build to a critical situation or they throw more hardware at it, or they manage to get some software enhancements where they'll just read in bigger chunks of data at the same time. Or they'll get software that allows them to reorganize at the same time that you have the applications running, which is a lot more risky in concept, but it exists.

The more intelligent companies are beginning to realize, and I'm speaking from a business perspective not an academic or a scientific one, but in the business community there is a certain resistance to change. There is a certain resistance to innovation to bring in new tools and naturally there is a desire to do it on the cheap. Economic pressure, tradition, ego, a combination of forces keeps the system from functioning at the level it should. Even technical managers may not really understand what they're being offered when it's a new approach. If somebody tells you it takes 20 hours to reorganize a database, you have to shut the thing off, bring it down, back it up, sort it out, and put it back out there. Then suddenly someone tells you that you can do this in 20 minutes, and of course you think that you're getting sold snake oil. Now if you're the chief information officer, responsible for the company's information, including what the image of the company is to the outside world, what do you do? Well, you try to find somebody else that's done it very often. But that's like kind of a circle, going around. So then somebody says, "Well, we'll do it for you quicker and easier."

S: There must be some serious proprietary issues connected with such interventions.

B: Yes, and you have the additional question, "To whom do the software and data belong?" There are companies that design software specifically for these kinds of solutions. So sooner or later when the pain gets to be great enough, this sort of solution is brought in and then a reorganization has to happen. Don't forget we're in this 24/7 world. So you eventually have to reorganize your legacy databases. You have to go after these things and find a way to handle them quickly. Either you're going to make smaller databases or you're going to keep the large one, but then how do you get the data you need? You've got to have the tools to do it.

S: Let's talk for a moment about the field of education. As a result of what's happened in the computer industry and with the Internet in particular, I see as utterly inevitable that there will be distance education. How do you see things developing in this area?

B: I agree with the inevitability aspect of your question. It's kind of like the buggy whip and the automobile. Manufacturers of buggy whips could have kept manufacturing, but the automobile passed them by. Yes, academics should brace for the change and shape it rather than resist it, because it's a tidal wave. It's already out there, particularly in the technical fields closest to developing computer operations and so forth. They recognize what they themselves could do. Educators should get themselves in the position of gatekeeper in terms of what educational materials go in and out over the Net, who has access to it, what the fee structure should be. While the Internet as a free medium is a wonderful idea, it can't be free in all cases, because after all, if someone is a musician or an artist or author and this is how they made their living in the past and now their material is on the Internet, I would think that they're still entitled to some royalty or copyright fee or some subscription fee and so that could likely become a model for academia. Academics shouldn't be worried about the money aspect of it because there have always been tuitions, there always have been fees and charges. The only difference is now it will happen in cyberspace. Nonetheless, there will still be times when people will need to come together face-to-face to discuss what they have to do.

S: As we have done.

B: As we have done. For academia to just put up its wall and pull in its drawbridge and then flood the moat, no, they'll be overwhelmed. Instead, the best thing is to figure out how to float the moat to the right height, how to lower the bridge, and welcome the hoards and dispense the cherries that are about to be picked, and charge, of course, for all of these things in the proper way so that everyone can make a living.

S: Thank you for your insights.

B: You're welcome.

CHAPTER 3

SENDING MESSAGES
ACROSS THE NETWORK

LEONARD SHYLES

The ability to *transmit* binary code is not the result of computers alone. Rather, it is the integration of computers and other digital devices with broadcasting and telecommunication technologies that permits message sharing among distant users. Without the public switched telephone network (PSTN) and similar (i.e., private) network infrastructures, and the various broadcasting technologies now used for telecommunication transmission, e-mail and the Internet as we know them could not exist.

The purpose of this chapter is to explain how digital information (including voice, data, and images) is transmitted, making communication possible. A central topic therefore is *bandwidth*,[1] or the capacity of a channel to move digital information from one place to another in a given period of time once a connection is made. I describe some of the communication technologies that transfer messages from point to point, including wire and cable facilities (copper, coaxial, and fiber optic), and wireless facilities using modulated radio energy (terrestrial microwave and satellite transmitters); all are currently used in telephony (including voice, image, and data transmissions) and/or broadcast programming.

Related to bandwidth is the topic of how telecommunication networks give users *access* to one another by providing connections through complex switching architecture. Another is the *signaling* system that alerts both users and exchange offices that connections have been made or terminated.

I also describe how the digitalization of content increases the capacity and flexibility of telecommunication channels. Topics include packet switching for Internet communication, multiplexing, and signal compression, all designed to make more efficient use of available bandwidth. I also outline some of the advantages and disadvantages of digital versus analog modulation, as well as quality control issues, and error correction features designed to ensure that messages received are the same as those that are sent.

As technology develops, so do our objectives for its use. Greater bandwidth increases the capacity for the delivery of more products and services to users. And although such developments are positive, they present uncertainties that both challenge and threaten vested interests wishing to maintain their customer base, audience, and the status quo. Further uncertainties (to both consumers and equipment manufacturers) are manifested by a lack of agreement on standards as new technologies emerge to compete in the marketplace. As a result, political, social, economic, and legal issues arise, all of which influence development.

Because analog television receivers are so plentiful in the United States, for example, it will likely be many years before we see a full transition to digital broadcasting.[2] This is because set owners are often reluctant to invest in expensive new systems that may fail to become standard. Some believe that because of economic limitations, the conversion to a digital broadcasting platform may never happen in the third world. Frequently, the adoption process is slowed by incompatibilities across competing systems vying for acceptance, market share, and licensing for spectrum space.

In addition, legal problems at times arise with chilling effects whenever new technologies force a reinterpretation of relevant laws. For example, the digitalization of audiovisual content, which enables users to copy and distribute artists' work worldwide in a few seconds, has put new strains on our copyright law, leading to costly litigation (e.g., the Napster case).

The analog-to-digital transition that we see in broadcasting and media industries is also transforming telecommunications.[3] Of course, the notion of transition implies incompleteness; that is, the digital revolution is still a work in progress. For example, to provide the connection or *local loop* between central offices and subscriber households, the PSTN still uses twisted-pair copper wire, a 19th-century technology originally designed only for analog voice traffic. Since its inception, however, the telephone network's switching technology has been continually upgraded (from electromechanical relays to vacuum tubes to digital solid-state equipment) to increase efficiency; for this reason, it is clear that technological change is nothing new to telephony. Yet these advances have left the local loop and its medium of delivery (twisted-pair copper wire) largely undisturbed; that is, *switching* became digital before *voice transmission* did.

Since around 1990, however, telephone companies have embarked on a more fundamental transformation, a functional expansion away from carrying just analog voice signals toward carrying digital content through the adoption of 21st-century technologies not even dreamed of when they started, including *T-1* and *T-3* lines, optical fiber for long-distance voice and data transmission, digital subscriber lines (DSL), high-speed digital modems and fax machines, and digital voice coders (*vocoders*) for cellular telephones. Thus, beyond using digital technology merely for switching, phone companies have begun digitizing voice and other signals once they leave the local loop, transmitting digital signals between central offices, a change that offers more flexibility and efficiency for message transfer than ever before. In other words, for the past decade, the *only* part of the PSTN that has remained analog is the local loop. And although existing copper infrastructure has been successfully adapted for many digital functions (e.g., both computer data transmission through modems and digital voice calls originating from cell phones must still be capable of reaching wire line phones through the local loop), the local infrastructure is not suitable for everything (e.g., broadband[4] applications such as television-quality streaming video). Thus, in terms of the connection from central offices to households, in telecommunications, the transition to a fully digital infrastructure is not yet complete.

Although deployment of a broadband fiber-optic backbone for long-distance telephony has been progressing for more than a decade (making it possible for a single line to carry thousands of telephone calls simultaneously through *multiplexing*, a technique that will be explained later), the local loop (or the "final mile" as it is called) still uses the same technology that inaugurated the telephone network more than a century ago. As a result, the current infrastructure cannot deliver to most households high-speed Internet service for real-time interactive[5] video and other products requiring high capacity.

In summary, the idea that we have completed the transformation to a fully digital telecommunication platform is simply false. Nevertheless, the eventual transition to a fully digital system for both broadcasting and telecommunication is inevitable. It is only a matter of time before the digital platform becomes capable of delivering to households all of the mass media content and telecommunication services we have come to enjoy, plus a cornucopia of new services as yet unimagined.[6] Until that time, we continue through a transition period rife with social, economic, political, legal, and technological challenges.

For now, however, to fulfill the goals of this chapter, I first describe how the telecommunication infrastructure permits users to gain access to one another for the purpose of exchanging messages. To set the stage, the chapter begins with some historical perspective.

■ CONNECTING USERS: ACCESS

When Alexander Graham Bell first demonstrated that his invention worked, he used *two* handsets but only *one* wire between them to complete a call. Bell used what amounted to a private line connecting two telephones.

As the telephone became popular, and more instruments entered service, the number of physical connections required for each phone to reach the others increased, making it impractical to use a permanent hardwire connection for every unit (see Figure 3.1).[7] Nowadays, with hundreds of millions of phones in service in the United States alone, such an approach, aside from being practically impossible, would also be a huge waste of resources—and this is so even before considering transnational service. To accommodate demand, a *switching* plan was inaugurated to maintain the viability of the system.

The telephone network's switching plan still provides a *dedicated* line between users and a central office. This means no others can use an engaged line while a call is in progress—the line is devoted to just the call connecting the users at each end to the exclusion of all others.[8] When a call is completed, the connection is broken, and the line becomes available for others.

The system is also designed to perform *signaling* functions: to alert parties that someone is trying to reach them, to alert the switching office that a connection is desired and when a call is completed, and to inform callers trying to reach parties engaged in a call that the party they are trying to reach is busy. In this way, the system is made practical. How are switching and signaling done?

Telephone Switching and Signaling

The practical arrangement for routing telephone calls uses a central office (called a *telephone exchange*) in a given service area where all lines from the area are brought. Once there, electrical cross-connections are made to connect instruments with one another upon request.

At first, human operators made the physical connection between two telephones at the exchange by routing calls through a switchboard using plugs physically connected to every phone in the area. As Noll (1998) tells it:

Each operator had about 18 cords that could be used to make connections. About 120 incoming lines terminated at the operator's switchboard at answering jacks. A lamp at each jack would light indicating that the line desired service. The operator would plug-in and answer the call. The calling party would give the name, and later the telephone number, of the called party. The operator would then complete the call by connecting the cord to one of the perhaps as many as 10,000 subscriber

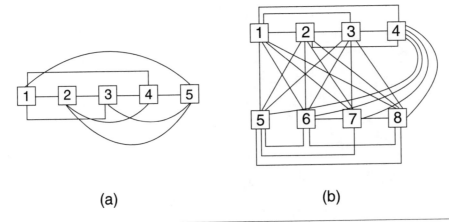

(a)   (b)

Figure 3.1   Hardwire lines required for dedicated service among telephone subscribers for five and eight units. (a) Fives units require 10 lines. (b) Eight units require 28 lines.

multiple jacks within reach. Lamps associated with each connecting cord indicated when parties had completed a call. (p. 138)

In this arrangement, a human operator made a temporary hardwire connection of one phone to another through the use of a switchboard (Figure 3.2).

The routing of calls through a central switching office is a practical means of connecting subscribers in a local area. Eventually, connecting calls between two central offices was accomplished over *trunk* lines, which expanded the switching concept to permit telephone communication between more distant areas. For trunk line service, a human operator in one central office reached an operator in another central office to set up each call. Later, the same approach was used between *toll* offices to handle long-distance service between cities.

Over time, a switching hierarchy was established for call handling. In the past, calls processed through the PSTN were sent from a central office (called a *class-5* office) to a toll center (*class-4*), to a primary center (*class-3*), to a sectional center (*class-2*), to a regional center (*class-1*) before reaching their destinations.

In the United States, there are currently about 20,000 central offices and about 20 regional centers providing service for the United States and Canada (Noll, 1998, p. 131). Today, however, a strict hierarchy is no longer followed for long-distance phone calls. Instead, the system views all toll centers as equal, and to increase efficiency, calls are routed based on feasibility and available capacity at the time they are placed.

Figure 3.2   Switchboard operator at work. Temporary hardwire connections between telephones were at first done by human operators.

SOURCE: Horowhenua Historical Society Inc., Levin, New Zealand. Reprinted with permission.

As the telephone network became established, its infrastructure included exchange offices, copper wire, switchboards, and human operators, not to mention telephone poles, installation and maintenance personnel, and number directories. By far, the most costly element of the infrastructure was the human labor pool of switchboard operators.

The Move From Human to Machine Switching

Manual switching was not only expensive, it was slow. It was also allegedly capricious and prone to playing favorites, especially in funneling business to operators' friends in some places. This tendency is apparently what led undertaker Almon B. Strowger to invent the first automatic electro-mechanical telephone exchange. As Walters (1993) tells it:

> A rival company was collecting nearly all the available funeral business. Naturally, the telephone system . . . was manually operated. Fortunately for Strowger's rival . . . [the] phone company was run by his wife. Hence, if some bereaved person called and wished to be connected to a funeral director, it wasn't Strowger that got the call. (p. 6)

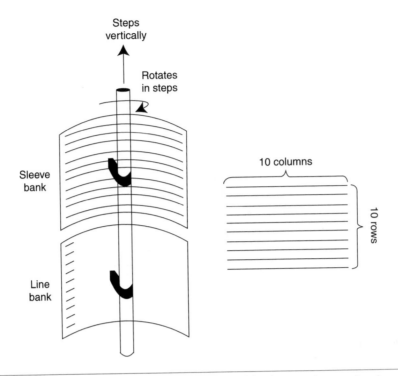

Figure 3.3   The Strowger switch eliminated the need for human interaction in call switching. The switching is accomplished through the use of relays, which control the movement of a wiper arm and contact banks to make the desired connection.

SOURCE: Reprinted with permission of Lucent Technologies, Inc./Bell Labs.

Strowger's invention entered service in 1892. It consisted of two motion selectors (see Figure 3.3) connected to a rotary dial[9] that produced electrical pulses to establish calls between users (see Figure 3.4) and was adopted by the Bell System in 1919. Strowger's invention completely eliminated human intervention in call switching and quickly became the backbone of the world's telecommunication network, dominating the field for more than a century.[10]

But regardless of whether switching is done by human hands or mechanical means, somehow it is necessary to provide a way for the system to recognize when a particular party wishes to place a call and to identify and alert the party being called. How does the system do these things? To answer this it is necessary to understand how the local loop is powered.

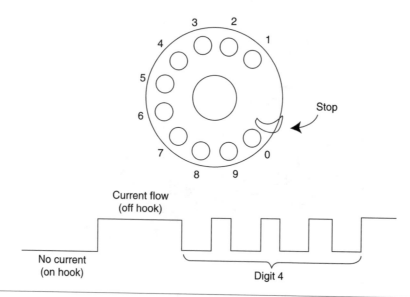

Figure 3.4   Diagram of the rotary dial, the device that delivered electrical pulses to the Strowger switch, and the crossbar system that followed.

NOTE: The rotary dial puts out 9-11 pulses per second. Each pulse cycle interrupts the flow of direct current. There is .7 second between dialed digits.

Alerting Subscribers and Offices About Call Status

At first, instruments were connected with a single wire, using the earth as ground to complete the circuit. Unfortunately, because power companies and others used the ground for their own circuits, that arrangement allowed a significant amount of noise to impair signal quality.[11] To reduce interference, in 1881, John J. Carty, a Bell employee, introduced a twisted pair of copper wires to replace the single-wire arrangement, eliminating the need to use the earth as ground to complete the circuit. The new arrangement formed a loop with the telephone subscriber's premises and the local telephone exchange, and came to be called the local loop.[12]

Since the inception of the telephone company, a direct current (DC) 48-volt battery from each central office has powered all telephones, as it does today. When a subscriber raises the handset from its cradle, a switch-hook closes and a DC electric current is made to flow over the local loop, identifying the party requesting service. The current flow is sensed by a line relay at the central office. On every telephone, a ringer is connected across the phone line. When a phone rings, and a party picks up the handset, its switch-hook closes, allowing DC current to flow through the unit. The central office then senses that a party has answered, and stops the ringing.

Telephone service is made two-way by the presence of microphone and earphone components in every unit, originally known as transmitter/receiver components. The microphone converts sound to electric currents used for signal transmission; the earphone converts the currents back into acoustic signals as they are received.[13]

In summary, the essential purpose of a telephone system is to provide connections for subscribers so that messages can be transmitted among them. To provide users access to one another, a switching function is needed to complete connections. Along with switching, signaling functions are needed to alert called parties that calls are being attempted, and to alert callers when called parties are busy. Signaling must also inform the central office when a called party has responded, and when a call has ended so that the line can be made available for other calls. To accomplish all of these objectives, it is necessary to equip each instrument with a ringer, a switch-hook, a dialer, a transmitter, and a receiver. In addition, the central office must be equipped with a power source to support signaling functions, to sense line status, and to maintain connections once they are made.

The switching and signaling infrastructure has changed over time, but the basic objectives are the same. In particular, switching, once accomplished through the use of electromechanical relays, or vacuum tubes, is now controlled by solid-state digital computers. This change has made it possible to monitor the entire system to determine when and where the heaviest loads are so that switching functions can be distributed over the telephone network more evenly to improve efficiency. Back-up switching routes can be programmed to keep the network running even when there are breakdowns (i.e., power failures) in some sectors.

Signaling and switching, once initiated through the use of rotary dialers, are now done through the use of a digital Touch-Tone system using a push-button assembly called a dial pad. This much faster technology generates a unique combination of electrical frequencies for each digit dialed, produced from a set of low-frequency tones (all below 1 kHz) and a set of high-frequency tones (all above 1 kHz) arranged in a matrix of four rows and four columns, respectively (Figure 3.5). Equipment at the central office senses each frequency sent from the dial pad and determines the digits dialed based on the sequence of frequencies it receives.

Recent Advances in Service and Handset Design

Digital switching and monitoring of network activity have made possible some noteworthy advances in telephone services; some refinements in handset

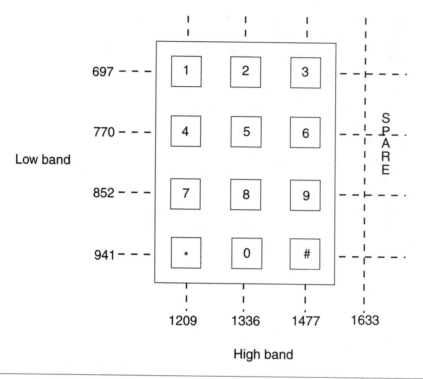

Figure 3.5   The dial pad replaced the rotary dial.

NOTE: The digital Touch-Tone system generates a unique combination of electrical frequencies for each digit dialed. Notice the last column on the right is a spare.

design are also worth mentioning. New services available for subscribers now include conference calling, call waiting, call forwarding, and other conveniences that direct calls through the network in multiple steps based on contingencies that may be requested by users rather than merely making initial connections between them.

In addition, over the years, instruments have become more functional and attractive, with designer looks to match room decor. Virtually all are equipped with printed circuit boards to reduce their weight and size. Contemporary units come equipped with jacks to accommodate multiple locations in the household. Many have microprocessors to allow users to record frequently dialed numbers. Many have a visual display for incoming numbers, providing a caller ID function. Ringers are no longer made of hammers and bells, but may consist of microprocessors that make music. Cordless units connected to a traditional phone line that uses radio energy tuned to a base station are common, permitting users to move throughout the house; many feature scrambling capability to protect users' privacy. Other features include headset attachments to allow hands-free operation, speakers for conference calls, automated answering and recording, and voice mail.

We now consider in greater depth developments that have led to the conversion from analog to digital content and carriage of both mass media and telecommunication products and services. These developments have increased the flexibility and efficiency of telecommunication systems by making better use of available bandwidth.

FROM ANALOG TO DIGITAL TRANSMISSION ■

With exceptions,[14] digital transmission is a relatively recent phenomenon. Before voice signals were converted into digital data streams, most of the content and carriage across the PSTN were analog. Likewise, for decades, our major commercial television networks distributed thousands of hours of programming to hundreds of affiliate stations coast to coast in the form of analog video signals via high-bandwidth coaxial cable provided by the telephone company. The first transcontinental distribution of television broadcasts began in 1951, using AT&T coaxial cable to carry analog video signals.

By contrast, since the early 1990s, we have seen a transition from analog to digital transmission in both wire and wireless technologies. Why the change? What technologies have fostered the growth of digital transmission of content over lines originally built for analog service? What are the advantages of digital transmission that make it an attractive alternative over traditional analog service?

Digital transmission was really the result of the development and success of digital computers—binary code is the only kind of information computers can understand. However, the pressure to convert from analog to digital signals in communication industries (i.e., telephony and broadcasting) is not the result of brute demands by computer moguls lording technical hegemony over their rivals; rather, it derives from the promise of a quantum leap in capacity (and by implication, profits) for those industries that convert to digital delivery of their products and services.

Differences Between Analog and Digital Signals

In the beginning of this chapter, I defined digital bandwidth as a measure of the physical amount of information that could pass through a communication channel in a given amount of time. However, in the early days of broadcasting (where the term *bandwidth* was first used), bandwidth was primarily defined not as a measure of information capacity, but simply as the frequency range assigned to a specific broadcasting channel or service (e.g., short-wave radio; AM and FM radio; and later, television).

Analog bandwidths were allocated according to both the physical limitations of the broadcasting technologies available at the time they entered service and the needs of the services that were to be carried.[15] Some services needed wider bandwidths than others to deliver acceptable signals. For example, television channels were bigger than radio channels because they had to deliver both audio and video signals; therefore, they were assigned greater bandwidth. However, once a service was assigned a bandwidth, spectrum allocations were fixed; that is, radio stations provided just radio programs, television channels provided just television programs, and so on, and there was not much further reason to discuss bandwidth issues.

Today, we live in a very different world, with deep implications for the notion of bandwidth. Digital transmission permits a more flexible and efficient use of bandwidth in both the electromagnetic spectrum and hardwire systems. First, digital transmission is more *flexible* than analog because binary code, unlike analog signals, can represent voice, text, data, images, and/or video (called multimedia), either alone or in combination with one another in any size channel and in any part of the frequency spectrum. Therefore, the bandwidth used to carry digital information can be any size, need not be restricted to just one type of service, and need not be limited to just one part of the spectrum. Second, digitizing enables analog signals to be sent without noise or loss of fidelity after they are digitized, preserving the original signal quality no matter how many transmissions they undergo. Third, digital transmission is more *efficient* than analog because, unlike analog signals, binary code, before being transmitted, can in some cases undergo data compression without signal loss, allowing more information to be sent over the same channel in a given period of time. For this reason, using radio spectrum for analog signals is nowadays considered wasteful. The implications of this for business, put simply, is that with increased flexibility and efficiency, *digital transmission can make greater use of available bandwidth, potentially resulting in greater profits.*

Another fundamental difference between analog and digital signals is that analog signals correspond to the phenomena they represent by copying directly some aspect of the original information, whereas digital signals do not. For example, in the real world, bright images have more light reflecting from them than dark images; similarly, analog TV signals vary in direct proportion to the brightness information they represent.[16] In contrast, digital code renders all phenomena, light or dark, soft or loud, audio or video, into sequences of 0s and 1s bearing no manifest resemblance to what the sequences represent.

Furthermore, analog signals are continuous in nature, whereas digital signals are discrete and discontinuous. For example, an analog signal of a carrier wave modulated by sound captured from a microphone proceeds continuously through time; by contrast, digital code representing that signal is a finite series of discrete samples captured and rendered into sequences of code thousands of times per second. Therefore, while a sound sampled at , any two consecutive instants is successfully captured in a digital signal, the representation of that sound at any instant in between them is not. Thus, for digital signals of sounds and images, some part of the original is always lost through sampling.

The Benefits of Digital Signals and Transmission

But what is gained from translating audiovisual phenomena into binary code?

To understand the benefits of digital signals and transmission, it is again critical to remember that digital bandwidth is defined as a measure of the amount of information that can flow from one point to another in a given amount of time. The fundamental measure of digital bandwidth is therefore *bits per second (bps)*.[17] We may also speak of thousands of bits per second (kilobits per second or kbps), millions of bits per second (Megabits per second or Mbps), billions of bits per second (Gigabits per second or Gbps), and so on. By contrast, analog bandwidth is understood not in terms of bits per second, but as a range of frequencies measured in cycles per second (cps), otherwise known as *hertz (Hz)*.[18] In analog terms, we speak of bandwidth in terms of thousands of cycles per second (kilohertz or kHz), billions of cycles per second (Gigahertz or GHz), and so on. Thus, the term *bandwidth* means completely different things when used to describe analog versus digital transmission.

Digital coding yields several advantages regarding signal quality. First, digital code avoids noise, interference, and distortion problems that often plague analog signals. This makes it easier to store, manipulate, and transmit digital signals without degrading the signals that are retained. This is because digital copies need only reproduce a string of binary numbers, and therefore do not have to imitate an original stimulus to preserve the desired information. In contrast, for analog signals to be transmitted, they must be copied, and each time a copy is made, additional noise and distortion further degrade the signal.

Moreover, analog signals require a dedicated circuit for each type of signal, must remain intact during transmission, and must be transmitted and reassembled in the same order in which they were created, whereas digital signals may be sent over any type of connection, may be transmitted in parts that may be received out of order, and then are reassembled into the original at the receiver. For example, the digital code representing a high-bandwidth one-hour television program may take several hours to send over a low-bandwidth telephone line via a modem and still be retrieved in its original form.

Packet Switching

Perhaps one of the greatest advantages of digital over analog transmission is that since digital signals can be intermixed with one another and then separated later (assuming they are sent with the necessary *header information*[19] to the various receivers about how to treat them), they do not require separate channels to carry them. This transmission capability has led to a form of data handling called *packet switching*.

Packet switching is a method of transmitting digital information in bundles or small units of data. Each bundle contains not only a segment of the information you wish to send but also information about the bundle itself, telling, among other things, where each should go and how each should be handled once it gets there. The advantage of packet switching is that it allows a transmission line to be shared by millions of users; it reduces quiescent periods, making the entire system more efficient. Messages traveling the system do not need to occupy their own circuits from start to finish to survive transmission (in the language of the telephone company, packet-switched digital messages do not require dedicated lines). Rather, different messages can be sent through the same wire or wireless transmission line sequentially without concern that they will be confounded with one another. As mentioned, because there is no need to segregate messages, a more efficient use of the available pipeline is achieved.

Both the traditional PSTN and the newer integrated services digital network (ISDN) introduced in the United States in 1992 use the same twisted-pair copper wire infrastructure between homes and central offices. Both were designed for continuous voice carriage. However, ISDN makes the local loop digital by connecting directly with digital technology at the central office. This means that unlike the traditional analog telephone service, ISDN lines eliminate the need for digital content to undergo analog-to-digital conversions in order to be transmitted.

Unfortunately, both the traditional local loop and ISDN are circuit-switched connections that function exactly like a dedicated line—that is, when engaged, they serve just the parties connected to that line, to the exclusion of all others, even when no data are being sent. This arrangement is wasteful whenever the connection is used for data transfer rather than voice transmission (i.e., e-mail or downloading Web pages), because in such instances, unlike continuous voice communication, data are sent in bursts, with frequent quiescent periods when the line connecting them is not used at all (i.e., when users are reading messages or attending to other activities). It is for this reason that data transmissions are characterized as *bursty*, meaning that times of transmission activity are intermixed with times when no activity is occurring.[20] During such periods, other users of the network *could* be using that line for data transfer, but because it is tied up or dedicated in a circuit-switched arrangement, it is unavailable. For bursty data, it is a more efficient use of network assets to use transmission lines in a packet-switched arrangement to accommodate simultaneous transmissions for multiple users.

Historically, the impetus behind packet switching as a mode of data transfer is generally attributed to a 1964 U.S. Department of Defense project by the Advanced Research Project Agency (ARPA), whose charge it was to develop a computer network called ARPAnet, the precursor of the Internet. By the 1980s, other networks sprang up based on the ARPAnet model. By the mid-1990s, these were absorbed into a network of networks, now called the Internet. By 1998, the number of computers connected to the Internet grew from 4 million to more than 30 million (Lu, 1998, p. 24). During that time, local area networks (LANs) were brought online to connect computers in a local area to allow sharing of data and hardware.[21]

The ARPAnet project connected a number of powerful computers located at several research sites around the country to one another through the use of modems. It was through modems that the telephone network was first extensively used for digital data transmission.

Modems

It should be obvious by now that the telecommunication environment now deals in two disparate commodities: voice and data. Anyone who uses his or her telephone for more than speech functions (e.g., banking, accessing online libraries, receiving a credit history, or calling up an airline schedule on the Internet) knows that a great deal of information is stored in computerized data banks. What may be less obvious is that access to such databases is frequently gained through the PSTN.

The reason the telephone company is the most used infrastructure for accessing computer data banks is simple: The PSTN is the most ubiquitous system available for such functions. Among its most valuable assets is that it has hundreds of millions of telephones already in place providing access to both wire and wireless[22] connections for the transmission and exchange of both voice and computer information.

Unfortunately, because computers can process only digital code, and the phone company was originally designed to handle only analog speech signals, there are clearly some technical challenges that must be met to reconcile these two essentially incompatible modes of communication. Nevertheless, the PSTN has, with adjustments, proven to be a feasible conduit for a lot of digital traffic. What makes it especially attractive is that it is the least expensive and most pervasive network available for such service. The alternative, namely, building a separate digital network of comparable magnitude, is less attractive because, among other reasons, it would be prohibitively expensive to build one with coverage comparable to that of the PSTN.

The best solution therefore is to develop technology that augments and adapts the extant telephone system for digital functions. And that is exactly what is being done. One way to send digital information over the analog local loop is by converting digital signals into analog sounds that can be carried over telephone lines. The first device built for this function was the modem.

The term *modem* stands for modulator-demodulator. When placed between a computer terminal and a telephone line, it produces tones from carrier signals modulated by binary data, performing translation functions between them. Because the telephone system was set up for two-way communication, modems perform both modulation and demodulation processing of the tones. By way of a computer, a modem, and a telephone, users can access a vast array of computer databases.

Modems can be categorized in terms of how quickly they can send and receive digital data. Modems with speeds of 1,200 bps began appearing in 1980. Advances in chip technology doubled this speed by 1984. By 1991, 14.4-kbps modems were not uncommon. Three years later, that speed doubled to 28.8 kbps; by 1996, modem speeds had grown to 33.6 kbps (Lu, 1998, p. 22).

Faster modem speeds are possible over copper wire. In 1996, for example, 56-kbps modems began appearing. However, switch and signal relay circuits impose limits of their own.[23] In addition, FCC-mandated rules on transmission power also impose nontechnical legal limits on modem speed.

Throughput

Digital bandwidth is measured by *throughput*, a measure of the amount of bandwidth carrying meaningful data compared to the overall information capacity of a device or transmission line. In other words, throughput is the proportion of total bandwidth used for carrying content rather than meta-code in a channel.

Recall that in addition to message content, packets also carry meta-code—address, source, and protocol information telling receiving computers how data should be handled. As it turns out, the laws of physics dictate that meta-code also requires some channel capacity; therefore, space must be allocated for it. That leaves less bandwidth for actual message content. The amount of bandwidth left for actual content is called throughput, which is less than the total bandwidth a channel can pass.

In modems, some available bandwidth is used for non-data carriage functions (e.g., quality control). Therefore, modem throughput is always less than maximum capacity. For this reason, currently a 56-kbps modem delivers content at a rate of only about 36 kbps.

In addition, modem speed is conditioned by the capacity of the modem it is "speaking" to. That is, if a fast modem is sending data to a slower one, they must operate at a mutually acceptable level, which is the fallback rate of the slower modem. To do this, modems are equipped to monitor this aspect of their interaction, and this negotiation at the beginning of their interaction (called a *handshake*) determines the data rate that is used.

Digital systems, as mentioned, feature a method of checking for errors in transmission, known as a *checksum* calculation, with further cost to throughput. The checksum process has an originating computer calculate a sum for a packet or cluster of packets based on the binary information they contain, and that information is transmitted to receiving computers. Receiving computers then calculate a checksum, which is compared to the one sent. If there is a discrepancy, a request is issued for the packet to be transmitted again. Similar error checks may be made at several points along the path to avoid sending inaccurate, flawed, or corrupt files across the entire network.

In digital systems where interactivity is not possible (e.g., in compact discs or DVDs), a receiving computer cannot request that information be sent again if an error is detected. In such cases, a *forward error correction* method is used to maintain quality. In such systems, redundant information is sent for purposes of comparison. If discrepancies are detected, the system can then substitute code for data that fail to arrive intact. Some digital video satellite systems use forward error correction methods to maintain quality.

For all these reasons, raw bandwidth should not be taken as the true measure of channel capacity. Rather, quality control features must be taken into account to get a more accurate picture of a bandwidth's throughput.

Digital Compression

Meta-code, error correction procedures, checksum calculations, and adjustments to monitor fallback rates are not the only issues that can alter channel capacity in digital transmission systems; the ability to compress data files before they are sent can also have an influence. But unlike the items mentioned above, which can all reduce throughput, data compression actually increases it. For example, some high-bandwidth digital content (e.g., a video teleconference) can exceed a channel's transmission capability. In such cases, a practical solution is to translate long strings of repeating binary code into shorter strings before they are transmitted, and then include meta-code telling the receiving computer how to retrieve the original content. This strategy of data handling is called *digital compression.*

Digital compression takes two forms: *lossy compression* and *lossless.* Lossy compression refers to digital compression that results in some loss of information when a data file is retrieved. As an example of lossy compression, imagine a video teleconference featuring a static image of a group of executives seated around a seminar table with a gray wall in the background. In this case, the video image may feature the same code for color and location for 90% of the pixels comprising the video for a significant period of time. Because much of the image is static for long periods, it makes sense to employ an image algorithm that reduces the code specifying the refresh rate of the video transmission for those parts of the signal that remain the same for long periods, thus reducing significantly the bandwidth required to maintain an acceptable picture. When a motion occurs that interrupts the status of the pixels (e.g., an executive moves to the podium to give a report), the portion of the video image affected by the motion can be refreshed once again.

In this example, some signal loss of the beginning of the new motion is lost, but the loss is insignificant. Therefore, the compression algorithm used is called lossy because losing certain parts of the signal is acceptable.

However, sometimes *any* signal loss resulting from compression is unacceptable. In such cases, the compression algorithm used must be capable of retrieving the original signal in its entirety. Such compression algorithms are called lossless. An example of lossless compression is when a replacement algorithm specifies a short code to be used in place of a longer code, as when the letter X is substituted for a long and complex calculus formula appearing repeatedly in a math book. After transmission of the text file, an algorithm reverses the process so that every appearance of X is replaced once again by the calculus formula. Such a compression algorithm would be lossless because none of the information in the original message is lost. Lossless compression is necessary whenever any loss of the original data could be fatal to the meaning of the message.

■ GROWTH OF THE TELECOMMUNICATION NETWORK

Since the inception of telecommunication, new technologies have been added to expand network coverage. Beyond twisted-pair copper wire, the current infrastructure now includes additional cable and wireless technologies; each increases available bandwidth for products and services.

Conduit connections for additional network carriage now include coaxial and fiber-optic cable. Wireless connections include terrestrial microwave and satellite radio transmitters. Since the appearance of these technologies, improvements have increased their capabilities at an impressive rate. Here I briefly describe these technologies and their contributions to the telecommunication enterprise.

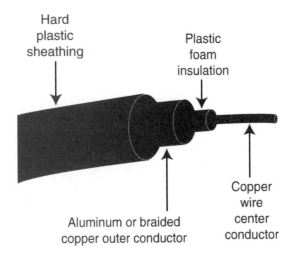

Figure 3.6   Exposed view of coaxial cable used in transmitting signals for telephone and video traffic.

Coaxial Cable

When first developed, coaxial cable was used primarily for antenna connections. Shortly after World War II, it was used to assist in the expansion of the growing telephone industry. In place of twisted-pair copper wire, coaxial cable or "coax" (rhymes with "no tax") uses two electronic conductors. One is a center copper wire sheathed in a protective layer of insulating material called a dielectric. The second is a wire mesh made of copper or aluminum wrapped around the dielectric. An outer layer of plastic shielding forms the outer body of the cable, providing insulation (Figure 3.6). The diameter of coax cable varies from as small as .8 mm to more than 2 inches. Coaxial cable is named such because it has two wires with a common axis.

Coaxial cable can be fitted to carry DC power that will energize amplifiers on the other end of the cable to boost the signal, making it capable of transmitting long distances with relatively little signal loss. Its shielding reduces interference usually present in standard wiring. Its structure also makes it possible for it to handle signals well into the GHz range, while minimizing spurious radiation.

Coax can handle thousands of telephone conversations simultaneously, or several dozen television signals in a cable television system. To offset signal loss that does occur, amplifiers (called repeaters) are added at regular intervals throughout the distribution system.

Many types of electronic communication may be carried through the use of coaxial cable, including telephone, television, and data services. For decades, U.S. television networks delivered programs to their affiliates through the use of coaxial cable provided by AT&T, the nation's long-line telephone company. One reason coaxial cable has been used for this service is because it delivers high-frequency signals more efficiently than standard copper wire, which permits high-frequency radio energy to leak into the surrounding atmosphere. Coaxial cable prevents such leakage by trapping high-frequency radio signals in its enclosed space.

Coaxial cable has been used to deliver long-distance analog telephone service since 1946. However, only one-way voice traffic is possible on a single coaxial cable, because the amplifiers used to boost signal strength are one-way systems. Therefore, two coaxial cables must be ganged together to make a two-way pair for interactive telephone service. Over the years, successive generations of coax telephone technology have increased capacity at an impressive rate, while distance between repeaters has progressively decreased as costs have come down for such devices, improving signal quality significantly.

When used for telephone service, a buried master cable containing up to 11 coaxial pairs may be used. The most recent such system entered service in 1978. It uses integrated circuit technology with repeaters spaced every mile. Each coaxial pair can handle 13,200 channels or voice circuits. With one coax pair set aside as a spare to be used as a replacement if a line in service goes down, 10 pairs are available for active service, providing capacity to handle 132,000 two-way voice circuits at a time (Noll, 1998, pp. 65-66).[24] Coaxial cable is now being replaced by fiber-optic cable.

Optical Fiber

Fiber-optic cable uses flexible glass in place of copper or aluminum, and light pulses in place of electrical signals, to transmit digital information (Figure 3.7). The basic principle on which fiber-optic cable operates is to use a pipe to carry light. As it happens, a light ray passing an optical boundary will be reflected at that boundary if the angle of incidence is less than some critical angle determined by the refracting abilities of the two materials. The angle at which a light ray bends is proportional to the relative indices of refraction of the two materials. This principle is known as Snell's law of refraction.

In line with this principle, if you take a strand of glass (in practice roughly the diameter of a human hair), and surround it with a glass coating with a lower index of refraction, then a light ray entering the strand at the proper angle will be repeatedly reflected until it exits the strand as if it were reflecting

Figure 3.7 Fiber-optic cable with its light-carrying capability clearly in evidence.

SOURCE: Reprinted with permission from Masterfile.com. © Brian Kuhlmann.

from a flawless mirror. Signals through fiber-optic cable may be encoded using either a laser light[25] or light-emitting diode (LED), and decoded by a photodiode at the receiving end.

The advantages of using optical fiber in telecommunication applications are many. First, glass is lighter, cheaper, and more plentiful than copper or aluminum. Second, and more important, brute capacity for encoding information with light is unsurpassed by any other conduit used for message transmission. For example, because light is electromagnetic radiation ranging in the hundreds and thousands of billions of cycles per second, it offers extremely large signal capacity. Its high frequency means that it can be turned on and off at a fast rate, making it capable of carrying a great deal of information in a short amount of time over a single fiber. Thus, a single glass strand of optical fiber has more than 600 times the capacity of a coaxial cable; in short, fiber-optic cable has huge bandwidth, with all of the attendant implications for economic competition, even against satellite technology (discussed below). Third, electrical interference is nonexistent in optical fiber; this means clearer signals for both audio and video. Fourth, optical fiber does not radiate its signal into the surrounding environment at all, even if damaged. Finally, when properly installed, very little signal loss (*attenuation*) occurs with fiber transmission, so fewer amplifiers (called regenerative repeaters) are needed to maintain signal strength. These benefits are attractive to both cable television and telecommunication companies, who long for technologies that offer virtually unlimited capacity. For these reasons, optical fiber is *the* transmission medium for intercontinental and interoffice telecommunication. In time, it may become common for local connections, eventually replacing the twisted-pair copper wire that now constitutes the local loop.

Of course, optical fiber technology has its downside. First, conversion from metal to glass is labor intensive, and therefore expensive. In addition, connecting and switching fiber-optic transmissions can be tricky, as the glass used in the lines must respect the physics of light by, among other things, not including any impurities. Furthermore, the frequencies of natural light are too incoherent to travel effectively through fiber; therefore, lasers or LEDs must be used. Yet another problem results from the fact that the light waves traveling through the pipe take different paths—some travel straight down the axis of the pipe whereas others reflect and bounce their way through. Because all these paths have different lengths, signals arrive at their destinations at slightly different times, resulting in what has come to be called *smearing* or *pulse spreading*. This factor bears directly on the rate at which data can be sent over a line without being corrupted. The integrity of the materials used in fiber-optic installations and the integrity of the installations themselves are therefore key.

Nevertheless, the move is on to make the switch. As of 1994, the regional Bell operating companies, or RBOCs (rhymes with "car locks"), had already installed more than 2 million miles of fiber-optic cable while the major cable television companies, all of whom now use fiber in some parts of their systems, had laid over 100,000 miles (Dominick, Sherman, & Copeland, 1996, p. 126; Dominick, Sherman, & Messere, 2000, p. 68).

In transnational applications, in the 1980s, a consortium led by AT&T began installing submarine fiber-optic cable to supplement undersea copper telephone cables. In 1988, a 4,000-mile transatlantic fiber-optic cable was deployed with a capacity to handle 8,000 voice circuits. A new line was added in 1991. Since that time, cables across the Pacific have also been laid. Such deployments offer a cost-effective option for intercontinental delivery of television programs instead of satellite systems.

Since their inception, the increase in service capacity of fiber-optic lines has been truly impressive. For example, AT&T's first system, installed in 1979, featured a bandwidth of 45 Mbps and could carry 672 voice circuits. Seventy-two pairs were placed into a single cable, with six reserved as spares. The remaining 66 supplied 44,352 voice circuits. By 1986, a 400-Mbps system entered service, each capable of carrying 6,048 voice circuits. Today, systems operating at 2,000 Mbps are standard (Noll, 1998, pp. 113-114). According to Noll, the upper limit of a single fiber-optic channel is about 200 Gbps, or 200 billion bits per second, enough to carry 4,000 television signals. At this rate, if all of the light spectrum that could be harnessed for optical fiber were used, the theoretical capacity would be 50,000 Gbps or 50 Tbps (Terabits or trillions of bits per second), enough to supply carriage for a million television programs (imagine the reruns).

One difficulty with fiber-optic systems as they have developed over the years is their incompatibility with one another. Interconnecting fiber systems built to different specifications means that special interfaces must be designed for handing off signals from one to another. An interface standard called synchronous optical network (SONET) now provides standards for optical fiber technology, simplifying interconnections between systems in Europe and the United States.

Terrestrial Microwave Transmission

Radio transmission in the form of microwaves (in current terms roughly from 1 GHz to 50 GHz, practically speaking) is used to carry broadcast signals, telephone traffic, and a myriad of satellite and mobile and fixed radio services in the United States. Some frequency bands within the microwave portion of the radio spectrum have been assigned for transmission of telephone traffic across continents and oceans via terrestrial and satellite routes, respectively.

In terrestrial microwave transmission, radio waves are sent between antennas using microwave dish antennas and/or horn-shaped metal pipes called *waveguides* (Figure 3.8). Examples of the bandwidths set aside for such use are 3.7-4.2 GHz (called the 4-GHz band) and 5.925-6.425 GHz (called the 6-GHz band). Each is 500 MHz wide. The 4-GHz band is subdivided into 20-MHz-wide channels; the 6-GHz band into 30-MHz-wide channels. Some of the uses of microwave bands are for long-distance telecommunication, cable broadcasts, and cable point-to-point transmissions.

As is well known in broadcasting, the nature of microwave radio energy is such that it must follow a line-of-sight path; it is blocked by physical obstructions. Therefore, communication between antennas is possible only if there is an unobstructed view between them. For a microwave radio signal to cross the country, therefore, terrestrial towers must be spaced at no more than about 26 miles from one another to avoid having their signals blocked by the curvature of the earth.

Microwave signals also dissipate relatively quickly. Therefore, to maintain signal strength, repeaters must amplify signals frequently along their path. The usual practice is to beam a signal from a waveguide to a target antenna, where its frequency is shifted to a different channel to avoid jamming. Then it is amplified, and sent on its way through another waveguide.

The first microwave system to be used for analog voice traffic, called *TD-2*, was installed by AT&T in 1950. It operated on the 4-GHz band and used

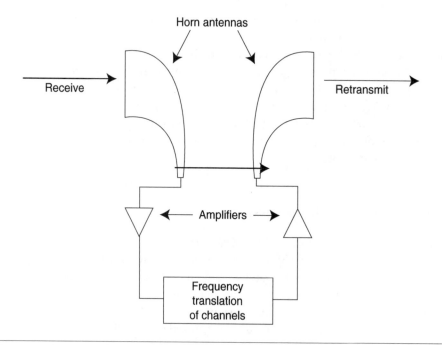

Figure 3.8   A diagram of a terrestrial microwave transmission system.

NOTE: Microwave relays receive radio signals, change their frequencies, and retransmit them.
Adapted from A. M. Noll (1998), *Introduction to Telephones and Telephone Systems*, 3/e. Reprinted
with permission from Artech House.

25 channels, each 20 MHz wide (such wide bandwidths were selected to
accommodate FM modulation because of its natural noise immunity). To
avoid adjacent channel interference, every other channel was unused.
Channels were unidirectional, so pairs were needed to provide two-way
circuits. This set-up yielded six voice circuits overall; five entered service and
one was reserved as a spare. Four hundred and eighty voice circuits were
sent over each channel. Across the entire 500 MHz of the 4-GHz band, a total
of 2,400 voice circuits were in service. By 1953, capacity of each channel
increased to 600 voice circuits, yielding 3,000 two-way voice circuits overall;
this figure quickly doubled due to technological advances (Noll, 1998, p. 69).

Through polarization techniques using special antennas, adjacent channel interference was eliminated as a problem in 1959, leading to full use of
the system's 24 channels. This doubled its capacity, yielding 6,000 analog
voice circuits. By 1968, solid-state components again doubled its capacity,
yielding 12,000 circuits. Around this time, a technique called frequency division multiplexing or FDM (explained below in the section on cellular telephony) was introduced with the effect of again increasing capacity to 19,800
two-way voice circuits.

In 1961, a different transmission system for voice traffic, called *TH radio*, entered service in the 6-GHz bandwidth using vacuum tube technology and dual polarization.[26] Sixteen channels were available for use, yielding eight two-way voice circuits. Six were actively used; two were reserved as spares. Capacity of this system was 10,800 voice circuits overall. In conjunction with the TD system already in use, a total capacity of 30,600 voice circuits was achieved (Noll, 1998, p. 71).

By the early 1980s, the TH system was replaced by one called *AR6A*. It featured a bandwidth suppression capability that allowed an increase in efficiency and an attendant increase in the number of analog voice circuits that could be carried in the allotted spectrum space. AR6A packed 6,000 voice circuits into each channel. Overall, with seven active two-way channels in service, 42,000 voice circuits were carried. In conjunction with the TD system, total capacity was 61,800 two-way voice circuits. Eventually, these analog systems using frequency division multiplexing were supplanted by digital systems using several different multiplexing techniques explained here in the section on cellular telephony.

Satellites

In some situations, it is either too costly or infeasible to build a series of terrestrial microwave towers for delivering broadcasting and telecommunication products and services to audiences and subscribers. For example, sparsely populated rural areas are not cost-effective investments for such infrastructure, and stringing towers across oceans is simply impractical. In these cases, placing a microwave transmitter up in the sky aboard a satellite is the answer.

Satellite technology enables microwave signals to cross the ocean in one hop (Figure 3.9). By placing satellites over the equator in geosynchronous orbits (meaning that they stay above the same spot on earth at all times), they must be at an altitude of 22,300 miles. When deployed this way, satellites takes 24 hours to make one revolution of the earth.

Radio transmission between a satellite and a ground station is constant and reliable when the satellite maintains the same position relative to the earth while in orbit. This is a great advantage because ground stations do not have to be readjusted to maintain contact and signal strength with the satellite. Satellites can then receive reliable signals, amplify them, shift them to a new frequency (to avoid interference), and then retransmit them to ground stations thousands of miles away. Circuits that do this are called transponders; satellites usually carry 24 transponders for multiple services.

At first, frequencies used for broadcast and telephony satellite transmissions were from 5.9 to 6.4 GHz for uplink transmissions (from the earth to

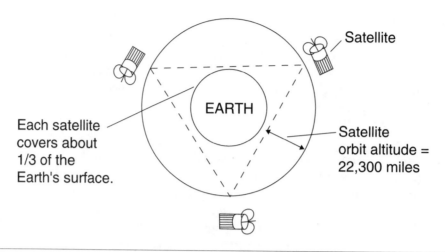

Figure 3.9 Diagram of satellites in orbit in relation to the earth.

satellites) and from 3.7 to 4.2 GHz for downlink transmissions (from satellites back down to the earth). This set of frequencies is called the *C-band*. A newer set of frequencies called the *Ku-band* uses 14-14.5 GHz for uplink and 11.7-12.2 GHz for downlink transmissions. A third band called the *Ka-band* uses frequencies in the 30-GHz part of the radio spectrum for uplink transmissions and the 20-GHz band for downlink satellite transmissions (Noll, 1998, pp. 77-78).

The parking spaces for geosynchronous satellites are nearly full. At 22,300 miles altitude, the distance between satellites providing different services using the same frequencies must be set at some minimum to avoid interference problems; that is, signals beamed from the earth to a satellite must not be received inadvertently by others. Both signals beamed from earth and the antennas used to receive them aboard satellites require narrow operating patterns to avoid jamming others in the vicinity. Spacing for satellites is therefore set at about 2 degrees, or about a thousand miles. Tighter spacing allows for more deployments, but with more transmission problems.

The effective coverage area of a signal beamed to earth from a satellite is called a *footprint* (Figure 3.10). Access to the satellite's signal varies as a function of the size of the footprint, which is in large part determined by the satellite's transmitting power. One fundamental advantage of satellites over older terrestrial relay technology is that whereas repeaters on land can link one location with only two others, a satellite can link a group of program or service suppliers (e.g., television networks or telecommunication companies) to an unlimited number of ground stations in multiple locations at no extra cost. For this reason, satellites are called *distance insensitive*.

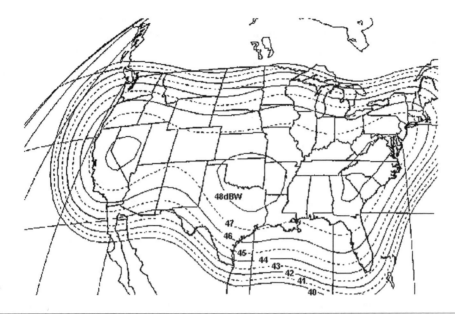

Figure 3.10   Satellite footprint showing area of strongest signal strength in the central portion of the coverage area.

C-band radio channels are 36 MHz with 4 MHz for a *guard band*, or unused portion between channels to serve as a buffer to reduce or eliminate adjacent channel interference. To minimize noise problems and work better with weak signals, FM modulation is used. A single transponder can deliver one color television signal or 1,200 voice circuits, or a digital signal with a 50-Mbps data rate.

When a signal is processed, it takes about ¼ second for it to travel up to and down from the satellite. Such delays, while insignificant for bursty data, can be annoying for an interactive telephone conversation that may take nearly a second from when speakers complete speeches to when they hear a response. For this reason, satellites are not the best choice for voice transmission. However, they are quite viable for one-way distribution of television signals (called TVRO for TV receive-only signals) among networks, cable companies, and affiliate stations. In addition, there is growth in direct-broadcast satellite (DBS) programming from program suppliers directly to homes.

Unfortunately, in reality satellites deployed in geosynchronous orbit are not perfectly fixed in relation to the earth; they require adjustment. To do this, noncommunication (*telemetry*) signals are traded between satellites and earth stations to make corrections using fuel and rockets aboard the satellites. Eventually, the fuel runs out. When it does, satellites must be replaced.

In recent years, the signal capacity of satellites has been surpassed by fiber-optic technology, with its remarkable broadband capability and its lack of delay involved in real-time delivery. One impact of this is that there has been a slowdown in the development of new satellite systems as demand for satellite circuits has declined (Head, Sterling, & Schofield, 1994, p. 165).

■ CELLULAR TELEPHONY

Without doubt, the success in recent years of wireless cellular telephone service has been among the most impressive developments in digital tele-communication. Evidence of this is found in the fact that in 1990, six years after cellular service began in the United States, there were 5.3 million U.S. subscribers. By 1996, that number had grown to more than 44 million. Today, the number of U.S. subscribers has topped 110 million (Noll, 1998, p. 215).[27]

Access to the World Wide Web via cell phones is also on the rise. It is estimated that by the end of 2001, the number of subscribers capable of access-ing text-based content available on cell phones (or personal digital assistants, PDAs as they are called), was nearly 100 million. By 2004, according to some estimates, the worldwide number of cellular wireless Web-surfers will grow to 743 million. In America alone, some analysts predict that by 2003, the number of Americans with Web-enabled phones will quintuple, from 8 million to 40 million.[28] One need only imagine collecting a monthly fee from hundreds of millions of subscribers to realize the immense success of cellular technology.

Cell phone technology connects users to regular wire and portable (wireless) telephones using two-way radio transmission. In the 1980s, the most popular system was called AMPS (advanced mobile phone service), an analog technology.[29] All new systems today are digital. Among the choices are GSM, or global system for mobile communication, a European system recently adopted by the U.S. carrier Cingular; digital AMPS or DAMPS; and code-division multiple access or CDMA, used by U.S. carriers Sprint and AT&T. All have fundamentally different operating systems, which makes standards a big issue, especially between countries that have adopted differ-ent approaches. Within the United States, systems vary to the detriment of the ideal of universal service.

In the early (pre-cellular) days of mobile telephony, a few dozen channels in an area provided telephone service with a single transmitter covering a 25-mile radius. Access was limited because if a user engaged a frequency, it was unavailable for anyone else until the user completed a call. This approach quickly led to congestion problems.

The introduction of the basic principles of cellular service, developed by Bell Labs in the 1940s, solved the congestion problem. However, it wasn't until the 1970s that the technology became available to make cell service viable.

In 1975, the FCC made part of the UHF television spectrum available for cell phone service by opening 40 MHz of the 800-MHz band to any qualified common carrier. In 1983, the FCC drafted regulations that brought competition and development to the nascent cellular telephone industry; it called for there to be two licensees in each area, with one required to be a purely wireless carrier. Thus, by design, traditional phone companies were put into competition with new wireless companies in each locale, and each was granted ½ of the spectrum allocated for such service.

Two frequency bands are designated for cellular service: *band A* for the wireline carrier, and *band B* for the non-wireline carrier. With each channel 30 kHz wide, each operator has 416 channel pairs. In addition, one or two control channels in each cell area are used for call management (to identify the cell phone requesting service, to assign a channel for each call, etc.) (Lu, 1998, p. 134).

Technical Principles

In cell service, the big improvement over early mobile telephone technology is the reuse of channels to increase access, permitting the same frequencies to handle thousands of calls at once. In some systems, a 50-MHz bandwidth is allocated from the 800- to 900-MHz part of the radio spectrum, yielding more than 800 two-way voice circuits for use in each area. The ability to reuse channels is due to a scheme that places a low-power transmitter or base station into a small area (called a cell) inside the larger service area (Figure 3.11).

Mobile Telephone Switching Office

Cells are typically 6 to 12 miles in radius. Each base station is equipped with a low-power (less than 100-watt) transmitter and receiver controlled by the service provider's mobile telephone switching office (MTSO). The low power of each transmitter means that the same frequency can be reused in other parts of the service area without causing interference.

The MTSO directs all call activity (Figure 3.12). When a cell phone initiates a call, a control channel receives a signal to assign a channel pair for service; if available, the MTSO assigns one. As the cell phone moves from one cell to another, the MTSO tracks its movement through adjacent base stations, all of which can sense the signal strength of the cell phone's transmitter.[30] The base station receiving the strongest signal assumes service.

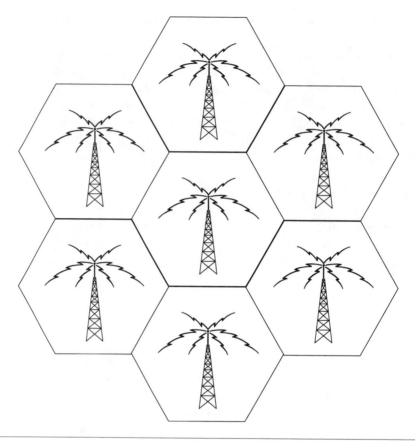

Figure 3.11 Diagram of a scheme for placing low-power transmitters into small areas for carrying phone traffic.

NOTE: Cellular telephone areas are ideally shaped like hexagons. Six are placed on a circular arrangement with a seventh in the center; each has its own low-power transmitter.

Hand-Offs

The assumption of service by an adjacent base station is called a *hand-off*. To reduce interference, adjacent base stations use different frequencies; this way, clusters using the same channels are separated in a kind of leapfrog allocation pattern. That means that the channel a user is tuned to during a conversation changes as the user changes locations. For this reason, during hand-offs, users may notice momentary interruptions in service.

Ideally, each cell is shaped like a hexagon. Six are placed into a circular arrangement with a seventh in the center. The cluster of seven cells is repeated throughout the larger service area. Of course, in practice, the ideal hexagonal shape is rare. Variances occur due to environmental conditions (weather, terrain characteristics, etc.).

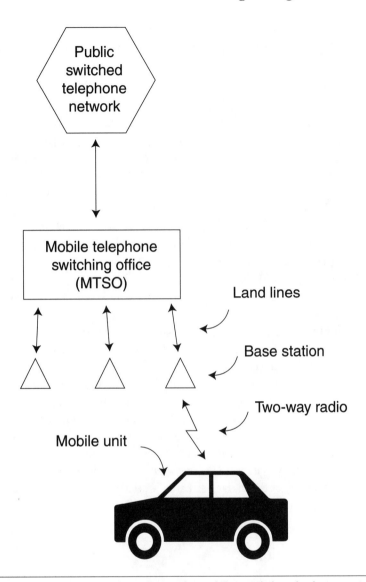

Figure 3.12 Diagram illustrating the relationship of the mobile telephone switching office (MTSO) to the public switched telephone network (PSTN) and cellular telephone subscribers for call handling.

NOTE: Each cell phone communicates via two-way radio with a base station. Base stations communicate over landlines with the MTSO, which maintains communication with the PSTN. Adapted from A. M. Noll (1998), *Introduction to Telephones and Telephone Systems*, 3/e. Reprinted with permission of Artech House.

In terms of strategy, cells in more densely populated areas are allocated more channels. From an economic perspective, because systems are expensive to build and install, their deployment is determined in large part by the potential number of users in an area. Therefore, densely populated areas tend to be better served than sparsely populated and remote areas.

Vocoders

The newer digital cellular systems differ from the original AMPS service in that voice signals are digitized before being transmitted. Aside from the advantage of rendering conversations more private and secure from electronic eavesdroppers (after all, binary code is itself a form of encryption), digitalization allows twice the number of channels (and sometimes more) to be used through the use of signal compression. The key to compression in this case is a voice coder (or *vocoder*) built into the cell phone unit.

Vocoders operate on the principle that speech signals have a great deal of redundancy in them. The analog bandwidth of the human voice is therefore reducible by analyzing and converting speech signals (through sampling and quantizing) into a reasonable copy that requires less bandwidth, with an accompanying reduction in the digital data rate representing it. Once transmitted, a receiver equipped with the proper code reader takes the data stream and converts it into a synthetic speech signal.

Different vocoders perform the conversion using different models of speech. One, called a *channel vocoder*, operates according to the audio spectrum of the human voice. It can transmit a speech signal at a digital rate of only 2 kbps, a huge savings compared to the 64 kbps normally used for voice transmission over a standard high-quality telephone circuit. Others include *formant vocoders*, which use resonant peaks of the speech signal to model the voice, and *LPC vocoders* (for linear predictive coding), which can potentially reduce data streams associated with voice signals to as low as 1,200 bps.

Multiplexing

Obviously, in all digital wireless communication industries, any method that can save bandwidth while preserving the utility of signals will receive serious consideration from service providers. This is because available bandwidth is so limited, and as demand for service continues to increase, it brings with it the promise for still greater profits if growing demand can be satisfied.

The fundamental infrastructure used to support cell service is the same as that used in all of the wireless personal communication services (PCS) (e.g., cell phone, data and paging services, beepers, wireless Internet). All are digital, and all compete with one another to acquire bandwidth for their operations. Currently, there are six PCS licensees sanctioned for operation by the FCC in each market in addition to the two wireless cellular companies, making eight such entities in each U.S. market (Lu, 1998, p. 138).

All PCS companies (cellular included) use advanced *multiplexing* techniques to extend the utility of the limited bandwidths granted them for service. Multiplexing is the simultaneous use of a transmission channel to carry multiple signals. Several incompatible techniques are now used to perform digital multiplexing in wireless systems. One is called frequency division multiple access (FDMA); a second technique is called time division multiple access (TDMA); a third is called code division multiple access (CDMA) and a fourth is called groupe special mobile (GSM), a form of TDMA used extensively around the world.

In FDMA, a number of signals to be carried by a service are each assigned their own band of frequencies within the larger bandwidth granted for service, thus multiplying the number of channels available for transmission. In TDMA, the entire bandwidth allocated for service is shared equally by all users, but with short durations of time granted to each user in turn for transmission. In CDMA (which uses "spread spectrum" technology), every signal to be transmitted is assigned a unique code; then all signals are sent out on the same radio channel using the entire bandwidth, and when received, only the signal matching the receiver code is retained and decoded (Figure 3.13).

As of this writing, some experts believe that spread spectrum technology will eventually win out over the others and become the multiplexing technique of choice among digital wireless service providers. The reasons for this are that this technique does not need more than one receiver to decode every signal, which is an obvious cost saver; in contrast, FDMA requires separate receivers to handle signals at different frequencies. In addition, CDMA is currently viewed as superior to TDMA because it allows for a greater number of signals to be transmitted, thus providing a more economic use of available bandwidth. Predicting is difficult—to know what the future holds, stay tuned.

CONCLUSIONS ■

To have a full understanding of how technology enables us to create, store, transmit, receive, consume, and manipulate audiovisual and textual information through both wire and wireless means, it is essential to know something about broadcasting, computers, and distribution networks. All three infrastructures are critical to commerce in both mass media products and services, and personal communication of digital messages. Without all three, digital telecommunication would not be what it is today.

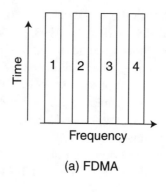

(a) FDMA

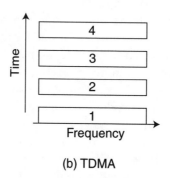

(b) TDMA

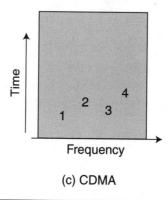

(c) CDMA

Figure 3.13 Diagram of three methods of multiplexing signals to make better use of available bandwidth in telecommunication. (a) In frequency division multiple access (FDMA), each signal corresponding to a telephone conversation gets its own band of frequencies for a call. (b) In time division multiple access (TDMA), the same band of frequencies is used by all callers via short bursts of digital data from each conversation sent sequentially through time. (c) In code division multiple access (CDMA), digital signals are given a unique multiplicative code, which is then spread over the entire spectrum. All the signals are then sent over the entire spectrum simultaneously and then decoded at the receiver.

Adapted from A. M. Noll (1998), *Introduction to Telephones and Telephone Systems*, 3/e. Reprinted with permission from Artech House.

NOTES ■

1.   See the interview in this volume with Michael Young, who discusses bandwidth issues and the differences between the analog world of the past century and the digital world of the new millennium.

2.   To promote the diffusion of digital television in the United States, the Federal Communications Commission (FCC) has ruled that all four major television networks were to have had a digital affiliate in each of the top 10 markets by May 1999; by November 1999, rules required that they broadcast in digital in 20 additional markets, thus reaching 50% of all U.S. households. Analog broadcasts are tentatively scheduled to end in 2006; this deadline is now viewed as optimistic at best.

3.   It is likely that as the digital conversion progresses, functional distinctions between these industries will disappear.

4.   The term *broadband* refers to the ability of a channel to pass data streams requiring large bandwidth. For example, in the United States, a single AM radio channel uses 9 kHz of radio spectrum, whereas a single analog television channel uses 6 MHz (666 times larger than the AM channel). The television channel requires more space because it has to pass more information, including signals for sound, pictures, and color, among others. Channels are therefore either narrow or broad, depending on how much information they can pass. In general, voice channels require less bandwidth than those carrying sound, pictures, and color information. Internet traffic featuring television-quality streaming video would therefore be considered a broadband service. The fiber-optic backbone is capable of delivering it, but the local loop is not.

5.   Recent estimates suggest that there are more than 250 million television sets in the United States alone. Unfortunately, television's unidirectional characteristic (i.e., its ability to send signals *to* households without any mechanism for receiving signals *from* households) means it is difficult for television to provide two-way interactive service. To do that, we need to look to the telephone network, which was built to provide two-way service, but with a relatively low channel capacity compared to television. With the addition of DSL and cable modems, it could be argued that high-speed digital service is already being provided directly to households, but full-motion broadcast-quality color video is still not possible via such services. It will require fiber-optic technology or something new with fiber-optic channel capacity to make real-time interactive broadcast quality color video service directly available to households. The infrastructure required for that type of broadband digital carriage to individual households is still years away.

6.   Perhaps the strongest operational definition of when the transition to the digital platform will be complete is when individual users in households can routinely *exchange* high-capacity messages and media products with one another in real time beyond instant messaging, e-mail, and mouse clicks (e.g., live high-definition color video featuring natural motion).

7.   Determining the number of hardwire lines that would be required for every unit if a private dedicated line were to be permanently connected from every subscriber to every other follows the formula $(N-1) + (N-2) + \cdots$, where N equals the number of subscribers. So, for example, if there were five subscribers, the number of lines would be $4 + 3 + 2 + 1$, or 10 lines. For eight subscribers, the number would be $7 + 6 + 5 + 4 + 3 + 2 + 1$, or 28 separate lines. With hundreds of millions of subscribers, this method of connecting subscribers soon gets unwieldy.

8.   The exception to this was the *party* line, where a number of phones were connected to one line to allow a number of subscribers to participate in a call. But even in this case, once a connection was achieved, there was no way to reach any other telephone engaged with another line.

9. Rotary dials specify the telephone of a called party at the central office by creating interruptions in DC current that are sensed and counted by the switching equipment. They use a spring winding and a governor to control the rate of rotation. They send pulses at a rate of 9-11 per second; each interruption lasts about 60% of each pulse cycle. About $\frac{7}{10}$ second elapses between each dialed digit.

10. The Strowger switch eventually was replaced by other electromechanical devices, including a crossbar system. Currently, telephone switching is performed by digital computers programmed with monitoring capability to distribute traffic evenly across the network.

11. Transmission impairments include all unwanted signals. For example, *impulse* noise from humanmade sources such as nearby motors turning on and off; *sputtering* caused by loose wire connections; and *crosstalk*, or leakage from one signal into a nearby circuit, all present noise that degrades signal quality.

12. Twisting the copper wire further reduces interference from surrounding electrical sources by balancing the impact of ambient electrical stimuli on the circuit, effectively canceling out unwanted signals.

13. Originally, some of the transmission signal leaked into the sender's earphone, resulting in a problem called *sidetone*. Sidetone occurs when the signal of one's own voice leaks from the transmitter through to the receiver and is heard in the speaker's earpiece. Balancing the circuits greatly reduces sidetone. Some sidetone still remains, however, because not all lines have the same impedance, which can differ because lines are almost always of different lengths. Hence, not all sidetone is eliminated through the use of balanced circuits. Nevertheless, some sidetone is considered good because it lets callers know that their phones are on.

14. Both telegraph and fax machines are examples of digital communication. Arthur Korn invented the fax machine in 1902; it could send a picture electronically over a wire. In 1913, the Berlino fax machine enabled faxes to be distributed via phone lines. In 1974, the United Nations set the first international standard for fax machines, called *Group 1*, allowing a page to be transmitted over phone lines in six minutes at a resolution of 98 dots per inch. In 1980, the *Group 3* standard was adopted, allowing a 200-dots-per-inch page to be sent in one minute; eventually this time was whittled down to 30 seconds. By the 1980s, faxing had become widespread.

15. Accidents of history and technical limitations assuredly played a role in how the radio spectrum looks. For example, AM was the first form of audio modulation, and therefore was assigned spectrum space without having to compete for it against FM stations. It is an accident of history that Edwin Armstrong's invention of the FM demodulator came years later than AM. Hence, it is plausible that had FM preceded the development of AM, the spectrum allocation chart would look different from the way it looks today. In addition, when broadcasting (namely, radio) was first instituted, the vacuum tubes that provided oscillating circuits for radio transmitters were unstable at frequencies greater than 50 MHz, leading to allocations of station bandwidths below that upper limit.

16. Unfortunately, with analog signals, there is always some discrepancy, however small, between the original stimulus (i.e., a sound or image) and the copy that is produced—that is, perfect fidelity does not exist; hence, there is always some degree of distortion or noise between the original and the copy, just as there is always some degrading of the signal when going from an original document to a photocopy.

17. Remember from Chapter 2 that *digital information* derives its meaning from Claude Shannon, who, based on the work of George Boole, defined information as a series of binary choices expressed in terms of 0s and 1s, called binary digits, or bits.

18. The term *hertz* is used in honor of Heinrich Hertz, who in 1887 demonstrated that electromagnetic waves at stable frequencies could be propagated and then detected through the use of oscillating circuits. It is the modulation of such waves that makes it possible to produce analog radio and television signals.

19. Put simply, *header information* is code about code—that is, meta-code about the data being sent telling receiving computers how to treat the data they are about to receive. Header code includes *source* information identifying the sender, and *address* information designating the destination(s) of a message, similar to address information on an envelope of a letter. In addition, data packet information is also provided, indicating how message content is to be treated. Data packet information includes *priority*, *protocol*, and *assembly* information, telling receiving computers how to process the information once it is received.

20. Of course, there are many instances when human speakers using the telephone for natural conversation do not speak, leaving quiescent moments when other data could theoretically pass through the channel. This is a good example of the inefficiencies of a circuit-switched line. However, in this instance, the connection between human speakers is kept continuous and uninterrupted to maintain the pace and sense of normal conversation.

21. LANs feature coaxial, fiber-optic, or traditional twisted-pair copper telephone wire to interconnect an organization's computers so that information such as e-mail and other computer files could be shared along with hardware such as printers. One advantage of using LANs is that traffic between computers is much faster over lines with greater bandwidth than a modem. More recently, wide area networks (WANs) using high-speed telephone lines have appeared connecting organizations with multiple locations miles or even continents apart that need to share information continuously.

22. Since the inauguration of telephone companies, twisted-pair copper wire has been augmented by additional wire and wireless technologies to provide more widespread network service, including coaxial and fiber-optic cable, and satellite and terrestrial microwave relay stations. One of the most successful new services (discussed later) is cellular telephony that uses wireless digital technologies to provide mobile voice and data services.

23. If a modem were capable of sending more information through a channel than a relay circuit could handle, a buffering mechanism would be needed to keep the information from overloading the circuit. In general, the functional bandwidth of any channel is only as wide as its narrowest part. Currently, the limit on data transfer from modems over copper wire is not the copper wire, but other components along the transmission path.

24. As a baseline of comparison, in 1946, using vacuum tube technology and repeaters spaced every 8 miles, route capacity for cables containing four coax pairs could handle only 1,800 two-way voice circuits.

25. *Laser* stands for light amplification by stimulated emission of radiation. A perfect laser machine generates a controlled beam of coherent light at a single frequency with all rays parallel and in phase with one another.

26. Radio waves can be polarized using special horn antennas to transmit either vertically or horizontally to reduce or eliminate adjacent channel interference. Polarization permits full use of the bandwidth allotted for service, increasing system capacity.

27. See also http://www.nwfusion.com/research/2001/0702featside.html.

28. See http://www.wright.edu/web/access/information.html.

29. Because of limited channel capacity, analog systems are slowly being replaced by fully digital ones. However, AMPS phones continue to be manufactured. Therefore, it will be some time before the switchover is complete. To speed up adoptions of digital cell phones, providers are offering lower rates.

30. Cell calls from high altitudes can result in less than optimal service because signal strength from the unit's transmitter may be received with roughly equal intensity by more than one base station simultaneously, confusing the system.

CYBERINTERVIEW

Charles Ehlin

On January 12, 2001, I spoke with Charles Ehlin, electronics engineer and software developer for Foliage Software Inc., in Burlington, Massachusetts. Ehlin's first job had him building computers designed to control moon landings by Apollo astronauts. Since that time, he has designed software for a number of companies in Massachusetts, the silicon valley of the East Coast. Ehlin's experience enables him to contribute insights about cyberspace that can come only from one with broad knowledge of the field of digital communication technology.

Shyles: How long have you been working with computers?

Ehlin: Over 20 years. I started at PRD Electronics in Syosset, Long Island, doing hardware design on military projects to support F-14 test equipment. I also developed hardware for the Apollo mission landing modules and radar systems. I relocated to Massachusetts in 1972 where I worked at a company called Analog Devices. They made analog-to-digital and digital-to-analog converters. I developed measurement and control systems. They are a big company and very successful now. I was with them about 13 years.

S: What made you leave?

E: I wanted to do something on my own. And Analog is where I got into software. It was my first step in that direction. One of the computers I designed had a lot of firmware in it, that is, the programming inside the hardware of the computer. So I started programming.

S: You were not trained in college to do this.

E: No. I had one Fortran course in college at Polytechnic Institute of Brooklyn.

S: Where else did you work?

E: When I left Analog, I went with someone I formed a software company with—a colleague—called Summit Software. We created a product called Better Basic, which at the time broke some of the boundaries of some of the Basic computer language. You used to not be able to have a program that was bigger than 640K. We developed an extensible language. You were able to add your own modules to it. It was a big breakthrough, but then Microsoft took over. I was there for two and a half years. Then the company ceased because it could not compete with Microsoft's product line. The problems were not in how good something was as much as how good the marketing power somebody has. Their marketing budget for a week was probably our yearly marketing budget.

S: What did you do after Summit folded?

E: I went to a company called Metra Byte, which was another measurement and control hardware company, and I started up their software department. There were a lot of base-level drivers.

S: What is a base-level driver?

E: Metra Byte sold hardware boards and they supplied drivers to go along with them to perform rudimentary operations so that someone wouldn't have to go in and figure out how to actually make the hardware work. We developed measurement functions and repeat management functions and timing functions designed to help the user. I was there for nine years. From there, I went to a company that made very large NT service materials—Windows NT. They were multiprocessor assistants. They had 16 processors in them. They had 40, 50 drives of hard disk. Very large, meant for high-power service systems.

S: It seems to me these are all very different jobs. Did any job ever intimidate you, making you feel, "Oh I really don't know what's going on here, it has such a high learning curve"?

E: I think that's what I thrive on.

S: You don't get intimidated?

E: Yeah, I get intimidated, but it doesn't stop me.

S: How do you get up to speed with that sort of thing? What do you do? When you have a new thing can you always fall back on your electronics training?

E: I think the foundation is education. Education has taught me how to solve problems and it's irrelevant what they are. I learned that from one of my mentors, who was an aeronautical engineer, a software genius, a physics genius. He taught me that if you learn how to learn, you can pick things up.

S: Then you came here?

E: About four years ago.

S: What are the reasons your current boss hired you?

E: First, a little history. I picked this company out on the Internet. I had been searching for companies featuring diverse types of work, including things related to the Internet, things in COM service, things in webs. [The company] Foliage was all over the place. They did things for aviation. They did things for the financial markets. And I was interested in them and I came in and they liked my experience, but they didn't like my price. We haggled. I started here with a cut in pay with the attitude that I would show them that it would be worth it for them to pay me my asking price after they saw what I could do. And that has worked out. They liked the fact that I had COM experience.

S: What is COM?

E: Common object module model architecture. It allows you to share objects and relate one object to another. It allows a user to run an object on one machine while looking at it on another. An object can be anything, say, a clock, and you want to be able to see it on a machine that's running but you also want to be able to see what the clock looks like on another machine that's running on the other side of the world. COM does that. It's not a trivial thing. There are a lot of pitfalls and many things that can go wrong. A lot of people can use it, but very few actually get to understand it.

S: If you had your dream project to be working on, what would it be?

E: Anything that's new and different.

S: What are the backgrounds of the people you work with?

E: It depends on their ages. For workers in their late 40s and early 50s, there was no computer science. So anyone that age into computer science and programming came from someplace else: mechanical engineering, electrical engineering, chemical engineering—problem solvers. They got into it because they started to use a computer in whatever it was they did. And mechanical engineers had programs to work with. Most of the younger ones are trained in computer science.

S: What part of the field are you glad you're not in.

E: I would not want to work on stuff that other people have done. So anything that's legacy I will never do.

S: How has the field changed since you entered the field?

E: It depends on how you look at it. When I look at trying to solve a problem using the tools at hand, say, trying to solve the problem rearchitecting something else using new technology, what usually happens is that you have new technology that allows you to do things better and faster, so you end up adding things that weren't in the original. It's a syndrome, actually.

S: It may be even faster.

E: It may be faster and more complex.

S: And that defeats its elegance?

E: It can. One of the hardest things as an engineer to do is to know when it is worth it, when it's not, and when to stop. And that's the biggest argument that engineers will have with marketing departments. Marketing departments want bells and whistles.

S: The complexity issue suddenly strikes me as being more difficult to deal with, which brings me to the question of documentation. You have a certain cognitive style to the work, but another engineer might have a completely different way of working. In light of such differences, how do you document your work? In other words, if there's turnover in the job and you've worked with ten people and five of them have left the company, they've left some legacy behind them; how do you deal with that difference in documentation?

E: You're right. You can't get away from that issue. I am fortunate in that I don't have a lot of legacy because most of the things I make have a finite life span. It's not as if you were doing programming for some financial institution where there is legacy software 20 years old. That's just not the case. As elegant and as wonderful as some of the things that I work on are, they have a life span after which they are no longer relevant. So legacy problems are not so critical for me.

S: Do your clients want documentation?

E: Yes, and they will all get documentation.

S: You write it personally?

E: I write parts of it. It depends on how many people are working on the project. I can give you an example of how things work here because this is unique. We have the customers here asking us to do software for them. We don't sell it. It's not our software. Once it goes to them, it's theirs.

S: They own it.

E: So they want not only to have the software, they want to know how it works, and their contract transfers all the knowledge on how it works. So there's a documentation defined right up front. Another advantage working for a company that's doing this kind of business is when you sit down and sign the contract to do the software, there's a document that clearly specifies the customer's expectations. The client relationship fosters documentation much more than if it was software that was just purely inside a company.

S: Do you work closely with quality assurance (QA) people to put the finishing touches on a project?

E: Only in fixing what they find. They have to document everything.

S: Does the QA department ever look over the documentation and come back to you and say, "This is wrong"?

E: Yes. They fix documentation too.

S: Do you like the fact that they have input on this?

E: That depends on when and how much they find, whether they're going to be too nitpicky or not. There's a relationship and a trust that you have. There are some people who will annoy an engineer and vice versa. And there are other people who mediate should there be a controversy.

S: Does the client get involved in that?

E: No. That's behind the scenes. The clients would get involved if the product you gave them didn't meet their QA; I mean they're probably going through some QA too. If it's failing their QA and it's passing ours, all hell would break loose.

S: Without naming any names, what kinds of firms are you dealing with? You mentioned that there were about ten or so.

E: There are financial institutions, some semiconductor manufacturing firms, several aviation firms dealing with navigation systems, some heads-up display groups, and all kinds of elaborate navigation systems that have become more popular economically.

S: What about digital telecommunication and Internet-related companies?

E: There's a fair amount of Web design going on for sports franchises and leagues. E-work in HTML (Hypertext Markup Language), XML (Extensible Markup Language), ASP, and Java.

S: And you also work with C++?

E: My strength is in C++ right now. It's built upon a machine that does a compiling and takes what you are writing and creates assembly language code for a specific machine. But the C++ code, theoretically, could be run on any machine if you compiled it for that machine.

S: Let's turn to some of the engineering issues, the transition from analog to digital. The cell phone industry, for example, is digitizing voices now. Do you have any sense as to why the transition from analog to digital happened the way it did?

E: I can only give you speculations. The reason that it started in that industry is that it was swamped with magnitudes of lines, and normal switching couldn't handle the sheer size of the demand. That was the bottleneck; that's why they all went to digital. With digital, you don't need a switch for every line to multiplex. You don't have to have a huge room with a bazillion relays. And the systems are reliable.

S: We see people here and we see so much talk about what we call convergence, which is the marriage of broadcasting and computers and telecommunications, where people say that once you turn all of the signal information into binary code, you have completely interoperable systems. That's what we mean by *convergence*. Do you see that being a reality?

E: Not without a real standard. In order for anyone to access all of this information, it has to be packed in some way and it has to be unpacked in some way. And standardization is what allows that to be done across different media whether it is voice, music, or whatever. You have to have standards that allow it to be coded and decoded properly.

S: I have heard you say, "One is a beautiful number in engineering."

E: Yes. There are two ways of looking at the utility of a medium. One is that its architecture is exquisite. It's the best. It's the highest performance. The other is, how is it used, what makes it easiest to get the job done. And I find that efficiency emerges when everything uses the same standard. So, if everyone is using that, the architecture and design may not be as beautiful, but it *works* beautifully. Microsoft is an example of that. The reason that so many people can sit down at a computer and use a word processor is because Microsoft dominated. An IBM PC wasn't IBM PC for very long. It came to be made by many companies, but it was made to follow a relatively universal specification. They all perform the same way. As a result, you could take a board from one and put it in the other. You can take software from one and put it on another. By contrast, the Mac was a more elegant machine, but it didn't have the volume.

S: That's a marketing issue.

E: And a pricing issue. The fact is, if you're going to design software, it's best to design it for the machine that's most plentiful in the marketplace, even if it's an inferior machine, because there are more of them available to buy and use it. And that's why the IBM is a better machine than the Mac in terms of getting a job done. It may not be a better machine, but it is the most ubiquitous.

S: What are your views about the direction of the field in terms of which products are headed for success as you look into the future? I know it's hard to crystal ball.

E: I think that the biggest change I see for people is in the financial world, with banking and how people will buy things. E-commerce. The amount of online banking is already increasing enormously. I just saw somebody who was programming from a bank that allows you to send money to someone else. Business-to-business financial is going to be really big with the payment of bills rather than having to send checks.

S: What about the risk factors involved in electronic funds transfer, especially with really large sums? How does an engineer meet the security challenge? What would you be asked to do by a financial institution to secure privacy and security and firewalls? How would you go about that? Is it encryption, double-key systems? What do you do?

E: You use the latest and the best that you can. And will there be someone who can hack it? Yes. Will it happen that they do something dangerous? Perhaps. Security is a problem just like it is with armored cars. But the more that gets done, the better the security will become.

S: Are you familiar with this thing the government wanted called the Clipper Chip? What's your personal take on that? Should the government have that "Big Brother" kind of back door into the account and the transactions going on? Should they have access?

E: I am really torn. They can order a phone tap. So I can see that, and that seems to be accepted. I'm torn. No one likes to be looked at. The problem is it's something new. They can see a lot more. So the question is, "Do you believe they will use it properly?" And if it's used properly, I have absolutely no problem with it, but there's no guarantee. I think if something happened where I was being monitored I would be vehemently opposed.

S: Does that influence the way you conduct yourself via e-mail in the world? Do you say things, do you guard your typing?

E: No. But I don't know that I have anything to say to anyone that I have anything to worry about. I'm not planning anything. I am not plotting anything.

S: Right. How would it make you feel to know that the people at your company read your e-mail?

E: I would be upset with that. But my company is not concerned with how many times I hit the keys on my keyboard. They don't monitor like that. They monitor my output. But I won't say there aren't companies that might.

S: Do they have a right to do it, do you think? The law says now that the companies own the machines, so they can look.

E: Legally, I believe they can, but morally I don't think that they should, unless there's a reason. I mean if they are finding that there's a great deal of theft going on, or there's something going on here or if there's pornographic material suddenly popping up on somebody's computer.

S: What is the breakout in terms of gender among your workers? There is somewhere around a hundred-plus people here. Is there a fifty-fifty split, or?

E: No. There are very few women.

S: Why do you suppose that is?

E: I don't know. It's never been that way before in the companies I've worked for.

S: It's always been a fifty-fifty split?

E: No. It hasn't been that. Engineering in general is a guy thing. I don't think there are as many women graduates. What's made up for that is all of the other jobs that are around tended to have a lot of women. In the financial areas, or human resources, or nontechnical engineering job positions, it is closer to fifty-fifty—or maybe more—women in those particular areas. Our human resources department is one with many female employees.

S: Let's try a technical question. When are hardware upgrades preferable to software upgrades?

E: It's preferable to do it in software, usually, because it's the cheapest. Hardware upgrades could mean a board layout change, which means that we'd have to go out and manufacture all new boards, make a new layout, and it could be quite expensive. However, there are times when software can't fix the problem you are trying to solve. Like when you can't get enough information to make a decision. Sometimes a change can't be done with software. Then it has to be a hardware change. And hardware is more permanent, so you don't want a quick, rash, slap-it-together fix in hardware. You want to make sure before you do a hardware change. If you have to do a redesign in hardware, you're accepting a certain amount of cost, so it's important to do it right and maybe make sure that you're covered for other things. The other way to go is kind of in between—you can have what I call firmware, which is a certain amount of programmability in the hardware that allows you to change its functionality by switching a chip, which could be on a socket, and that's easy. But still the software is preferable. The software upgrade doesn't require you to open the machine up, to pull a chip out, to worry about plugging in the chip wrong, wondering whether you got all the pins in properly, and so on. There are lots of things that could go wrong.

S: What about the issue of throughput? Do you consider that as a significant issue in your work?

E: In general senses. I know that it's used a lot in the cellular telephone industry. There are issues of compression, latency, and various other factors that influence throughput, that is, the speed at which a signal makes it through the network, especially as you go, say, from copper to fiber and back again. There is a delay time. Sometimes it's a very short time and sometimes it's a long time, like when you go through a satellite. In such cases, a signal is relayed and converted, then retransmitted, perhaps at a different frequency. In addition, the signal is multiplexed, and that involves processing time. So signals can become dysfunctional for voice when they are perfectly functional for data transmission. For a phone conversation, you don't want to have even a 1-second delay. Because if you said, "Hello" you don't want it to be a second before you hear it because you're going to think something's wrong. So it depends on what you're doing. If you're transferring bank information as data, you don't care that it takes a second or two. Sometimes you use buffers, because data can be coming in faster than you can put them out.

S: For example.

E: If there were a piece of equipment you were using to receive numbers and you had to compute the sum of them or a running sum for a string of numbers and send them out, there's processing going on. If the processing took longer than the time it took to receive a new number, you would need to start buffering the numbers coming in so that you can keep processing. That means the buffer would have to be deep enough so that it didn't overflow until you got all of the information without losing any of it. And depending on the data flow, you could either handle it successfully or not. So to build a good buffer, you make one capable of signaling the sender when it gets filled up saying, "I can't take any more right now." Then when it's ready to take more it will say, "OK, give me more."

S: So that's another circuit and so what we're dealing with in that case is the issue of maybe error correction? Will that fall into that category?

E: It certainly could. You can take data in to see if they correlate.

S: And that reduces the capacity of the channel, doesn't it? That is, you're now going to send a signal back saying, "Wait, don't send it." Well, that's taking some of the capacity, right?

E: Yes. But to minimize that problem, what happens with error correction is that it's not done on a piece of information at a time. It's usually done on packets of information.

S: And they'll look at the last digit?

E: Or sometimes it'll look at all of the data and compute what it thinks the word should be.

S: And it matches it up to see that it comes out right?

E: And if it isn't, then it requires a retransmission of the whole packet over again.

S: Yes, and so that takes a certain segment of the channel capacity?

E: Yeah.

S: So if someone says that this is a 54-kilobyte, or kilobit per second, capacity, but a hunk of that is used for error correction, then it really has less than that in useful capacity?

E: Yes, but the overhead for error correction is pretty small especially when it's done on a per-packet basis. For example, if for every byte you sent you said a word that told you to compare to see if it was correct, you would be doubling the amount of capacity that you need to send that information, but if you sent a correction for every hundred bytes of information, then you are only using 1% of the capacity for that function. If you did it on a thousandth, then it becomes only .1%, so you can make it smaller. And then the only time you pay the penalty is when you do detect an error. Then you have to retransmit that packet.

S: Well, that's pretty much it. Thank you for your insight.

E: You're welcome.

PART II

MARKETS

CHAPTER 4

CHILDREN IN CYBERSPACE

Mark R. Banschick

Josepha Silman Banschick

THE CHILD/INTERNET INTERFACE ■

We can't talk about the world of the 21st century without considering the Internet. So much of contemporary life, for an increasing number of people, is happening online, and it's just a matter of time before nearly everybody will be connected.

Today's children are being raised in a new environment, one that did not even exist ten years ago. Young people, who often seem at the forefront of innovation, are quickly mastering this new environment and increasingly inhabit it. At the same time, many of their parents are being left behind, struggling to understand.

By the end of grade school, an ever-increasing number of children are introduced to the Internet either through school or at home. In 1997, a Gallup national survey (in conjunction with CNN, USA Today, and the National Science Foundation) found that 55% of teens said they have used the Internet and less than one third (29%) had access to the Internet at home. More recently, a Grunwald Associates (2000) survey found that 40% of American children and more than 70% of American teens are using the Internet. It is where (if the notion of location is appropriate in this context) they play, communicate with friends, and get exposure to the world outside their communities—for better and for worse.

Even though it is still in its infancy, the Internet is progressively becoming more commonplace, as its role in such life functions as banking, shopping, communicating, studying, playing, and working illustrates. Yet it is still a chaotic space, where the roads are often unmarked and anarchy rules. It has its own dialect and etiquette, its own culture, and perhaps its own perspective.

Children growing up today are influenced and shaped by this environment. Parents, educators, and public policy makers need to learn about this "neighborhood" and how to master its ways. They need to understand how the Internet affects the minds, the values, and the behavior of young people if they are to become a directing force in the lives of children. On a more urgent note, school administrators, parents, law enforcement professionals, and even children themselves need to understand the risks of Internet-related violence and sexual predators.

The Internet, like other historic technological leaps before it, brings both opportunities and dangers, particularly for the youngest among us. Unlike the invention of the car or the printing press, the Internet is a technology that is just as available to children and teenagers as it is to adults (perhaps more so). It opens wonderful new vistas as well as new problems.

Before the advent of the automobile, there were no head-on collisions at 80 miles per hour. Before the printing press, hateful propaganda had a limited audience. But the invention of the automobile and the printing press changed our world toward what most consider a better life. Increased literacy and communication meant more knowledge and power among an ever-widening number of the population, enabling democracy to thrive. The invention of the automobile effectively reduced travel time and allowed the population to spread over the country while maintaining access to their families.

Similarly, the Internet offers a monumental step forward much like the printing press and the automobile. And likewise, it is a democratizing force. It brings information and power to groups of people who are otherwise removed from the centers of power. One such group is children. It puts children within reach of information that was not easily available to them before. It also bridges spaces that the automobile created and makes community a thing one can experience without leaving home.

But the Internet also exposes people, particularly children, to new dangers, both obvious and subtle. Sexual predators can now target children more easily; children can become detached from and reconnected to places in the outside world with a click of a mouse.

The benefits and risks of the Internet are dependent on how it is used. One thesis we advance is that the Internet functions as an *amplifier*: It increases our potential for good and productive work as well as for inappropriate and immoral endeavors. Its freedom and anonymity offer a vast world of experimentation that can be liberating but also can promote unhealthiness.

Ultimately, a technology is only as useful as the intentions of its users. A student fueled with ambition and curiosity can quickly and easily find vast amounts of information online, which would have taken much longer to assemble in the past. Yet the Net can also be easily used by students to get by with shallow research and even plagiarism.

Both the freedom and anonymity of the Internet allow shy users to connect to others online, leading to a widening of the repertoire of social intercourse. However, this same freedom enables pedophiles to venture from the world of thought to the virtual world of chat rooms, where they can target victims without ever leaving home.

In this chapter, we first focus on the processes and attributes that shape the child/Internet interface. These include multitasking, blurring, amplification, virtuality, and anonymity. Next we discuss three crucial aspects of child development affected by the Internet: intellectual development and education, social development, and identity development (including the formation of a value system). In each section, we cover the opportunities and dangers the Internet poses for children, adolescents, and young adults based on the literature and clinical experience.

Multitasking

In some contexts, multitasking refers to the concurrent operation by a system of two or more processes. That is, multitasking is a term used in computer operations—the ability of a computer to do a number of tasks simultaneously (in reality, the computer executes the tasks sequentially, but very quickly). However, as a result of the technologies that allow multitasking (or perhaps the other way around) humans have incorporated multitasking into their lives.

People multitask not only on computers. They do it when they simultaneously wash dishes, talk on the phone, and watch television. But the ultimate multitasking environment—one that allows simultaneity in a great number of operations—is the Internet. Simple multitasking may have preceded the Internet, but the Internet is pushing it to its ultimate limits in terms of both human and machine capacity. And the current generation of children is growing and developing in a multitasking environment, where they do their homework, socialize, play, consume entertainment, and shop, all at the same time.

Does multitasking affect the developing mind of children? Recently, scientists at the National Institute of Neurological Disorders and Stroke (NINDS) have used imaging technology to map areas of the brain responsible for branching (multitasking)—doing several tasks sequentially while remembering the goal of each task, which is a uniquely human capability (Koechlin, Basso, Pietrini, Panzer, & Grafman, 1999, pp. 148-151). They have located that area in the anterior prefrontal cortex. According to Koechlin et al., branching appears to play a key role in human cognition. This area of the brain houses the executive functioning required for decision making and staying on task, even when multitasking. Without an effective executive function, multitasking breaks down into ineffective multiple projects and distractions. Burgess (2000) suggests a connection between deficits associated with the frontal lobe area, such as disorganization, absentmindedness, and problems with planning and decision making, which are typical of attention deficit disorder (ADD) and exposure to situations that require multitasking.

Some educators see a connection between multitasking and ADD as well. They worry that the result of multitasking on the Internet will be an increase in ADD-like behavior among children. Teachers are already complaining about shortened attention spans (Healy, 1998, p. 183) and difficulties with sustained attention. Others speculate that such behavior will be adaptive in the future, that children will eventually adjust to the new demands and still be able to attend with the same ability they had before being exposed to Internet interaction. "Today's 'difficult' students . . . may actually be showing us the way into hypermedia's new world of parallel processing," says Healy (1998, p. 153).

Blurring

In their 1999 book *Blur*, Davis and Meyer describe the effects of the Internet on the economy. They argue that the Internet blurs the traditional boundaries between buyer and seller, between product and service, and between tangibles and intangibles. The world of *Blur* requires flexibility and multiple talents; business needs are not seen as static or even slowly evolving but rather quickly shifting requiring new management styles and a more quick-footed work force.

But the concept of blurred boundaries may be applied to other sociocultural aspects of the Internet, and not just to those of the world of e-commerce. And the blurring of boundaries may affect children even more than adults because of children's lack of experience with culture in general.

Some blurring may be a consequence of multitasking. Engaging simultaneously in different tasks brings about the blurring of boundaries between them. Examples of Internet blurring are the following:

1. *Work and social life*. It is not uncommon for even grade school children to conduct research or write an essay on the computer while responding to *instant messaging* from a number of friends.

2. *Personal and commercial*. While writing papers and corresponding with friends, young surfers are frequently exposed to unsolicited advertisements. Thus, the private world and the world of commerce blend together.

3. *High and low content*. Boundaries blur with regard to the kinds of information children can access. With a mouse click, they can access sites with serious and/or dangerous content (e.g., bomb-making recipes) or with the lewdest pornography. They may even view different kinds of information at the same time on their screen.

4. *Family roles*. As children gain hegemony over this new technology, family roles blur with regard to the Internet. Youngsters understand the Internet and operate freely within it, much like someone who grows up speaking a language versus someone who has to learn it as an adult. Many parents are unable to control the Internet with equal facility. This shifts the power structure in the family, making parents often dependent on their children.

5. *Age boundaries*. Blurring of traditional age-related boundaries among children is becoming more common online. One middle school administrator told us that the adjustment to high school seems easier in the past few years, at least in part because middle school-aged children are in contact over the Net with their counterparts in high school. "They seem to be better prepared and know what to expect," she said.

6. *Generational boundaries*. By exposing children to adult content (news, adult chat, pornography, etc.), the Internet blurs traditional generational boundaries. Meyrowitz (1985) noted more than 15 years ago a similar effect brought about by television:

> Television removes barriers that once divided people of different ages and reading abilities into different social situations. The widespread use of television is equivalent to a broad social decision to allow young children to be present at wars and funerals, courtships and seductions, criminal plots and cocktail parties. (p. 242)

This overexposure through the media to adult issues forces children to ask questions about issues that are not yet relevant to their lives.

There are also interactions across generational lines that occur on the Internet often around common interests. Young people have the opportunity to correspond with experts and mentors who were not available offline. They also interact with adults in chat rooms, because the anonymity of the Internet makes it difficult if not impossible to determine the identities of the participants. Predators often take advantage of this to make contact with children.

7. *Community*. The world has gotten smaller because of the Internet. A child's sense of community is blurring because of instant access to friends who are not contained within traditional geographic boundaries.

8. *Social hierarchies*. The Internet blurs the social lives of children in some new and interesting ways. Even in the pre-Internet world, social hierarchies and cliques have been common from about age ten. The Net further promotes natural groupings of children through special interest chat rooms and through buddy lists. One might expect these lists to be small, like cliques. But this is not the case. Instead, many middle school children have as many as 80 or more names on their buddy lists. Because of the privacy of the Internet, they can experiment with talking to people whom they normally wouldn't be paying attention to in school.

9. *Blurred identity*. The Internet presents users with a particularly good opportunity to explore questions of identity. Children test different facets of their personality online with a great deal more latitude than might otherwise be possible. They do that by adopting a style online that is different from their real-life personality. They often allow themselves to be more expressive or outrageous, more cutting, more erotic, or even more thoughtful than in their real lives. This is a normal part of exploring identity in adolescents, and to some extent occurs in the real world as well. However, extensive involvement in chat rooms and role-playing games can result in a weakened identity because fantasy play online is a poor substitute for working through one's issues in the real world with real people.

10. *Appropriate and inappropriate*. What is appropriate and not appropriate is blurred in the nebulous space of the Internet. Some children and adults allow themselves aggressive and abusive behaviors online that they would not dream of using in the real world. Children are exposed on the Internet to a myriad of attitudes, some courteous, some insulting, some inappropriately seductive, often in the very same Internet site. This can lead to confusion about what is proper and what is not.

Beyond the above impacts, the Internet is a *democratizing* force. "On the Internet everybody is equal," says Douglas Both, principal of John Jay

Middle School in Katonah, New York. The boundaries of country, race, and religion are broken on the Internet. People's looks, socioeconomic status, or gender are blurred or effectively erased entirely in cyberspace. This may reshuffle many users' preconceived notions about race and gender and force people to adopt new criteria for evaluating others that are not based on external cues. Perhaps, Internet use will help reduce racism, sexism, and other prejudices in future generations.

Amplification Lowers Entry Barriers

The Internet has a psychological impact that affects users much like an amplifier. It tends to exacerbate inherent difficulties and augment existing strengths. Apparently, easy and anonymous access to cyberspace lures users into dropping some of their inhibitions and adaptations that shield them in real life (or shield society from them). Thus, users who tend to harbor hostility in real life may explode with anger in cyberspace. People already inclined to isolation may be lured into becoming even more isolated as online users. In a story in *U.S. News & World Report*, a young man relates how the computer and the Internet increased his isolation from the world while growing up. Being shy to begin with, he preferred staying home with the computer and playing games. The Internet "gave me a reason why I didn't have to go out," he said (Kleiner, 2000, p. 52).

Another aspect of the Internet that contributes to the amplification effect is the *lowering of entry barriers*. The Internet makes it easier for users to venture into areas previously out of bounds for them. Pedophilia predates not only the Internet but also probably civilization itself, and people probably do not become pedophiles because of the Net. But the Internet lowers the barriers of entry for people inclined to antisocial behavior, such as pedophilia, by increasing access to child pornography and simplifying the targeting of potential victims. Pedophiles who may not have thought about getting into their car and seeking young victims on the street can't resist the ease with which they can now connect to targets online.

The Internet lowers barriers of entry for both criminal acts and creative endeavors thus amplifying the incidence of both crime and productiveness. The trade in stolen credit card numbers has mushroomed since the Internet provided new ways for hackers to crack confidential databases. Unfortunately, the Net, with its anonymity and access, has made it possible for hackers to abuse the system, invade privacy, and steal information and property. One wonders what information is safe online and for how long?

Conversely, the Internet also lowers barriers to legal commerce. People who may be disinclined to engage in business (including children) are now able to start their own businesses on lower budgets and without leaving their homes. Many young people have become Web designers, creating Web pages for other people and for companies.

The amplification effect appears in various aspects of children's lives. In education, for instance, the Internet tends to amplify existing tendencies in students, rather than change the course of their academic trajectory. It allows serious students, who use it well, to enhance their scholarship and knowledge by giving them easy access to many diverse sources. Alternatively, it allows children who are passive students to get away with even less work than before by giving them easy access to summaries and by making plagiarism a simple affair of cutting and pasting.

Amplification of Commercialism and Invasion of Privacy

Unlike television, which promotes comparatively passive viewing, the Internet is interactive. People use the Net to find what they want. But the Internet also uses them. Many Web sites, particularly of commercial companies, gather information on visitors and track their activities online. They use this information to create user profiles, so that they can better target them with advertisements. And who is more vulnerable to custom-tailored solicitation than children? Promoters learn about their wishes and desires, at times presenting irresistible offers.

Increasingly, Web pages, including both commercial and nonprofit sites, come decked with flashing banner ads targeting children with marketing appeals. They are solicited, seduced, bought, and sold. The Internet did not invent advertising, of course, but it widens its scope and makes it more pervasive, immediate, and for heavy users, ubiquitous.

Media Consumption: Reality and Virtuality

Today's children are growing up in a world in which mediated experience frequently occupies more space and time in their lives than direct experience. The problem with mediated experience is that it replaces real life. Time used consuming media is time away from direct human interaction, and away from physical involvement with the world.

To understand the tension between reality and virtual reality as it occurs in cyberspace, we must start with a review of television consumption, because television offers an early form of virtual reality that has been around much longer than the Internet. Even before the Internet, there was a societal concern about the amount of time children spent in front of the television. According to the National Center for Education Statistics (NCES), in 1984, 52% of fourth graders and 39% of eighth graders were watching 4 hours or more of television a day. By 1996, the numbers declined to 34% and 28%, respectively. The same survey indicates that most children spend less than an hour doing homework (Snyder & Wirt, 1998, pp. 118-119).

Unfortunately, although the decline in TV watching may seem promising, it is accounted for by a pick-up in video game use and Internet involvement. A Stanford University survey shows that for every additional hour on the Net, people report further decreases in time spent with traditional media, reaching 65% for those spending more than ten hours a week on the Net (Nie & Ebring, 2000, p. 6). According to a study by the Kaiser Family Foundation, 33% of children aged 8-18 said that if they had to choose which medium to bring to a desert island, they would bring a computer with Internet access. Only 13% chose television. The rest chose videos, video games, CDs, tapes, radio, books, and magazines. The same study shows that the average media use of children 2-18 is a staggering 5½ hours a day (amounting to 38 hours a week, with the biggest chunk of media time taken by TV, at nearly 3 hours per day), whereas time spent reading came to only 44 minutes per day. Children 8-18 use 6¾ hours of media a day. And they may be multitasking, using more than one medium at a time (Rideout, Foehr, Roberts, & Brodie, 1999, p. 73).

These statistics tell us that after school and homework, many children just plop in front of the TV or the computer screen, spending most of their leisure time consuming electronic media rather than getting involved with the world around them. And increasingly, they are spending their time in school in front of a computer screen. For these reasons, their development from childhood to adulthood increasingly occurs in a mediated space, or in virtual reality rather than in the real world.

This behavioral shift is part of a cultural trend toward increased media consumption coupled with increased automation, culminating in intelligent machines that threaten to replace a wide variety of human cognitive functions. Some scientists believe that this may well be the next stage of evolution: intelligent machines replacing human beings and human beings becoming more machine-like by downloading their consciousness into computers (Hayles, 1999, p. 1).

Postman (1986) argued that television determines our cultural discourse and is the "culture's principal mode of knowing about itself" (p. 92), just as typography dictated a shift in cognitive styles away from memorial processes and toward one largely dependent on reading. Yet a new shift is under way in our style of discourse as a result of the advent of telecommunication. As Postman puts it, "Television now takes command. In courtrooms, classrooms, operating rooms, board rooms, churches and even airplanes, Americans no longer talk to each other, they entertain each other. They do not exchange ideas; they exchange images" (pp. 92-93).

In some ways, today's Internet mode of presentation is developing along the same lines as television, and the impact of this new medium on our cognitive style of apprehending the world is developing along with it. Web sites present serious material in entertaining ways. Although it is interactive, unlike TV, and much of its content is presented typographically, out of necessity, the Internet still uses an image-based presentation meant to please as well as to inform. And the days of predominantly typographical presentational formats online are probably numbered. As technology advances, the Internet will move rapidly toward more audiovisual and graphically based presentations.

But precisely because of its interactive nature, the Internet presents some unique problems. The TV viewer is in a position of spectator, outside the circle of events unfolding onscreen and without power to influence them directly. This position guarantees some distance between the viewer and the spectacle being viewed, even during live and "reality based" programs (e.g., *Survivor*). By contrast, on the Internet, users can watch events unfold and can participate in them also (MUDs or multiuser domains, and metaworlds), thus diminishing the distance between themselves and the event. This shift creates an experience of immersion in the cyberworld not found in the world of TV viewing, and can alter users' sensation of reality. For many, their experience is not illusory but real. Some online communicators argue that their experiences in cyberspace are as real as any.

The phenomenon of a mediated simulation of reality has come to be called *virtual reality* (VR). Although watching a drama on television can be described as a form of virtual reality, the term usually refers to cyberspace role-playing games and 3-D simulation technology. The ultimate VR experiences are those involving 3-D simulation technology, such as IMAX. This technology creates a feeling of immersion: Viewers or players feel as if they are inside the virtual space, as if they are surrounded by it, similar to the way the natural world surrounds us in real life.

However, a major aspect that currently separates 3-D virtual reality from reality itself is that the virtual events are preproduced and the participant must go along with the script. Perhaps eventually, technology will be perfected to the point that one would not be able to distinguish between virtual reality and reality. Nevertheless for the moment, it is clear that in the real world, unlike VR, many daily events are not programmed in advance; rather, they unfold naturalistically. So, for example, even though the event of attending a wedding may be highly ritualized, with invitations sent out weeks in advance, and the timing highly choreographed for all the participants, it is still possible for the bride's car to break down on the way to the ceremony, and so on.

The movie *The Matrix* describes a world in which people live their entire lives in VR without realizing that their lives happen only in their minds. As one of the main characters in the original script asks, "If the virtual reality apparatus, as you called it, was wired to all of your senses and controlled them completely, would you be able to tell the difference between the virtual world and the real world?" (Wachowski & Wachowski, 1996). The answer according to the movie is arguably no.

Some experiences on the Internet have come to be known as VR as well, even though they are different from the 3-D simulation technology variety. Users participating in Internet fantasy games known as MUDs or their outgrowths (MOOs or multiuser domains, object oriented; MUSHs or multiuser shared hallucinations; and metaworlds) are creating in cyberspace a whole world, complete with characters, relationships, even objects. To many, the interactions of fictional personas within a given MUD are as real as reality itself. In her book *Life on the Screen: Identity in the Age of the Internet*, Turkle (1995) describes a MUD inspired by the television series *Star Trek: The Next Generation*, in which participants spend up to 80 hours per week in intergalactic exploration and wars:

> Through typed descriptions and typed commands, they create characters who have casual and romantic sexual encounters, hold jobs and collect paychecks, attend rituals and celebrations, fall in love and get married. To the participants, such goings-on can be gripping; "This is more real than real life," says a character who turns out to be a man playing a woman who is pretending to be a man. (p. 10)

Although cyber VR does not yet possess the sophisticated 3-D graphics of IMAX, to some degree it shares with it the sensation of immersion.

If VR seems as authentic as reality to some adults, how much more does it seem so to children, whose personal boundaries may still be relatively flimsy? Turkle (1995) describes children in their teens who feel that the animals they create in SimLife could be alive and that the organisms in the computer get their energy from the electric plug. When asked about robots, one 11-year-old girl said she felt that robots were alive in the sense that Pinocchio was alive even when he was not a real boy (pp. 169-170).

As Internet use begins to overtake traditional TV viewing, children may interact more with anonymous users whose online personas may or may not accurately reflect their real identities, as when users engage in role-playing games (RPGs).

Some scenarios raise disturbing questions. Will children be able to distinguish between what's authentic and of value and what's not? Would children prefer the exciting world of VR to the physical world of playing ball? Can the Internet increasingly distance children from the physical world, turning their lives into a long digital hallucination? Will children conclude along with Cypher from *The Matrix* that life in VR is preferable to real life?

Turkle (1995) feels that the experience of VR online should be understood only in the context of the larger culture:

That context is the story of the eroding boundaries between the real and virtual, the animate and inanimate, the unity and the multiple self, which is occurring both in advanced scientific research and in the patterns of everyday life [as scientists create] artificial life [for] . . . children "morphing" through series of virtual personae. (p. 10)

In cyberspace and elsewhere, our society is moving toward disembodiment: disconnecting sensory experience from our physical bodies.

According to Hayles (1999), we are evolving toward what she calls the posthuman, which "privileges informational pattern over material installation, so that embodiment in a biological substrate is seen as an accident of history rather than an inevitability of life" (p. 2). Is this the kind of world we want to bequeath to our children? Should we mindlessly follow the lead of technocrats, who dream of cyborgs and disembodied consciousness, or should we actively stake our claim to the physical, real world?

Anonymity

The relative anonymity of the Internet is an essential part of its appeal. It is conceivable that in the future we may be forced to disclose our identity when logging on. But for now, anonymity accounts for at least part of the traffic in chat rooms and in online RPGs. It also accounts for much of the traffic in pornographic sites and for some Internet crime.

Some aggressive and inappropriate discourse online, from both adults and children (see discussion on social life) can be attributed to anonymity. Users tend to be less inhibited online because of perceived anonymity, much like drivers who tend to exhibit aggression behind the wheel because of relative anonymity of the driving situation.

The major concern that anonymity poses in regard to children is its effect on the development of a moral sense. Children develop morally in a context of an observing society. But what happens in an environment where one's identity is hidden, where words and deeds can be brought about without consequences? Would we have to deal with hackers and crackers if the Internet were not so anonymous?

The other side of anonymity is that it liberates users from the constraints of convention and from the fear of being judged negatively by others. This has an amplifying effect on human imagination. Users have greater freedom to express themselves in ways they would not have in real life. It opens up numerous possibilities for human interactions and exploration of identity that are not possible in real life. This can have a positive effect on identity development for many adolescents (as long as they don't get carried away by it).

Each of these processes—multitasking, blurring, amplification, virtuality, and anonymity—has a role to play in the development of children, as the Internet increasingly occupies a larger place in their lives. But the impact of the Net on child development is a broad area. The next section looks at the Internet's effects on child development in more specific terms, namely, in the areas of education, socialization, and identity.

INTELLECTUAL DEVELOPMENT ■

Does the Internet affect intellectual development? To answer this question we must first understand how the intellect develops. Piaget believed that intellectual growth of children is achieved through their own physical action, rather than simply sensory perception. From Piaget's theoretical perspective, children's active participation in the world is key. Using their bodies to explore their surroundings by moving and touching helps generate questions in children's minds, which they then attempt to answer through further exploration in the concrete world. The process is active, worldly, multisensory, and ultimately, useful. This is essential even in the formation of the logico-mathematical structures (Piaget & Inhelder, 1969, p. 155).

If Piaget's theory is correct, it follows that there is little point in putting small children in front of the computer, certainly not before the age of seven, when they have learned to read and can start processing typographical information. At the present, the main function of the Internet in the service of the intellect is as a provider of easy access to information. How the Internet affects intellectual development depends on the processing and utilization of the information by the users. A parallel holds with books in this regard. Simply acquiring books will not make children any smarter until they have read, processed, and then somehow used the information contained within the texts.

Surfing the Internet for information and games by older children is fine as long as it takes only a limited portion of their time. But it does become a problem when children favor the Internet at the expense of other significant activities. By spending hours in front of the screen, many children miss out on important developmental tasks that can be best achieved through actual physical involvement in the world. There is nothing on the Internet that matches constructing a fort with Lego blocks or, on a larger scale, building a tree house, in terms of exercising problem-solving skills.

John Dewey (2000) also believed in the importance of physical involvement in the intellectual process. He was critical of the separation of mind and body in schools. As Dewey warned, "A separation of the active doing phase from the passive undergoing phase destroys the vital meaning of an experience.

Thinking is the accurate and deliberate instituting of connections between what is done and its consequences" (p. 157). It is worth pointing out that Dewey directed his criticism toward the traditional school setting, in which children are forced to sit quietly for hours and absorb information divorced from its physical context, and as such, lacks practical meaning for them. Today's schools are not much changed; children are still required to sit quietly much of the day and listen to lectures about subjects that may be as relevant to their lives as quantum mechanics is to a dog.

It is conceivable that the Internet can help bring relevance and active exploration to the classroom, if used appropriately. As virtual reality technology develops, it will be possible to conduct virtual experiments on the Internet. Although real-life experiments are preferable, sometimes they are not feasible in a school setting. Dissecting a virtual cadaver online would be a lot more interesting than memorizing the various parts of the human body. Constructing and firing a rocket online will surely help in understanding the physics of trajectory rather than just computing the math formulas involved. As it stands now, however, the Internet and digital media in general provide mainly passive sensory stimulation that does not require much active involvement, unless one considers moving the mouse around to be movement.

Healy (1998) suggests that digital media promote a style of learning by trial and error at the expense of following directions in sequential order, which helps develop one's analytical thinking (p. 149). But although this style of learning is helpful to some children who have attention problems, it can be detrimental to others if it replaces traditional methods that require decoding written text, because it fosters poor analytical ability and ultimately stunts cognitive development by favoring the concrete over the abstract.

Digital Learning

For children endowed with great curiosity, the Internet provides access to unparalleled volumes of information. "The Internet brings the world into the classroom," says Doug Both, the principal of John Jay Middle School in Katonah, New York. "The accessibility, not only to information but also to expertise, is extraordinary." Students find opportunities to "communicate with people in specific fields of education . . . an example would be the opportunity to communicate through the Internet with a scientist in Antarctica, on the spot, live" (personal communication, September 2000).

The Internet is particularly helpful to children who are self-starters. One student told us how the Net helped him advance his knowledge and expertise in music while attending high school. By downloading a library of music through the infamous Napster Web site, he had become more sophisticated and varied in his tastes. He also established e-mail contacts with important music critics from around the world—something that would have been significantly harder and more expensive to do in the days before e-mail. "Adults," he told us, "respond to the reliability of the written word. You would be surprised who might respond to a well-written e-mail" (personal communication, September 2000). He now spends many hours a week chatting with other music enthusiasts from around the world and discussing music with critics and music professionals, who are much more inclined to respond to e-mail than to traditional letters sent via "snail" mail.

Through the Internet, he has had contact with a Japanese musician he would never have known about had he been limited to the brick-and-mortar world of the traditional classroom and the retail music store. Although that musician's CDs are not available in the United States, he is able to purchase them directly from Japan—through the Internet, of course. Now a freshman in college, he uses all his accumulated knowledge and connections to organize, schedule, finance, and coordinate concerts on campus.

The Internet at its best is an educational tool that serves as an amplifier of students' abilities and interests. Students who come to the Internet equipped with imagination and interest can find relevant material and get deeper into a subject, prodding and plowing the Net for detailed information.

But this use of the Net requires a focused mind. Surfing without a focus and jumping from link to link brings students nowhere. It can lead to a diffused and inchoate learning, which ultimately leads to meaninglessness. Gavriel Salomon (1997) puts it well in his article "Of Mind and Media": "Students may start exploring the life cycle of elephants in Central Africa but very quickly find themselves following a lead that takes them to the biography of Napoleon or to the political situation in Turkey" (p. 379).

The multitasking nature of the Internet environment poses additional risks to scholarship and learning. It is common today for children to conduct research or write papers on the Net while responding to ongoing instant messaging from friends and playing online games on the side. But such activity blurs into the social and recreational activities and focus is often lost. As Healy (1998) points out, "Much of today's technology fragments children's experience instead of integrating it and distracts their minds from the job of sense-making" (p. 137). Once again, one wonders about the impact of multitasking on brain development, most specifically that of frontal lobe executive functioning.

Long before the Internet, educators tried to adapt electronic media for didactic purposes by introducing audiovisual learning aids in the classroom—with mixed results. Unlike the linear, integrated delivery of book learning, visual images are delivered as separate packets, loosely tied together, and arranged in sequences moved by the visuals rather than by the text. Postman (1986) noted, "We face a rapid dissolution of the assumption of an education organized around the slow-moving printed word, and the equally rapid emergence of a new education based on the speed-of-light electronic image" (p. 145). Such image-based education can easily lead to a shortened attention span among children, a situation already observed by many educators. Television's main contribution to educational philosophy, according to Postman, is the notion that "teaching and entertainment are inseparable" (p. 146). The multimedia capabilities of the Internet help promote the notion that education has to be entertaining. Children today expect to be entertained all the time. Healy (1998) cites a teacher who complains that "the worst sin today is to be boring. . . . I am tired of these children expecting to be entertained—they don't have the patience of a flea" (p. 137).

Television and digital media have for years shortened the attention span of children. Some experts feel that the Internet exacerbates this problem because much of the information on the Web is delivered in short, easily digestible, and graphically enhanced packets. As a result, many children now find it difficult to assimilate information unless it is delivered in short digestible packets. Studies have shown a rise in incidence of ADD in recent years. According to a study from the University of Pittsburgh School of Medicine, attention problems in children ages 4-15 have increased from 1.4% in 1979 to 9.2% in 1996 (Kelleher, McInery, Gardner, Childs, & Wasserman, 2000).

According to Healy (1998), teachers believe that the "media-blunted brains" of children are a factor in the recent rise in attention problems (p. 183). With MTV videos getting shorter and more stimulating, the typical teenage viewer has become habituated to attending best to highly charged inputs rarely seen in the classroom. The multitasking and blurred nature of the Internet environment (with instant messaging, illicit sites, and aggressive games, e.g.) have probably exacerbated this trend.

Some educators accommodate universal shortened attention spans by serving children jazzed-up materials via VCR, Internet, closed-circuit video, and other multimedia offerings. But this may only increase the problem. Such practices may convince children that learning is fun, but such learning may be useless in preparing them for college. When they get to college and have to study thick volumes of real text, the fun, entertaining visuals they were served up in school will not help them assimilate a body of coherent, complex material.

Healy points out that computer games and activities on the Internet are frequently not open-ended. Resolutions and outcomes are preprogrammed, and the user's task is to find the preexisting solution rather than to think up an innovative one. But life *is* open-ended. Selecting from a menu of offerings may therefore stunt creativity because children learn that there is only one solution and their task is to *find* it rather than *invent* it.

In short, digital media do not promote problem-solving skills. The user's task in a digital game, whether online or on any other digital platform, is to find the spot on the screen and click on it at the right moment, so that he or she can move to the next level. This kind of activity promotes a trial-and-error style of learning rather than analytic processes.

Some people believe that Internet games enhance children's hand-eye coordination. However, although such arguments may at times be valid, it is a fair question to ask how much of a childhood should be spent perfecting hand-eye coordination. Others claim that children need to spend a lot of time on computers and online to prepare them for the future job market. Not so, say some industry leaders. In an article in the *Atlantic Monthly*, a spokeswoman for Hewlett-Packard told Todd Oppenheimer (1997) that "the company rarely hires people who are predominantly computer experts, favoring instead those who have a talent for teamwork and are flexible and innovative" (pp. 45-62).

Perhaps the best way to exercise children's intellect and prepare them for the future is by engaging them in the real world. Learning how to nail two boards together and figuring out how to build a chair or create an object from real materials require more mental effort and may teach a lot more about problem solving than most things that could be done online. In fact, many users find that learning to surf the Internet or use a computer program does not require more than two weeks of training. There is no need to spend precious educational time and resources for what can be acquired in only two weeks.

Digital Scholarship

Whereas the Internet can be a haven for serious students looking for information, it can also be an educational hazard for students who are less motivated, by allowing them to get by with shallow work. According to a 1997 Gallup poll, 77% of teens would prefer to conduct research for a school report by surfing the Internet than by using books and magazines (Gallup, 1997). Carnie (2001) calls the recent phenomenon of relying on the Net for research *cyber-sloth*. In a recent article in the *Chronicle Review*, he tells of the numerous e-mails he gets with requests to answer questions that can easily be found in reference books in the library. On a recent trip to that "anachronistic" institute—the library—he discovered that one of his students, a senior in her final semester, had never activated her library card. "Many young people," he writes, "think that if information can't be found in cyberspace, then it can't be found at all" (p. B14).

A mother of a sixth grader told us that her daughter does not read books anymore. When assigned a book, she simply looks for the book excerpt online and uses it to write her report. But electronic *Cliffs Notes* is not a viable alternative to primary sources.

Cheating is another immediate educational hazard posed by the Net because it reduces the entry barrier for plagiarism. Children who cut and paste from their online sources often turn in work that is more complex than what they are capable of producing on their own. The effort required to copy a paragraph word for word just with a simple mouse click is even less than that which was once required through the use of a traditional typewriter. Thus, although it is true that the problem of plagiarism is as old as writing itself, it has never been so easy. If students' tendencies today are to get by with as little work as possible, they may choose to copy and paste their way to a good grade.

Middle and high school students are highly vulnerable to abuses of scholarship standards. And worse, college students can buy assignment work online from a variety of vendors such as schoolsucks.com. One student told us, "If your friends plagiarize and get to have fun while you are in your room trying to write your paper the right way, you begin to feel like a fool" (personal communication, September 2000).

Information Glut

People call the present era the "information age." And indeed, we are currently flooded with information. The Internet has increased the flow of information to millions of households and offices by a magnitude of thousands. We have yet to assess the full impact of this information glut. But clearly, it has changed the way education is delivered and assimilated. According to one middle school principal:

> The critical piece here is that there is so much information out there, that there is no way that we can teach information the way we used to teach it. We used to have a curriculum and it had content in it. Now content changes every day, and there is more and more content. What we are finding is that we need to be selective about the content we want children to know and more in-tune with helping children understand where they can find content, how they can use it, and how they can determine what's appropriate, reliable, and truthful. (personal interview with Doug Both, principal of John Jay Middle School, Katonah, New York, September 2000)

Other school administrators point out that because of the vast supply of information now available online, children have to be better at sifting in order to find what is most pertinent to their project. Said one,

> From a teaching perspective, it is certainly much more unpredictable. If you used to bring your class to the school library, you pretty much had a sense of what was available for the children to research; now you have no idea. And they are going to hit sites that are appropriate and sites that are inappropriate. One of the things children learn in computer class is

that if it's a dot.gov it's a safe location, or if it's a dot.org it's also pretty safe, but if it's a dot.com, they have to be more concerned about it. (personal interview, September 2000)

Mastering databases will require that children develop new skills of sorting and organizing information. Perhaps this will ultimately be the redeeming educational value of the Internet, as it will push people to develop new skills. "If our children are to stay afloat in the information sea, they must become accomplished users of high-level cognitive strategies. They must learn to take massive amounts of data and information and convert them into something meaningful and useful" (Healy, 1998, p. 138).

Learning Style

The engine of learning is curiosity. That's what motivates children in their learning process and drives them forward. Other sources of motivation, such as wanting to please one's parents, or a competitive drive, are also predictors of learning success, but are not as sustainable as curiosity. Some children come equipped with a voracious appetite to learn new things and master what they can of the world. Others need to be motivated. The Internet can be useful in tailoring an educational program to a child's needs.

Learning styles are as varied as people. People exhibit different learning styles and different intellectual endowments, interests, and capabilities. Some are visual-spatial learners and take easily to blocks, puzzles, and later to engineering problems. Some have high verbal capacities and do well in traditional school settings. Some are social learners; others are natural introverts with creativity located within themselves and not in groups.

Traditional learning often requires the capacity to sit still for long periods and assimilate material through engaging written texts. Imagination, linear thinking, and commitment of time have been the classical characteristics of successful learning. It seems that the Internet, when used properly, can help children with learning styles different from the traditional model; it offers visual stimulation to the visually inclined and audial stimulation to the audibly inclined, and it can help those who work well in teams to maintain contact with their teammates.

Learning Disabilities

An important learning motivator is history of success. Unfortunately, this is where many children get stuck. By the time children are presented to a child psychiatrist or a pediatrician with ADD or a learning disability (LD), much damage has already been done to their self-image as competent learners.

Children with ADD, ADHD (ADD with a strong hyperactivity component), or LD often come with a long history of school underfunctioning. They may know that they are as smart as their peers but they can't attend, are often disruptive, and lean toward giving up at school.

The Internet can help youngsters who have difficulty in traditional settings become more productive and successful. ADD is characterized by inattentiveness, restlessness, and impulsivity. The requirements of sitting in a library for hours or at a desk with pages of text staring blankly back make ADD children feel antsy and helpless. The Internet, with its multi-stimulatory environment, may in some cases actually help the ADD child to focus.

This blurred world of image, movement, knowledge, and verbal interaction with friends offers a heightened stimulus that may help or harm focus and learning, depending on the child. Some children with ADD do well in this environment. They often learn better from visual cues and through kinesthetic experiences of handling the mouse and keyboard.

Healy (1998) believes the world is moving toward a learning style that favors perceptual stimulation over cognitive function:

> Newer technologies emphasize rapid processing of visual symbols . . . and de-emphasizing traditional verbal learning (e.g., expository writing, text reading) and the linear, analytic thought process that accompanies it. Sequential argument, reflection and "making pictures in your mind" are diminished in favor of immediate experience. (p. 142)

Children predisposed to learning from visual cues and kinesthetic experience may learn better from Internet-based content than other children. In fact, we suspect that many of the people involved in creating the Internet have ADD.

Finally, of utmost importance in a child's education is the concept of modeling in the framework of loving adult relationships. Children require parents who read and study themselves, and who display curiosity about the world. Stanley Greenspan (1997), author of *The Growth of the Mind*, argues that such a matrix of love, attention, and learning actually fosters and accelerates intellectual growth.

Children, including adolescents, watch adults in their lives and internalize important lessons. They learn right and wrong from how their parents behave and they learn to value their minds by appreciating how adults around them behave and use their own thinking skills.

■ INTERNET AND THE SOCIAL WORLD

Among the social aspects of the Internet's impact on children is the way in which the Internet has contributed to the transformation of the world into a "global village." What used to be on the other side of the world is now a mouse click away. In a sense, children are gaining back the social freedom they lost when issues of safety compelled parents to keep their children indoors. Such global reach makes old notions of near and far obsolete. What's near now may lie physically on the other side of the planet; what's far is now the supermarket and other brick-and-mortar buildings that require getting into a car and driving.

Although the notion of a global village is not new, and has been attributed to the global reach of television and other electronic media (McLuhan & Fiore, 1967), the Internet, because of its interactivity, has brought new meaning to this concept. It is different from the phone that has connected children to each other for decades. It is more casual. It offers a rich, multilayered environment in which friends come and go at leisure, and one can meet strangers from other places and other lands just by entering a chat room or playing a game. It offers vast access to entertainment, which one can enjoy while attending to other tasks (e.g., homework). It is also less involving than the telephone, more impersonal and less demanding. On the phone, you must speak with your own voice and you must listen attentively; you must share the intimacy of your vocal tones, which may be quite revealing; and you must do it all in real time, with no time to edit your words. Not so on the Net.

In some ways the Internet is the same, at least in spirit, as the old-fashioned neighborhood. In such communities, children can go out on the street and find somebody to ride bikes with, or knock on a friend's door and drop in for a visit; they can walk a couple of blocks to do homework with a school buddy, go to the park and throw a ball around with a friend, or explore the marsh at the edge of town.

This kind of freedom is inconceivable in many of today's suburban neighborhoods, in which people zealously guard their privacy and children spend their afterschool hours in supervised activities to keep them safe from predators. The irony is that although the Internet can build up the social lives of many children, many of whom would otherwise be isolated in real life because of circumstance or personality, it also insulates children from the world, by placing them in front of the screen for hours on end. Social worker Marianne Johnson worries that because of the vast amount of time children spend online, they are not developing healthy, adaptive social skills. "[They miss] experiencing the normal day-to-day human-to-human contact and all the intellectual, emotional, psychological, and verbal stimulation that is there just by sitting across from somebody" (personal interview, September 2000).

According to a study by Kraut et al. (1998), the use of the Internet has led to less social engagement and poorer psychological well-being of participants during the first two years of cyberengagement. In addition, greater use of the Internet has led to declines in family communication (pp. 1017-1031). However, the study did not find a relationship between initial loneliness and subsequent Internet use. Interestingly, economic status turned out to be a factor in increased loneliness, with richer individuals being affected more than poorer ones. (The findings of the study should be considered preliminary since the sample, although diverse, was not large—only 169 individuals participated—and the period measured was short.)

The authors say that although people use the Internet for interpersonal communication, their social interactions on the Net are not the same as their real-life relationships. They distinguish between strong and weak ties that people maintain on the Net. Strong ties involve deep feelings of affection and obligation, and tend to buffer people from the upsets of life and contribute to psychological health and well-being. Weak ties, on the other hand, are superficial and tend to be transitory. Whether Internet socialization produces positive or negative effects depends on the balance of strong and weak ties that people maintain on the Internet, according to Kraut et al. (1998).

Some children get stuck in their development because they spend so many hours in front of the screen, to the exclusion of other activities. The danger is particularly acute for children who tend to be isolated anyway. An article in *U.S. News & World Report* describes a child who has been hooked on computers since he was 7 years old:

> For a shy child like Adam, the computer was a godsend. It allowed him to overcome his awkwardness and hang out with virtual pals, and the fact that he was the tech whiz in his family built confidence. But the 18-year-old now recognizes that it caused some problems, too. "It gave me a reason why I didn't have to go out," says the Auburn, Alabama native, noting that he never had many real-world friends. He also stopped playing sports and slacked off in school. (Kleiner, 2000, p. 52)

There is an inherent problem with spending much of one's social life on the Internet. Despite its wonders, the Internet can't replace real life. It does not present the same challenges and the same feedback encountered in real life. Children can't fully learn from online interaction how to behave in human society. As Turkle (1995) puts it, users (of MUDs and other VR sites) get "caught in self-contained worlds where things are simpler than in real life, and where, if all else fails, you can retire your character and simply start a new life with another" (p. 185).

At best, the Internet should serve as an extension of real life, a space where children can continue to interact with their friends, and possibly meet other people, who may expand their horizons. But parents should be mindful of the time children spend online. Providing real-life opportunities for children to interact is the best antidote to being stuck in virtual reality. It requires effort on the part of parents and children, but is necessary if we want to raise wholesome children, able to manage and negotiate the complexities of a real-life society.

Intimacy and Anonymity

Ironically, anonymity may be an excellent starting point for intimacy. Many who have trouble establishing intimate relationships appear to be quite adept at getting into short-term relationships with complete strangers and baring their souls to a degree that rarely happens between even close friends. Bartenders often report that it seems easy for complete strangers to reveal private intimate information to them. They carry with them the secrets of many regular and one-time clients. Clearly, self-disclosure seems to thrive in such contexts.

It now appears that the anonymity of the Internet provides just such a context. People can say whatever is on their mind without ever revealing their true identity or even their face. This may be a godsend for many who experience problems with intimacy, particularly middle and high school students, who are often shy and insecure.

However, when they are not shy, they may be busy posturing. Children report that on the Internet they are often more thoughtful and/or expressive than in real life. Gardner (2000) quotes a child saying: "It's easier to express yourself online. . . . When you say it face-to-face, your stomach begins to grumble" (p. 40).

Yet virtual interaction is not equivalent to the real thing. Real-life relationships tend to be more rewarding and long-lasting. They require maturity, ability to compromise, patience, and tolerance. And they involve risk taking, such as the risk of being hurt or rejected. But because on the Internet children do not have to reveal their identities, they can avoid the awkwardness and unpleasant feelings that sometimes accompany relationships. Unlike real life, where children have to manage difficult moments, online connections can be severed more easily, especially if things somehow don't work out with an e-friend. An endless stream of new friends is there to replace old ones.

Children tend to have more than one relationship online (often communicating with them simultaneously through instant messaging or *IM-ing*). Having these relationships as a whole may be important to them, but few individual relationships are all that important. As the saying goes—easy come, easy go. If one relationship gets spoiled, another will spring up to replace it. The availability, ease, and lack of consequence of Internet relationships seem to be turning intimacy into a commodity.

The "commoditization" of friendship has a hallucinatory quality, perhaps because it is not anchored in any physical environment. Children float in and out of chat rooms like clouds, to be endlessly replaced by other clouds. For example, spot123 says, "G2G" (got to go) and disappears in the middle of a conversation, and tiger456 comes online and asks, "WUZUP" (what's up). Big789 drops his chat with ba_be to answer tiger456, whom he met online a couple of days ago. Ba_be is trying to communicate with big789, and he is trying to maintain the conversation with big789 while engaging tiger456. Suddenly, tiger456 types "POS" (parent on shoulder) and disappears. There are many conversations going on at the same time, and to the uninitiated who drops in it looks like disconnected strands of thought, which it arguably is.

Unlike real life, online chats lack the visual cues that accompany real-world interactions, as well as paralinguistics and other cues that can serve as feedback for zeroing in on deeper meanings in human relationships. Online chatters, aware of the problem, try to compensate by using keyboard symbols to express their affect, such as :-) for a smile, :-(for being sad, and ;-) for a wink. But that can hardly replace the rich, nuanced nonverbal communication that accompanies real-life conversation. In the end, the information users get about others is comparatively limited.

"MUDs, like other electronic meeting places," says Turkle (1995), "can breed a kind of easy intimacy. In the first phase, MUD players feel the excitement of a rapidly deepening relationship and the sense that time itself is speeding up" (p. 206). Yet often when users meet their online partners in real life, they get disappointed. "The lack of information about the real person to whom one is talking, the silence into which one types, the absence of visual cues, all these encourage projection. This situation leads to exaggerated likes and dislikes, to idealization and demonization" (Turkle, 1995, p. 207).

Blurred Barriers

The Internet clearly blurs barriers between children. Age boundaries get blurred because it doesn't really matter that you talk on the Internet to someone who is much younger or older than you are. This can be potentially harmful if as a result smaller children are exposed to issues that they are not prepared to tackle with yet, such as sex.

Unfortunately, the freedom and anonymity of the Internet that blur users' identities can be used by predators for such unsavory purposes as exploiting children sexually, selling them drugs, and getting them involved in other illegal activities. The best way to avoid this danger is for parents to monitor Internet use to make sure their children stick to conversations with other children they know from real life. At the very least, children should be taught never to reveal any identifying information online.

Some educators observe differences between the experience of middle school and high school children on the Internet. Whereas high school children are more confident and knowledgeable about the online environment and are more selective about who they talk to online, middle school children are comparatively more eager to make contact with anyone who will talk to them and are thereby more vulnerable to danger.

The Internet blurs financial boundaries as well. Children who may not get together because they are not in the same socioeconomic group are now connected. In this way, connections occur between disconnected groups, bringing with it a cluster of possibilities both felicitous and potentially dangerous.

Cliques and Peer Pressure

The middle school years are a time when children (especially girls) form cliques and struggle to fit in. This struggle continues on the Net. In his article "Is AOL Worse Than TV?" in *New York Magazine*, Gardner (2000) reports that children aspire to have as many names on their buddy lists as possible. Some children have more than a hundred names on their lists, yet "buddies" are not necessarily friends. They may have the names of friends of siblings on their lists, or names of children they met briefly on a weekend vacation, but that doesn't matter. What matters most is how long the list is, which apparently is a measure of their popularity. Conversely, being left out of such lists is social death. When a child wants to hurt another youngster she announces that her "friend" is no longer on her buddy list (Gardner, 2000, p. 40) and encourages others to follow suit.

The Internet also seems to promote cruelty displays that children seldom exhibit in real life. Children can easily harass each other online, via gossip, rumor mongering, *flaming*, and even through direct threats. Such behavior is not new; it just finds easy access online. Gardner (2000) reports that the Internet "allows children to travel daily . . . to a world where parental supervision is almost impossible and where a *Lord of the Flies* ethic rules" (p. 39).

Clearly, the Internet offers an easy way for children to hurt one another because they can be anonymous. Some users can maintain anonymity while slandering others or playing pranks and then assigning blame to a third party. For instance, children have sent e-mails or instant messages posing as a popular girl to their mark (a boy they know to be interested in the girl), making it sound as if the girl they are impersonating is interested in him. The "joke" humiliates the target when it is revealed that he has been duped.

Flaming and Violence

Instant messaging and e-mail encourage a type of discourse that often fosters the escalation of unhappy feelings. Wallace (1999) explains that "because people experience disinhibition on the Internet and feel relatively free of serious consequences because of physical distance and reduced accountability, they often use tactics that go far beyond what they might use in person" (p. 118). This often leads to flaming (as in inflaming), a practice in which children (just like adults) use aggressive and inflammatory language on the Internet. Flaming can evoke retaliation leading to back-and-forth flaming, sometimes spreading to others.

Although inflammatory language occurs frequently outside the Net environment, there are a number of reasons why it is particularly prevalent online: The "Send" button facilitates the release of impulsive messages. Perhaps this is why the Internet originally had a "Retract" icon for e-mail. The one-step and relatively instantaneous transmission of e-mail or instant messages does not leave much time for reflection, unlike traditional (snail) mail, which requires senders to put their messages into an envelope and place it in a mail box.

Although children use the Internet for casual communication, these text-based messages lack body language and paralinguistic cues of ordinary speech, which can mitigate meaning and rouse psychological functions in the participants. By contrast, online text tends to obscure anger and other forms of hostile intent and can result in less inhibition regarding the consequences of such communication. Similarly, retaliation for negatively received information may be unleashed in more virulent forms online than might otherwise result during in-person encounters. Thus, the Internet amplifies possibilities for extreme behavior by obscuring emotional extremes.

The false sense of anonymity that the Internet projects entices e-mail writers into thinking that they are writing something of a private nature on their computer. In reality, once sent, the instant message or e-mail becomes a document that can have a wide audience of unintended recipients and can lead to severe legal ramifications.

Children often share troubling e-mail with friends. As a result, private spats can mushroom into a public scandal. Private humiliations between friends that become public knowledge only reinforce the injured party's exposure and shame.

The escalation of school shootings and related violence (e.g., Columbine in Littleton, Colorado, and more recently, in Santee, California) raises the issue of the potential impact of flaming on intemperate reactions by children. It is not uncommon for a middle or high school-age child to say something inflammatory over the Internet during an impulsive or angry moment. Here's an example of a fictional communication that escalates into a flaming incident:

Sandi64:   HI
(no response)
Sandi64:   Helloooooooooooooooooooooooooooooooo!
(no response)
Sandi64:   Question. . . .
Chris23:   What?
Sandi64:   so r we friends?

Chris23:	not today
Sandi64:	WHY?!
(no response)	
Sandi64:	We were friends when u needed me for finals!!!!!
Chris23:	Not anymore . . . I made it up
Sandi64:	COWARD
(no response)	
Sandi64:	Maybe Jill is right about suicide
Chris23:	I can't deal with u. . . . u r nuts
Sandi64:	who do think made me nuts
Chris23:	You and your family
Sandi64:	so maybe I should buy a gun . . . . . its logical if im nuts
(no response)	
Sandi64:	HEYYYYYYY
(no response)	
Sandi64:	don't worry, Im not goin to do anything
Chris23:	I think u should get some help

Meanwhile, Chris23 has forwarded this e-mail to other children. Note how Chris23 escalates Sandi64 by not responding when challenged.

Once a child sends a message such as, "I wish you were dead" or worse "I'm going to get a gun and _____," all responsible adults should act swiftly and decisively. We have seen school districts respond more quickly in recent years to inflammatory e-mails. But the nub of the problem lies in sorting out which threats are of public safety concern and which are innocuous—no easy feat. Because of the violence associated with such communications, cases of violent intent documented over the Internet constitute a thorny and scary public health problem. It is not a simple task to identify which child falls into the benign category and which child is dangerous. A lot is at stake in making a correct evaluation, and in some cases there may be no easy way out of this dilemma that is both social and psychological. Suspending a "benign" child for a long time can increase the child's humiliation and sense of isolation, and may result in a serious trauma, whereas failing to take aggressive action with a truly dangerous child can put whole communities at risk.

Independence and Rebellion

A direct consequence of the online life of children is their increased independence. They can manage online and at home a great deal more than was once possible before the advent of the Internet. Tapscott (1998) observes that today's children "begin to develop self-reliance at an early age: they can find what they want and what they need quickly, easily, and honestly" (p. 87).

Children's increased independence is in part due to their increased technical acumen, which is often superior to that of their parents. Their computer expertise gives them confidence and a sense that they can manage the world. Such independence narrows the gap between children and parents and blurs the power structure within the family, often causing surprising and dramatic role reversals. Hence, parents often become dependent on their children to accomplish tasks online, or to figure out what's wrong with the family computer. Long before the advent of the World Wide Web, Meyrowitz (1985) observed that the power structure within the family had shifted as a result of children's exposure to television. TV brought the world into the home, diminishing parents' control over their children's access to information.

Concern about the exposure of children to media actually started well before television. In the early 20th century, critics pointed out how radio (then the new technology) would break up the family by drawing children away from their families into the world of radio. It was also argued that the radio exposed children to inappropriate programming (Wartella & Jennings, 2000, p. 33).

It seems that mass media, by its very nature, exposes children to the world of adults (including magazines and to some extent, newspapers, since they include visual images). By contrast, in the pre-mass media era, children were barred from adult information because books, the conduits of information, were written for different levels of readership. Children could not easily decode information written for adults. They had to grow cognitively and acquire education to be able to understand adult books.

Television and now the Internet have erased this natural barrier to information. The image-based information purveyed by TV and PCs is easy to digest even for little children. Parents who may try to supervise their children's exposure to such media find it extremely hard to protect them from inappropriate material, because it is so ubiquitous. It's in news programs, which show wars and crimes; it is in nature programming, which exposes nature with all its cruelty, danger, and sexuality; and it is even in prime-time network television programs, such as *Married With Children*, where sexuality and relationships between parents are exhibited.

Television has permitted children to gain outside perspectives from which to judge and evaluate family rituals, beliefs, and religious practices. Says Meyrowitz (1985):

Parents could once easily mold their young children's upbringing by speaking and reading to children only about those things they wished their children to be exposed to, but today's parents must battle with thousands of competing images and ideas over which they have little direct control. As a result, the power relationships within the family are partially rearranged. (p. 238)

The intergenerational boundary is a key concept in the current psychological understanding of wholesome family functioning. Parents are on one side of the boundary and children are on the other. But as Meyrowitz aptly points out, this state of affairs has been changing for some time.

Now, the Internet destabilizes power relationships within the family even more than television. It further reduces children's dependence on their parents. The results of this power shift are starting to appear in the guise of children increasingly challenging authority. Parents are faced with rebellious children at an earlier age. "'N-Geners' are more likely to raise controversial subjects with their parents and other adults," says Tapscott (1998, p. 88). They seem to mature faster, have more self-confidence, and seem to know what they want earlier than previous generations.

It would be wise to remember that children, no matter how savvy they seem, are still children and need adult guidance, supervision, and support. It is up to parents to assert their authority, including their authority over media use. The most effective way to do that is by becoming a real presence in their children's lives, and not abdicating the job of raising them to the media.

IDENTITY FORMATION AND THE INTERNET ■

Several issues illustrate the impact of the Internet on children's identity formation. What is identity? *Identity*, *ego*, and *self*, often used interchangeably, refer to an internal organizing mechanism that integrates one's preferences, experiences, and so on, into a coherent whole. According to Erikson (1950), "The emerging identity bridges the stages of childhood when the *bodily self* and the *parental images* are given their cultural connotations; and it bridges the stages of young adulthood, when a variety of *social roles* become available and, in fact, increasingly coercive" (p. 235, emphasis added).

During the first few years of a child's life, identity development primarily involves the attainment of mastery over his or her body and separation from the mother. Mahler (1971) called this early stage of development a time of "separation and individuation." Mahler and those after her (see especially Bergman and Pine) found that when children work or play to separate from their mother they are simultaneously constructing their nascent self through a process they identified as *individuation*. A young child that has just learned to stand and to walk gains a new perspective on the world. A toddler "enhanced by the upright position has potential for *identification with the parents*. Mastery over locomotion leads to elation, an affect that enormously promotes the sense of *self-esteem* and that propels a leap into the object world" (Blanck & Blanck, 1979, p. 22, emphasis added).

Mahler (1971) documents that the first few steps a child takes are actually away from the mother, the drive to separate and individuate being powerful and primal. Thus, with the advent of locomotion the toddler immediately engages a profound developmental task, the thrust toward autonomy and separation from his or her parents. Mastery and the striving toward independence continue to be developmental themes throughout childhood, adolescence, and even into adult life. But the tasks required for mastery quite naturally shift with age. The tasks of locomotion and separation from the mother, so important to the toddler, are replaced for school-age children by the task of fitting into social norms among their peers. Adolescents, in turn, continue to work on social mastery and on finding their appropriate place among their peers, but with the added excitement (and confusion) of sexual development and early struggles with adult responsibilities. Self-esteem becomes increasingly tied to one's status in the social milieu. Human development is thus a changing dynamic, where each stage has its own set of tasks to master. With mastery comes a well-earned identity.

In considering the impact of the Internet on identity formation, we examine the effect of the Internet on mastery, social roles, and by implication, on self-esteem in general. We also examine the role of the Internet in shaping moral development, since the set of values that people adopt is an integral part of their identity.

Mastery and Play Online

Children spend most of their free time playing. Why? Because it is fun. Play is found throughout life and serves a number of functions at the same time, all in the guise of having fun. "All play means something" (Huizinga, 1950, p. 1). Some play allows a child to safely master fears while experimenting with the fantasy of being a grownup. The game Cops and Robbers is a good example. By playing alternatively a cop and then a robber, children get to dramatize ongoing tensions within themselves (e.g., am I good or bad?). Hide and Seek tackles the problem of separation anxiety. It is a way to be found and lost and then found again with safety, and—we may add—with glee.

Play requires a conscious suspension of reality. In children's role-playing games, this suspension of reality can be called "make-believe" or "pretend." Children know that they are not robbers but nevertheless benefit from the joy of being "bad" *as if* they were robbers.

This is an important point in regard to the Internet because formal role-playing games as well as role experimentation (i.e., on e-mail and instant messages) is ubiquitous in this setting. Competitive games such as baseball, soccer, and chess all require this suspension of reality. To play baseball, players must suspend the arbitrariness of life and enter a world of strict and enforceable rules. They accept a nonambiguous standard of what is fair and what is foul. The game imposes order on the universe, which feels very real and allows a healthy exercise of sublimated aggression in the form of competition, both as an individual and as a member of a sports team. Anyone who breaks the spell of this pretend world is considered a spoilsport. Huizinga (1950) argued that all play has its rules that determine what "holds" in the temporary world circumscribed by play. The rules are absolutely binding and allow no doubt. Indeed, as soon as the rules are transgressed the play-world collapses and the game is over. The umpire's whistle breaks the spell and sets real life going again (Huizinga, 1950, p. 11). Play therefore becomes most real and "serious" when the participants know that it is a world of pretend.

The Internet is filled with opportunities to play. Children play a wide variety of games online including board games like chess, field games like baseball, first-person shooter games, and role-playing games. In the Internet play-world, children know quite well what is fantasy and what is not because they understand the make-believe nature of play. Children play online for the same reasons that they play outdoors—it's fun.

But the Internet also invites more subtle and important kinds of play. The anonymity of the Internet allows children, particularly teenagers, to experiment with the nuances of how they present their persona to others including "playing" with mood, style, and even gender. Furthermore, Internet play can contribute to a deepening sense of mastery when it operates along the same lines as traditional play, creating a space defined by its own rules and requiring achievement of specified goals.

However, from a developmental point of view, the Internet can cause harm when it becomes a substitute for working out conflicts and aggression in real life. Whereas fantasy is a useful adjunct in mastering fears and feelings of inadequacy or anger, it is a poor substitute for dealing with these conflicts through face-to-face interaction. Aggression is managed more productively through individual and team sports and through interpersonal interaction via academic competition and other social involvement (e.g., club membership and participation).

Freud (1961) wrote in *Civilization and Its Discontents* that "sublimation of instinct is . . . what makes it possible for higher psychical activities, scientific, artistic or ideological, to play such an important part in civilized life" (p. 44). True sublimation of aggression requires shifting one's anger or rage from primitive and violent acts to competitive and socially sanctioned ones. And here video and Internet shooter games do not quite do the trick. They indulge aggressive fantasies, but the motives and feelings of aggression remain. Hence, the experience is ultimately merely narcissistic, meaning that it involves just oneself and a computer screen. In contrast, playing soccer, for instance, truly sublimates aggressive feelings, because the aggressive urge is directed toward nonviolent aims. The aim becomes scoring a goal instead of hurting someone else. Thus, players feel competitive, not just vengeful. In addition, team sports, unlike video and Internet games, dilute a person's narcissistic preoccupations by encouraging cooperation and teamwork, sacrifice and bonding with other team members—all important skills for survival in civilized societies.

Occasionally, Internet play deteriorates into Internet addiction. Addiction is compulsive in nature and does not have the gratifying sense of fun that is so characteristic of play. The amplifying nature of the Internet can encourage maladaptive fantasies, which may pull a person away from this world and away from real life. Signs of addiction include feelings of desperation when forced to be offline and compulsive preoccupation with the computer during most free moments.

Finally, the Internet itself can give children a sense of mastery. They know that this technology will be part of their future—and some are quite adept at it. Tapscott (1998) argues that the Internet gives children a sense of mastery because as they learn to navigate they become increasingly independent. It is an arena for children to learn and exercise new skills, which are valued by society. Some children learn to design Web pages, some learn to create objects in MUDs, and others enjoy the power of using the Internet for a variety of interests such as music, art, and movie production.

Social Roles

During adolescence, children are involved in exploring and identity formation to a greater extent than at any other time. Adolescence is the time when children exhibit their quirkiest behavior. They spend much time behind closed doors, daydreaming and talking to their friends; they play "what if" scenarios in their heads, and experiment extensively. Experimenting with drugs, smoking, wearing outrageous outfits and hairdos, and piercing body parts are all part of the process of finding out who and what they are and are not.

According to Erikson (1950), "The adolescent mind is essentially a mind of the *moratorium*, a psychological stage between childhood and adulthood, and between the morality learned by the child, and the ethics to be developed by the adult" (pp. 262-263). During this stage, adolescents experiment without really committing themselves to anything in particular, and without assuming responsibility for the consequences of their behavior. For instance, children can get into intense emotional relationships without really committing themselves to the other person. According to Turkle (1995), society, mainly in the 1960s, tacitly tolerated such behavior (p. 203). But even during other periods, children have experimented, and society has been tolerant. This semisanctioned suspension of responsibility allows children freedom to jump into a variety of situations without worrying too much about the outcome. Sometimes, unfortunately, reality is not as forgiving as parents, and some children end up paying the price by getting involved in deadly accidents, drug addiction, or unplanned pregnancies. Nevertheless, intense experimentation facilitates the working-out of identity issues and the emergence of a more solid adult identity.

Turkle suggests that the Internet provides an additional moratorium for children. Its anonymity, wide access, and relative exemption from consequences allow children to experiment with all sorts of relationships, different personas, and even a different gender. It is an excellent place where children can explore who they really are and who they wish to be. It provides them what Erikson calls a "toy situation," which allows them to reveal parts of themselves safely, and play with varying levels of commitment (Turkle, 1995, p. 184).

Experimenting With Personas

A great deal of identity experimentation happens in virtual environments such as MUDs—sites on the Net where people play characters in an imaginative world, and on MOOs, metaworlds, such as Active World, and chat rooms. "In MUDs, each player makes scenes unfold and dramas come to life. . . . As with reading, there is text, but on MUDs it unfolds in real time and you become the author of the story" (Turkle, 1995, p. 194).

People who play in MUDs do not know who the other players are. They present a persona by which they want to be known. Personas are usually based on characters that belong in the fantasy world of the particular MUD. For instance, in a MUD based on J. R. R. Tolkien's stories, a user may choose to become a troll.

Players create characters within the parameters of the MUD. They also create the environment. Some people work with several personas at a time. These personas often have very close relationships with each other.

Role-playing allows children to experiment with different sides of their personalities, or to express a side of themselves that they do not usually express. They can even adopt new traits and new personalities and try them out. The most obvious benefit is to shy children, who feel free, because of the Internet's anonymity, to become more assertive online, and sometimes even outright aggressive. Here is what one of Tapscott's (1998) young interviewees said: "I'm very shy unless I know a person very well. This does not happen though in cyberspace. On the Net, I am one of the most outgoing people I know" (p. 93).

According to Straus (1959), even real-life interactions are a form of role-playing, because they involve the constant conscious and unconscious evaluation of the way the self is presented to the world. We act out dramas in real life with real people. Straus reported:

> Identity is connected with the fateful appraisals made of oneself—by oneself and by others. Everyone presents himself to others and to himself, and sees himself in the mirrors of their judgments. The masks he then and thereafter presents to the world and its citizens are fashioned upon his anticipations for their judgments. The others present themselves too; they wear their own brand of mask and they get appraised in turn. (p. 9)

Role-playing serves an important function in the psychological life of children and adults. Jacob Moreno founded a school of psychotherapy called psychodrama, which presupposes that adult personalities are a function of roles requiring a "dramatic" working out of conflicts as a method of healing (Blatner, 1985, p. 15). Blatner notes that people play many roles in real life. Most are implicit or explicit social contracts. A woman can be mother, wife, executive, socialite, and weekend actress. In each of these roles she is a different persona.

Role-playing did not start with the Internet; Greek drama was popular more than 2,000 years ago. More currently, people have been getting together on weekends to play Dungeons & Dragons since the early 1970s. In this form of theater, participants assume fictitious personas and play out adventures together. Participants often show up at these gatherings dressed in elaborate costumes, and the event can spread over a whole weekend.

Psychodrama and face-to-face role-playing serve an important psychological need. According to Straus (1959), we constantly play out roles, dramas, and scenarios in our heads as preparation for real-life interactions:

> As with children, the line between adult day-dreaming and "doing" is sometimes very slight: for instance, college instructors who are new to teaching sometimes day-dream elaborate dramas in which they speak to their classes. This is one way to discover how to give the lecture and what to say and not to say. A common kind of daydream is preparatory: you imagine how an encounter will work out. If it is important enough, you may play the scene several times, much like a movie director will repeat his scenes. (p. 66)

Online role-playing games are therefore a continuation of real-life role-playing and serve an important psychological need in the service of building identity. "The Internet has become a significant social laboratory for experimenting with the construction and reconstruction of self that characterize postmodern life. In its virtual reality, we self-fashion and self-create" (Turkle, 1995, p. 180). Role-playing fits well in the modern concept of identity, which views the self as multiple. Many contemporary people experience identity as a set of roles that can be mixed and matched with diverse demands that require a good deal of negotiation.

It is useful to consider in this context Lifton's (1993) concept of the protean self—an experience of self by contemporary men and women as being multiple, flexible, and changeable, yet striving for meaning. According to Lifton, the protean self is an evolutionary adaptation by humanity to a world that is constantly and rapidly changing. The self of the contemporary person is made fluid in response to the surrounding fluidity of the world (p. 21). It is a self that is better defined by what it does rather than what it is.

Lifton (1993) explains that the "protean self seeks to be both fluid and grounded. . . . Proteanism is the balancing act between responsive shapeshifting, on one hand, and efforts to consolidate and cohere, on the other hand" (p. 9).

Viewed from this perspective, the Internet fits naturally with the sensibility of the postmodern person and can serve as a training ground for preparing youngsters for a world that requires a fluid identity for survival.

However, rapid shifting from persona to persona can undermine reality testing and lead to a fragmented self rather than a fluid self. Although many theorists in addition to Lifton believe that the self is constructed of multiple identities, it is fair to say that most people are able to maintain a feeling of a coherent self that is continuous over time. Although we can't weigh it, there probably is an integrating quality to the ego that attempts to hold the personality in a more or less cohesive whole. Under the force of the online environment, this sense of coherency and continuity can be jeopardized, especially if one is constantly changing roles, and particularly in virtual reality, away from the checks and balances of real life. For a vulnerable young mind, the Internet can contribute to confusion about one's core identity and values and to the blurring of one's real identity with imagined identities. While such a condition is extreme and pathological, we do not expect such dramatic consequences for the majority of children on the Net. Once again, the safety or danger of a technology is dependent on the user of that technology. For every adolescent indulging a malignant preoccupation online (e.g., the perpetrators of the Columbine massacre in Littleton), there are surely many more using the technology to experiment with their emerging identities in adaptive and creative ways.

Sex, Children, and the Internet

Children experiment with virtual sex from around age ten, according to Turkle (1995): "Social life involves online flirting, necking, petting, and going all the way" (p. 26). Some parents are alarmed by sexually oriented activities of their children online. And indeed, the Internet increases access to sexual content and may lead to premature sexual activity. But it can also lead to better sexual decision making (Subrahmanyam, Kraut, Greenfield, & Gross,

2000, p. 137). The Internet actually provides a safer environment for children's sexual explorations in some cases. Children can explore sex without ever giving up the physical safety of their home. In other cases, the Internet provides an easy launching pad to real-life sex with all the natural consequences for those youngsters who lack the maturity to handle it.

Virtual sex may have the positive effect of forcing children to explore aspects of sex beyond the physical. It brings thoughts, feelings, and reflection into the sexual experience that often get short-changed in real-life sex. And unlike other aspects of virtual reality, which threaten to replace reality, there doesn't seem to be a danger that children will end up giving up the real experience. Instinct prevails. Internet sex therefore has the potential to be carried over to real life and make real sex a richer experience.

Some children prefer Internet sex. A 13-year-old girl says that her partners are usually boys from her class. But while in real life they tend to be more "grope-y," on the Internet they tend to want to talk more (Turkle, 1995, p. 226).

Turkle (1995) also describes Rob, a 14-year-old who says that he finds online flirting easier than in school or at parties because at parties he feels pressure to get close and touch, which he craves but also dreads. Online, he does not worry about being rejected or embarrassed by his physical excitement. Online, he says, "I am able to talk to a girl all afternoon—and not even try anything [sexual] and it does not seem weird. It [online conversation] lends itself to telling stories, gossiping; much more so than when you are trying to talk at a party" (p. 226).

A 13-year-old girl says that she has learned a lot from older children online, children she wouldn't normally hang out with. She feels safe to go online and talk sex with older children and even adults because she can always disconnect.

Sex is also a way for some adolescents to boost their self-esteem. Sadly, often the drive behind promiscuous activity, especially for girls, is the wish to gain attention. On the Internet, these children can gain as many sexual fans as they want without having to bear the physical consequences, as long as they don't venture beyond the Internet. Girls can be as brazen as they want to be without having to fear the consequences of their behavior. Boys can get as excited as they want with less fear of rejection.

Some sexual experimentation on the Net involves gender swapping. Gender swapping is not unique to the Internet. Children explore their gender identity in real life as well. Many children who turn out to be heterosexual experiment with homosexuality during their adolescence (Lewis, 1982, p. 293). The Net often makes it safer for children to explore sexual identity in total anonymity and usually without physical consequences. Nevertheless, parents should be in close contact with their children and become acquainted with details of their child's activities online as well as offline.

Social Acceptance and Self-Esteem

How does self-esteem develop? The most important period regarding self-esteem is during latency, a period between the ages of 6 and 12, when the child is busy building skills, accomplishing tasks, and forming his or her social status. Failure to master this stage successfully often leads to insecurity and feelings of inferiority.

Although self-esteem may be influenced by many factors such as academic success, accomplishments in sports or other fields, and one's body image, one of the most important factors is social success. But what happens at this stage of development when the Internet is where much of contemporary children's social life plays out? It is there where youngsters may struggle to fit in the social hierarchy of their peers. Hence, the Internet may have a significant impact on the success of self-esteem development.

According to Tapscott (1998), chat groups seem to boost children's self-esteem because "children can always have another chance—they can adopt another self" (p. 92). By contrast, in real life, children can have only one persona, which they can't hide. Their social status is determined not only by their personality but also by their looks (in face-to-face settings, an overweight child can be ridiculed—such is less likely to occur online), by their level of outgoingness, and by whom they're friends with in school. Hence, in face-to-face situations, a nasty nickname can take years to shake, but in cyberspace, if a child doesn't like how he has been characterized, he can adopt a new identity.

Of course, children can still get hurt on the Net. Flaming, bullying, harassing happen on the Internet just as in real life. Children may be ridiculed in chat rooms even more harshly than on school grounds. Middle school and high school professionals tell us that they spend many hours a week defusing Internet fights, misunderstandings, and flaming episodes from the night before. Perhaps a significant amount of such bickering and insulting behavior occurs more in situations where the online participants already know one another (or know of one another) interpersonally.

Moral Development in Cyberspace

Does the Internet influence the moral development of children? The anonymity of the Internet, which spares users from the consequences of their words and deeds, raises questions about what the Internet does to users' sense of morality, particularly younger ones who are still developing.

Children report that they use language online that they would not dream of using in real life. They are more aggressive online and more profane. The use of screen names creates in children the feeling that they are not the ones who are interacting. Hence, there's a feeling of amorality with regard to their activities online. One may wonder if the distinction between behavior online (a pretend world of sorts) and offline will eventually get blurred, and the freedom from restraints that children allow themselves online will spill over into real life.

This laxity of personal standards seems to characterize many activities online. For instance, children do not feel the same compunctions about questionable moral behavior (i.e., plagiarizing homework) online. Many report that they do not feel that there is anything wrong with it.

The allure of anonymity and lack of consequence have given rise to a new class of young delinquents, who did not exist before the advent of the Internet—hackers. This class of offenders is new both in terms of demographics and the types of offences they commit. Children who become hackers are technologically knowledgeable and usually come from middle-class and affluent families. They justify their wrongdoing by claiming that no victims are involved in their crimes. Many in business and government would strongly disagree. Such comments on the part of hackers imply that they may be no better than any other sociopath who uses others as objects for their own ends.

Morality is something that human beings develop in the context of society. A newborn has no sense of morality. A kindergartner has only a rudimentary sense of morality. According to Piaget, morality is a developmental process, and like all such processes, a moral sense emerges through interactions with the world. Children start their moral development by rigidly adhering to rules and obeying authority (Piaget & Inhelder, 1969, p. 127). The motivation for this stage is basically fear of punishment.

Older children regard social rules as mutual agreements among peers that could be changed by a democratic process. As children increasingly interact with others, they move into an autonomous stage in which they become less egocentric and are able to consider others' points of view. They apply rules more discriminatingly and in accordance with their desire for cooperation and mutuality. They learn to postpone immediate gratification, for instance, when they learn to take turns using a toy, and they learn to tolerate frustration when they don't get what they want. Both qualities are important in the development of a moral sense and are crucial to the well-being of a society.

It seems that the Internet can be detrimental to the development of these qualities. By its nature, the Internet thrives on its promise and delivery of instant gratification. Want to buy a toy? In a second you are connected to a number of retailers, where you can view products, compare prices, and make purchases. Feel lonely and need to chat with someone? No problem! There is always someone available online.

If children spend increasing amounts of time in front of a screen, getting their wishes constantly fulfilled, one wonders if they will get enough experience of situations in which they have to delay gratification or experience frustration. According to Freud, civilization is built on renunciation and management of instinct. "This 'cultural frustration' dominates the large field of social relationships between human beings" (Freud, 1961, p. 44). Without sublimation of instinct and tolerance of frustration society begins a slippery slide toward self-indulgence and exploitation of others.

To be sure, the Internet is not the only culprit in creating an impatient generation. A prosperous economy coupled with conspicuous consumption and a culture that is hooked on entertainment have done their share. One could indeed speculate that the recent rise in children's violence has something to do with this trend of decrease in frustration tolerance.

Thirty years ago, if a person committed a mass shooting he or she was almost certainly psychotic. But most of the children involved in the recent schoolyard shootings have not been psychotic children. They may have been unhappy or suffered from abuse or extreme character problems, but they have not been overtly psychotic. The threshold for violent acting out has gone down. A small problem like reduced frustration tolerance may contribute to this problem. Now a person doesn't have to be psychotic to go on a shooting spree.

Increasingly, children receive the message that being unhappy is bad. The commercial world bombards us with feel-good products. Entertainment is available 24 hours a day and the choices are vast: TV, Internet, video games, videotapes, pay-per-view, and so on. There is even increasing pressure to dispense education in fun formats. Children today are increasingly exempt from enduring even the effort of listening to a "boring" lecture from a teacher and having to make sense of it.

Seel (1997) argues that electronic entertainment challenges healthy character formation because it's a medium whose strong suit is artificiality and triviality. He quotes a Hunter and Bowman (1996) survey of young people, where nearly two thirds of respondents claimed to base their ethical judgments on how it made them feel or whether it helped them get ahead. And that is exactly the kind of attitude promoted by the media (Seel, 1997, pp. 17-32).

The Internet promises children an illusory escape from frustration. Like electricity or water, children often choose the path of least resistance. If it's too difficult to write a paper, they don't have to deal with their difficulty and learn from it. They can simply copy information from the Internet. Both educators and parents should be concerned about the outcome of such an upbringing. Which children will grow up able to face hardship and frustration? Who will be prepared to deal with the world with patience and perseverance? Who will be vulnerable to being amused to death?

The physical isolation of being online creates another obstacle in the development of moral character. Children do their homework in isolation anyway, but increasingly they are doing their work in isolation at school as well. Piaget (1971) believed that schools should promote teamwork and cooperative problem solving as a way to help children move from concentrating on the self toward a broader perspective (pp. 109-126). But putting children in front of a screen, even if their work results in a communal project, does not achieve that. It further accentuates their egocentrism.

Healy (1998) points out that flooding children with so much indiscriminate information does not leave room for thinking and reasoning: "Will our children's minds become so saturated there is no room left for moral reasoning?" she asks (p. 191). In our information-worshiping society, access to data is often confused with knowledge, knowledge with wisdom. But having access to information is not enough to form a moral sense. What is required is real-life experience, with real-life people followed by reflection and reasoning.

Another factor that interferes with normal moral development is the ambiguity of online encounters. In MUDs, it's clear that the identities of players are often fake. The purpose of the MUD is to role-play fantasies. However, in chat rooms users can never know how real or how fake the person is with whom they are interacting. The personas can be real, fake, or partially fake.

Several problems arise from this. One is that children, as well as adults, can get hurt by engaging in relationships they believe are real and then find out were a hoax. After experiencing several such encounters, they may get the message that relationships are just a game.

What is the effect of blurred boundaries between real (person) and fake (persona)? For an adult who understands the nature of online interaction, this is perhaps of little consequence. But for a child who does not yet have a full grasp of reality, this may present a problem. Surrounded and saturated from a young age by online encounters and other audiovisual media, which increasingly serve to replace reality and which increasingly blur the boundaries between reality and nonreality (e.g., docudramas, unscrupulous infomercials), it may become difficult for children to distinguish between reality and fantasy. They may carry behaviors glorified in their fantasy world into the real world. We can see this happening already in the increased aggression by children, which many studies attribute to media violence.

According to a news release by the American Academy of Child and Adolescent Psychiatry (AACAP) from August 2000, data from more than 1,000 studies suggest that there is a pathological effect of entertainment violence on children. A joint statement by AACAP, the American Academy of Pediatrics, the American Medical Association, and the American Psychological Association concludes that viewing entertainment violence can lead to increases in aggressive attitudes, values, and behavior, particularly in children. In agreement with this view, Fraiberg (1959) described the effect of a TV diet on children:

Johnny is afforded the privilege of most nice children in nice homes of being entertained and educated by gangsters, dope addicts, sadists and morons in his own living room . . . human values are debased in these stories, and in endless repetition of these stories and their themes, they undergo some debasement in the child's mind, too. (p. 268)

The media seem to try to arouse viewers' compassion by showing gruesome scenes of war. But paradoxically such displays of human misery, particularly in the context of today's entertaining delivery of news, can numb viewers' feelings. Children (particularly boys), even more than adults, are exposed to violence and brutality. Not only do they watch it on television and in films, but they are also exposed to it in their video and computer games, and now, on the Internet. There is evidence that such repeated exposure to violence and aggression may desensitize children to human suffering (Subrahmanyam et al., 2000, p. 134).

CONCLUSIONS ■

As we mentioned at the beginning of the chapter, the Internet serves as an amplifier of existing tendencies. For the most part, the Internet is not good or bad in and of itself, but rather it allows people to expand their horizons. Whether children benefit or suffer by the Internet will vary, depending on their personal inclinations, their environment, and their family.

Other media have elicited similar concerns when they first appeared, and studies on the effects of film, radio, and television have concluded that media affect individual children differently, depending on such factors as age, sex, predisposition, and parental influence. For instance, studies on the effects of television conclude that "the relationship is always between a kind of television and a kind of child in a kind of situation. When children have unsatisfactory relationships with their family members or peer groups, they are more likely to retreat to television and to fantasize about what they see" (Wartella & Jennings, 2000, p. 36).

In the beginning of *Technopoly,* Postman (1992) tells us how writing, one of the greatest human inventions in history, actually exacted a heavy cost from humanity, reducing the scope of human memory. Digital media may be as powerful a force as writing itself, and will probably in the course of time change the meaning of what it is to be human. Early signs indicate that it has as much potential to harm as to benefit. Perhaps there is a more apt analogy available—the invention of gunpowder. After all, gunpowder was initially used for fun.

CHAPTER **5**

SOCIAL AND PSYCHOLOGICAL USES OF THE INTERNET

JoAnn Magdoff

Jeffrey B. Rubin

A rapidly expanding global network, an "information superhighway," the Internet is changing our lives. But is it merely transforming an old way of doing things or is it creating a new "social and cultural sensibility" (Turkle, 1995, p. 22)? It is too early to make predictions, too soon to collate statistics. But we can add to a growing conversation about how the Internet affects the way we relate to ourselves, to our lives, and to each other.

Potentially, the Internet can open new forms of communication, relocate and reshape how and where we work, expand our definition of community, and transform and augment our deepest sense of ourselves. This chapter focuses on key ways we see the Internet affecting our sense of mind, body, and self—the psychological impact of the Internet on people who use it. Our data are drawn from both clients in psychotherapy and individuals who spend a large proportion of their work and leisure time engaged in online activities. We begin with an overview describing how the Internet is used by different age groups; next, we explore a variety of psychological uses of the Internet. We then describe the worldview of young teens—Gen Z'ers—Internet users emerging along with the Internet itself. Our concluding remarks summarize certain crucial social meanings and psychological functions of the Internet.

■ WHO USES THE INTERNET?

Broadly, there seem to be three general categories of people who use the Internet: the *cyber-savvy*—an elite group that includes people who upgrade their systems as soon as they become outdated and who are extremely facile with Internet use; the *cyber-clumsy*—the bulk of Internet users who use it only for e-mail or other simple, instrumental functions (they do not explore every avenue that could be open to them and struggle with the intricacies of the Internet); and the *cyber-innocent*—often the poor for whom any gateway or access to the Internet would be paid for on a per-use basis, for whom owning their own hardware is a dream, at least so far.[1]

There is a well-documented trend toward increasing access to and usage of the Internet by individuals at home and at work. A recent Stanford study on the Internet and society claims that people are adding work hours by accessing the Web from home (Rowe, 2000). The percentage of U.S. households wired for the Internet will surely grow from the more than 50% currently with access to such service. Many experts suggest Internet penetration will eventually reach every household in America.

However, all access is not equal. Just because people can get onto the Net doesn't mean that they will all receive equally fast and clear access to available services, even though capacity increases as bandwidth (through both wire and wireless technologies) expands.[2] Different users will be connected on faster or slower modems, be inundated with fewer or more unsolicited advertisements, and so on. In some cases, users will have "free" access, but they will pay in other ways (e.g., "free" or ad-bearing e-mail, banners, or being "cookied").[3] They may or may not be able to find out which of the sites provide the most reliable medical or financial information, or emotional advice.

Different Age Groups Make Sense of Cyberspace Differently

"But where is cyberspace, exactly?" the 85-year-old father of one of the authors asks. He and his cohorts are comfortable with the culturally reassuring, unexamined, and familiar. When his generation can integrate the concepts of laptops and desktops with preexisting models engendered by telephones and electricity, when they can see wires plugged into wall sockets and in back of machines, the machines are no longer mysterious anomalies. Building on this analogy, we suggest that the same is true for many people when they interact with a computer. As long as people experience a recognizable transformation of what they already think of as text, audio, or video, they accept this new resource as just another means of conducting business as usual. The Internet becomes merely a different way to browse the personals; a cheaper and faster way to make hotel reservations or plan a trip; a more convenient way to buy books and records, gamble, dip into pornography, or bid on auction items, without leaving home. For some, shopping on the Internet takes up as much of their time as they spend going to the store.

The way the Internet is being assimilated into daily life is one with which anthropology is familiar. People "fit" new technologies and experiences, "make sense" of new information, new worlds, by analogy: "Oh, this (new thing, concept) is like that (thing with which I am already familiar)." For example, during World War II, the indigenous population of the northern New Guinea highlands assimilated what they had learned from the GIs to preexisting cultural practices and beliefs. Cargo cults developed around newly introduced items. Locals tied models of airplanes and other Western goods to trees, believing that would result in actual planes delivering actual goods. When the Internet was introduced to the American public, they "made sense" of it by analogy, as good natives anywhere would.

Internet Use: Direct Translation From Real-World Activities

The first generation of PC users maps sets of already conventional activities onto the new medium much like the cargo-culters who tied symbols of airplanes onto trees. The most prevalent categories of buying and selling, *B2C* (business-to-consumer) and *B2B* (business-to-business) transactions, the models of TV, movie clips, music, magazines, books, dating services, gambling, accessing pornography, auction houses, mortgage brokers, buying discount food, and purchasing diamonds, are all fairly direct translations from transactions engaged in before there was a Web. These are familiar activities, unremarkable to most of us. On the Web, the "dirt world" storefront is transformed into the cyberspace-based "virtual world" storefront. Many businesses or destination sites on the Web therefore are modeled after prototypes in the real world—like the everyday world of going to the mall, filling out a form for a dating service, or receiving mailings from travel agencies. The familiarity of categories means that people visiting a site, such as Amazon.com, can easily respond, "Oh, this is like a bookstore. I know about going to a bookstore." After discovering how to find the title they want, or being induced (or enticed) to purchase a book, they figure out how to traverse the payment and shipping protocols. By then they have made the site and the activity promised by the site their own.

Internet Use Varies Greatly by Age and Less by Gender

Overall, the percentage of the U.S. population over age 55 is growing, as is the percentage of computer use among women. Currently, more women than men log on and make purchases on the Internet. More than 50% of Internet users in the first half of 2000 were women (Flynn, 2000). Preliminary assessment indicates the way in which people use the Net varies only slightly by gender; more significant variations occur across age groups.[4] Clearly, who does what on the Web differs as a function of age. Perhaps this is because older adults feel more challenged by the Internet.

Generation X

Gen X'ers, now the 30-something generation, use their computers all the time. It has become their standard medium for information gathering; making travel arrangements; setting up dates; purchasing clothing, books, and stocks; downloading music; buying movie tickets; calling long distance; and sometimes meeting potential partners either for business or fun. For this age group, the Web is a utility tool.

But more than that, in contrast to their elders, when this younger generation sits in front of their computers, or use their PDAs (personal digital assistants, such as Palm Pilots), they also take advantage of things they haven't seen before, adding new links and applications as they see them appear—downloading music, videos, books. They also program and experiment with multiple self-representations, or versions of themselves, online, going far beyond the cargo-cult model. Gen X'ers learn to use the Internet for novel applications including entertainment and diversion, not just utility.

Generation Y

Generation Y represents even younger high school and college students and recent college graduates. Characteristically, Gen Y'ers take computers for granted. The computer is more transparent to them. It is more naturalistically woven into their daily lives. They use the Net to play games, visit chat rooms, download music and videos, and conduct group research projects for school, in addition to copying what their older brothers and sisters in Gen X do. Gen Y'ers presume there is an Internet to be used. They engage the Internet for more social functions, for more emotional involvements than mere entertainment and diversion.

Generation Z

For Gen Z'ers, preteens, the Internet is what they have always known. It is utterly transparent to them. Possibilities within it have evolved and have continued to increase ever since they clicked a mouse and explored cyberspace for the first time.

We suggest there is an epistemological shift between how those of us over age 35 think about and use the Internet and how the Gen Z kids do: They have grown up in a postmodern environment in which, compared with the older generations, there is no fixed reality that people share. They do not even expect people to agree about the status of the world, for more often than not they do not see the world through the same set of lenses, even among themselves.

The members of this age group are acutely aware that each person sees things from a different, subjective frame of reference. Because they accept the validity of many unique viewpoints, Gen Z'ers can carve out a place in which each one can affirm the legitimacy of his or her own subjective vision. Because no one perspective is privileged for them, they are free to do what adolescents do: transform their subjective perspectives on themselves, their friends, and the larger social context. This group takes gender-bending even more causally than their Gen Y older brothers and sisters do. Gen Z'ers are growing up along with the Internet, discovering and creating new uses for it.

WHEN THE WEB RESEMBLES THE REAL WORLD ■

Web-based interactions (outside of the realm of business) may initially be apprehended to resemble non-Web communication, at least on the surface. They may occur in chat "rooms" of like-minded people (or people like-minded enough to agree to disagree), who will discuss anything from what are the best fly fishing locations to what they are experiencing as parents of an autistic child, to political issues such as whether pornography on the Web is covered by the First Amendment. They "chat" by typing in their comments about a topic of mutual interest and reading other typed comments on the same subject.

Information sites proliferate. Many relate to medical or behavioral issues. At these Internet locations, people can share what they know or learn what the latest research may be on a topic they have selected.

Also, importantly, there are sites that function as support groups for people going through difficult times. One potential drawback to support sites can also be one of their greatest strengths: anonymity. This is because people often feel freer sharing their deepest fears when no one in the group knows their real-life identity. This is a perfect example of anonymous intimacy, where self-disclosure can at least appear to happen safely without embarrassment or threatening repercussions. Membership in one of these groups may be temporary, transient, or longer term.

For example, a recently divorced woman in her 30s with two young children visited an Internet site targeting divorced parents: "I'm having a hard time explaining to the kids where I go when I'm out on a date, or who I'm talking to when a guy calls me. I don't like to lie to them, but I don't know what I should be telling them. Anybody out there with any ideas?" She can expect responses ranging from the humorously encouraging: "I went through that. I told my kids I was having a grown-up play date. That worked fine." Or the sanctimonious: "Mothers should stay home with their children!"

Several sites provide ongoing support for people with mental health diagnoses. Some elicit powerful reactions. Someone logging on to one of them can expect and receive targeted, specific information as well as more general "hang in there!" support. For example, one man said: "I'm bipolar. Lithium isn't working for me. My psychiatrist wants me to try one of the drugs that are anticonvulsants, which are usually given to people with epilepsy. Does anybody know about these? Has anyone tried them? What kinds of side effects do they have? How bad are they? What other options do I have?"

Exploring the Internet as a new tool that permits often quicker, anonymous problem solving may be one of the first ways people dip their toes in the ocean of cyberspace. Game playing is often an entry point for Generations Y and Z. Many people start and stay with games they know, such as solitaire. For the subset of users known as *gamers*, Internet game playing can rapidly take on the lure of gambling, becoming so seductive a pastime that it feels almost impossible to stop. With gaming involving real-time global Internet opponents, universal scoring, and brilliant graphics, the compulsion to play seems likely to increase.

Cyberaddiction

The summer of 2000 found a rash of articles detailing what authors labeled *cyberaddiction*—a new phenomenon in which people feel driven to spend increasing amounts of time online. Like the metaphor for which it is named, such addiction can have different content: trading, gambling, game playing, even pornography and visiting chat rooms. Calling it an addiction presumes both that it is harmful—to relationships, bank accounts, one's job and/or health—and so compelling that it becomes painful to stop.

One of our patients was quite concerned about his increasingly costly and time-consuming use of Internet pornography. Drawing an interesting parallel, he said he felt that he was consuming cybersex much the way one of his uncles had dialed up phone sex ten years earlier.

We understand cyberaddictions as substitutes for something vital that is missing from someone's life. That "something" may be feeling understood and valued by others or feeling meaningfully connected to people that one esteems.

How do people know if they are "addicted"? Does the person logging on to a site have trouble walking away from it? Does time spent online disrupt major relationships? Does it interfere with parenting or work? If yes, there might be some addiction involved.

If both marriage partners are in bed going through a nightly ritual in which they feel impelled to check e-mail on their laptops, and if the user feels his or her computer is more compelling than the person sharing the bed, that person may be cyberaddicted. The cyberspace sites to which people feel addicted may share key features with the world they know: The venues are familiar—for example, a hand of cards laid out for blackjack, a pornographic story in which they play the verbal hero. Or they may be driven to revisit a virtual world obsessively, either in a game or as part of an ongoing story. These virtual worlds may prove, if not addictive, often irresistible.

The Web and the Enhanced Worlds of MOOs and MUDs

In the realm of pure fantasy, players can participate in any one of a number of games from violent, action games to elaborate ongoing stories of increasing sophistication and complexity. The first games (played in cyberlocations called MOOs [multiuser domains, object oriented] or MUDs [multiuser domains]), such as Dungeons & Dragons, were originally text based. Players wrote down descriptions of their individual personas (called *avatars*), the character that represented each of them when they were playing the game. They described where they were and what they did. Until the advent of action games—in which players move avatars around the screen, finding hidden ammunition caches, blowing up monstrous opponents—descriptions of players' venues, actions, and feelings always had been written on the screen. For example, "Georgie [a large pink rabbit of indeterminate gender] hops playfully into the center of the den. 'Anyone for tennis?' s/he asks giggling. Winking at the Archduke Michael, Georgie looks down, demurely."

Players often assume a persona, or avatar, with little resemblance to what they present in daily life. People represent themselves with any avatar imaginable: human, idealized, humanoid, as well as a pink rabbit. Clearly, on the Net you need not necessarily be who you were when you turned on the computer. Logging on to the game, giving a name you have chosen, your identity for the scope of play (either just one time or repeatedly, whichever you choose to play), you may switch gender, shave years off your age, or, as seems to happen with adolescent boys who have time but not much experience, add years onto your chronological age. You can be beautiful, hideous, or unremarkable; change height, weight, national origin, or skin color. You can be anyone you can convince other players to believe you are. The range of possible identities goes from Barbie to a monster from hell, like Grendel's dam in the classic epic poem *Beowulf*.

■ RE-CREATING IDENTITY

New possibilities in the ways in which people posit their identities in cyber-space are being created by constant advances in computer technology. The technology that underlies the Web is *emergent* (a concept that has been developed in complexity theory).

We will describe how we see emergence and complexity later. For now, let us call something emergent when it is unexpected and unforeseen, instead of following a linear, predictable path. Interacting and intersecting in surprising ways, units from different levels dance. As their music is created, their choreography forms structures in real time, with their own unique rhythms and motifs.

Internet II chief scientist Jaron Lanier writes:

When [and how] will the Net change? My guess: two years from now rich people in the United States and northern Europe will make substantial use of video chat with the ability to see each other on screens that are located in different places; five years from now elite companies will have tele-immersion in special meeting rooms (virtual reality without head-sets or goggles, using cutting-edge optics); ten years from now elite users will be able to feel things at a remote site; ten years from now tele-immersion will become a home phenomenon; fifteen years from now home tele-immersion will get the sense of touch. (personal communi-cation via e-mail, April 29, 2000)

Technological breakthroughs are coming each day. The tiny camera created by Eyematic, a hardware and software company in Los Angeles, which places a tiny camera on top of the computer, is illustrative. The lens of the Eyematic camera focuses on the face of whoever is at the keyboard. It maps the facial movements and expressions it sees onto any face—like an avatar—a great way for grandparents to interact visually, in real time, with far-away grandchildren. With a little creativity, and a few simple tweaks, the image on the screen becomes the face of anyone, anything. Grandpa can be an Angry Beaver, a character from the cartoon show of that name, or maybe Humphrey

Bogart, while grandma turns her avatar (her character) into Glenda the Good Witch from the *Wizard of Oz*, or perhaps the next Marion Jones, Olympic star in the 2000 Olympics in Sydney, Australia.

This technology, which potentially bypasses the need for external "armor" (gloves, body suits), is a first step in total body representations via images, from camera to screen. The implications, short term, for game players are tremendous. We don't know how the experience of having one's expressions, quirks, and movements show up in the environment of screen fantasy worlds will affect game players psychologically. Voice recognition has been around for some time. Soon, it will be possible to share one's voice with others, and chat rooms will be as full of vocal interruptions as they are now full of typed ones. Again, one's voice may reflect one's speaking voice or the voice of one's character in a game. (Later we consider the question of which, if either, is one's "true" voice.)

Fears and desires can trigger the assumption of a new Internet identity. Sometimes these choices are spurred on by developmental changes, as when adolescents "try on" unexplored self-expressions that they may or may not act on later in the real world. Some choices are made in response to one's most profound fears of exposure, of inadequacy. Often the process itself is used to regulate the amount of intimacy and the form a connection to someone else will take—be they therapist or friend. Happily, many avatar choices are simply playful.

We'll begin with the selection of a new body.

Body Image and the Internet

Want a perfect body? It's possible to have one, that is, a virtual body, online. For many teens as well as adults, a general social and cultural emphasis on the desirability of having and displaying the right kind of body provides ongoing pressure to conform to and attain an ideal that, for many people, simply is not possible. In our world, self-commodification is an accepted and unremarked upon fact. But it is spelled out most directly via the self-sculpting of one's body via cosmetic surgery, extreme diets, or multiple hours in the gym.

The Internet could not have been a more perfect invention for addressing the desire to present a perfect body (that is, a perfect *virtual* body) to the world. Having an ideal virtual body is attainable immediately on the Internet, where one's desired physical self can be enacted: You "are" who you seem. For some, the mediation of a computer affords a more protected, more private environment, which feels liberating. It is a place that seems created for interacting, for pretend. It bypasses the daily experience of a gawky adolescent boy who feels he could never impress a particular, special girl unless he were able to show her he is someone who he is not. Self-protective, online identities hide adolescent shame, often manifested in large pimples, excess weight, or bad hair.

Although it serves the positive function of offering a respite from searingly self-critical feelings, unfortunately the assumption of a patently untrue identity seems unlikely to foster self-acceptance and the elusive but crucial goal of growing up—some kind of psychic integration. Seeking to escape isolation, adolescents use the Internet as a transitional space between being alone and being physically with others. It can be great, but it can also result in perpetuating one's difficulties in living rather than resolving them.

The Presentation of Self in E-mail

Adolescents present special treatment challenges. For some therapists of teenagers, e-mail sessions are a stratagem of desperation. For others, communicating online feels like an appropriate use of new technology because it dovetails with a diagnosis. Some Gen Y'ers participate in a recent phenomenon, which we are calling "adolescent e-treatment."

We are among a growing number of therapists with adolescent clients who conduct real-time sessions using e-mail. Every year, practitioners report conducting more sessions online. Teens, sitting in their bedrooms at home or writing from their dorm rooms, say they feel "more in control" when there is a computer screen that functions as a literal screen between them and their therapist, when they can neither see nor be seen by the therapist. Often it is not the therapist's eye that is off-putting. For some of these adolescents, leaving the house, presenting themselves to the world, feels psychologically dangerous. They feel vulnerability and shame about their appearance, their weight, the condition of their skin, and so on.

One of us (JR) treated a young woman who moved abroad in the midst of treatment because her father changed jobs. We maintained regular contact via e-mail. Because I could not see her, she felt less ashamed to show her emotional vulnerability. When she felt a sense of urgency, she e-mailed me. My quick response was unlike anything she had come to expect in between our twice-weekly sessions in person.

With the built-in distance afforded by e-mail, for the first time she had the experience of being responded to when she needed and asked to be. As a result of having felt safe, psychological intimacy with me when an ocean lay between us, when she resumed face-to-face therapy it quickly reached a deeper level than it had before her move to Europe.

Controversy surrounds doing psychotherapy on the Internet.[5] We've seen that e-mail sessions may be a good psychological "fit" for some adolescents. They were for this one.

Sophisticated Internet users can regulate effectively what, and how much of themselves, they reveal to others, as well as what part of themselves they acknowledge to themselves, by how they use Web-based interactions such as e-mail and instant messaging (*IM-ing*).

When Gen X'er Michael moved to Seattle, I (JM) thought that like most people I'd worked with in therapy, he would schedule weekly phone sessions for about six months. After that, distance, time zones, and lack of face-to-face contact would probably result in a gradual termination, with perhaps a referral on my part to a therapist in his part of the country.

However, once he was settled, Michael began to e-mail me relevant pieces of information about himself and his life: press releases, interviews, letters from his ex-, and e-mails forwarded from his father. The communications were quite informative, containing other people's points of view about Michael, something we had seldom included when we had seen each other for weekly sessions. Forwarding e-mails of his choice to me helped him to feel in control. Michael dealt with his overly intrusive father simply by not responding to his e-mails or calls. Michael experienced the Internet as a safe and reliable presence, one he felt he could use as and when he needed and that would always remain accessible, reliable, and interactive, without being invasive.

Michael used the computer to maintain psychic boundaries and ward off anticipated invasion. By using his peripheral vision, changing appointment times, "disappearing" for brief periods, he took charge. By maintaining distance, he felt in greater control. With the computer screen in front of him, he believed nothing could attack him.

However, like any symptom, the psychological gains Michael's computer use achieved were accompanied by psychological losses. Michael felt that he could not maintain psychic integrity without the ability to use the computer to maintain a safe distance. Unable to discuss his underlying feelings, Michael retreated.

Ultimately, this proved a stumbling block to his treatment, which was not easily resolved because of his sophisticated, defensive use of the computer.[6] At the same time, the computer allowed him to engage immediately with others in real time (via IM-ing) or not to send anticipated e-mails and so remain remote, enabling him to keep his sense of self intact.

Thus, e-mail and cyber-interactions allowed him to interact with others using the part of himself with which he felt safest.[7] Hence, clearly the computer can be a social and psychological aid to users.

A Generation Y Programmer

A Gen-Y girl, an excellent programmer, says she feels unself-consciously "at one" with her computer, that it allows her to regress to an earlier age, when she felt more connected to herself. Because she is aware of her programming competence and creativity, her self-esteem and self-confidence have grown.

Programming can be an isolating, lonely experience or it can be an avenue leading to creative self-expression and grounded self-esteem, as it was for this college student. Karen, a programming 19-year-old, attends one of the universities linked to Internet II. She is one example that clearly counters the Stanford study's conclusion that Internet time is less psychologically valuable than face time.

As she told one of us (JM), "I lose myself in the game. No matter whatever else I'm doing, I'd rather be there." In the game, Karen is a strong player and getting better. Other players whom she respects know her and welcome her when she joins them. Being in the game is a very different experience from her ordinary, more constrained daily reality. "I can go there whenever I want; I can stay as long as I want. If I don't feel like participating I can watch. No one makes me do anything."

For an honors project, she proposed programming a new game. This proposal was rejected by her adviser as "impossibly ambitious." Nevertheless, her delight and prowess in programming provided a strong attraction for her. Karen's computer was an extension of herself through which she found creative expression. Like a baby's treasured blanket, Karen's computer soothed her. Sitting at her keyboard, Karen felt she was in a closed, safe space, where she felt whole.[8] Whether writing code or adopting a persona different from her real-life identity while she played a game, working on her computer added to her growth and transformation, particularly as it permitted self-expression. When she programmed, she described being in a benign state, using simple, almost childlike language to talk about her experiences. She described her prowess as a programmer—implicitly linking herself to the most advanced, fastest technology and software she could find. It was a symbolically rich process, buoying her up, continually setting challenges that she could meet and overcome.

When she was creating code, she was open to the actions and reactions of other players and the code itself. That seemed to be a more growth-promoting environment for her to inhabit; her sense of self-worth was enhanced by programming activity.

Karen's treatment focused on "play" time and "programming" time. She became more and more involved in her time in front of the screen. It was more therapeutic for her to write code, concretely changing something, than for her to interact in real time with her cohorts. When she was online, Karen did not feel that she was creating an alternative persona to inhabit; she felt like Karen, "only good," as she said.

Karen was able to "become" someone or something else as a game player, although the process seemed trivial to her. She assumed changing identities was a symbolic option open to her. Like many of her cohorts, she took for granted the possibilities of gender switching, of thinking herself through sets of characteristics usually assumed to be exclusively female or male. A very different experience is had by people who feel worthwhile only if they "become" someone else.

Gay on the Web

The anonymity of Internet communication can provide a safe environment to explore parts of oneself that have remained hidden. The adolescent in this case used it to explore sexual preference.

Always identified by family, friends, schoolmates, and teachers as a jock, when the captain of the high school football team realized that he was gay, he kept it to himself. Embarrassed, ashamed, and fearful of discovery, he was terrified that if he were to tell anyone about his sexual orientation he would be ostracized by teammates and friends. Alone with his computer, he searched online until he found several chat rooms geared toward people who seemed to be going through similar experiences. After a period of just "listening in," he began to add comments of his own as well as writing responses to others' stories. In one chat room, he found someone who seemed to be a kindred soul, an athletic high school student who was in a similar situation. They began a cross-country e-mail relationship. Through their developing, although anonymous, budding cyberfriendship, he gradually felt more accepted and less like a pariah. At the beginning of his senior year in high school, he "came out of the closet" and told his teammates. Despite his fears, they were understanding and respectful, directly opposite to the reaction he expected from them. He credits the deep support and acceptance that he received through his relationship with his online friend with enabling him to be more honest with other people as well. The anonymous cyberrelationship gave him the acceptance, support, and courage to be more open about his secret.

WHAT IS THE TRUE SELF? ONLINE AND OFFLINE ■

Being able to present oneself in a way that is different from one's ordinary, everyday self, that is, the construction of an alternative persona, can open a potentially enormous sense of personal freedom.

A lonely, isolated teenage boy eats by himself in the school cafeteria, but when he is online, has more girlfriends than he can handle. These "girlfriends," however, have permanent quotation marks around them. They are *virtual* girlfriends. Offline, he appears to observers and to himself like the same isolated boy he was when he sat down in front of his computer and logged on; his online self, however, is transformed in his and others' imaginations into a buff 20-year-old.

These crucial questions arise: Is he the same person he was in person before he logged on to have these experiences? Are there psychological ramifications of "becoming" someone else and being treated like that new someone?

Exploring a self who one "isn't" can lead to a deepening sense of who one might be, or might become. But can such exploration also confuse one's identity? For a brief period of online time, one can take on the attributes of an admired alter ego, in effect, "trying on" idealized identities. It can be an affirming and cathartic experience.

Long before the digital world of the Internet became available, children growing up in the real world have played similar games. They do so when they pretend to be Superman or a Pokémon or Wonder Woman. It is common to watch teenage girls appropriating their version of the latest style, which they replace serially. During the summer of 2000, many young girls wore blue eyeshadow, emulating the young pop singer Britney Spears. Who knows what 2005 will bring? For teens, trying on a new style, which is rapidly substituted for another, having a new haircut, wearing a new set of clothes, assuming different values and goals (and sometimes, it seems, personalities) are part of figuring out their future identity. Because a normative part of adolescent activity is to take on such "serial selves," the psychological impact when they transform themselves, assuming a new identity online, may not be a foreign experience to them. It may be just one more avenue to exercise such normative adolescent activity.[9]

Body Image, the Internet, and the "True" Self

Sometimes the Internet serves a reparative function that may not be transferable to the real world, raising complex issues of projecting what is often called a "false self." For example, one of us (JM) treated a teenage boy who was severely, inoperably disfigured. Poignantly, when he assumed his gaming avatar, he felt, he said, like a "real person" at last. After much exploration, a treatment goal became to find places for him to go that were not psychologically toxic to him—that is, situations in which he was not constantly reminded of his distorted face.

On the Internet, he could create and sustain relationships with other people's avatars. Exchanging dialogue with people at other sites provided affirmative responses that reduced his shame and made him feel more whole. On the Net, he was accepted by others—they told him he was fun, helpful, kind, and insightful. He kept records of these dialogues and referred to them when bad feelings about himself threatened to overwhelm him. The recorded texts were like talismans serving to remind him that there were places where he could find acceptance.

This adolescent boy's experiences raise the vexing question of true and false selves. Many people assume that they have an essential, buried True Self that offers a "blueprint" for how to live. "I am large," writes Walt Whitman, "I contain multitudes." However, because we are all multidimensional, there is no single, essential, authentic self that guides our lives. Although certain behaviors and actions feel deeply opposed to who we think we are—even false and inauthentic—there is no single "True Self" for us to discover within ourselves (Rubin, 1998). Instead, the self emerges during the process of interacting with others—people, pets, a paintbrush, the world, a computer screen. In short, the notion of the self is not a static construct but a dynamic process. Our view is one of multiple possible, serial, diversely connected "selves" that might be conceptualized with reference to complexity theory's idea of "emergence" (Magdoff & Barnett, 1986).

EMERGENCE AND COMPLEXITY ■

Here we briefly return to discuss the concept of *emergence* in greater depth, then look at how some Gen Z'ers' sense of themselves and of the world seems emergent, reflecting what we believe are models engendered partly in cyberspace.

When disparate units, people, ideas, or even bits of computer code connect and link in unexpected ways, many more unexpected and unplanned connections may be triggered. This phenomenon exemplifies a notion of emergence as it has been developed in complexity theory. Like any herd animals—for example, Congo parrots that have learned to hunt antelope as a group, an activity never before documented in the wild—computer programs can initiate unanticipated outcomes not possible when operated separately and for which they had not been programmed.

In this context, we may define an activity as emergent when it happens among a collectivity of interactive units (called an "ecology"); it has not been previously programmed or anticipated; it is either hardwired into human, animal, or mechanical brains or results from software or previously learned experience; it takes time to unfold, although when it finally coalesces, it can seem instantaneous, like mercury drops "finding" each other and turning into a ball and, once a critical mass has been reached, additional drops "find" this new shape seemingly at once; and the new mass or pattern does not follow major "cause and effect" sequences.

The Internet has these characteristics. As a social and psychological phenomenon, the Internet appears to generate heretofore unforeseen possibilities, amplifying opportunities for users to engage in sociocultural behaviors unanticipated before emerging in practice. The result is that the Internet exhibits the texture of what Thomas Kuhn has called a paradigm shift, signaling radical changes in the cadence of social activity, shifting cultural perspectives, and affording users the means to leap to novel levels of interaction.[10]

■ CONCLUSIONS

Psychologically alone or while interacting with others—people or things—Internet users are actively engaged in exploring and enhancing their sense of themselves. We have seen the Internet used to try new identities; create transitional spaces and templates for sites in the real world; establish self-enhancing voices; create virtual selves; forge "safer" self-regulated worlds.

As a working hypothesis, we assume different generations of Internet users will continue to integrate cyberspace as they have in the past: The first generation of PC users maps sets of already conventional activities onto the new medium; Gen X and Gen Y each find themselves more immersed in the Internet than their elders, logging on and staying on, integrating more of their everyday activities through the Web; Gen Z perpetually undergoes a sea change, typically sharing generally unarticulated assumptions about how their world works and mapping their interests and life activities more broadly onto varied forms of interaction, whether they are among, or driven by, software (computer code), hardware (computers themselves and/or related devices), or in the future, "wetware" (biological and/or biochemical effects related to the human body itself[11]).

Gen Z sensibilities are captured by content, as well as ways of approaching content, and a characteristic subjectivity. At one extreme, when immersed in subjectivity, the world they see easily shifts images and shapes without presenting discomfort. It appears as though these age cohorts assume they, and their world, have a certain malleability in more areas than body image and gender identity. Morphing is a common trope for them; it ranges from shape-shifting to taking on many possibly opposing roles and points of view serially or simultaneously, without experiencing the shift as psychologically discordant. To these users, the Internet offers an obvious new venue for ample exploration of serial selves, the trying-on of different identities long noted as normal in the course of development among adolescents.

This does not mean that Gen Z'ers feel free to do anything at all. We also observe that morality does count to these avid Internet experimenters. They apply their sense of right and wrong to specified areas or causes, for example, gun control, the rain forest, animal rights. To be prochoice or antiabortion is deeply important to many of them. But they are not of one mind; they do not cluster around any particular set of causes or values. Each value is a monad and that is not seen or felt to be a problem. They grew up with hypertext, the ability to customize, change, and find alternative readings of a specific text. To have only one narrative alternative seems to them to be, if not precisely ungrammatical, a bit weird. Gen Z'ers seem more comfortable living with the assumptions of Einstein's special theory of relativity than their elders. Glossed by Brian Greene (1999) in a book about string theory, "The essential concern of special relativity is to understand precisely how the world appears to individuals, often called 'observers,' who are moving relative to one another" (p. 24). Elaborating subjective perception he goes on, "In the precise way delineated by Einstein, special relativity resolves the conflict between our intuition about motion and the properties of light, but there is a price: individuals who are moving with respect to each other will not agree on their observations of either space or time" (p. 25). Likewise, Gen Z emerges from a symbolically fluid world in which there are fixed points that appear different, depending on where one is standing at any given moment. The fixed points appear to move with them; they are subjectively experienced, like the way we were taught to understand relativity.

From a Gen Z perspective, what can it mean if your avatar looks and sounds like "you" or like a cartoon kitty or like the actor Will Smith, since any of those choices is a moral equivalent, reflecting a mood, a shift in vision? Choosing one or another persona depends on a different rationale operating at a specific time. The selection of any avatar, whether to chat, play a game, or visit an Internet virtual world, brings with it a unique set of boundaries and attributes. It transforms the user's self, *but only while that avatar is used*. Another persona may be selected by the same person at any time. Online, whether game playing, chatting, or using e-mail, only a part of oneself is available for others to interact with. Adding an ontological dimension, Jaron Lanier, who coined the term *virtual reality*, comments:

The interesting thing about Net kids to me is that they have the option of discovering how other people are in parts rather than as wholes. You can talk to people in chat without having to smell them, without having to reveal much of yourself. Their experience of growing up will potentially be more self-directed in that they will have to decide how deeply to explore other people and when they are ready to do it. They'll have to make active sacrifices to develop long-term relationships by being available at specific times and physical places, instead of being anywhere anytime and always online, while previous generations were thrust into close contact with others by circumstances. This is what Silicon Valley is already like—anything other than isolation has to be actively sought. The good news is that it *is* sought. (personal communication, April 29, 2000)

For Gen Z'ers, neither the world of online reality nor the real world is privileged over the other. At times, one or the other is more "real," more important to them, and they can and do differentiate between them. That multi-dimensional perspective provides the epistemological basis of both films such as *The Matrix* and an *X-Files* television series episode in which a game-dwelling, stellar, Amazon Barbie fighter becomes the mistress of the game and gives battle to a human game player. Following the trend, the title character of a TV series introduced in Fall 2000, *Dark Angel*, is a technologically "enhanced" woman. Interestingly, for the casual viewer, it is not clear if she has been augmented like a cyborg (e.g., increased speed) or had her biology modified by the addition of animal characteristics (e.g., exceptionally acute night vision).[12] When asked, Gen Z'ers seem unflapped by the notion that they, or future generations, might be similarly enhanced. As one said, "It will all happen." To her and to her friends, cyber- and biochemical additions to the human body appear inevitable. Will the end result be "human"? This may prove a nonquestion to them. If Gen Z and following generations continue to act according to the set of premises we have identified, *enhanced humans* will be treated as human if they act human. How the edges of "humanity" will be determined remains to be seen: If one has the night vision of a cat, and not that of a traditional human being, is one still human? Where does humanity stop?[13] Gen Z takes for granted alternative moral frameworks; shifting, personally defined contexts; having serial selves including possible gender shifts; a future that contains enhanced bodies—both biological and cyber based.

Judging from these trends, what it means to be human looks like it's about to change.[14] In short, Gen Z'ers' lack of adherence to consistent bodies, visions, and standards may be our issue, not theirs. And it is increasingly their world.

Where Gen Z and the Internet are going is anybody's guess. Emergent systems are like that. We sense that the Internet is intrinsically value free. It can prove psychologically restorative or be perverted to pathological ends. Being online can effectively isolate one from essential interactions with others, or it can provide a much sought-for, vital, *virtual* community. It promotes both interaction and avoidance. And it offers unprecedented possibilities for the transformation of the self.[15]

■ NOTES

1. As Esther Dyson has pointed out repeatedly, the economically poorest group of computer users gives the lie to any complacent assumption that we currently have a Web that is truly "worldwide." This may change as companies begin to offer computers or Internet access at affordable rates in exchange for information about consumers' online behavior.

2. Wireless broadband means more available bandwidth.

3. To be "cookied" means to be tracked as a consumer, and perhaps targeted for future marketing campaigns. It is a subset of ECRM, electronic consumer relationship management, a euphemism for gathering and using consumer data.

4. Regarding gender, many women over age 60 first use computers to e-mail their grandchildren. They also use their computers to pay the household bills, potentially following a path leading from e-mail to online banking to trading.

5. Some contemporary interactive software treatment packages based in cognitive therapy are a comfortable choice for a subset of adult clients. See Wallace (1999) and Turkle (1995). Lee Van Horn participated in what must surely have been among the first group therapy sessions online in California in the 1980s (JM, personal communication).

6. For a contrasting use of e-mail in treatment, see Gabberd's account of e-mail used to express an erotic transference.

7. His "mind object," as Corrigan and Gordan (1995) have described it.

8. Karen's computer shared aspects of what psychoanalyst Kohut called a "self-object" and Winnicott a "transitional object." Although these concepts are different, in both theories the object serves a reparative or developmental psychological function for the user (e.g., see Turkle's 1995 generalization of Winnicott's notion of the transitional object to include aspects of user-computer interaction).

9. This concept was elaborated in Magdoff and Barnett, and in different terms by Lifton (1993) as the *protean self*.

10. If we are right, how will complexity theory replace the conceptual bedrock underlying our worldview? Until postmodernism began to shake them, the basic tenets of modernism were heir to epistemological assumptions that were the foundation of the 18th-century Enlightenment. These include an abiding belief in linear, logical thinking, and its child, the scientific method; and the quest to improve the world, to increase freedom, through reason and reflection. Even if we keep or modify the scientific method and the desire to improve the world, or at least, ourselves, what surprises might be closer than we think, when we legitimize a postmodern subjectivity that results in a profound splintering of what constitutes "improvement"?

11. Recently, this has been expanded to include biological and biochemical media. Computer theorists are engaged in hard-, soft-, and wet-experimentation (see Eisenberg, 2000, on using bacteria; Austen, 2001, on using light; and Rosato, 2000, on using quantum distances).

12. It turns out her DNA is "enhanced."

13. This raises the intriguing possibility of a next cultural oscillation, the ascendance of defining what is human via a code for conduct, rather than inhering in some substance—blood, DNA, a "real" essence that separates each individual or group from each other independent of action. See Barnett and Silverman (1979).

14. Sherry Turkle, who has been instrumental in shaping the field of human/computer studies, is conducting research suggesting that young children may be inventing a subset: the "almost alive" (Hafner, 2000).

15. JoAnn Magdoff would like to thank Napier Collyns for inviting her to present an earlier draft of this chapter, at a Global Business Network Meeting on e-commerce in Montreal (May 2000). Provocative questions on this draft were posed by Elizabeth Friedman and James Hawley. Glen Goddard generously e-mailed his paper. As usual, the extensive comments, insight, and support of Steve Barnett and Jaron Lanier proved invaluable. And thanks, Jeff. Jeffrey Rubin is grateful to Mary Traina for her support, feedback, and labor on this chapter and to Len Shyles for his patience and professionalism.

CYBERINTERVIEW

Marvin Kane

On February 13, 2001, I spoke with Marvin Kane, Web designer for CYRK Incorporated, a promotional product and marketing firm headquartered in Wakefield, Massachusetts. His e-commerce experience is in the area of B2B (business to business), providing Web sites for business clients. His position in Web design came after working for five years selling cable advertising for a cable television rep firm. His insights are about how businesses use cyberspace for marketing, client service, and e-commerce.

Shyles: Web design is new, but you've been in the work world for a while. What did you do before you came here?

Kane: I was with National Cable Communications for five years, a cable advertising rep firm selling advertising time on cable stations. I did a lot of things in that company. I started as executive assistant to the CEO. I didn't have a lot of skills at that point. I came from a musical career, and I realized I needed a more solid career with better money. So I looked at the possibilities, and it seemed that one place there was growth was in information technology. At the time, the Internet wasn't big. It certainly wasn't big at National Cable. But what I always had was an artistic eye, and I used to create Word documents and Excel spreadsheets. I had a certain feel for layout, and as the Internet grew I got into Web development. When I transferred to computers and information technology, it was largely self-taught. With Web design, if you're looking at an Internet page and you go to the menu bar and click "view source" you can see the code that created the page. I started doing that a lot. I copied and cut the code into my own editor, and I examined to see how it affected the page. Then my company funded some HTML (Hypertext Markup Language) classes for me.

S: Why did your current boss hire you?

K: The Internet development group was expanding; he needed people. But there was a lack of understanding of the artistic, graphic, and creative side of Internet development. They had a staff of programmers in one building. In another building, there was a graphic arts staff with product catalog publishing experience, but there was little or no communication between them. When I interviewed, it was clear that I could speak both of those languages. So I was a bridge between the two groups.

S: What kinds of projects are you involved in now?

K: We are the Web-development group, serving the sales force. We create a Web presence for established companies with well-known logos. We aim to be their one-stop promotional marketing company on the Web.

S: Who are some of your companies?

K: Peterbilt, Accenture, Philip Morris, SAFECO, Caterpillar, Delphi Auto, Volvo, Genuity, Enterprise Rent-A-Car, Fidelity.

S: OK, and they'll come to you for what?

K: Let's say Accenture is sponsoring a youth golf tournament. They may ask that we develop T-shirts, apparel, hard goods, watches that they'd like to have as a part of their promotional campaign. Then we brand all of that merchandise. We put the Accenture logo on it.

S: And HTML is useful in doing that?

K: Before Web sites, there were merchandise catalogs. Accenture has one. But now everyone wants an online catalog also.

S: So customers can see product lines online before ordering.

K: Exactly. That's how they order.

S: And you make the Web sites that feature the company's goods.

K: Yes, we create a program for Accenture, for example, consisting of a print catalog, or a Web catalog, or both. More often it's both.

S: Do you meet with the art department to plan the approach?

K: Yes, we build e-stores for companies that already have a corporate Web site. The Web site we build appears to the user as visually seamless with the one already in existence. For example, you might be on Accenture's corporate Web site and there might be a link saying, "merchandise." When you click on that, you've gone to the one we developed but you don't know it.

S: Does the money your company makes come from the sale of promotional and campaign items and from new Web pages you design?

K: Yes. And we also make money manufacturing product; we source the product, we procure it, and we do all the client follow-ups.

S: Do you go out in the field and talk to these clients?

K: Yes. There is a growing sales component to my job. I talk to clients, explain what we do, and am involved in sales meetings. I bring a laptop and show sample Web sites. I generally start with a PowerPoint presentation, and what I always say is: "Here are the advantages of having a Web-based shopping experience, so forget the PowerPoint.

Let's look at some Web sites." Then I pick the ones that highlight particular kinds of functionality relevant to them. It is a B2B function. Sometimes there's B2C (business to consumer).

S: Do you ever get asked to produce things in poor taste? Do you ever come into any ethical conflicts about the production of materials or First Amendment problems?

K: Not too much, although recently we have been contacted by our own legal department because there are rights issues that have not yet been decided on the Internet and we need to be somewhat careful about some legal issues.

S: For example.

K: We had some generic boilerplate verbiage that would be on every shipping page where we'd say something like "orders placed today will be shipped in three days." Our legal department pointed out that unless you can guarantee shipping in three days, you can't say that. So, now, our Web sites have a footer on every page with links to disclaimers, terms of use, privacy policies. And this is something you're beginning to see more and more on e-business sites. We don't create that content. We just provide links to them. And our group gets electronic copy from our legal department, which types it; then we take, say, a Word document, and cut it and paste into our code.

S: Are there high-pressure deadlines?

K: Most definitely. But we try to oversee the process up to and including delivery of the Web site. And we try to be realistic about timelines. So when production people ask how long a job will take, we consider the entire process, and then add on a nice bumper time to avoid missing deadlines. We need to build in time for unforeseen delays, and for testing by the quality assurance (QA) department. We work in a strong team environment and all the different groups cooperate, but sometimes after building codes for hours until your eyes are falling out of your head the QA department comes and says, "It doesn't work." It's the job of the QA department to break the Web site. Their job is to try to break it because if they can't break it, our client isn't going to either. It's embarrassing if the client breaks the Web site. So for example, the QA guy will type "1,000,000" into the "quantity" box asking customers how many blue shirts they want just to see what happens. And based on his findings, we'll have to go back and fix things.

S: The companies you serve don't get to see all of the stuff that you sweat through and you don't want them to.

K: Exactly. We didn't have QA when we were smaller. We all wore many hats. And that's an advantage in some ways because you get to learn a lot, but as you get bigger and better, you can't have the lead programmer be the QA guy because he's looking at it too long. You need fresh eyes on it. In the past, our clients were our QA people because they were the ones trying out the site. That is, before we had QA, our site went live, and we didn't test it. We'd say to the client, "We're done as far as we can tell. Now you go play with this and tell us your reactions." Now we do all that internally.

S: So what do you do when you're the Web site designer and you hit a loggerhead and you just can't solve a problem?

K: I take it to a higher authority and say, "I can't figure this out. I have tried it in every version of browser, every vendor, and I can't figure out why this is doing this." There are people who know more than I do about certain things. So if I can't fix it, someone else generally can. There are problems in Internet development that are difficult to deal with. For example, no matter what you do in Web site development, there's no guarantee what kind of browser users are going to have. It's beyond our control. So we have to design Web sites to degrade gracefully, which means you don't always use cutting edge technology that's dependent on browser support because if you're using something that is really fancy but only works on some machines, then some people can't access it. Not only that, but they can get all kinds of error messages. So we make it a point to use open standard technology. That is, when we spec out the project, we have initial meetings with the client and draw up a plan based on what the client is likely to be using. Is it for Intra-, Inter-, or Extranet use? What systems are the clients using?

S: Please describe what you mean by Intra-, Inter-, and Extranet.

K: Internet is basically accessible by anyone with a browser and an Internet connection. An Intranet is an Internet site developed with all the same technology as an Internet site, but intended specifically for people within a company. That is, only insiders can see it. If you're an outsider, firewall security won't let you in, so you can't view it. Intranets are typically platforms where companies post all of their HR (human resources) documentation and other proprietary information.

S: It seems to me that you don't need any local database if you have that. It can be somewhere else and you can access that.

K: That's definitely one benefit. And also it's paperless and changes are instantaneous. You need only make a change in one place and it's changed everywhere. And that's a huge benefit. So that's the Intranet. Then there's the Extranet. Extranet takes the Internet model one step further. For example, we built a site for Volvo. On their site, they recognize three classes of users: regular retail people like you and me, Volvo dealership owners, and Volvo employees. Now when you arrive at the site, the first thing you are asked to do is identify yourself, and depending on your answer you will then be restricted to a particular part of the Web site you are visiting. You will only be able to see and purchase certain kinds of material. Or you will get certain kinds of pricing. So if you own a dealership you can click on a link, and verify that with a password. And from then on, every item you see is geared to the audience of Volvo dealers. So the Extranet is like a secure channel between the Web site provider and your group. Extranet benefits are in e-commerce, of course. If your business supplies auto parts, for example, then you can, within the larger Web site, maintain several Web sites that serve as channels to different dealers. And if you own a parts company but you buy parts from us, we can have an Extranet between us; then you can see the parts you need, but Joe Blow who owns a body shop can't see the same stuff you can see.

S: You can do a lot with a single keystroke now. Individuals now have the power to change the content of documents in a lot of places in an instant. What do you see as the impact of such capability on the way we do business?

K: So many things are different. How we get information, and what we do with it, has dramatically changed. We get information almost instantly now. Eventually, the different media will converge; that is, several different technologies will become one huge technology. We will get to a point where people will have an ID number that can route information to their watches, to their car phones, Palm Pilots, to their cars. People will be able to buy things, find out the weather, and get theater tickets. Using Extensible Markup Language (XML) will make it possible to take subsets of data from larger databases and present it in new ways so that you can take a file, ship it anywhere, and depending on who's receiving it, reformat it for various purposes. So programmers only need to do one piece of work getting all of the data into an XML file and it can be sent to, say, a bank, and on their end, they'll render it a certain way for their purposes; at the same time, the same data can be sent to private clients and they will be able to retrieve what they want. Through XML, data will be customizable. So beyond mere availability of information, I see a great leap forward in functions. In the future, a lot more chores will be done for us, as machines become programmed to respond to voice commands to do the most mundane tasks, like get us a cup of tea.

S: What are you doing on the computer these days?

K: Producing Web pages, programming, working with HTML. Inside a given Web page, there are other things going on. There's Java script that makes a link change color when you roll over it. There's ASP code that queries a database and brings back results almost instantly. There are creative issues like the color of the background, images, pictures, photos on the page, and so on.

S: Do you use support software when you work?

K: Sometimes. Typically, we use Microsoft technologies to develop our Web sites. We use a platform called Site Server, a Microsoft environment we find effective for building e-commerce Web sites. It has programming functionality so that we don't have to reinvent a lot of tasks. We don't have to code from scratch. For example, Site Server already has built into it much of the "shopping cart" and credit card functionality. We can, without any modifications, crank out generic e-commerce sites. But we can also take that code and modify the way it looks. It provides us with basic functionality but enough freedom to make the site look the way we want for our clients. It supplies most of the code so we don't have to build from scratch. Its language is built around the active server pages technology, and the language is called VB script. It uses SQL (Structured Query Language) to query a database. We also use Java script, which is a client-side scripting language. It's not a robust object-oriented programming language. It's more of a lightweight scripting language that allows you to do things just with the browser. We use that for visual effects that have become standards for Web sites now. For example, nowadays when you roll over a link it almost always changes color. If you go over a link on a Web site and it doesn't change color, you would think something was wrong.

S: What other visual devices are standards now in Web design?

K: We are always talking about "usability." Particularly, we are in the business of developing e-commerce Web sites. So we're most concerned with the kind of experience the user has. It's not just information. The point of our work is to make the user's experience on the Web site enjoyable, clear, and simple. We want the user to see what the categories are, for example, apparel, outerwear, caps. Some items need to be top level because our clients say to us, make the user want to make a purchase.

S: So there is psychology you must design for.

K: Oh, absolutely, it's called marketing psychology and it translates in our world via information architecture. For example, you don't want to put apparel in the bottom right were you have to scroll to see it. You want to put it right there where it's the first place the user's eye goes. Studies show that the eye goes to the top left corner of the page. So there are levels of information. Primary information has to be seen immediately. That means all the available shopping categories have to be right there on the top left. Also, you don't want important information to be what we call "under the fold," taking a phrase from the newspaper world. In the Internet world, if you have to scroll down to see it, that's below the fold, and we'd rather design the page so that everything fits squarely in the browser window without scrolling. Sometimes that's impossible; then you try to put the most top-level information above the fold. Things below the fold might include links to privacy policy. We also like to show all of the available items for sale if possible, but if, for example, the client is selling a hundred different kinds of hats, and you can't show all of them, you put three or four of them in a row and then you don't allow the page to keep scrolling forever. What we've instituted is a three-rows-is-the-most-you-can-have-on-one-page policy, and then we have a "next" button, which takes you to the next page of three rows, and so on. We believe that makes for a better user experience than having endless scrolling because by the time users reach the end they have forgotten what was on the top row. Another technique we use is called *user indicators*; that is, users should know where they are and always be able to get anywhere else without getting lost. There are many studies about user issues. Users can get disoriented if the shopping experience is confusing or inconvenient. So we try to make it comfortable. If it's not, people will go through the whole Web site and then they won't click the last button that says, "Buy now." They just won't do it. So you have to make them comfortable. One way to do that is to minimize the number of click-throughs because you don't want to have 1,000 different pages until you finally get to the end. That's why sites like Amazon.com are so good. They have great functionality. They feature an option called one-click shopping, available after registering the first time. You just do one click and, boom, you're done. That's what users expect now.

S: What are the visual indicators?

K: Let's say you click on "apparel," which may be the first link you click to. The next page may show you a series of thumbnail images, each a hundred pixels square of an item for sale. When you click on it, the next page is dedicated just to that item, with available prices, fabrics, colors, sizes, and so forth on that page. But as you keep going, you want to have some means by which you can look to the top of the page again. To make that easy, we use what we call *bread crumbs*, icons that show where you've been and how you got to where you are so that you can always know the trail you've taken. That's a big issue, always knowing where you are and how you got there. One way to do that is to have a link you have clicked on to be in the *on* state; it might be red telling you visually that you're still in apparel. Those are some examples of the visual indicators we use to make navigating easier for users. We are always e-mailing each other back and forth if somebody reads something about a new way of doing something.

S: You sound enthusiastic about your work. But from musician to Web designer, this must have been quite a journey.

K: Yes, but I'll tell you where the common thread is. What's really been going on with my attraction for what I'm doing right now is that it parallels in many ways what music has always been. It's similar emotionally because it is creative. In Web design, you can look over the code and it looks so arcane and ugly really, but all you have to do is go back to the browser view, and see how nice the Web page looks, and that equates practicing scales with the beauty of a finished musical composition. Practicing scales is a pain. But when you're on stage, and you're warmed up, you make music. So that's what attracts me. And there are more parallels. In music, I went for years being self-taught until I got to a point where I just wanted to be better than I was, and I couldn't teach myself to get any better, so I had to go to school. With Web design, it's the exact same way. I've taught myself a lot, read books, and taken courses, all to get in the full environment and get a more solid foundation.

S: It is a very broad field. There must be some parts of it where you say, "I'm glad I don't do that job."

K: Yes. I'm glad I'm not a network administrator. I don't know or care to know stuff about connectivity and how to connect into a network. Another thing that's not for me is working the helpdesk. I wouldn't like QA because, again, that's not me; although you know as I said earlier on, in this company we're all doing a little bit of everything.

S: And I'm sure some people would say that doing QA is quite creative.

K: Absolutely. So QA folks will go through a site and come up with a list of things that need to be fixed. Now the way my mind works, if you come to me with a list, I will go through it item by item and fix everything. Fix, check it off, fix, and check it off. I can do that because you laid it out for me. I don't have to go and hunt for the errors. But if I were in QA, the job of testing would be tedious to me.

S: Is all your company's Web design done internally?

K: Not all. Sometimes we work with an offshore developing group in India. We create templates for some of our pages and then send them off for programming, and they send the files back to us through the Internet.

S: And that process works efficiently?

K: For the most part. Sometimes we get files back that don't look right. Something has been broken, or they have ignored some kind of code that I wrote. So it is very good programming practice to provide some documentation for your code.

S: What do you do that is in most demand? What do you see as your own future in the field? Where is the big money? How has the field changed since you came into it?

K: Well those are questions I ask myself all the time. I think the industry is so segmented, and there are so many special areas within the Internet world. My world is e-commerce. And e-commerce itself is expanding. It's gone from e-store to e-business. There is so much more now than just going online and buying something. Now there are all kinds of online loyalty programs and point redemption plans and communities and groups where Web sites are entire environments. For example, we do some work for NASCAR, and if you're a NASCAR fan you can go onto their Web site and buy NASCAR-branded merchandise. You can talk to racing personalities in chat rooms. You can redeem points from previous purchases. Web use is expanding way beyond just buying merchandise, and along with this expansion is new technology. So it's hard to know sometimes what is leading what. Is it the need to do more things that creates the technology, or is the technology creating the desire to do new things? I mean it's just leapfrogging.

S: Do you trust the technology personally? Do you feel it is able to protect your privacy and allow secure business transactions?

K: I don't have many problems with it because I am in the industry and I feel it's OK. Look, is anything fail-safe? No. Is it possible for some hacker to get in there and get my credit card number? Yes. It's also possible to cross the street and get hit by an 18-wheeler. So I'm not overly concerned. At the same time, the need to preserve online privacy is huge because it's recognized as an area of concern for consumers, and anything that blocks a consumer from buying must be addressed right away. Now I am not an expert by any means on Internet security, but I know what we go through. We apply for what's called an SSL, which is secured socket layer, one of the many different ways to ensure security and privacy on a Web site, and we are extremely concerned with our users' privacy because we want to stay in business. There is encryption, there are algorithms that are configured so that it's virtually impossible to break those, and again, it's not fail-safe, but what I'm really saying is that I feel secure enough that those who know about it are attending to it. They're making Web sites secure. And for e-commerce and e-business to proceed in the direction it's going, this *has* to be taken care of. I mean I just don't see e-commerce coming to a screeching halt because we can't figure out how to be secure. Ultimately, it's in the interest of the e-business community to make things safe in order to keep the system viable.

S: Do you have a personal, political stance on the issue of, say, allowing the government to have access to all Web sites via the Clipper Chip, a trap door, into each and every Web site because of the need for national security?

K: I am uncomfortable with the government having the ability to do that, but I can see why they'd be uncomfortable not being able to do that. I am a strong First Amendment guy, and one of the attractions of the Internet early on was that this is a new frontier and the government's not there yet. Eventually, I know that they are going get their arms around it. It's too big of an area for them to allow it go without their control. I am almost resigned to it. So my philosophy is that I wish that they didn't have to do it but I know they will.

S: Thanks for your insights.

K: Thank you.

CHAPTER 6

CONNECTED LEARNING IN THE INFORMATION AGE

THOMAS A. MCCAIN

LEIGH MAXWELL

THE INFRASTRUCTURE OF EDUCATION ■

Communication technologies have always been introduced to society with bravado and hyperbole. Advocating communication media as a means to improve education has been a familiar theme since the 1920s (Cuban, 1986). Often new media are viewed with hope and promise as well as apprehension and suspicion (U.S. Web-Based Education Commission, 2000). History is rife with projections regarding the role of media in society; many turn out to be overly optimistic at best, far from reality at worst. Consider Thomas Edison's 1922 vision for movies: "The motion picture is destined to revolutionize our educational system and in a few years it will supplant largely, if not entirely, the use of textbooks" (quoted in Cuban, 1986).

Sorry Mr. Edison, nothing close. According to a publishing industry newsletter, in the 1996 higher education market, 80% of all expenditures were on books; the rest was split among other, "new" technologies. The Association of American Publishers reported more than $25 billion in sales in 2000; all audiovisual products were included in the "other" category and made up just 2% of sales (see http://www.publishers.org/home/). Thus, books continue to be important.

The networked computer is the most recent revolutionary communication technology for education, but unlike many previous innovations, policy makers from federal, state, and local levels believe this one to be true. Is the Internet the most transformative technology in history, reshaping business, media, entertainment, and society?

This chapter argues that new and emerging digital media should be introduced into colleges and universities primarily to facilitate reform and transformation in meeting the needs of contemporary society. We argue that digital media should be used to alter higher education, even at the expense of old educational systems and goals, and that the needs of the contemporary adult learner should guide the transformation. Accordingly, educational systems must try to balance change and continuity in achieving this goal.

Several assumptions guide our thinking regarding the relationship between learning and digital media, and provide a framework for action. They are based on our experience in teaching and learning with technology over several decades. They have been informed and enlivened by a host of collaborators, students, and critics to whom we are indebted forever.

Definitions and Perspectives

What should you call this technology stuff? One of our colleagues simply calls it all "goo," and everyone seems to know what he means. *Cyberspace, emerging digital technologies, communication technology, new communication technology, networked computing, computers, digital media, digital technology, new media,* and *digital telecommunication technology* are all useful for describing contemporary communication and learning activities mediated by technology. We use these terms interchangeably throughout this chapter. This is not to argue that what things are called doesn't matter. In fact, some terms used to describe technical phenomena in this field may mislead. *Cyberspace* and *distance education,* for example, suggest that new media are primarily about spatial phenomena (space, distance). Once in the "space" of the Internet, however, most learners who spend time with "distance education" experience alterations in speed, reaction time, pace of interaction between users, access, convenience, and so on. Thus, the networked world appears to have more temporal ontologies than spatial ones.

Education Should Facilitate Learning

Theories and philosophies of pedagogy abound. Many offer important lenses for seeing the educational process from unique perspectives. Pearson (Chapter 7 in this volume), for example, provides a superb view of technology and education from the administrative vantage point. Our perspective focuses on the learner and the qualities of learners' lives that are enriched or constrained by the institutions of education, and particularly the use of emerging technologies. (See Figure 6.1 for a list of propositions and assumptions related to connected learning.) Certainly, there are social, economic, and political aspects to education just as there are in media. We think it is helpful to focus on the raison d'être of education—helping learners learn, that is, helping students achieve their educational goals and meet their needs, including some they may not know they have. Our focus on student learning draws from examples and research primarily concerning post-secondary students, particularly those seeking college educations.

A small liberal arts college's transformation to a learning community for the 21st century provides an example. It is based in part on a real school in a midwestern urban city. The college examined its mission and goals along with its needs for technology as a single opportunity that required thoughtfulness and integration. In the mid-1990s, the college pioneered using technology to enhance learning by wiring the entire campus and turning to its teaching faculty and educational consultants to design space, both electronic and physical, that would promote collaborative learning.

By 2001, the entering urban students each had laptop computers at an increased cost of about a hundred dollars a month. What the students found was that computers and the school's broadband network provided access to real courses, resources, faculty, and fellow students. The faculty had revised the curriculum to meet the needs of their students and community partners. By focusing on the learning needs of their students early, the college understood why and how the campus was to be retrofitted with a new network and with faculty resources responsive to this population of urban learners.

Faculty development seminars and curricular overhaul preceded the introduction of laptops. The need for connection, collaboration, and electronically enhanced learning experiences were all felt, if not articulated, by the students. The process of transforming the campus into an electronic hub for learning wasn't easy. But they got it right! Students, faculty, and campus buildings were all winners. They have given themselves permission to teach and learn via new ways of thinking about the education process.

Definitions and Perspectives

- ◆ Education should facilitate student learning.
- ◆ The critical components of learning include students, teachers, resources, and context.
- ◆ Contexts both constrain and facilitate learning.
- ◆ Connected learning is the preferred term to describe the dynamics of technology-mediated learning.

Contextual Issues of Digital Media and Learning

- ◆ The interdependence of technology, markets, and policies of communication media define their own unique spatial and temporal biases.
- ◆ Digital media have characteristics that distinguish them from other media resources and connecting devices for students and faculty including: interactivity, immediacy, multimedia and Hypertext, organizational culture and values, and digitalization.
- ◆ The trajectory of change in digital media is on an exponential development curve.
- ◆ There is tension in transforming higher education between the needs for both efficiency and creativity.
- ◆ Successful learning in information-rich contexts requires successful collaboration.
- ◆ Ownership of intellectual property is a major challenge for connected learning.

Learners, Content, Teaching, and Pedagogy

- ◆ The information society can be characterized as a context of information abundance. Most educational institutions are based on assumptions of information scarcity.
- ◆ Problem-based learning, constructivism, and educational reform all suggest that the connections between and among faculty, students, and resources require a different approach than the one that has been traditionally practiced by educational institutions.

Figure 6.1   Propositions and assumptions of connected learning in the information age.

Critical Learning Components

Student learning is best understood within the matrix of *students*, *faculty*, *resources*, and *context*. All intertwine in the enterprise of communication and technology. Student and faculty needs and competencies vary, as do the resources across different contexts. The "distance" between a faculty member and students in a lecture class is different from that in a small seminar. The context of the large lecture hall differs from that of the seminar room, and so does the learning. Via e-mail, students and faculty communicate in a context significantly less power differentiating than is found in most classrooms. Both spatial and temporal conditions of teachers, students, and resources should therefore be viewed as *contexts* for learning.

The importance of considering all components in transforming learning is provided here in a second example of technology and education. Here the vision of a dot.com billionaire and philanthropist provides the scenario of a new set of relationships among students, faculty, resources, and context.

Mr. Billionaire is concerned about the university and college experience available to students. Worried about the digital divide, Mr. Billionaire sets out to provide ways to provide the highest quality education to all, regardless of where they live, or what their social status might be. An initial pledge of $100 million is earmarked for creating the preeminent distance-learning program and virtual university on the planet.

The vision for this ambitious overhaul of higher education is to provide great lectures and courses from the world's preeminent scholars in their fields. His idea is to make a top-drawer education available to any student in the world with Internet access. His plan includes persuading famous people, such as Michael DeBakey and Steven Spielberg, to tape courses in their areas of expertise that could be broadcast on the Internet. A cyberlibrary of digital video would be made available to for-profit and nonprofit organizations to accelerate the initiative. The intent is to revolutionize learning by allowing "a cab driver in Bombay" to receive an Ivy League education.

But is it the kind of education we need in the 21st century? Are all cultures well served by a linear, top-down distribution of information from afar? Will students really sit passively through video lectures for all their education, even if it is Henry Kissinger on Vietnam? No personal interaction between professors and students will be required. Tests over the content of the video lectures, standardized and translated into all the languages of the world, will provide the basis for learning assessment.

Mr. Billionaire's vision will be learning "hell" because the focus is misplaced on the content and the teacher, not the unique learning styles of the learners, or their needs or ability to demonstrate that they can do something with what they know. Although it would be great to have access to expertise via video, this is but a small part of the educational enterprise. Mr. Billionaire is suggesting that external resources deliver education, like electricity delivers light to a bulb.

The notion that meaning and growth come from interacting with another human being is virtually discarded in Mr. Billionaire's model—his model assumes that the Internet, as a medium for communication, will transplant existing colleges, curricula, certification requirements, campus buildings, and a host of existing technologies, competitors, and policies that have emerged over many years. It's a false assumption and a bad idea.

Time

Space	**Synchronous**	**Asynchronous**
Same location	Traditional classroom	Libraries, computer labs
Different location	Television classes	Web-based courses

Figure 6.2   Learning contexts in space and time.

Contexts Can Both Constrain and Facilitate Learning

Acknowledging that technology can facilitate or constrain the educational process serves as a starting point for understanding the influence of distance education on the educational enterprise. Communication theory teaches that the context in which messages are sent and received is critical in understanding their impact. Distance between teachers and students is itself a learning context. The temporal dimension is another; clearly, the time that learning occurs matters.

In media-enhanced learning, it is useful to think of both space and time as critical factors that influence the learning context. As those factors modify learning, it is more important than ever to recognize that students and faculty have always used space and time differently. Figure 6.2 presents the intersections of place and time in terms of learning contexts.

As Figure 6.2 indicates, in the traditional classroom, learning is biased by events happening for all participants at the same time (synchronous) and in the same space. Students in traditional settings also learn by going to places where resources are predictably available (e.g., the library), but they are able to go at "their own time." Many early broadcasting models of distance learning were designed to have all students gather at the same time, but in different locations—hence the bias for the term *distance* education.

By contrast, the Web allows learners to be in different locations but also to access resources at different times, something that is difficult to do in the traditional classroom. Technology is necessary for learning at a distance; it is also often integral to learning "live" with other students in the classroom.

We prefer to think of the interdependency of students, teachers, and resources as contexts where media can enhance or detract from some aspects of learning. Chairs bolted to the floors of college classrooms are technologies designed to help the janitorial staff clean a classroom, not to help students learn.

Whereas all of us may wish to hear great minds lecture, Mr. Billionaire's learning model does not address the range of students' needs. By contrast, perhaps the college that transforms itself successfully for the digital age should start with student needs in forming its vision. That is, all the critical components of learning should be included from the start.

Connected Learning: The True Dynamic of Distance Education

Many authors characterize technology-mediated learning under headings such as *distance learning, asynchronous learning, distance education, or online education* (Holmberg, 1995; Kember, 1995; Willis, 1993). Moore (1990) describes distance education as consisting of "all arrangements for providing instruction through print or electronic communication media to persons engaged in planned learning in a place or time different from that of instructor or instructors" (p. xv). Shale and Garrison's (1990) definition of distance education focuses on education, not distance. Steve Gilbert offers a slightly different orientation, one that focuses on processes rather than elements. He advocates the use of the concept of *connected learning*:

> In this view, individual learners, teachers, and related support profes-sionals connect better to information, ideas, and each other via effective combinations of pedagogy and technology, both old and new.
>
> Connected education captures a vision deeper and broader than dis-tance education, asynchronous education, or online education. The latter three describe conditions or media associated with certain kinds of teaching and learning. However, distance, asynchronicity, and being online are not educational goals. Fortunately, new applications of infor-mation technology make it possible to teach and learn more effectively than ever before at a distance, asynchronously, or online—and doing so can help achieve *connected education*. (http://www.tltgroup.org/gilbert/NewVwwt2000—2-14-00.htm)

Connected learning refers to contexts where teachers, students, and/or information are separated by either time or distance. It suggests that distance and time modify education by enabling new possibilities and relationships among and between participants. Thus, teachers can still be lecturers, they can still be in physical proximity with learners, but they can also be working at a distance (e.g., NASA scientists, archaeologists at a dig). Learning materials may still be textbooks, class notes, and library resources, but they can also be files from distant databases, or satellite maps from the National Weather Service, and so on. And fellow students can be in the same physical classroom or on a global computer teleconference. What changes (on occasion) are the time and spatial relationships between resources, teachers, and students; in short, what changes are the learning contexts. Thus, digital technology changes relationships among these essential components of education, making available new places to explore and new cubbyholes in which to become immersed. Digital technology allows immediate answers to questions, but also facilitates interaction among students, teachers, and resources.

Media Technology, Markets, and Policies Define Contexts

Bell (1979) notes that control "is not in the technology per se but in the social and political . . . [contexts] in which technology is embedded . . . technology does not determine social structure; it simply widens all kinds of possibilities" (p. 44). Technology can either facilitate or constrain; depending on the choices made by members of the social system, technology can intensify the degree of centralized power or empower individuals to pursue diverse interests. Political and social demands match education output with workforce input, influencing choices in the use and design of technology.

This holistic view of communication technology is among the root metaphors of this book. To understand the relationship between emerging technologies and learning requires a perspective that considers correlations among (1) markets (i.e., costs of technology and learning, media and education ownership, and what technologies most people adopt for use); (2) technologies (i.e., capabilities and functions of new tools for distribution, storage, and creation of messages); and (3) policy (i.e., asymmetric power relationships of communication in both private and public spheres).

In the field of education, the relationship between particular institutions and networked computing must deal with processes of continuity and change; often forces and interests are at significant odds. As an essentially human process, adopting new methods and tools in complex organizations such as colleges and universities is disruptive; it challenges the status quo. For these and a host of related reasons, the transformation of higher education into a technology-rich learning environment will be a "slow revolution" (Gilbert, 1996). This is because many core stakeholders view such transformation as potentially dangerous.

The midwestern college discussed earlier understood in both conceptual and practical ways that as a small liberal arts college it needed to serve the needs of the student constituencies as part of the marketplace where there were increasing options. The college worked with existing suppliers of technology to help it design and build an infrastructure that was available, dependable, and affordable. The college president, a dynamic leader, understood that the school's vision for the future required an approach that included changing policies and technologies to continue serving students.

By contrast, most attempts in history to provide "experts from afar" as resources for learning have not succeeded in transforming educational institutions (instructional radio, television, film, computers, CD-ROMs, etc.). Instead, such resources historically have been used as supplements to existing courses and practices. Mr. Billionaire will have to consider the necessary requirements of educational institutions for specific courses, majors, credentialing rules, and the existing technologies that are already in place.

THE UNIQUE QUALITIES OF DIGITAL MEDIA ■

Communication media present new means for broadening the scope of knowledge and conveying old knowledge in new forms. They also cultivate new skills for exploration as they allow us to envision knowledge with new internal representations (Olsen, 1974). The characteristics that seem most critical in understanding digital media as facilitators or detractors of student learning are interactivity, immediacy, multimedia/hypermedia, organizational culture and values, and digitalization (Ball-Rokeach & Reardon, 1988; McQuail, 1991; Rafaeli, 1988). Implicit in the ensuing discussion of cyberspace and learning is the fundamental assumption that media are not neutral.

Interactivity

Interaction is about feedback and control. Media structured to encourage distribution of information from one to many, as do traditional mass media (i.e., broadcast radio and television), engender a host of expectations and design demands. Likewise, digital media, especially those that are networked, present possibilities inherent to their nature for interaction and participation. The Internet and emerging media give comparatively more access and freedom to select content and activity according to the students' and teachers' intent and convenience. A shift away from producers and distributors of mass media content and toward users is but one characteristic of digital media that is profoundly transforming teaching and learning. Both students and faculty become authors on the Internet, becoming more responsible and involved in their learning.

Emerging media may not match the level of interaction supported by face-to-face communication, but they do provide forms of communication experiences generally not available with other forms of communication technology. Some scholars argue that there is equivalent interaction in computer-mediated communication; it just takes longer to establish the relationships in the mediated setting compared to face-to-face (Walther, 1992).

Historically, changes in communication patterns have contributed to social change. When a new factor is added to an old context, the result is not the old context plus the new factor, but instead a new environment (Fischer, 1992; Meyrowitz, 1985). Computer-networked media allow a model of communication that expects interaction—one biased toward information flowing two-ways between users.

If you were taking a course at Mr. Billionaire's school, interaction would be unimportant; instead, mastering what the video experts say would be privileged. By contrast, at the midwestern college, the practice of students writing each other and their instructors would be expected and facilitated through e-mail, threaded discussions, and chat environments. The Internet encourages participation through its network design and two-way capability.

Immediacy

Digital communication technologies value timeliness and currency more than their counterparts in traditional media. Although the nature of some content in newspapers, radio, and television requires currency, these media have deadlines, after which changes are not easily made. Production must begin sometime. By contrast, when contemporary learners want the most current information, they turn to the Web, which is prone to more frequent updating; it is by nature more malleable in terms of content than some of the media it "replaces." For example, the New York Times Online changes its front-page picture every few hours, something its printed version cannot do. Although this places an enormous burden on content producers, meeting audience expectations for current news and information is one of its central advantages. Emerging media operate with technology to facilitate storage, delivery, and quick access to current information. Does such immediacy lead to new biases in the nature and quality of the information commodities it provides? We think it can.

The structure and bias of the Web favor using information that allows learners to *do* something. In learning circles, this is sometimes called "usable knowledge" (Argyris & Shon, 1978). The book, by contrast, emerged over centuries as a resource that requires a more reflective attitude from users (Hesse, 1996); it is a more passive medium. Contemporary online students, therefore, find it ironic when required to read books in a fast-paced learning environment. Hesse notes that in the contemporary setting "knowledge is no longer that which is contained in space, but that which passes through it, like a series of vectors, each having direction and duration yet without precise location or limit" (p. 31). Both students and faculty have an *action bias*— there is immediate pressure to demonstrate what they know to themselves and others.

Some learning in the new age of cyberspace may actually be biased against reflective processes, an aspect of education that has been part of the pedagogical process for centuries. Traditional learning models have been characterized by drill, practice, rote memorization, standardized testing, and segmented curricula designed to serve the needs of an industrial age aimed at producing an educated workforce. But the importance of having more ephemeral knowledge bases (called *just-in-time* information), current facts, and expertise available "24/7" has grown; such new curricula are taking their place alongside traditional ones and are becoming an important aspect of education for contemporary students and teachers.

Colleges, viewed as places where people go to learn, fit the spatial bias of traditional learning media, particularly the book. But digital media shift users away from a space bias—that is, learning can happen anywhere, at the convenience of the learner, rather than according to an institution's room assignment and "bell schedule." From this new perspective, it becomes possible that learning, ironically, may be interrupted by the act of "going to class." To facilitate learning in the information age, therefore, institutions must recognize a shift in the time/space bias, and recognize both reflection *and* action as expressions of learning under the new arrangements wrought by digital media.

Of course, the impact of the Web's immediacy on teaching and learning is double-edged at least. Although incorporating the latest and most exciting findings into a course is intellectually stimulating, it also requires continuous time and effort in planning. Combining the immediacy of the Web with interactive capability does not happen by chance. Teachers may have to relinquish some control over the class and the materials used in order to maximize the Web's resources.

But teachers must also maintain quality. Managing the cross-pressures of the new arrangement can be tricky. Veteran teachers (perhaps those least likely to adapt to new innovations) may be those best qualified to make the shift—a learning irony to be sure.

Multimedia and Hypertext

One attraction of Mr. Billionaire's cyberuniversity is the ability to gather contemporary information from the greatest minds and deliver it to students everywhere, thus extending access to high-quality resources nearly instantly. It is more difficult for local instructors to find such dynamic resources at the midwestern college.

Communication media are known by their predictable form and content (McQuail, 1991). Newspapers provide text, images, and other graphics on paper. Television provides text, images, animations, audio dialogue, and other sounds, much of it offered in narrative form. The WWW provides visual images, animations, live-action video, interactive features, sounds, and a variety of interactive and layered applications.

The capability to offer not only information but also interactivity through both sight and sound has an impact on education in novel ways. Hypertext and multimedia are robust enough to support multiple learning styles. More senses are involved including sight, sound, and even touch. Learning environments that offer individuals multiple forms for grasping and applying concepts can lead to deeper involvement and perhaps deeper understanding than older media forms were able to offer (Brown, 1993; Gardner, 1991; Means, 1994).

New multimedia also allow learners new options for demonstrating their learning. Those with language intelligence can use words and text to show what they have learned. Those with artistic intelligence can display their work using nonverbal tools. Such customization and individualization of processes within teaching and learning can engage users more actively than older media forms could do.

Hypertext allows users to organize information into customized units. An instance of a hypertext unit is an Internet link or hypertext link connecting an audio source with a particular text. Hypertext is a pipeline to databases of content connected by links, the defining feature of the World Wide Web. With access to the Web, learners have a variety of media and information sources available to them that they can use in a variety of ways. In addition to finding multimedia forms, users can surf the Web to locate relevant materials with relative ease.

According to communication historians, the move from oral communication to print media led to new habits of thought—more linear, cause-and-effect thinking, and more of a one-thing-at-a-time cognitive approach to the environment (for better or worse) (Innis, 1951; McLuhan, 1964; Nunberg & Eco, 1996). What new thought processes might develop as a result of hypermedia and the integration of the WWW to academic pursuit?

Research in the Apple Classrooms of Tomorrow found that learning activities that took advantage of new media's characteristics influenced the way learners represented and processed information; such change may result in an increase in the variety of and types of learning that can occur (Bass, 2000; Tierney, 1992). For example, it appears that students shift their views of documents as communicating ideas in a linear form to a more layered arrangement and therefore shift their ideas of themselves from workers to creators. Thus, hyper- and multimedia seem to facilitate the development and expression of new forms of learning that unbind thinking from linear modes. Such new media challenge teachers and learners to think anew about knowledge and learning assessment. The experience with students in the Living in the Information Age course at Ohio State University demonstrates this engagingly. Students' homework, class presentations, and research projects included a variety of forms, and significantly altered the learning process.

Organizational Culture and Values

The organizational cultures out of which digital media are emerging differ significantly from those that accompanied traditional mass media. The newspaper, radio, and television industries were shaped during the industrial age; by contrast, digital networks are forming in a political economy of an information society. It is therefore likely that the structures, processes, values, and ways of conducting business will differ accordingly (Bell, 1979; Fischer, 1992; Tapscott, 1996).

Organizational cultures include those practices and values that are often unspoken, but nevertheless characterize the climate and procedures for doing work within an organization, whether a dot.com, school, or cable company. Culture fundamentally conditions the way people use language and other symbols to communicate. In new media organizations, cultures often differ from those of traditional media because "the way things are done around here" is dynamic and emerging.

Comparatively speaking, organizational cultures within emerging media organizations often reflect more of the characteristics that contemporary business theorists advocate for information organizations: flat, nonhierarchical units, more clearly focused on specific outcomes, featuring multitasking among both managers and workers. Such units are more project centered than process centered, and they exhibit long-range vision, short-range strategies, and a bias for action and innovativeness (Drucker, 1993; Gilder, 1989; Pinchot & Pinchot, 1994). One lesson of 1990s mergers and acquisitions in communication industries was recognizing the difficulty understanding cross-industry convergence. Microsoft's culture of casual clothes, pizza, caffeine, late-night hours, and video games allowed the employees to get things done. But in the early days of the company, among the difficult things for them to accomplish was to work with the employees of IBM, where suits, ties, white shirts, formal conversation, and strict schedules characterized IBM's culture. It was a difficult and often contentious relationship early on, one that Microsoft's Bill Gates characterized as "riding the bear."

In terms of education, American schools similarly reflect the structure of the industrial age (Marshall, 1992; Means, 1994). Ironically, in the current climate, some of the cultural characteristics of emerging media organizations may serve as a model of the learning enterprise. Educational culture has developed over a long period with a host of stakeholders and vested interests that will not transform easily. After all, the process of healthy transformation is one of both efficiency and creativity—"automating" and "informating," in Zuboff's (1984) terms. But emergent cultures among educational institutions must respond to society's needs for both reflective thinkers and action-oriented problem solvers. The cultures of educational institutions and emerging media must understand each other in order to derive optimal benefits from each other; presently, the cultures are in conflict.

For Mr. Billionaire, the culture for learning seems to emphasize structures featuring one-way learning models. For the midwestern college, the structure of the school and the functioning of the faculty are being transformed to meet the needs of the students—they are creating a new culture together.

Digitalization

Digital technology sends and stores messages encoded into discrete packets composed of bits assembled by users' software on their computers. To arrive intact, digital signals carry messages in the form of binary data, as well as data about that data, which helps define and direct that information. It is the information about itself that allows digital information to be transmitted, searched, and categorized in virtually endless ways. This arrangement enables information to be manipulated using key words or even concept searches using search engines. By contrast, text cannot be manipulated in a textbook the same way; nor can traditional analog audio and video signals be so manipulated. Digital codes therefore offer overwhelming advantages by permitting users to combine information in new ways. Thus, creative power is placed into the hands of both teachers and learners as never before.

Of course, such changes come with a price: The disadvantages include susceptibility of information to being copied, diluted, erased, manipulated, hacked, and infected—in short, meaning can be changed and destroyed as well as created. Traditional notions of authority, ownership of intellectual property, and credibility regarding publishing rights are challenged as never before in the digital environment (Maxwell & McCain, 1997; Strangelove, 1994). Thus, the constraints and enhancements of learning via digital media are conditioned by policy regulations regarding who owns information, how information may be used, and who has legal access to it.

Media Development and Information Capacity Is Growing Exponentially

The brute amount of information currently available to students and teachers is clearly more unwieldy (and certainly more difficult to absorb) than it was only ten years ago. In addition, the speed with which it is generated has increased significantly as has the rate of invention for communication technologies.

There is evidence that prehistoric humans were using technology to express themselves at least 45,000 years ago (Marshack, 1999). Some 20,000 years later, people left paintings on cave walls in France at Lascaux telling stories about their beliefs and their relationships to other animals. Too bad the alphabet hadn't yet been invented so we could understand more clearly what these early authors were saying. It was around 3500 B.C.E. that the Sumerians began writing. Thus, it took human beings more than 41,000 years to invent writing, a length of time nearly unfathomable by today's standards for technology development. Assuming that the average human lifespan was 30 years, it took 1,300 lifetimes for humanity to develop from speaker to speaker-writer. The printing press was invented in the middle of the 15th century, some 5,000 years after evidence that we could write—or another 167 lifetimes.

The speed of invention and the changes in communication technology in the past century is significantly different. More innovation to help us extend our world with communication technology has occurred in the past hundred years than through the prior 450 centuries. The title of Bill Gates's (1999) book reflects the contemporary conception of time: *Business @ the Speed of Thought: Using a Digital Nervous System*. The pace of change is accelerating even as we try to make sense of it. More people are able to communicate in more ways and have access to more information than at any other time in human history. But the rate of change for communication technology is not paralleled by a similar rate of change in economic principles, or the rate at which people can read or become wise.

Thus, the information explosion is no myth. The growth and diffusion of digital telecommunication infrastructures have made available to contemporary society an unprecedented abundance of information. As the literate population has increased, so have available materials for information consumption. Today's learners face a blizzard of information and not enough capacity to process it. Students are consequently overwhelmed with information rather than comforted by it. As Nobel Prize winner Herbert Simon (1997) has noted, "A wealth of information creates a poverty of attention." This turn of events makes choosing among sources an intellectual achievement in its own right; how to make strategy decisions and what to spend time with is its own cultural challenge.

The implications for higher education are profound. Information overload is the operative mode in which students and faculty find themselves. Clearly, the strategies and methods for learning in an era of information abundance require different approaches from those that can be provided by institutions and traditional processes designed for a bygone time of relative information scarcity.

Kurzweil (1999) visualizes a breathtaking increase in machine intelligence in coming decades, presenting an elaborate argument that by the year 2020, computers will exceed human intelligence. When computers become so fast (and so small) that massive information storage becomes totally portable and accessible, learning and teaching will enter an unusual new context. What will learning be like when the full text of the Library of Congress, and all the video produced over the past 50 years, becomes available to students, who will also be able to access all known recorded music at the same time?

Digital Media Offer Education Both Efficiency and Creativity

The adoption of digital communication technologies by educational institutions comes with an inherent tension. On the one hand, digital technology is used for efficiency—doing old things more cost-effectively, faster, more safely, with fewer mistakes, and with less of the drudgery that accompanies patterned, repetitive activity. However, networked computing is intimately tied to human communication processes and requires creativity to help develop new ways of thinking about and doing things. But "efficiency" and "creativity" are often diametrically opposed in organizations. It is this tension that helps us recognize some of the problems facing colleges committed to adopting new communication technologies.

Digital technologies do more than improve efficiencies of current processes (transferring messages by the billions; offering online courses by the thousands); they can also change the nature of what is being done because they provide new contexts and redefine what we mean by accomplishing work, particularly intellectual work. The necessary condition for this transformation, according to Zuboff (1984) and others (see Nonaka & Takeuchi, 1995), is actual hands-on experience, skills development, and mastery.

Thus, it is not only the processing of information that makes the Internet an important and powerful element of change in the academy. On another level, it is the multimedia nature of messages, the interactive message production capabilities of the Web, and the demand for immediacy that are transforming the shape of knowledge and the learning process. The production of content in new forms requires both new tools and practices with these tools.

One great promise of networked media is that they provide tools that equalize the power relationships between sources and receivers. But how does this democratization occur? What skills and competencies are needed to promote literacy and understanding in the new environment? How should users of networked technologies learn to use these tools? What dimensions of the networked computer promote its becoming a mass medium of dialogue rather than a medium of mere transmission? What kinds of knowledge and experience are needed for becoming adept at using this potentially transforming tool to liberate rather than constrain? The history of social adoption of technology provides some insights to these questions.

Both *efficiency* and *creativity* are significant qualities of communication technology and organizational change. The propensity to see new things through old glasses is a normal human way of processing information. Students, teachers, and administrators are all influenced by their own past personal experiences with technology as a starting point. Zuboff (1984) calls this propensity the "natural attitude." A person's natural attitude conditions his or her capacity to act and react without thinking or making natural actions problematic—we call this inclination "habits." But new communication technologies challenge natural attitudes and distract or help learners think about themselves and what they wish to accomplish—they help users evaluate their habits.

The history of work and of humanity's relationship to technology may be viewed from both physical and mental perspectives. Different kinds of knowledge, *explicit* and *tacit*, are critical for understanding the impact of technology. Explicit knowledge is language based. Knowing facts explicitly means information can be assessed linguistically. Explicit knowledge, therefore, has explicit form.

But tacit knowledge, the unspoken cultural practices associated with different folkways related to the work-world, explains the deeper knowledge that comes with experience (Nonaka & Takeuchi, 1995). Tacit knowledge is that kind of understanding that people have that words cannot express—the feeling of a kiss, the sound of wind on a sail, the understanding that you need to reboot your computer—these are things learned only through acting on and acting with these phenomena. They are often the knowledge that society values most, the deeply held knowledge that provides insight and creativity when actors are engaged with a partner in a kiss, a boat on the water, or a computer online.

Tacit knowledge is that which is revealed to actors in the time and moments during interaction. Digital media challenge the taken-for-granteds of when and where things can and should be done. Because of this, they are excellent tools for facilitating, encouraging, even demanding users to change. As Zuboff (1984) notes:

> The technology takes over for a certain amount of human activity, even as it renders that activity in text. Action-centered skills (acting-on and acting-with) are built into the technology as it substitutes for bodily presence—that is automation. At the same time, activities are made transparent. They are exposed in detail as they are textualized in the conversion to explicit information—that is Informating. (p. 181)

Perhaps this is why written text in newsgroups and MUDs (multiuser domains) are excused from the demands of proper grammatical form: Technological substitution for bodily presence frees users from having to participate in the demands of "proper" expression (and the lengthy investment in associated skills). That is, new digital media free students and faculty "from" as well as "to." In short, the latitudes of freedom are amplified.

New parameters for expression or knowledge depend on at least two conditions: first, the presence of individual competence, and second, the opportunity to express that competence. The development of competence with networked computing comes only from experience with the technology and its ability to perform as an interactive medium. Users cannot develop interactive skills akin to literacy skills in reading merely by watching computer screens printed or scrolled online. Rather, the interactive aspects of the medium can be learned only through active participation with all of its features. Zuboff (1984) notes:

> Knowledge associated with action-centered skill could remain largely tacit throughout the course of learning and execution, but the knowledge relevant to intellective skill development must be made explicit in the learning process and can only become tacit when an individual has attained a high level of expertise. Even then, it is unlikely that form of knowledge can become only partially tacit and is readily accessible to explication. (p. 191)

The ability of digital media to aid in transforming the educational process and to displace old media necessarily requires that users have experience online. We regularly have students with different skill levels in our Web-based course, Living in the Information Age. To be sure, students with extensive experience display higher levels of competency with the tools than do the *newbies*. More important, online experience increases students' overall sense of control, competency, and creativity with the technologies (McCain, Morris, Green, & al-Najran, 1999). For this reason, one goal for transforming higher education should be to celebrate the efficiencies of digital media as well as the creative aspects and to give potential users the necessary experience with the technologies to prepare them for creative applications in both play and work settings.

■ ADMINISTRATIVE CHALLENGES

The emergence of digital media presents significant administrative challenges to higher education. These include balancing the efficiency and creativity potentials of digital communication technology; colleges and universities must also juggle seemingly contradictory demands from social expectations and economic requirements. Socially, colleges and graduate schools are expected to teach how to manage today's information abundance, and meet the demands of business in terms of relevant skills and knowledge. Higher education must also expand its "customer base," enrolling and teaching more students more cost-efficiently.

Fortunately, digital technologies may be an ideal solution for both the social and economic challenges. More institutions now offer online degree programs (see, e.g., www.ecollege.com for a directory of such institutions); in addition, administrators are increasingly encouraging faculty to incorporate online elements into their courses. Wiring classrooms, upgrading computer labs, and even requiring or providing laptops to students are becoming the academic norm.

As the cost of higher education increases, pressure mounts to find economically sound solutions. Many of the early proponents of distance education have argued that new technologies would bring great economies of scale, making the learning enterprise more cost-effective. However, a recent comprehensive study of the World Wide Web for learning (U.S. Web-Based Education Commission, 2000) concludes that there are few cost savings regarding Web-based learning; in fact, there is a need for more expenditures in order to enjoy the creative potential of new digital media.

Research claiming "no significant difference" (NSD) between courses taught with electronic media and those taught traditionally are often interpreted as a support for administrators' edicts to improve efficiencies by going online (Russell, 1999; http://teleeducation.nb.ca/nosignificanctdifference/). NSD research compares educational outcomes (usually test scores) between students in traditional classes with students in mediated classes and finds no measurable difference. That is, the delivery strategy does not appear to influence academic test performance between online and face-to-face students. However, this thinking is faulty on a number of grounds. First, the NSD findings support the conclusion that there is insufficient evidence to assert a difference between in-class and virtual students' test scores. But this is not the same as claiming test performances are equivalent. A host of alternative explanations exists for these outcomes, the most prevalent being the differences in age and motivation of face-to-face students and their virtual counterparts (see Acker & McCain, 1993).

The manifold challenges for academic managers include, therefore, understanding the potential digital technologies have for transforming education; this includes recognizing the differences between merely transmitting information efficiently (à la Mr. Billionaire's mode) and enabling users to engage in more dialogic and interactive modalities. Administrators should therefore establish processes that assess both new learning economies and new modes of learning. To do this, administrators should experience new technologies firsthand. Tacit knowledge of administrators is essential for them to develop an understanding of and appreciation for the potential of digital technologies to alter current educational approaches. Besides, it's what community leaders are clamoring for (Maxwell, 1996).

Successful Transformation Requires Collaboration

Collaboration is a natural element of connected learning with digital technologies. For this reason, digital media require contributions that no one person can possibly provide. Making a difference with digital communication technology for learning requires an "other," usually many others.

David and Roger Johnson and their colleagues at the University of Minnesota study the effectiveness of collaborative learning (http:/www.clcrc. com/pages/cl-methods.html). They analyzed more than 160 studies, comparing collaborative learning to learning where competition or individual success was the primary focus. In achievement, collaborative learning was consistently superior. The results held for verbal tasks (such as reading, writing, and oral presentation), mathematical tasks, and not surprisingly, procedural tasks (such as swimming, golf, and tennis). The research on achievement also found that high levels of cooperation promoted greater intrinsic motivation to learn, more frequent use of cognitive processes such as reconceptualizing, higher-level thinking skills, meta-cognition, cognitive elaboration, networking, and greater retention of the skills learned.

Intellectual Property in the Connected Learning Environment

Of course, the altering effects of digital media are not restricted to shifts in the balance of control in space and time, nor is their effect felt only in the institutions where they are introduced. They are also having a profound impact on the legal status of the content that traverses the network. One of the biggest challenges facing society, and education in particular, therefore, is in the area of copyright law, the control over content, and the ownership of intellectual property.

Copyright protection balances the legitimate needs of society for access to material with the rights of creators to be compensated for their work. Access to worthy content is critical to society because it enriches all our lives. Nowhere is this balance more salient than within the institution of education, where livelihoods depend on both the access to and protection of intellectual content (Maxwell & McCain, 1997). Fundamental to education is the creation, preservation, and dissemination of ideas, and our most fundamental values are reflected in the ways scholars find, respect, and build on the ideas of others. With technological advances transforming the means for creating, storing, and exchanging information, the challenges posed to intellectual property and the need to reexamine its purpose and role carry serious implications for higher education.

Copyright law arose along with the printing press, capitalism, and the regulated publishing industry (Eisenstein, 1979; Nunberg & Eco, 1996; Schiller, 1994). The legacy of copyright includes a pattern of protection offered by government regulation that allows publishing industries to expand. At times, it has also resulted in censorship and monopolies of knowledge (Hesse, 1996; Innis, 1951).

Since copyright's inception, the ability to control access to and distribution of intellectual property has been fundamental to protection. Centralized production facilities made control a practical possibility. But in recent years, due to networked computing, and a transition from analog to digital platforms for content creation, storage, and transmission, production has become decentralized. The shift from the centralized communications of bookstores and libraries to the decentralized communications of computerized households and offices has resulted in a proliferation of information creation, storage, and distribution facilities that is virtually impossible to control (Maxwell & McCain, 1997).

Copyright was also founded in an analog era. The copy machine challenged copyright's control; however, the lower quality of copies (compared to the original) combined with the time involved in their production limited the extensiveness of their reach and the threat to copyright. This is not the case for digital media. Information technologies not only have the capability to improve production and dissemination efficiencies but also to alter information into new forms.

The printing press automated the production of books. The copy machine automated the copying of books, articles, and so on. The computer automates the production of texts, but also "informates" by providing a digital record of the text that can be cut, copied, pasted, and time stamped. When the workstation or cell phone is connected to a computer network, the text can be distributed to a virtually unlimited number of sites for storage, modification, redistribution, and repeated dissemination (Barlow, 1994). Thus, not only can a copyrighted work lose its traditional form, its digitalization makes it possible to translate it into forms with contrary meaning (Dommering, 1992).

Historically, policy has acknowledged the need for teachers, scholars, and researchers to have access to information as indicated in the doctrine of *fair use*. Fair use refers to a reasonable amount of copying when it is socially beneficial and the overall effect of the copying does not threaten the economic interests of the author (Coyle, 1996; Ginsburg, 1992). Decisions on fair use are not objective, but require weighing a number of factors including the purpose of the copying (for commercial or nonprofit use), quantity copied, nature of the copied material, and the impact of that copying on the market for the copyrighted work (Gorman, 1998). The capabilities of new technologies are forcing policy makers to reexamine how fair use is to be defined (Coyle, 1996; Maxwell & McCain, 1997; Samuelson, 1996).

Individuals arguing for stronger protection of copyrighted materials claim that the potential of the National Information Infrastructure (NII) will not be realized if the content is not protected effectively (Coyle, 1996; Lehman, 1995; NII Task Force, 1994). They suggest that owners of intellectual works will not be willing to put their interests at risk if they cannot control the terms and conditions under which their works are made available to the world. Consequently, learners will not use the services available online unless access to a wide variety of works is provided under equitable and reasonable terms. The essential purpose of the control is to ensure economic gain from the information. But this combined with shrinking educational budgets could mean a decline in learning, which is precisely what Innis (1951) warns about when describing the danger of monopolies of knowledge and the mechanization of education.

With the rapid emergence of Internet-based distance learning programs, course content is a hot commodity, and a renewed debate over who owns course content is just getting started. Does course content belong to the professor teaching the course? To the university that offers the course? Is there a hybrid solution that will satisfy both sides?

Universities want to distribute and profit from course content developed under their auspices. Professors want to retain control over their authored material. Copyright law is at the crux of the debate. For instance, the California legislature passed Assembly Bill 1773, signed into law in September 2000, prohibiting the recording of all or part of a professor's lecture without his or her permission. Some institutions are taking an "unbundling" approach, under which neither the university nor the professor owns all of the rights to copyrighted material. At the Stevens Institute of Technology, professors are paid to develop online courses but the school keeps the copyright, and course developers receive a third of the revenue from course licensing. Some purists have serious doubts about this unbundling approach, claiming that it blurs the role of university with that of publisher. It will take years and probably courts and legislatures to sort out the answers to the many questions regarding course content ownership (*May the Course Be With You*, retrieved from http://www.linguafranca.com/print/0103/feature_ strikes.html).

Finding a reasonable balance between the needs of the users of intellectual works and the creators is just one challenge facing policy makers, content providers, and users of new communication technologies. Attempts to argue for the free flow of information may not be considered seriously by policy makers convinced that without economic incentive no information of any value will be created. With the Internet becoming more and more commercialized, and higher education institutions seeking ways to become more marketable, the traditional academic model that puts society's needs ahead of commercial goals may change (Gorman, 1998). By viewing communication and the teaching and learning process as social activities built on individuals creating and sharing meaning, two guidelines are suggested in an attempt to find a balance between the needs of users, specifically faculty and students, and the owners of intellectual property: (1) Redefine educational licensing arrangements, and (2) modify fair use guidelines (see Maxwell & McCain, 1997). Decisions over how to protect intellectual works in an electronic and digital world will have long-term implications for social interaction, creative thought, intellectual breakthroughs, and technological advancements. The federal government is constantly working on approaches to solve the dilemma (see http://lcweb.loc.gov/copyright/).

New Connectivity Options Foster Nontraditional Approaches to Education

Two approaches to fostering relationships between students, content, and teachers represent opposite ends of a pedagogical continuum. These are known by many names. Our nomenclature favors a communication bias—*transmissional* or linear, one-way approaches, versus *dialogic* or more interactive approaches. However, it is important to note that pedagogy and technology are not inherently linked. That is, it is possible to use transmissional methods with or without technology (an in-person lecture is an example). Similarly, dialogic methods are not inherently linked to technology either (student with a tutor is an example). A summary of the polar differences in these models is presented in Figure 6.3. Both approaches have their place in higher education, including in the information age.

Our contemporary education system is largely based on a transmissional model resting on assumptions that stem from behaviorist views of learning and a factory model of instruction (Berliner, 1992; Daggett, 1994; Marshall, 1992; Means, 1994; Wood & Smellie, 1991). In this model, knowledge is viewed as a static body of information to be transferred from teachers and textbooks to students; teachers are experts of subject matter, lecturers, disciplinarians, and evaluators; students are viewed as passive recipients of knowledge who come to school ready to learn (Richter, Maxwell, & McCain, 1995). Teaching in this tradition consists of passing along facts and content identified as important from the past. Learning means acquiring what is already incorporated in books and the heads of elders (Dewey, 1938). Tests

Transmissional Instruction	Dialogic Instruction
• Faculty directs.	• Students explore.
• Instruction is didactic.	• Instruction is interactive.
• Students receive short blocks of instruction on a single subject.	• Students perform extended blocks of authentic and multidisciplinary work.
• Students work individually.	• Students work collaboratively.
• Faculty is knowledge dispenser.	• Faculty is facilitator.
• Students assessed on fact knowledge and discrete skills.	• Students assessed on performance.
• Knowledge is finite and measurable through objective exams.	• Knowledge is limitless and observable through performance.

Figure 6.3 Comparison of transmissional instruction and dialogic instruction.

SOURCE: Adapted from Means (1994, p. 6).

measure students' knowledge of discrete facts or mastery of particular skills (Means, 1994). The transmissional model is the approach inherent in Mr. Billionaire's solution to the digital divide that would provide great video lectures to students the world over.

Recent efforts to improve education through a transmissional model that emphasizes higher standards and universal assessment ignore cognitive research that challenges the traditional assumptions about teaching and learning. In his controversial book, Perelman (1992) is critical of the learning that occurs in contemporary colleges and universities. He notes that assumptions about teaching and learning that undergird curricula in higher education are flawed. For example, in response to the assumption that people learn best in school, Perelman finds that most learning occurs in real-world settings, in contexts where the skill or knowledge is used. In response to the assumption that school is preparation for working in the real world, research indicates that theoretical principles learned in school do not transfer to real life. As for the view that the teacher is the fountain, and the learner is the bowl, research indicates that students become deeply engaged, more motivated, and less of a discipline problem when their learning tasks are organized as collaborative discovery projects. Finally, whereas the traditional model of pedagogy assumes that learning is solitary, research finds that not only do students master subject matter better working collaboratively, they develop better social skills and higher self-esteem. Thus, the transmissional model of learning is similar to communication models that present messages as "magic bullets" able to inoculate audience members with their messages

(DeFleur & Ball-Rokeach, 1989). The research evidence is clear: It just doesn't work that way.

Dialogic models focus on education for learner understanding through active participation, not merely the transfer of information. According to Gardner (1991), this involves the ability to grasp concepts, principles, or skills in such a way that learners can bring them to bear on new problems and situations. The assumptions underlying this model of education are that learning occurs through experience, authentic and challenging tasks, involving shared understanding among teachers and students. This model calls for teachers to situate what is to be taught in terms of the students' experiences, and together they come to mutual understanding, creating new knowledge (Freire, 1993; Jones, Valdez, Nowakowski, & Rasmussen, 1995; Marshall, 1992; Means, 1994; Richter et al., 1995).

The dialogic model places greater emphasis on the idea that learning occurs through interaction among students and teachers as opposed to the transmission of facts from teacher to students. Central to this model are learning activities. Instead of blocks of didactic instruction on separated subjects, the dialogic model emphasizes extended blocks of "authentic tasks" that cut across traditional disciplinary boundaries and take the form of theme-based projects of collaborative work (Jones et al., 1995; Marshall, 1992; Means, 1994).

Assessment for dialogic instruction is based on continuous improvement and actual performance rather than one-time mastery of facts. The roles of the learner and teacher are made more fluid as students move from being passive recipients to active explorers. Teachers move from keeper and disseminator of knowledge to facilitator, coach, and colearner.

Tishman, Jay, and Perkins (1993) call for teachers to create a "culture of thinking" in the classroom. To accomplish this, they suggest that teaching be organized around three aspects of instruction: (1) providing exemplars, (2) encouraging and orchestrating students to engage in greater interaction, and (3) direct teaching. Teaching and learning need to rely on the strengths of both learners and teachers, activities that will vary across contexts.

The dialogic model is strikingly similar to the assumptions of progressivism articulated by John Dewey. He saw education in terms of individuals' effort to study the world and acquire cumulative knowledge of meaning and values (Dewey, 1938). Such knowledge then serves as the critical data needed for intelligent living.

Dewey's philosophy is concerned with the relevance of education and developing understanding to transfer knowledge acquired in school to situations encountered in and outside of school. He places learners' activities at the center of education. He and his followers downplay standardized assessment in favor of projects "through which children could come to know their world, achieve a fuller understanding of themselves, and begin to secure a feeling for the skills and concepts that lay at the heart of formal disciplines" (Gardner, 1991, p. 193).

We suggest that assumptions about the nature of knowledge, teaching, and learning that follow transmissional models of instruction can lead to choices about technology that can potentially constrain learning. Innis (1951) demonstrates that the mechanization of education for purposes of efficient transmission of information limits creative thought.

Transforming colleges and universities into exciting learning environments where students can develop the skills to continue learning throughout their lives requires rethinking traditional assumptions about the nature of knowledge, teaching, and learning from transmissional views to those based on dialogue and shared creation of knowledge. Therefore, if the goal of technology is to use it to facilitate learning, then traditional assumptions must be challenged and decisions must be conditioned by a greater commitment to dialogic assumptions of teaching and learning.

■ CONCLUSIONS

Connected learning seems relatively young on the surface, but it is centuries old. Ever since there was a teacher with something to teach and students with a desire to learn, there was some form of communication medium supporting the effort. The dominant communication media of the time always influence knowledge distribution and the commerce of ideas.

Many consider emerging digital media to be potentially the most transformative in history. They are already changing the ways we teach and learn. They widen possibilities. However, they may facilitate or constrain, depending on the choices made by the social system.

Digital media should be adopted by higher education primarily to serve contemporary society. The arguments presented here can guide choices for facilitating learning. Just as most communication media have traditionally centered on information transmission, so education has traditionally been concerned with knowledge distribution. But digital media can facilitate a shift in the balance of power and alter the role of student to a new level of participation in the learning process.

The transformation from a transmissional model of communication to a dialogic one should be viewed as a welcome development. New forms of communication media—their technologies, markets, and policies—are breaking the monopoly of knowledge held by transmissional models that served previous economies, social systems, and technologies. This shift can invigorate future learning.

Digital platforms can revitalize an education system that hears far more criticisms than compliments, but the potential can be realized only if we replace our industrial age practices and philosophies with fresh approaches. To maximize learning through the implementation of digital communication technologies, we must develop tacit as well as explicit knowledge of their capabilities so that we can engage future learners most effectively. We can also reach larger audiences beyond the traditional classroom.

Such change will require our pluralistic journey to cope with the immediate chaos. But in addition to the fear engendered by the change, we will all be invigorated by the excitement of working on such an important enterprise.

CYBERINTERVIEW

Rick Marx

On February 21, 2001, I spoke with Rick Marx, writer and senior editor for YackInc.Com (now Yack Media Services), a Web site for entertainment news. We met at his office at 461 Fifth Ave. in New York to talk about the dot.com world, the world of cyberspace, and the future of interactive media.

Shyles: Tell us about your job at YackInc.

Marx: I'm senior editor. I am part of a team responsible for finding and identifying content, and putting it up on our Internet program guide. We have two sites. One is a teen site, called www.yacksters. com, and it features music, TV, film, games, sports, fashion, and fiction. We cover live daily events. Another site we have is geared toward a broader audience, and covers culture and learning, technology, health and family news, and so on, and that's www. yack.com. Our company is based on the syndication of media to businesses and other Web sites that want to have listings. Cable companies are our service providers. My job in particular is to identify events on the Web, be it live events such as Webcasts or concerts, or events featured in archived video and audio files such as songs or radio shows that broadcast on a certain topic, or a video from a fashion show, or clips from online games.

S: You don't tell people about events that they can go to live, like a concert where they can watch it live?

M: We do that too. For example, here's a live chat room with a group called "A-One." If we go to the main site, there are more live events. If a concert is on the Web (for example, we have the Grammy Awards here) [he clicks away]—grammy.com has some enhanced coverage not available on TV, such as chats, or some other type of activity, then we can provide it.

S: How long has your site been up?

M: About a year, and the company has been around for two years, but we've really just kicked into gear, I'd say, in the last year and a half.

S: And you started with them from the inception three years ago?

M: No. I was in the newspaper business before, as a freelancer for years. When I started with computers, my first job was as a computer operator, but I always wanted to be a writer so while I was operating computers I started doing a lot of reading and some writing on the side and I sold some things. Selling writing was addictive for me. So for many years, I was writing for a number of publications, including *Box Office Magazine*. I reviewed films, and wrote for *Film Journal* magazine, also a film publication.

S: Nonfiction?

M: Magazine stories, fiction, and screenplays. A few years ago, I had a mild shift in career; I went into newspaper reporting and then became editor of the *Record Review* and a newspaper up in northern Westchester County. We won best paper in the state four years in a row while I was there. Then I came to www.yack.com, where I've been involved in many different phases of the company as we began growing in new directions.

S: How would you categorize your company in the world of the dot.coms?

M: It's a portal site. We direct users to other people's sites. We are not a "destination site." We therefore see everyone as a partner rather than competition. Our goal is to be comprehensive in our listings and have good-quality detail.

S: You must do a lot of detective work to find places to list.

M: Yes, I have about 70 sites I'm going through, looking for content. I also work on a print guide.

S: Do you need to ask permission to have sites appear on your site?

M: Yes, we have people here who handle rights. We have an event producer networking with other sites who contacts them and discusses listing their events and getting various permissions.

S: Do you pay them a fee for the right to list them?

M: No, they pay us to be part of our network, and that way they are assured of a listing, in a certain place.

S: What criteria do you use to include a company?

M: Basically, if they have streaming content, that is, on-demand material that can be seen or heard at any time by a user, then we can include it.

S: Motion visual?

M: Right, at any time, day or night 24-7. Of course, there are a lot of Webcasts that we don't list, including obscure ones from individuals who put cameras in their homes. We look for those we believe have newsworthiness—a broader interest.

S: Are there taste and other norms involved to avoid questionable or objectionable content?

M: Yes. We self-censor. We use a group called Trust-e for such functions. They've got certain standards, sort of like Good Housekeeping, so we put them in charge of that.

S: What do you physically have to do with your computer to get that site to pop over to yours?

M: We use a hyperlink that says, "jump to event," and it takes you right to the page [he demonstrates with a click as he speaks]. Here is an event directing people to the Grammys' official Webcast. Each has its own unique code.

S: Do broadcasters have rights to the Grammys that they're upset you're taking?

M: No. We're taking users right to their sites. We don't broadcast the Grammys. They broadcast the Grammys and we just guide audiences to them. We say, "Hey, they got the Grammys on over there, go watch them."

S: On the Web, or on TV? The broadcaster is the one showing the Grammys, right?

M: Yes, but on the Grammys site there are some extra features not shown on regular TV.

S: Do you get to see how many visits there were to each of your offerings?

M: We can see where people went and where they came from.

S: And you probably want to know that.

M: Yes, but I don't have much involvement with measuring traffic and click-throughs and such. Somebody else does that.

S: How many people work with you in this company?

M: About 75 people.

S: And about three years ago?

M: Six. There was an office in Emeryville, California. We have a lot of content editors in California, and production management. Now we've expanded operations to Connecticut and New York.

S: And what do the editors do?

M: We have the categories of music, TV, sports, film. Each has an editor based in Connecticut. I'm one of the few editors actually based in New York, and we have another office located downtown.

S: So what is your workday like normally, or is it normal?

M: There's no real normal.

S: Well, what did you do in the last week each day?

M: Well, this week I've been involved in a magazine, pretty much nonstop.

S: And these are printouts of the hard copies of what will be seen on the Web?

M: Exactly. This stuff is on demand, so it doesn't go away.

S: And you're writing as well as editing?

M: Yes, I do a lot of articles on stores and work on extras as well. I'll do feature stories for each of the categories I mentioned. I'm the senior editor. I meet with people in the morning for a 45-minute session to just work out what's going to happen that day. But even more, with the Internet, people communicate through e-mail all day and night, so although we do have meetings quite frequently, there's e-mailing flying all day long.

S: So you could be here any time, any place, and you could take the work home, obviously.

M: Yes.

S: What other companies are out there doing this?

M: There's TV Guide Online, there's a company called Channel Surf, there's a company called Yahoo! Broadcast.

S: Who owns Yack?

M: It's a private company. And it's a very volatile business because things come and go very quickly. Internet businesses in general are volatile. Keeping track of content is tough because there's so much stuff coming online all the time; it's growing, exploding.

S: No matter what you do there's more of it. It's like Mickey Mouse in *The Sorcerer's Apprentice*, with the buckets of water.

M: Exactly.

S: So you just have to cope with that.

M: You have to prioritize constantly.

S: Journalism is similar to that, with deadlines.

M: Yes, but the deadlines here are not quite as crucial because it's not news. Nevertheless, the deadlines here are very real because these are events that are happening now.

S: What is your take on the future of Yack and the technology you are dealing with?

M: Well, it's not the technology so much that you're dealing with, but the space within the technology that must be very solid.

S: You mean your niche space, not cyberspace?

M: Yeah, right.

S: You mean you must offer a desired content to succeed. There must be content there that people want.

M: Right. I think it is most important to provide sensible pathways for people who enjoy what's out there.

S: So talk to me about the revenue stream for this company without giving me actual numbers. I am just interested to know how it's set up financially. I mean, you are drawing a salary, 75 other people are drawing a salary, where does all that money come from?

M: Well, as I said, we syndicate our content.

S: Talk about that.

M: Well that's not my area of expertise, but let me say we have numerous partners that pay for our services that pay a monthly or weekly fee for our listings.

S: Currently, I'm thinking of how the NASDAQ dropped 53% in the last couple months and that a lot of people got killed financially, so I'm wondering whether people here are biting their fingernails, nervous about their future.

M: I think that everybody in this business is nervous. And I've been around the block, so I realize that life is generally filled with uncertainty. My view is that what happens will happen and I'm enjoying my work now, so I'll deal with it. I try and just stay loose.

S: What changes have you seen since you started in your computer-related careers?

M: Very fast connections. There is less waiting. In addition, kids today are enthusiastic about computers. There are definite generational differences. Kids don't question whether or not they will be using computers; they just know they will be using them. Another difference between the past and now is I think that personal storage will be eventually put on the Net.

S: Any other major trends?

M: Well, I think that places like Blockbuster (videotape and DVD rental stores) will become on-demand from the Web.

S: Video dial-up?

M: We won't be walking around with tapes from Blockbuster. Instead we'll type in a code and soon get whatever movie we want.

S: What infrastructure is missing right now that will be in place to make that possible?

M: I think the fiber-optic pipe, for broad bandwidth. It will make downloading faster and better. I think it's going to become just an everyday part of our lives, much like fashion. We'll also get more interactivity in general among ourselves. One thing interesting in terms of just a psychological perspective is it could change the nature of the way we become involved in society and politics. For example, on Napster today I saw a message that said, "Contact your Congressman about Napster." Up popped a little form to write in the date to send a message to Congress. I wonder if people are still going to become involved on a personal level, say, in school issues, environmental issues.

S: You mean people may turn off as a result.

M: Yes, it's mind-boggling what the effects may turn out to be.

S: Do you think magazines will stay paper?

M: For a while. I think that they'll probably go to a mock paper that will be on the computer. The *New York Times* is now a facsimile edition on the Web.

S: I look at it every morning.

M: In the future, the aesthetics of the Internet will become more sophisticated as more people get online. Programming languages are becoming accessible to more users. People are not going to be satisfied with just a plain HTML (Hypertext Markup Language) page. And as we get more cameras in the home it will certainly be a lot easier to engage in multimedia from the home.

S: So if users tune in to your Web site, they will get a listing of all the online activities that you mentioned. But as the technology stands today, generally speaking, who can take advantage of your offerings in the fullest way?

M: I would say music lovers have the best advantage because there's so much availability of music and concerts. In addition, there are events that are streamed and Webcast. Sports has made some leaps, but they have a ways to go.

S: Are you happy with the Napster-type services? Or in your view is their action a copyright infringement?

M: I think Napster and other such sites should be free. It's a great place to set up a line of music and find out about others. I don't think that it would hinder me from buying a CD.

S: And would you then generalize that to include Olympics video and things like that? You know, everyone should be able to watch everything for free?

M: Not everything, but I think that samples of songs from a CD is OK. I realize that people are downloading entire CDs. I am impressed with the European concept of putting a tariff on electronic parts to pay for creative works, and companies that create content like record companies and broadcasters.

S: Do you ultimately see TV as it is today disappearing into the computer?

M: Yes, but when it will happen is still unclear. I would say probably not quite as fast we think, probably 2010, 2012. I think that it will happen, but it will happen kind of slowly. I must say I like the concept of convergence and I like the concept of bringing people around the world together in terms of the events, be it entertainment, music, sports, or whatever.

S: I always like to ask people about their own comfort level regarding privacy and security. Do you use, say, your credit card on the Internet?

M: Yes. But you should know that long before the Internet, I had a mixup where somebody else used my social security number and I had a hell of a time getting that straightened out. That's just something that can happen. There have been some charges on my credit card, and I didn't know what it was and I had to go through it. Apparently, some computer just put it up there and they just took it off of my bill. It happens. Somebody can reach into a garbage can and pull out a credit card slip and steal your credit card number.

S: Right. In education there is now something called distance education, and I am just wondering—

M: It's huge—the university without walls. It's inevitable. What a great way to expose kids to a professor or a class that they may not otherwise be able to enjoy. The question is will people still do the job with students that they have to do to give them knowledge. There's no doubt distance education has a lot of potential. I would like to see how it actually functions in a real-world environment. For example, I wouldn't like my son to go to a high school like that.

S: Why not?

M: Because I think that he needs the society. That is, we need to maintain our humanity and our emotions, and yet at the same time utilize the tools that are available to us through the Internet. There are times to stare at the screen, and times to be involved with humanity, forming connections with others through the face-to-face interaction.

S: We need both.

M: Eventually, perhaps, here's where we're going: One day, we may be able to disassociate from our bodies and support our brains isolated in some sort of a chamber or something, and we'll be able to manipulate our needs and get a sense of pleasure and sense of delight from—

S: From electrodes?

M: Whatever it is, electrodes, and you know that could be where we're going.

S: I don't want that.

M: Well, that's the business I'm going into.

S: With virtual helmets?

M: We won't need helmets.

S: I think this is a good place to stop.

M: Slowly entering the realm of fantasy?

S: Yes. Thank you, Rick.

M: All right, Len.

CHAPTER 7

ADOPTING INSTRUCTIONAL TECHNOLOGIES

Judy C. Pearson

Today, in a time of unprecedented change, our challenge is to tap that energy and creativity to transform institutions . . . into entirely new paradigms. We must respond to the rapidly evolving needs of numerous and diverse stakeholders, question existing premises and arrangements, and eliminate unnecessary processes and administrative structures. Administrators should work together to provide an environment in which change is regarded not as threatening but rather as an exhilarating opportunity.

— James J. Duderstadt, President Emeritus
and Professor of Science and Engineering
at the University of Michigan (2000, p. B6)

In a world of increasingly rapid change in technology developments, what strategies can administrators use to select the most effective instructional technologies (IT) for their workplace? Adult learners, vocational trainees, and people with disabilities or without transportation particularly welcome

IT for its ability to extend opportunities as never before. Because of the potential democratization of knowledge, distance learning may well be one of the most profound outcomes that telecommunication technology can provide. However, IT presents problems in policies and practices.

Because the challenges and promises of IT adoption are highly varied, it is useful to outline the strongest critiques that have been offered as well as the most honorific goals. Readers familiar with IT issues can consider the principles presented here and reformulate them to fit their own organizational needs. The goals of this chapter are to demystify the administrative perspective on digital technology and to help future administrators make informed choices in selecting IT systems.[1]

■ BRIEF OVERVIEW

Distance education is not new. Since the 19th century, American distance education has been present in the form of correspondence courses. In 1896, the International Correspondence Schools in Scranton, Pennsylvania, offered one of the first correspondence courses to coal miners residing in outlying areas who were unable to attend classroom lectures. In the 1940s and 1950s, the advent of television made possible educational television programs. Courses have been offered at a distance through the mail, radio, television, video, and more recently, CD-ROM. Today, students in remote locations can regularly receive instruction through audio, video, and computer technologies.

IT is of particular interest today because of the possibilities brought on by the development of the Internet and the World Wide Web. Web-based content can be accessed asynchronously in any location in the world where connectivity and computers are available; in many places, synchronous capability is fast developing.

Definitions and Distinctions

IT is better understood when terms are well defined. For example, IT today features synchronous transmissions of video programs delivered live via satellite and, more recently, live teleconferences and real-time global-computer networking.

IT can be classified into forms that are *transmissional* or *dialogic*. Transmissional technologies engage users in noninteractive modalities such as watching television or listening to the radio. Common forms of transmissional education include audio- and videotapes, cable or satellite broadcasts, and online databases and reference tools (i.e., CD-ROMs and DVDs). The advantages of transmissional technologies are that they are familiar to people and widely available in people's homes; they are therefore perceived as user friendly. Such information is often available at a convenient location. However, such materials do have some obvious limitations. Disadvantages include that they allow no group interaction; users can neither ask nor answer questions, nor be provided with feedback.

By contrast, dialogic modalities allow for interaction with the material and between people. Common examples include the telephone and the teleconference; of course, audio and video presentations may all enhance the process. At this writing, the array of technologies used to disseminate such materials includes teleconferences, voice mail, cable and satellite television, point-to-point microwave radio communication, electronic blackboards, computer instruction, and more recently, computer-mediated communication such as e-mail, bulletin boards, and computer instant messaging and conferencing.

The advantages of dialogic over transmissional systems are clear: They allow interaction and feedback. A downside is that they are perceived as more complicated to use; they are also viewed as inconvenient because currently, people generally are required to be in a special location at a specific time to use them. Dialogic technologies are also generally more expensive than transmissional systems.

Dialogic systems can be further subdivided into those that are *synchronous*—the interaction takes place at the same time—or *asynchronous*—interaction may take place at different times and at users' convenience. For example, synchronous systems are typified by the telephone or the interactive audio or video teleconference. Asynchronous systems include voice mail and e-mail.

It is not wise to oversimplify the communication aspects of a technology. Dialogues and monologues are, in fact, human communication conventions, and technologies that enable such complex communication to occur over great distances are worthy of careful attention. We can understand the phenomenon it helps create in terms of persuasion, entertainment, or education, or some combination of these activities or processes, potentially in all settings, not just educational ones. Therefore, technologies can be maximized in their effectiveness when understood in terms of where they fit in the communication continuum, not only in terms of their setting or their technical qualities. Individual technologies may be placed on a continuum based on the extent to which each exhibits the following seven capabilities: (1) immediacy of response, (2) nonsequential access of information, (3) adaptability, (4) feedback, (5) multiple options, (6) bidirectional communication, and (7) interruptability.

Using this approach, communication need not be face-to-face to be interactive; indeed, even in person a large auditorium (familiar to many of us) is frequently not very interactive. Audiotape, which frequently features monologues, allows some immediacy of response, nonsequential access, and interruptability. It seems well advised to keep this continuum in mind as we consider Web-based and online interaction.

Web-Based Content

The development of the World Wide Web allows users to create electronic visual displays devoted specifically to serving particular needs. Web pages typically feature text, instruction, articles, and pictorial information with highly varied subject matter. Users can communicate with each other in a variety of ways. Software programs simplify the creation of Web-based content, eliminating the need to learn HTML (Hypertext Markup Language) code. Examples of such programs include WebCT, developed by a computer science faculty member at the University of British Columbia, and TopClass, which is used to create online instructional material and corporate training programs. TopClass was chosen by *PCWeek Magazine* as the best such Web-training tool. CourseInfo, a commercial product created by two graduates of Cornell University, is entirely Web based.

Online Interaction

Users can access online materials featuring both synchronous and/or asynchronous interaction. Online discussions may supplement, extend, or replace face-to-face discussions. Asynchronous discussions are frequently conducted through listserv software, Internet-based newsgroups, or other PC-based software such as Lotus Notes. Synchronous or real-time discussions may occur in a variety of local, national, and international environments, such as Internet relay chat, which uses the Internet to communicate with distant partners; MUDs (multiuser domains), MOOs (multiuser domains, object oriented), or MUSHs (multiuser shared hallucinations).[2] Platforms such as these enable users to present themselves in fictional contexts with pseudonymous identities. The Caucus system enables chats through networked personal computers and desktop PC networks when they can send and receive messages from other computers over the public switched telephone network (PSTN) via a modem.

Contemporary Developments and Current Use

Rationales for using IT center on the need to make content accessible to those who, because of time and/or geographic constraints, are unable to go to an actual physical location to receive materials. Demographic shifts and increasing pressure to provide workers with lifetime learning have generated new markets for IT instruction. Advancements in technology and the development of excellent programs have in some cases provided solutions to these constraints. For example, satellite downlinks, video conferencing, and Web-based content featuring desktop delivery now allow users to receive materials at home, at work, and at other locations. Thus, developments in IT, in general, have begun to offer more opportunities to access information in a wider variety of formats than ever before.

Thanks to digital telecommunication technologies, IT is flourishing. Some institutions, such as the for-profit University of Phoenix, currently offer entire curricula through such new technologies. Other institutions such as Western Governors University, which began operation in the fall of 1998, exist as "virtual universities" with no physical campus. They rely heavily on the use of computing technology to deliver interactive content. The Southern Regional Education Board's (SREB) Electronic Campus is really not a university at all but rather a directory of online courses offered by member states generally located in the southern United States.

In addition, huge increases in the use of IT may be found around the globe. For example, China Central Radio and Television University currently enrolls 3 million students; the British Open University currently boasts 215,000 students; and the University of South Africa has 120,000 students. Smaller facilities serve the same purpose in Asia, Europe, and South America at all levels, offering remedial courses, graduate courses, and professional certifications, all available on the Web.

The number of institutions offering distance education is growing at an impressive rate. For example, the National Center for Education Statistics (NCES, 1997) reports that in the fall of 1995, approximately a third of the higher education institutions offered distance education courses and another quarter had plans to do so within the next three years. By contrast, 42% neither had offered such courses nor had any plans to do so. However, in only two years, the NCES (1998) documented that 76% of institutions with 10,000 or more students and 61% of institutions enrolling between 3,000 to 10,000 students offered distance education courses in 1997. At the end of the academic year 1997-1998, 78% of public four-year schools and 62% of public two-year schools offered distance education courses. Enrollments in credit-granting college-level courses stood at 1,363,670 and a total of 54,470 courses were offered, mostly in college-level, credit-granting courses (NCES, 1999).

ASSESSING THE IMPACT OF INSTRUCTIONAL TECHNOLOGIES ■

Technology Can Improve Quality and Control Costs

One key rationale for IT adoption is to provide access, but institutions adopt technology for other reasons. Stephen Ehrmann (1995), from the American Association of Higher Education, writes that institutions are trying to solve a triple challenge: "to improve certain unsatisfactory educational outcomes, extend access to older and more diverse learners, and control spiraling costs" (p. 41).

For administrators, it is clear that the extension of access and the corresponding potential for new institutional income generally trumps other rationales. Whereas early adopters of IT often appreciate what they perceive to be more satisfactory outcomes, later adopters show concern for the greater investment of time and question the instructional benefits. In some cases, workers affected by the introduction of IT into the workplace fear they will be usurped and replaced by machines. Some users bemoan the greater responsibility that technology places on them to initiate and master new technologies but are grateful for the asynchronous quality that allows them to choose the most convenient times and places for using them.

In higher education, Duderstadt sees nine different models of the university emerging as a result of IT.[3] One of them is the *Cyberspace University*. Citing the University of California at Los Angeles (UCLA) and the for-profit University of Phoenix, he writes that such institutions are "well on their way to becoming 'knowledge servers,' linked into a vast information network, providing their services to whoever might request them." He adds, "As distributed virtual environments become more common, we might even conceive of a time when the classroom experience itself becomes a commodity, provided to anyone, anywhere, anytime—for a price" (Duderstadt, 2000, p. B6).

William Draves, president of the Learning Resources Network, a distance-learning industry group (retrieved from http://www.lern.org), predicts that online classes will replace traditional lecture courses and will enroll as many as 1,000 students per class within the next 20 years ("Distance-Learning Forecast," 1999). As a proponent of distance education, Draves believes that such large classes allow students increasing interaction with others. However, many faculty members on traditional residential campuses disagree with the view that mega-classes are advantageous, suggesting that interactions will be in a more brittle, limited channel, narrower than a classroom setting might allow.

From an institutional perspective, sprinkling some large classes within a degree program offers clear economic advantages and may not necessarily be harmful to students. Students will eventually learn to interact with large numbers of classmates technologically. On the other hand, although the "technologizing" of education has its advantages, it may not be effective to conduct an entire academic program that way. The nature of the subject matter, the importance of face-to-face communication, and opportunities for immediate and same-time feedback all affect the desirability of such a model in specific disciplines. For example, IT may fit better in disciplines such as engineering, math, and science than in fine arts and humanities where answers may not be so clear-cut.

Community colleges have also become more active in distance education. Carr (1999) writes, "Although most community colleges were created to think and act locally, increasing numbers are finding a niche in the global realm of distance education" (p. A37). Some community colleges in a number of states have joined with other four-year public universities to create consortia. For example, community colleges have been players in both the Southern Regional Electronic Campus and in Western Governors University. Three community colleges joined a group of four-year public universities in Massachusetts in 1999 to create a distance-learning consortium. Many four-year schools have increasingly come to rely on community colleges to provide basic requirements in a variety of agreements.

Some futurists urge caution about the changes brought by IT. The Association of Governing Boards forecasts that one third of the current independent American colleges and universities will close within the next decade. Dunn (2000) calculates that 10% of public colleges and universities and 50% of independent colleges will close their doors in the next quarter century because of changes brought about by digital telecommunication technology. Of course, neither the number nor the percentage of campuses that will close is known, but traditional institutions are facing stiff competition from IT providers, a number of which come from the corporate sector.

Dunn (2000) adds that almost all colleges and universities will be reshaped and reframed in radical ways because of the digital revolution. Whereas the number of degree-granting institutions may grow, traditional campuses may decline in number. Corporate software manufacturers will bypass some educational institutions and sell products directly to end users. Courseware applications will be available by 2005 for the 25 college courses that enroll 50% of all students. It seems likely that the higher education market will grow for adults seeking additional certifications throughout their careers.

Dunn (2000) forecasts that many distinctions that now exist will diminish or become fuzzy. For example, distance and local education will be less distinguishable as digital enhancements are introduced. High school, undergraduate, and graduate school lines will blur as students move through their programs at different rates. Distinctions among for-profit, nonprofit, public, and private institutions will eventually disappear.

Criticisms of IT

Some of the above trends are sobering to stakeholders. Not all institutions and businesses eagerly promote IT. Prohibitive costs, negative effects on training, poor comparison with traditional face-to-face experience, increased inequities among groups of people, inappropriate applications for some content, additional administrative burden, negative political or economic impact, and the usurpation of entrenched interests by outsiders are among the most oft-cited concerns.

Ehrmann (1997) explains that one unanswered question concerning the onslaught of the IT culture is the cost of digital databases compared to that of the traditional face-to-face setting. Unfortunately, such costs are difficult to assess. Global generalizations about cost are virtually meaningless for a number of reasons. Ehrmann (1997) writes,

> Howard Bowen, a noted economist . . . found that institutions . . . each raise all the money they can, spend all they get, and spend it in ways that relate closely to the way they spent the money last year. His 1980 study found little relationship in patterns of spending even among institutions that appeared on the surface quite similar. They spent rather different amounts . . . and they spent each dollar differently.

In agreement with Bowen, Ehrmann notes that determining costs is difficult due to different accounting methods from institution to institution and from situation to situation. In addition, the constant development of new and emerging technologies (with new and emerging price tags) makes calculations even more difficult in determining the cost of IT.

Although many administrators wish to adopt IT in part to offset spiraling costs, it is becoming clear that adopting IT systems can be expensive. In the past decade, we have seen that IT is not necessarily an inexpensive way to offer a program. For example, the California Virtual University (CVU), founded by the California Board of Regents in 1997, was closed in the spring of 1999 because it ran out of money. Peek (2000) observes, "Among many of its ambitious plans, CVU had planned to open the world's largest school of library and information studies. It has been reborn as the California Virtual Campus, serving as a gateway to courses offered within the California higher education system" (p. 30). Although the vision was substantial, the budget was quickly spent.

Similarly, the Western Governors University, a virtual university including 40 colleges and universities from 22 states, plus a university in Canada and another in Guam, illustrate that expectations for thousands of virtual learners may not be guaranteed simply because new distance media are employed. In the first year, only 12 students enrolled. In 2000, that number increased to 200, a disappointment after $13 million of expenditures. Thus, huge startup costs have proven to be a tremendous barrier. Average costs per user in the first years of operation often cripple projects.

On traditional campuses, costs for adding IT are also substantial. The experience at Virginia Tech is illustrative. The university began a university-wide program to integrate instructional technology in 1993. The effort was complemented by an investment in faculty known as the Faculty Development Institute (FDI), which provided faculty members an opportunity to integrate instructional technology in their courses. Participants received multimedia computers and high-speed network connections.

In a 1998 study conducted by California State University, comparative costs were identified. Combining the costs for the FDI, course conversions, and workstations, and assuming enrollment between 100 and 200 per term, costs were estimated to be $4,200 to $6,000 (roughly $30 to $42 per user assuming an enrollment of 140 per course). If one quarter of all courses were taken this way, the cost per student would increase to roughly $331 to $465. If one quarter of the courses were so transformed, the cost to the institution was estimated to be an additional $1.7 to $2.4 million per year. These estimates were conservative because they were based on courses with enrollments between 100 and 200 per term. Of course, as class size decreases, cost per user increases.[4]

On a per-course basis, some educators now realize that IT is not necessarily less expensive than traditional schooling. In short, good IT courses can cost more to plan and design than traditional classes. Hardware, software, and training for users add significantly to the overall bill, especially in the short term. However, once designed, such courses can handle large volumes of students, and in the long run, costs do diminish, coming more in line with the cost of traditional approaches.

Costs are also affected by rapid changes in technology; keeping current adds cost. For example, Internet II is a collaborative effort among a number of universities to go beyond the problems associated with current technology. The cost for membership dues for the 160 higher education members who belong to the consortium is $25,000 per year. In addition, each institution must upgrade the infrastructure, a cost estimated at $500,000 per year (Peek, 2000).

Some believe traditional institutions are the likely leaders in IT because they are seen as most able to absorb these additional costs; newly emerging distance organizations are showing early signs of fiscal insolvency and may not be able to supplant entrenched universities. It seems technology may ultimately become just another set of expenses for established institutions.

Effectiveness of IT

A second reason many administrators initially tend to embrace technology is to improve learning. Indeed, some proponents are so eager to adopt technology that they do not concern themselves with how they will use it. Ehrmann (1997) suggests that here may be another area of faulty comparison. He notes that teaching is a highly variable activity that often eludes categorization. That is, we simply do not know what criteria should be used for measuring, comparing, and validating effectiveness of IT programs. Furthermore, even "traditional" courses today often include digitized elements, which may or may not be considered part of IT.

Ehrmann (1997) paraphrases a talk given by Roxanne Hiltz, Distinguished Professor of Computer and Information Science at the New Jersey Institute of Technology, who reported on the early use of computer conferencing:

> I've got two pieces of bad news about the experimental English . . . course where students used computer conferencing. The first bad news is that . . . the experimental group showed no progress in their ability. The second . . . is that the control group, taught by traditional methods, showed no progress either.

This anecdote suggests that students may learn equally badly (or well) in both traditional courses and in those "enhanced" with technology. Some research on individual classes suggests that better learning outcomes accrue in courses that include digitized elements, but the jury is still out in terms of universal generalizations. Until we have comprehensive longitudinal data that examine new systems, we will not have clear answers. How should the efficacy of IT material be assessed? One way is to determine how successfully the material was before being digitized, and then compare outcomes in each condition.

Some theorists recommend replacing entirely the current model of learning that focuses on the transmission of information from one person to another with an interactive model of information sharing among users (Bork, 1999). The goal of such a change is to render learning more active as it is in a one-to-one situation with, say, a student and a private tutor. Furthermore, such instruction could be customized, capitalizing on some of the IT system's dialogic capabilities.

For Bork (1999), effective learning is highly interactive and should include a number of elements, many possible to varying degrees through IT. First, interaction should be frequent, such that whether students are learning in face-to-face settings or on computers, interaction occurs often—with students engaged in meaningful communication. Second, it seems desirable that the quality of interaction with computers should approach that of a human conversation. Such interaction might include the ability to give and receive feedback, to understand intent as well as content, and to understand paralinguistic elements of the "conversation." Third, long-range memory (highly possible with computer-based IT systems) is essential. Computers, like good human tutors, could be made able to recall both the learning styles and the past errors of particular students, and use that information to maximize student progress. Of course, whereas not all human teachers have the capacity for empathy, current courseware is even less attuned to such capability. But that may change.

From an economic perspective, providing learning via IT with high-quality individualized feedback is probably more expensive than is transmissional instruction featuring content that does not vary based on the audience and does not include feedback or any corresponding adjustments. By contrast, dialogic models focusing on individual learners through feedback procedures and multiple learning paths can benefit users, but may presently be beyond the economic reach of most individual institutions and perhaps even state governments. Therefore, for distance learning to develop and lead to positive outcomes along more elaborate lines, larger groups may need to unite to provide sufficient funding.

The United Nations and other international consortia need to lead the way in such endeavors. Regardless of the funding for IT developments, assessment of developing technologies is critical. We must develop valid comparisons across multiple methods to justify to funding agents the value of IT programs.

IT Versus Traditional Face-to-Face Settings

Distance learning critics often say that traditional educational experience including learning to share a room in a residence hall, meeting people from diverse cultures, communicating face-to-face, forging friendships and social relationships, and interacting in multiple situations in face-to-face real-time encounters simply cannot be simulated online.

Currently, few would argue with this view. People who rely solely on distance education clearly lose the richness of interpersonal experiences. Students educated at elite colleges and universities may be especially concerned about the loss of campus life. Undergraduate experience is more than the absorption of information. It is also interaction and the chance to dialogue with colleagues and peers, and to engage in the full gamut of extracurricular activities, such as sports and socializing, both on and off campus.

Many say that distance education can even lead to feelings of isolation and loneliness. In the fall of 1999, Supreme Court Justice Ruth Bader Ginsburg made this point. She focused on a program offered by Concord University Law School when she said, "I am troubled by venues like Concord, where a student can get a JD . . . without ever laying eyes on a fellow student or professor. We should strive to ensure that the Internet remain a device for bringing people together and does not become a force for isolation" (reported in Peek, 2000, p. 30).

Potential Inequities

Another concern is that IT may increase the divide between those who can afford to move to a campus and receive a traditional education, and those who cannot, and therefore must select distance options. If IT options are hardly better than no learning at all, as some maintain, they may be viewed "as an educational Band-Aid for underserved populations" (Peek, 2000, p. 30).

On the other hand, IT proponents declare how new technologies are "democratizing" education as never before by making curricula available to thousands who cannot now get to the nation's elite libraries. But computers may not be available to all. Hence, some people may remain disadvantaged. Ray Steele, former president of the nonprofit U.S. Distance Learning Association, notes,

> The Internet has grown phenomenally, but I think that folks get carried away when they assume that everyone is on the Internet and everything can be sent via the Internet, because they haven't looked at the numbers. Internet growth is tremendous, but you still have to look at how many houses have network-capable computing devices and how many houses are on services or [Internet service providers] so that they can actually participate. (reported in Carr, 2000b, p. A50)

IT's "Fit"

As mentioned, IT may not be equally appropriate for all subject matter and all learners. Currently, the Internet appears less desirable when face-to-face interaction, immediate feedback, and visual and other nonverbal cues are essential. This is especially relevant in situations requiring meeting management, small group process, and team building, for example, which appear to be more appropriate when done in traditional settings.

As for differences across individuals, the Internet appears most appropriate for those who are highly motivated and disciplined. Just as the microwave oven took its place in kitchens next to the conventional oven, not in place of it, IT applications might play an increasing role in education, but they probably will not replace all synchronous face-to-face learning any time soon.

Administrative challenges suffuse IT adoption, particularly when institutions become part of consortia. Articulation agreements, financial aid policies, library privileges, intellectual property[5] issues, and workloads and rewards head the list.

Both workers and administrators fear changes created by IT. In-house workers responsible for creating online content frequently spend significantly more time preparing materials than they had originally imagined would be needed. They worry about time taken away from other activities and the potential negative impact this could have on how they are evaluated.

Economic and Political Impact

Higher education has traditionally enjoyed a great deal of autonomy and freedom. Today, however, its institutions are under greater pressure than ever from business and industry as globalization and economic development have sharply increased demand for special training and nontraditional programs. Corporate sector IT programs have also begun to present new forms of competition. Business leaders now lobby higher education for "just in time" online courses, requesting that they be provided at lower cost than traditional classes. Business leaders argue that their industries require reduced training costs, available around the clock, to lower travel costs in both time and money (Garcia, 2000; Mottl, 2000; Yager, 2000).

Some institutions have therefore created partnerships with industry organizations to provide corporations with courses that meet these requirements. However, serious consequences arise from allowing corporate needs to drive IT developments. For example, the speed at which industry expects course development and delivery may lead to low-quality product.

Clearly, industry partners are results oriented. But for administrators, it is critical to avoid the mistake of adopting solutions that may be at odds with the needs of individual partnership members. For example, college professors are accustomed to a slow pace for course development. Curriculum committees, faculty senates, and other bodies approve courses after a long deliberative process. By contrast, people in industry have little patience for such efforts and demand immediate course development to serve their needs. In short, there is a basic lack of fit between these two worlds.

One way for administrators to bridge the policy gap and temporal chasm between these two worlds is to create an advisory board of carefully selected chief executive officers (CEOs) and educators who could meet, develop a relationship, and begin to understand each other's views and needs, and how their views and needs are conditioned. Then, mutually beneficial procedures and programs could be formed for adopting successful IT. Administrators, in such instances, should act as facilitators, taking care not to be identified too closely with either side.

Corporate partners can offer many advantages, including equipment, space, personnel, and funding. However, they can also become too demanding and can wind up exercising too much control and influence. Many businesspeople forget the goals beyond the bottom line that may be critical to educators.

Of course, even business leaders are not necessarily motivated only by the bottom line. VEP Computer Systems, Inc. president Vincent Pascale serves as an example. Pascale runs his company, at least in part, "for the good of society." VEP works with adaptive technologies—tools and devices that allow disabled persons to work productively with technology. Among the products developed by VEP are speech recognition products and video magnification screens (Forman, 2000).

Political leaders, too, have joined forces to encourage IT in business-education partnerships. Indeed, the governors of several western states started the Western Governors University. When Tom Ridge was serving as Pennsylvania's governor, he demonstrated that he was both pro-business and pro-education. As governor, he emphasized the importance of technology in reinvigorating his state. Ridge brought together the major universities in Pennsylvania to create the Digital Greenhouse, which serves to "commercialize" intellectual ideas and products (Gruman, 2000).

When educational institutions do not adapt quickly enough to changing educational needs, business and industry sometimes step in to provide their own IT programs. The lack of response from the education sector was the impetus for one such industry venture. Arcadio, a Seattle, Washington, start-up, hopes to become "a one-stop learning shop, the Yellow Pages of Erudition" (Hillis, 2000). Steve Sperry, its founder, proposes a Web-based classroom registration system where users can sign up for virtually any class they desire. He sees his venture as similar to a travel agency that helps customers buy airline tickets. Sperry notes that educational institutions are brick-and-mortar companies, for the most part, and are therefore not very strong on the e-commerce side.

Nicholas Negroponte, cofounder and director of the MIT Media Laboratory and Professor of Media Technology at Massachusetts Institute of Technology, argues that people can recognize and purchase superior products, including educational courseware, and will shop online for them.[6] This idea has implications for higher education. If the college experience is sought out for its social aspects, students will continue to come to campus. But if distance education comes to be perceived as a source of desired information that is as good as or superior to that which is found in more traditional settings, students may increasingly rely on digitized education.

Information technology vendors can also make big profits as educational institutions spend more on IT products and services. The International Data Corporation (IDC, www.idc.com) reports that U.S. higher education institutions spent $3.1 billion on such products and services in 1998 and will probably spend $5 billion by the year 2003 ("IT Spending," 1999). Hence, sharp competition for students will likely encourage colleges and universities to maintain an attractive and up-to-date technology environment. At the same time, institutions will make unwise decisions if they simply acquire the flashiest toys or those that appeal to the current vogue.

■ THE PROMISE OF INSTRUCTIONAL TECHNOLOGIES

Telecommunication technology providers and users make proud promises about the future of digitized education, suggesting that IT will eventually force a rethinking of the very notions of teaching and learning. They tout the democratizing effects of IT in reducing inequalities across gender, race, and income levels while making educational opportunities available to the disabled as never before. In short, one of the potential promises of the digitizing of education is the reform of the entire educational system for the general good.

Higher education, through the use of IT, can reach intended objectives: to teach more efficiently, reach additional students, and transform education. But technological developments also invariably have unintended impacts on institutional philosophy, accountability, and the way workers use their time. In short, IT adoptions influence the texture of the entire workplace.

In acquiring IT products, therefore, administrators should emphasize the importance of clarifying specific objectives as the motives for adoption. The intentionality of the implementation is paramount in the adoption decision. Users, for the most part, tend to be persuaded to adopt new products and practices based on their efficacy in light of the relevant issues present at the time. The adoption process itself is conditioned by the very discussion and the perceived needs of the stakeholders.

It is helpful if users focus on objectives, not on media, because a variety of media may be useful in achieving the same outcomes. For example, discussions can occur face-to-face, synchronously in a chat on the Web, asynchronously on an online bulletin board, or in a teleconference. A case study can be presented in person, via e-mail, or on videotape. Arguments can be presented orally, as e-mail attachments, or via Web pages. Hence, it is a mistake to believe that adopting a specific application is the only way to achieve a given objective.

It is important not to be seduced by the "gee whiz" aspects of new technologies. It is an all-too-common mistake to become enamored with technology for its own sake. Furthermore, missteps or software crashes can occur with any technology, even those that offer exciting, efficient, and often visually appealing material, but they can also be disappointing if they are adopted only for their novelty and emotional charge.

In adopting IT for an organization, administrators should therefore begin with two basic questions: "Which objectives are best?" and "What technologies will best support those goals?" Computer-based content may be useful for some kinds of subject matter, but not all. For example, if users are learning material for which questions admit of only one correct answer (e.g., mathematics, chemistry, or even car repair), computer-based tutorials may be highly effective. However, more ambiguous content may require different treatment, including human interaction or judgment. Such material may require different technology or the same technology used differently. Therefore, administrators must assess multiple methods and alternative technologies in their decisions.

IT Increases Reach

Several past developments in the United States have led to greater democratization of knowledge. For example, the First Morrill Act of July 2, 1862, donated public land to several states and territories for creating colleges for agriculture and mechanic arts. These provided opportunities for tens of thousands of people in rural areas to attend college for the first time.

Later, the Servicemen's Readjustment Act of 1944 (popularly known as the G.I. Bill) allowed U.S. military service veterans to attend college. Additional federal legislation created a comprehensive package of benefits, including financial assistance for higher education available to men and women. As a result of these programs, college and university enrollments swelled following World War II. Further federal legislation extended these benefits to veterans of more recent wars. Such legislation provided opportunities for populations not yet reached to receive an education.

Today, IT provides educational opportunities to people all over the world, including those formerly disenfranchised because of geographic immobility or economic disadvantages among other reasons. The opportunities made possible by the Morrill Land Grant Act and the Servicemen's Readjustment Act may pale in comparison to the potential effects of the Internet, which can literally change the world as it changes the meaning of such words as *student, teacher, learning,* and *education*.

Of particular promise is the ability of IT to deliver information to geographically isolated areas of the world. In South Africa, for example, the Gauteng and Environs Library Consortium (GAELIC) provides access to vast library holdings to consortium members in both large, well-established libraries, and in smaller, more remote, and historically disadvantaged institutions. Thus, the cooperative nature of GAELIC has overcome historically significant disparities for the first time (Edwards, 1999).

In the United States, IT has begun blurring the lines between educational institutions, yielding positive benefits. For example, some universities are now able to provide opportunities for students to begin coursework before graduating from high school while they are still in their own hometowns. One example is the Medina Project, which allows high school students to take classes at the University of Akron (Ohio) through distance learning. Eligible juniors and seniors can take undergraduate courses from the University of Akron for college credit; the Medina Project also provides opportunities for team teaching among the high school teachers and generates broadcasts of undergraduate- and graduate-level classes and seminars, which are made available to area residents in a number of nontraditional classroom settings. In such cases, all participants are winners.

Distance education also opens markets to nontraditional students. These include the homebound, busy midlife adults who want new careers but must have additional certifications to make the transition, retirees who want to continue learning over their lifetimes, and even young geniuses who want to begin higher education as children. Students at Virginia Tech who moved to campus because they wanted to enjoy the pleasures of campus life—beautiful surroundings, sports activities, fine arts and cultural events, and socializing—often enrolled in online classes. Their explanation? They did not want their academic schedules to interfere with extracurricular activities. Thus, IT reduces barriers to education including those of time and place, increasing convenience for users, and increasing the number of learners previously unserved.

IT Reduces Gender, Race, and Disability Bias

Unintended effects result from IT. Although people may not speak voice-to-voice or have visual access to each other (a situation viewed as a detriment to communication assuming that a great percentage of accuracy in communication occurs through nonverbal channels), nevertheless positive advantages accrue. For example, students who normally report bias in their interactions with others in traditional face-to-face settings report that their gender, race, ethnicity, attractiveness, class, or disability are no longer factors in the distance education setting.

CHALLENGES FACING ADMINISTRATORS ■

Given the immense breadth of the digital telecommunication revolution, how should administrators proceed in adopting IT for their organizations? Some principles are about philosophy; others derive from issues of utility and desirability of particular technologies. Still others derive from considering the effectiveness and integration of technologies depending on the immediate needs and circumstances that exist in the organization.

Improve Organizational Goals

Technology should be considered for adoption primarily to further the goals of the organization. For example, in the field of education, IT adoption should foster understanding and integration of course content; systems should not be acquired as ends in themselves. Trendiness should never cloud adoption decisions.

The decision to adopt a new system should be primarily based on a valid assessment of its value for meeting the needs of the organization, not primarily on perceptions of administrators of cost savings in selecting one system over another. Misperceptions of technology "savings" can include time considerations (because ironically more time is frequently needed to integrate technology during the early stages of adoption), cost per user (technology obsolescence means periodic and expensive reinvestment), and overestimation of acceptance (some users still use their CD-ROM drives as cup holders!). For these reasons, valid assessment in terms of goals is critical.

How best to adopt and use technology in the service of organizational objectives is a multivariate challenge represented by many stakeholders: primary users, administrators, managers, owners, and others. Multiple perspectives alter efficacy assessment, usually for the better. Some want to deploy technology to accomplish traditional objectives; others are more interested in making dramatic adaptations and creating new objectives. Often goals create cross pressures.

As the Boyer Commission on Educating Undergraduates (1998) notes, IT promotes situations where users can "explore deeply as well as widely, with which they can discriminate, analyze, and create rather than simply accumulate." In short, users become active participants in their work, not passive receivers. Hence, discovering and adopting IT systems that best serve the organization require monitoring and rigorous testing over time. Needs change; therefore, adopted IT systems need periodically to be readapted to new functions.

Reflect Strategic Vision

IT systems must also be consistent with both the institutional mission and its market. Overall motives for adoptions and/or upgrades should be clearly articulated in a vision statement developed through collective input. Ownership of the goals and vision for major changes is critical for effective implementation and long-term commitment. Involving administrators, staff members, and users early and throughout the development process can resolve many difficulties before they arise (Costello, 1997; for an example of an extended vision process, see Chrisman & Holliday, 1996).

Organization members are often suspicious of IT systems if they perceive them to be imposed by outside forces. Across the country, IT has often been championed by politicians who understand its popularity among taxpayers, especially in the context of higher education. Information technology companies who see large markets for their wares, and university administrators who hope it will save money, also tout new systems for the wrong motives. But external agents do not generate successful adoptions; rather, it is critical that administrators engage potential users in meaningful debate to determine how best to integrate new tools into their organizations.

Such deliberation can be varied depending on organizational culture. On one highly technical campus, traditional face-to-face strategic planning sessions were conducted with all of the stakeholders—advisory board members, administrators, faculty, staff, and students. The planning was methodical and extended over an entire academic year. Resulting documents were carefully crafted for consistency, logic, accuracy, and fiscal affordability.

On another campus, using external funding, the faculty engaged in seminars and luncheons over a two-year period. External experts and local "early adopters" made detailed presentations at meetings featuring catered meals. This "food for the soul" as well as for the body encouraged strong attendance.

Regardless of the approach, administrators should ensure that discussion be open to all interested parties and provide an honest effort to represent and incorporate all points of view. Also essential is ensuring that administrators agree at the outset on what will constitute a successful adoption process. Clear operational definitions of key terms should be developed as part of the process.

Many educational leaders were surprised when Amherst, Brown, and Williams colleges announced their consideration of an online consortium. Before Williams College began discussing their membership in the Global Education Network, a group of faculty studied the proposal. Their concern that the online consortium would take too many scholars out of the classroom was considered before administrators moved forward. The faculty agreed that the online courses would not be taken for Williams credit, but would be offered for continuing education units for alumni and advanced high school students (Carr, 2000a). Thus, multiple perspectives were solicited before a viable plan was adopted.

Promote Access and Training

On the macro level, digital telecommunication technology has the potential to reshape society while providing unprecedented educational opportunity, securing individual independence, and meeting economic and political goals. Therefore, equal access to IT is truly a question of justice. Access is a philosophical (as well as legal and federal) principle that has great relevance in large-scale adoption of technological innovations.

For basic fairness, adequate access must be provided for our citizens to use IT to work, experiment, and manage their lives efficiently, and this requires finding the best ways to integrate and adapt IT into our educational fabric. Exploring, learning new skills, and planning make a difference in improving the quality of life for all Americans (Yocam, 1996). These goals are a matter of our national interest.

Toward these ends, large investments in IT training are essential for the successful incorporation of IT into our national life. High-quality technical assistance and training can benefit the transition from face-to-face to digital modes of instruction. To encourage learning *with* media and technology rather than simply learning *from* media and technology will require implementing more philosophical, as well as technical, approaches. Administrators must therefore keep current with the full range of technologies available to make appropriate choices.

In 1995, the Clinton administration outlined four pillars of education and technology: hardware, connectivity, content, and training. The CEO Forum noted important progress in two of these areas—hardware and connectivity—but called for developing better methods of incorporating "content and training teachers" *(T.H.E. Journal*, 1998, p. 10). Faculty training is therefore seen as critical to the success of any widespread technology initiative. Faculty training involves not only introductory workshops but also follow-up training and ongoing collaboration among teachers and support from administrations. Teacher training cannot be successful, particularly in the area of IT development using short-term workshops. Rather, successful training requires teams of people training over long periods.

Training should be adaptive to areas of instruction and should build from immediate uses and gratifications to long-term incorporation. Development sessions should be designed so that users can learn how to do something they can use immediately; instant application maximizes motivation (Paul, 1994). Some short-term success can provide motivation for greater usage and integration.

Peer support is critical in fostering enthusiasm. Voluntary training sessions help generate peer support. Collaborative training and mentoring stimulate support and provide a reassuring atmosphere for adoption of innovative technologies (see, e.g., an institution-wide "ideabook," Dardig, 1997).

McDaniel and Klonoski (1995-1996) identify several principles learned from their training experience including training users on their own equipment, adopting a "need to know" teaching philosophy, focusing training on specific needs, and adjusting training to the learner. The authors note,

> Our model offered instruction on-demand that was individualized, peer supported, and delivered on-site. Electronic mail empowered learners to seek answers to more sophisticated questions, and trainers, who taught on a need-to-know basis in tutorials generously seasoned with specific applications, created the sort of bond that encouraged further contact. (McDaniel & Klonoski, 1995-1996, p. 65)

In addition, training should be continually revised, based on the responses of those being trained. Sherry (1997) observes,

When a staff development or training program is sensitive to the needs of its typical end-users, and when it takes their feedback into account when modifying tutorials, demonstrations, and hands-on exploratory sessions to meet stated needs, it tends to meet with a higher degree of success than a fixed, linear-design approach. (p. 70)

Information presented to users should be realistic. Time demands, changing roles, and development challenges should not be underestimated. Unrealistic and heightened expectations can crush enthusiasm and endurance if obstacles, challenges, and frustrations are not realistically identified.

Recast Roles

IT adoption promotes the recasting of the role of the organization members. Young (1997) explains that some new technologies are able to replace traditional tasks leading to questions of whether the diverse roles played by workers should be "unbundled" and distributed among a variety of other actors.

For example, workers who design content using online materials in conjunction with on-site meetings may adapt to the role as content designer. The traditional role of evaluator in assessing progress is another job that could be assigned organization members. The trick is doing so without engendering fear and resentment among other workers concerned about job security.

In short, new technologies can dramatically recast the traditional role of workers. Increased emphasis on worker as facilitator is a common experience in many organizations. Some users may balk at participating in such change, but if handled properly, they could also welcome the development of collaborative frameworks using IT.

Include Multiple Resources

Administrators should encourage broad-based adoption of information resources. Using a mix of databases—including the Internet, the library, CD-ROMs, and other technologies—ensures the development of varied information-retrieval systems, which helps improve the quality of the information gathered. Multiple sourcing is one of the best ways to ensure the quality of the information gathered and assessing its credibility, breadth, timeliness, bias, attribution, and so on. Separating the wheat from the chaff is still a difficult problem in determining intellectual efficacy.

Users need to develop skills to cope with the quantity of information now available. A blizzard of information can be frustrating and ultimately discouraging without critical skills. An essential challenge of the 21st century will be to develop citizens capable of managing large amounts of information quickly.

Ethical and responsible use of information must be cultivated along with developing the skill in using information technology. A culture of responsible use should be developed through ethical discussion, including discussion of copyright law and normative statements about the proper use of technology (Bain, 1996; Connolly, 1995).

Integrate Ongoing Assessment

To make the best use of technological applications, ongoing assessment is critical. We are still in an exploratory period with new technologies; very little research has been conducted that provides rigorous documentation of their benefits. Mechanisms for ongoing assessment and evaluation of technology effectiveness and effects must be an integral part of any serious effort. Because technology is continually evolving (with constant upgrades, improvements, and modifications), static evaluations and one-shot assessments will never provide the information needed to correct deficiencies and overcome problems.

Assessing effectiveness is conditioned by goals and objectives, as well as user satisfaction. Ehrmann (1991) suggests that in the area of technology, users should consider whether the technological changes they have adopted are central to their needs, or trivial and easily eliminated. One criterion Ehrmann suggests is the presence of *positive addiction* among users. For Ehrmann, positive addictions are evidenced by beneficial habits with respect to the use of new IT systems in the workplace.

Another criterion of success is when we increase productivity through reaching goals more efficiently or by reaching greater audiences through the use of IT. Most experts, including those highly critical of instructional technology, agree that technology allows us to reach larger audiences. But reach alone may not be enough. In the education setting, we should also determine how engaged and productive users are, and for how long, compared to how they would be without such technology. A mixture of quantitative and qualitative instruments should be employed for assessing technology effectiveness along the lines mentioned. Different forms of measurement yield different data, all of which are useful in providing an overall picture of technology effectiveness (see, e.g., Luna & McKenzie, 1997).

Offer Rewards

Large corporations, educational organizations, state and federal agencies, and nonprofit institutions have put programs into effect to reward excellence in instructional technology programs. Reward systems (depending on the type of organization) can include promotion, raises, training, time off, equipment grants, and so on.

Adequate support, recognition, and incentives should be built into the larger framework of technology adoption. Time spent learning new technologies and in exploring new functions for them should be recognized. Absent proper recognition and institutional valuing of this time allocation, users too often remain reluctant to commit the time and effort necessary to gain mastery.

CONCLUSIONS ■

In summary, in adopting IT systems, administrators should

1. Develop a vision statement of goals and objectives through collective input from stakeholders *inside* the organization; if IT systems are perceived to be imposed by outside forces, their chance for successful integration into the workplace diminishes dramatically.

2. Create an advisory board of stakeholders to develop the procedures for adopting programs and systems.

3. Emphasize organizational objectives, not media, as the motives for adoption; then decide which systems will best support those goals.

4. Assess multiple methods and alternative technologies in the decision process; do not focus on just one.

5. Recognize that over time needs change. Therefore, rigorous monitoring and testing of effectiveness of systems must be an ongoing process.

6. Develop a mechanism for keeping current with the full range of new IT systems that becomes available so that appropriate choices can be made in the future.

7. Not underestimate the impact of the integration of IT systems. This change alters workplace roles in both intended and unintended ways. To manage it to the advantage of the organization, reward systems, adequate support, recognition, and incentives should be established.

8. Continually engage potential users in meaningful debate to determine how best to integrate new tools into their organization.

9. Develop clear operational definitions at the outset on what will constitute a successful adoption process, and what will be accepted as "effective" use.

10. Know that users should determine the worth of the technology, but the user and not the technology is ultimately responsible for its effectiveness.

IT programs are multiplying and expanding into a variety of education, corporate, and nonprofit markets, forcing substantial reorganizations throughout all sectors adopting IT. What is emerging is a demand for lifelong learning, based on the continuing need for workers to develop knowledge and skills for a rapidly changing business environment.

IT systems enable the delivery of cost-effective programs to serve business, government, and education, making it an attractive financial opportunity for new players and new partnerships. Increasingly, corporate, university, government, and nonprofit partnerships are emerging with new training programs (Marchese, 1998).

The full impact of these changes is not yet clear. Yet a significant role for IT in the future is inevitable. Its worth will be found in its ability to supplement if not replace high-quality interactional processes, benefiting all regardless of age, sex, race, or socioeconomic status, across business, government, education, and nonprofit groups.

■ NOTES

1. As a university administrator, I directed the building and organization of a campus in the Washington, D.C., metropolitan area that provides graduate education to well over 2,000 students per semester. We used a variety of distance education and face-to-face approaches and were part of a large land grant university that prided itself on instructional technology development. Many of the programs on the regional campus focused on information technology. I served as graduate director, associate dean of a graduate school, and associate dean of an academic college, helping plan, organize, and implement distance education programs. Not all of these programs were in high-population areas. The principles that I have derived from my experiences are provided here to help future administrators cultivate productive approaches to their own circumstances in acquiring information technologies.

2. MOOs, MUDs, and MUSHs are all computer programs that a user can log onto in order to interact, engaging in instant messaging, creating objects to manipulate, or going to different "rooms." Such devices are useful in classes when the need for communication is more immediate than using asynchronous means such as e-mail. Real-time communication capability allows users a closer approximation to face-to-face talk in terms of immediacy, if nothing else.

3. Duderstadt's (2000) nine different models include the World University, the Diverse University, the Creative University, the Divisionless University, the Cyberspace University, the Adult University, the Lifelong University, the Ubiquitous University, and the Laboratory University.

4. This report was titled "Course Restructuring and the Instructional Development Initiative at Virginia Polytechnic Institute and State University: A Benefit

Cost Study." It was one of a series from a project funded through a Field-Initiated Studies Educational Research Grant by the National Institute on Postsecondary, Education, Libraries, and Lifelong Learning, Office of Educational Research and Improvement, U.S. Department of Education, with additional funding provided by Information Resources and Technology in the Chancellor's Office of the California State University. The project Web page is www.calstate.edu/special_projects/.

5. As developers spend more time designing online content than those in face-to-face settings, the question of the ownership of such materials arises. The American Association of University Professors (AAUP) recommends that virtual courses should be the sole property of the professors who develop them. However, some institutions have policies that grant ownership to the university, colleges, or academic departments. In other cases, state governments have intervened and have created different policies on ownership. The best solution may be to "cut the baby in half." Gail S. Chambers, a New York economist who helps negotiate partnerships among colleges and universities, recommends that institutions adopt a policy similar to that practiced with patented research. Patented research is owned both by the institution and by the researcher. Similarly, online classes could become a shared possession of the institution and teacher. Chambers (1999) suggests that such an approach would avoid jeopardizing public support for higher education while maintaining academic quality in higher education. Faculty members would maintain their roles in the governance of their institution, as well as their academic freedom. She adds that shared property rights would also lend themselves to shared reputations strengthening the bond between the institution and the faculty member. From an ethical perspective, perhaps all of the contributors to the creation of intellectual material should benefit from any arrangement that is adopted. Chambers's suggestion is like that of the global interdependence we find in our market economy today. A successful example of worker-owned enterprises is DynCorp, an information technology firm in northern Virginia. DynCorp was established in 1946 and is now one of the largest employee-owned technology and service companies in the United States. The company has $1.4 billion in annual revenues, a $4.4 billion contract backlog, and 20,000 workers worldwide.

6. Negroponte's columns, "Wired," are available online at http://nicholas.www.media.mit.edu/people/nicholas/Wired/.

PART III

POLICY

CHAPTER 8

LAW AND REGULATION, PART I

Individual Interests

KEITH LEE

JANESSA LIGHT

> *This case calls not for the judgment of Solomon but for the dexterity of Houdini. . . . The novelty of the use, incident to the novelty of the new technology, results in a baffling problem. Applying the normal jurisprudential tools—the words of the Act, legislative history, and precedent— to the facts of the case is like trying to repair a television set with a mallet.*
>
> — Justice Fortas[1]

J ust as Justice Fortas grappled with the interpretation of existing law in light of the then new technology of television, current Supreme Court justices struggle with applying existing law to the Internet. Justice Fortas's consternation over the application of existing law to new media exemplifies the reoccurring challenge courts face when a new form of communication is developed.

Adapting existing law to new technologies is not easy and does not occur overnight. Traditional legal principles must be reexamined in the light of new media such as the Internet. Sometimes these traditional legal principles may not apply to new technology at all, requiring the creation of laws. Courts may deal with the Internet by molding common law to this new technology. Congress may pass new laws and statutes applying specifically to the Internet. Currently, courts and federal, state, and local governments are struggling to decide how to apply the law to the Internet.

In this ever-shifting legal landscape of cyberspace, it is important for Internet users to be aware of their personal rights and remedies as they communicate over this new medium. The focus of this chapter, therefore, is to identify and explain the legal issues that concern a person's individual interests in cyberspace. Our discussion will entail a certain amount of speculation because, as one court noted, "the legal rules that . . . govern this new medium [the Internet] are just beginning to take shape."[2] The next section begins with an analysis of freedom of expression in the application of the First Amendment to the Internet, including filters and child pornography. The section following that deals with privacy on the Internet with concrete focus on the use of "cookies" and anonymous speech. Next we explore some legal ramifications of intellectual property[3] on the Internet, specifically, copyright violations in linking and framing, as well as music and video piracy.

■ FREEDOM OF EXPRESSION

Two years ago I sat down to begin a book mostly [on] freedom of expression on the Internet. Two years later I'm still writing it.[4]

Background

More than two centuries have passed since the passage of the First Amendment, which states, "Congress shall make no law . . . abridging the freedom of speech, or of the press."[5] The Supreme Court has continually interpreted the First Amendment in light of technological advances unseen by the Founding Fathers, including the telephone, radio, television, and the Internet. Before delving into the First Amendment's impact on various Internet issues, it is necessary to comprehend the existing status of the First Amendment.

Contrary to the absolutist tone of the First Amendment, speech may be limited or declared illegal. Subsumed under the rubric of "speech" is the commonly heard phrase "freedom of expression," although not explicitly stated in the First Amendment. Speech limited or forbidden under the First Amendment includes, among others, libel, defamation, fraud, obscenity, and child pornography. The government justifies such limitations as fulfilling a "compelling governmental interest," such as preventing children from being sexually molested. A "compelling government interest" is a rubric of First Amendment judicial doctrine, requiring the government to convince the court that its interest is so compelling that the speech restraint imposed by the government is justified. In addition, the First Amendment applies only to government actions.[6] Private corporations and individuals may impose almost any limitations they deem necessary.

Certain ground rules underlie government limitation of speech. Generally, the restriction may not be based on the speech's content or viewpoint. The government, for example, may not ban speech concerning airlines. Also, advocacy of a position generally may not be outlawed, unless such advocacy incites imminent lawless action.

The Internet, as a unique medium, challenges traditional interpretation and application of First Amendment principles. In applying these principles to the Internet, judges must keep abreast of the latest technological developments or risk the danger of writing decisions that impose an adverse, perhaps unintended, effect on the community.[7] Given the enormous scope of the First Amendment, this chapter will limit its focus to obscenity, child pornography, and filtering.

Obscene Material

Obscene speech is not constitutionally protected. Individuals have the right to *possess* obscene materials but may not "communicate, transport, distribute, or sell such materials," under the cloak of constitutional protection.[8] Federal and state criminal statutes forbid the distribution of obscene materials. Additionally, states may apply a different standard of obscenity to minors, to prevent exposure to minors of "material aimed at a primary audience of sexually explicit adults."[9]

In 1973, the Supreme Court defined obscenity with the *Miller* test, setting forth three elements that if met, would qualify the speech in question as obscene.

(a) Whether the "average person, applying contemporary community standards" would find that the work, taken as a whole, appeals to the prurient interest . . . ;

(b) Whether the work depicts or describes, in a patently offensive way, sexual conduct specifically defined by the applicable state law; and

(c) Whether the work, taken as a whole, lacks serious literary, artistic, political, or scientific value.[10]

This federal standard is applicable to the states via the Fourteenth Amendment. Differences exist between obscene material and material related to sex. "Obscene material is material which deals with sex in a manner appealing to prurient interests."[11] *Prurient interest* is "a shameful or morbid interest in nudity, sex, or excretion, and [material that] goes substantially beyond customary limits of candor in description or representation of such matters."[12]

With respect to *community standards*, the definition of such varies across state and local boundaries and may change over time.[13] One community, for example, may consider certain material distributed by a bookstore to be obscene, whereas another community, perhaps even one "down the street," may not. Additionally, geographic borders alone may not necessarily define a community. Radio and television broadcasts that could potentially transmit obscene material easily span such geographic boundaries. Regardless of the nature of the boundaries themselves, the fact that boundaries exist as part of the obscenity standard raises questions on how, if at all, community borders may be drawn. What may appeal to the prurient interest in one locale may not necessarily appeal to the prurient interest in another.

With respect to *patently offensive* works, the precise definition is dependent on state law. Patently offensive works are works depicting "hardcore sexual conduct" as defined by the relevant state law.[14] Similar to the problem posed by prurient interest, the standard of patently offensive varies among states.

Assuming that a work appeals to the prurient interest and depicts hardcore sexual conduct, that work may not be obscene unless the work, as a whole, lacks serious literary, artistic, political, or scientific value.[15] Unlike the first two elements of the *Miller* test that apply a community-wide standard, the last element employs a "reasonable person standard."[16] In other words, a community standard may be held "unreasonable" if a minority of the entire population agrees that the work has redeeming value.[17] Depending on how "community" is defined, a controversial work located in the country's heartland may not necessarily be banned if people from the coasts find the work has redeeming value.

Statutory Application of the Obscenity Standard to the Internet

One famous example of a statutory application of the obscenity standard to the Internet is the Communications Decency Act of 1996 (CDA).[18]

Congress, concerned about the proliferation of pornography on the Internet, passed the CDA with the goal of preventing "unsuspecting or unaware Internet surfers from accidentally happening upon sexually explicit materials."[19] The CDA enabled the prosecution of any individual who knowingly made available to minors "indecent" or "patently offensive" material. The statute also allowed the prosecution of those who dealt in obscene material and child pornography over the Internet.

One of the more prominent criticisms of the CDA was that the language was too broad. Although pornography fell under the statute's scope, organizations seeking to educate children about sexually explicit topics such as contraception, pregnancy, and AIDS could also be prosecuted under the CDA. The American Civil Liberties Union (ACLU) challenged the CDA on the grounds that the "indecent" and "patently offensive" clauses were too broad. The ACLU declined to challenge the obscenity and child pornography provisions. Even with the indecency sections of the CDA struck down by the Supreme Court, the language regulating obscene materials remains standing. Thus, the CDA remains somewhat in effect.

Congress attempted to bolster the strength of the CDA with the passage of the Child Online Protection Act of 1998 (COPA).[20] COPA's intent was to protect minors from exposure to sexually explicit material on the Internet. COPA imposed on entities supplying such sexually explicit material over the Internet the responsibility of ensuring that minors remained unexposed to it. The ACLU challenged COPA on the ground that it was a content-based restriction. COPA forced those entities who would provide such content to enact credit card or adult verification schemes on their Web sites.

Courts, in essence, prevented COPA from passing.[21] The court agreed with the aims behind the statute, but disagreed in the *manner* in which those aims were achieved. Specifically, given that COPA forces the implementation of age verification schemes, anonymity could be lost and such schemes could be financially burdensome on, for example, nonprofit organizations intent on educating teenagers about pregnancy. COPA, therefore, could force content providers to censor material considered harmful to minors—an impermissible "chilling" of speech rights, the court concluded.

Case Applying the Obscenity Standard to Modern Computer Telecommunication

Although it dates prior to the explosive growth of the Internet, *United States v. Thomas* remains the seminal case concerning obscenity standards and cyberspace.[22] In 1993, the defendants, located in California, operated an adult bulletin board.[23] A bulletin board system, or BBS, is a computer accessible via modem access and was a popular means of communicating messages and data before Internet access became easily accessible. A Memphis, Tennessee, jury convicted the Thomas couple for transmitting sexually explicit photos digitized for computer viewing and transmittable over phone lines. Access to the bulletin board's adult content was restricted to members, who were required to sign a form asserting their age. A Tennessee postal inspector, receiving a complaint from another citizen, used a pseudonym when he applied and was granted access to the Thomas bulletin board's adult content. The inspector downloaded the sexually explicit images that formed the basis for charges against the Thomas couple. They were convicted of, among other charges, transporting obscene material through the telephone company in interstate commerce. Upon appeal, the Thomases asserted that Tennessee's community standards of obscenity should not be applied to them because the nature of computer telecommunication made it difficult to determine the final destination of the material the Thomases disseminated. The appeal was denied on the basis that the defendants knew that the inspector was calling from Memphis, Tennessee.

In *People v. Barrows*, another case relevant to Internet obscenity, the defendant was convicted of violating a New York statute prohibiting "use of the Internet to transmit sexually explicit pictures to encourage minors to engage in sexual activity."[24] The court found that statute unconstitutionally vague as it failed to explicitly define what was "patently offensive." The court additionally concluded that there was no way to effectively apply the statute to the Internet. Given the nature of the Internet, the court found it "impossible for the sender to control with certainty the route or ultimate destination of his message."[25] Thus, Barrows's conviction was overturned.

Similarly, the court in *ACLU v. Johnson* overturned a New Mexico statute criminalizing the use of a computer system to distribute or send sexually explicit material to minors.[26] Given that the entire Internet is accessible from New Mexico, anyone who sent such material could be prosecuted. In addition, there still remains the problem of accurately identifying recipients of such material given the decentralized nature of the Internet and the anonymity inherent within it.

To summarize, state laws attempting to regulate Internet communication by criminalizing the use of the Internet to disseminate obscene material to minors will most likely be struck down. The reasoning is that in attempting to regulate Internet communication conducted intrastate, the statute, due to the nature of the Internet, attempts to regulate the *entire* Internet. This is not to say that all statutes regarding the Internet and content would be considered unconstitutional. Using the Internet to persuade a minor to engage in sexual activity is a criminal activity unprotected by the Constitution.[27] First Amendment protections were not implicated as the issue was *not* the sending of sexually explicit materials, but the solicitation of a minor to engage in sexual activity.

Impact

Nearly a decade later in the midst of the explosive growth of the Internet, the afterglow of the *Thomas* and related decisions casts a forbidding pall. As Congress has the authority to ensure commerce is not "polluted" with obscene material, that seems to imply Congress has the authority to prosecute the sender, even if the sender has no idea who the recipients are. This authority, however, is tempered by First Amendment protections that Congress must abide by. Balancing the two to the Internet medium is a difficult if not impossible task, given the nature of the Internet.

Unlike the era in which a person needed to take deliberate steps to dial and access an adult bulletin board system to obtain sexually explicit photos, all a person needs today is an Internet service provider (ISP). The Internet, unfortunately, grants a shroud of anonymity that may disguise the origins of senders and recipients alike of such explicit material. No longer may one positively identify the actual person sending the e-mail message or picture.

In addition to the difficulty of identifying Internet users is the fact that the Internet is a global medium typically accessible for the price of a local phone call. A person accessing the Internet from his or her home may access and retrieve information from computers located worldwide, via Web sites, file transfer sites, Usenet newsgroups, and chat rooms. Thus, obscene material is globally accessible, and therefore it is nearly impossible to discern the original geographic origin of such material. Even if the geographic origin were identifiable, American courts would have little, if any, jurisdiction over computers located outside the United States, as discussed in Chapter 9 in the section on jurisdiction.

Note that although cookies may allow tracking of users' Web-browsing habits, the identities behind *sources* of Internet traffic may be disguised (see the discussion of cookies later in the chapter). That is, there is a difference between tracking users' current activities and identifying who is *behind* the Web sites that the users browse. The decentralized nature of the Internet and the fact that computers are continually being added and removed from the Internet makes locating a source, for example, that is sending pornographic material, difficult, if not impossible. There are innumerable methods for disguising one's point of origin on the Internet. For example, sites such as http://www.anonymizer.com and http://www.safeweb.com filter out identifying data, including cookies, thus preventing Web sites from identifying and tracking visitors, and in return, granting those visitors cloaks of anonymity. E-mail additionally may be sent using special software and/or computers that "anonymize" the sender's identity.

Not only may senders remain unidentified, but recipients may receive such material even though it was not requested. Entities, colloquially known as "spammers," may e-mail hundreds of thousands, if not millions, of people with unsolicited advertisements, typically sexually explicit in nature. The manner in which the Internet transmits data precludes easy identification of those spammers, ensuring that the geographic source of those entities may remain hidden or disguised.[28]

It is unclear what, if any, community standard applies when an individual receives through the Internet sexually explicit material considered obscene within that individual's community. It is currently uncertain whether a standard should even apply given the Supreme Court's decision in *Stanley v. Georgia* allowing a person to possess obscene material within the home.[29] One commentator suggests that the answer might be yes, but declines to directly address the technological issues that would arise with this standard—such as the potential extra-national origins of such material and the fact that origins may be disguised or counterfeited.[30] Given current technology, a person transmitting information over the Internet has the capacity to remain unidentified. It is a safe assumption, however, that most users of the Internet lack or require such capacity or knowledge.

As noted earlier, private entities, such as corporations, may control access to any material without any First Amendment repercussion. America Online (AOL), for example, the popular Internet access provider, was able to prevent a company from using AOL computers to send 1.9 million unsolicited e-mail advertisements a day.[31] The court noted that AOL is a private company in upholding AOL's right to restrict the type of Internet content flowing through its computers.[32]

ISPs, in addition, generally have the right to remove any Web sites that may violate their policies. The ISP MindSpring, for example, shut down a controversial Web site referred to as the "Nuremberg Files," as it contained the names and addresses of doctors who performed abortions and advocated that these doctors be tried for crimes against humanity. In response, however, a suit was filed against MindSpring, claiming that the ISP had no right to take down the site, noting that it was under no legal obligation to do so.[33]

Child Pornography

Material depicting child pornography may be legally banned. Courts, unlike their struggle in defining and regulating obscene material, have not encountered such difficulty regarding child pornography. Federal law prevents the knowing transmission or receipt of visual depictions, generally pictures or movies, of minors engaged in sexual conduct.[34] States, the Supreme Court ruled, may prohibit depiction of minors engaged in sexual activity as the equivalent of sexual abuse of minors.[35]

The courts, with the caveat that the alleged possessor must have knowingly possessed or distributed the material, have upheld laws prohibiting the possession and distribution of child pornography. Those who operate Internet or content service providers and know or have reason to know that such material is passing through their computers are also potential distributors. Should providers fail to take immediate action, such as notifying the authorities, then they may potentially be held liable under the law. The "knowing" requirement is significant, given the vast amounts of information that flow through computers each minute.

The problem with multimedia depictions of minors engaged in sexual activity is determining whether the depicted individuals are truly minors. Adults could be masquerading as minors or images and movies could be digitally altered to make adults appear to be minors. There is also the question as to whether it is a crime to possess images modified by computer to present the impression that the persons engaged in sexual activity are minors. Issues also exist as to whether possession of computer-generated child pornography, where no "real live" people are involved, constitutes illegal possession. Courts must examine such issues prior to ruling on Internet pornography cases.

Indecent Speech

A fog of confusion surrounds the quagmire that is indecent speech. Unlike obscenity, the courts do not define *indecent* as succinctly. The Supreme Court has stated that indecent speech describes in terms "offensive as measured by community standards . . . sexual or excretory activities and organs."[36] As mentioned previously, in 1996 Congress passed the CDA, designed to protect children from indecent material. Immediate controversy erupted, with the main vein of complaints being that "significant educational, political, medical, artistic, literary, and social [speech was prohibited under the act]."[37] In short, the act was termed "overly broad." The CDA's relevant statutory language in question follows:

> A person in interstate or foreign communications who uses a "telecommunications device" [is prohibited from] knowingly making, creating, or soliciting "any comment, request, suggestion, proposal, image, or other communication which is obscene or *indecent*, knowing that the recipient of the communication is under 18 years of age, regardless of whether the maker of such communication placed the call or initiated the communication."[38]

In *ACLU v. Reno*, a number of civil rights organizations challenged the statute, on grounds that the language was "overly broad." For example, organizations seeking to educate teenagers about safe sex would be held liable and subject to imprisonment and/or fines under the CDA. Specifically, the

CDA barred all indecent speech, which included speech that may be indecent yet have "serious literary, artistic, scientific, or educational value."[39] It appears Congress no longer had the wherewithal to defend to the death our right to say it. The Supreme Court agreed with the petitioners and held that this provision, among others, was unconstitutionally overly broad. Although the Court has allowed the government to regulate indecent speech with respect to television and radio, the government may not do so with the Internet.[40]

Underlying the prohibition of indecent speech in television and radio is the "scarcity of available broadcast frequencies" and the "invasive nature of broadcasting." Whereas there are limited frequencies over which radio and television can be broadcast, the same may not be said of the Internet. Although there was once a concern about bandwidth—that there would not be enough capacity to transmit information over the Internet—that is no longer the case with improvements in Internet data "traffic control" and inexpensive fiber-optic communication lines.

Similarly, although minors have easy access to television and radio broadcasts, the Internet is not so pervasive that minors may not avoid access to it. Broadcast media "intrudes [sic] into the home so that it is practically impossible to keep minors from experiencing its content." Unlike broadcast media, however, active steps are needed to access the Internet, unlike the "flip of a switch" with television and radio. Such active steps, the Supreme Court notes, include turning on the computer, connecting to an ISP, and specifically retrieving the information. This decision, however, presaged the novelty of WebTV, a device connected to the Internet that literally with a flip of a switch connects a user to the Internet. Such a device, however, still requires that the user actively retrieve the requested information.

There remains the practical problem of regulating indecent speech even if the Court had found otherwise. Unlike radio and television stations, where broadcasts originate from one physical locale easily subject to regulation, the Internet is a medium allowing any participant to transmit media. Every participant on the Internet has the capability of being a transmitter as well as a receiver of information. Given the Internet's interactive two-way nature and unlike the one-way nature of radio and broadcast mediums, regulation of the end user/potential broadcaster is more difficult given current technology.

Filters

Filters, however, do allow end users to censor information they would not otherwise wish to view. Private individuals, so long as the state remains uninvolved, may determine what material is filtered.[41] Several software packages exist that are designed to "filter" Internet material deemed unsuitable by the end user. There are several practical problems with such filter software.

Perhaps most important is that such filtering software cannot recognize whether *images*, and not just text, are obscene or indecent. By parsing the content of the Web site, filter software may censor words, but not pictures or other forms of media such as movies and audio files. Given that the majority of pornographic images consists of multimedia, most filter software prevents *any* type of access to Web sites it decides are adult in nature.

The problem with such software packages is that the end user is generally unaware of what is being filtered out. Due to competitive pressures, filter software companies keep such information proprietary. In other words, as such information is kept secret, one company's filter software may restrict access to a Web site whereas another may not. In addition, sometimes the software is too aggressive in that it may prevent legitimate research, such as biological behavioral research or birth control/abortion information—regardless of the Web site's position on such issues. The primary concern among civil rights organizations is that end users employing such software are *unaware* of Web sites that they may not access.[42] Finally, given that the Internet is always changing as new Web sites are continually added, filter software will always lag behind in keeping abreast of Internet content to filter until the company issues an update to its software.

Although problems exist with filter software, it is a step in the right direction, preventing minors from viewing material deemed objectionable. As parents may set the "viewing standards" for the Internet, end-user filter software also avoids constitutional problems inherent in government regulation of Internet content.

CONSTITUTIONAL RIGHT TO PRIVACY ▪

The right-to-privacy concept may be traced to an article published in the late 19th century.[43] The concept soon branched into two schools of thought: (1) The right to privacy was a common law right, and (2) the right to privacy was a constitutional right, even though it is a right not explicitly stated in the Constitution.

Common Law Right to Privacy

The common law privacy right protects the individual from four activities: (1) intrusion upon seclusion, (2) appropriation of name or likeness, (3) publicity given to private life, and (4) publicity placing a person in a false light.[44] The right to privacy is not an absolute one. Some examples include that the right to privacy does not prohibit publication of a matter that is of public interest or where the person being published about consents to the publication.

The first common law privacy claim against an online content provider occurred in 1995, when Howard Stern, a radio talk show host, sued Delphi, an online system, for misappropriation of his likeness.[45] Specifically, Delphi used Stern's photograph without permission in an advertisement for an upcoming political debate by Delphi subscribers. The photograph of Howard Stern wearing leather pants that "largely exposed his buttocks" was published in New York magazines and newspapers. The court found that the service Delphi provided was equivalent to a newspaper. "The First Amendment . . . protect[s] the ability of news disseminators to publicize, to make public, their own communications." The impact of this decision seems to be that ISPs are allowed to disseminate newsworthy information under the shielding wing of the First Amendment. Stern's lawsuit was rejected, as Delphi qualified as a news disseminator.

Constitutional Right to Privacy

The constitutional right to privacy protects individuals' privacy from being invaded by the government. The constitutional right to privacy only prevents the government, not private entities, from invading a person's privacy. The Fourth Amendment's protection against unreasonable searches and seizures and the Fifth Amendment's protection against self-incrimination create an impermeable constitutional bubble of privacy around an individual. Generally speaking, the government must obtain a warrant in order to prick that bubble and legally invade a person's privacy.

E-mail may very well have a right to privacy. In 1995, a U.S. Air Force court held that the defendant, involved in child pornography, had a right of privacy to "any email transmissions he made so long as they were stored in [an AOL] computer."[46] Specifically,

> [The defendant] clearly had an objective expectation of privacy in those messages stored in computers which he alone could retrieve through the use of his own assigned password. Similarly, he had an objective expectation of privacy with regard to messages he transmitted electronically to other subscribers of the service who also had individually assigned passwords.[47]

In this case, the court found sufficient Fourth Amendment justification for a warrant issued to search AOL's computers to retrieve the defendant's e-mail. Note that a private corporation may have the right to review an employee's e-mail if that e-mail originates from a corporate computer.

In the case of *Steve Jackson Games v. United States Secret Service*, the Secret Service seized the plaintiff's computers in the belief that it contained an illegally obtained secret document.[48] The court ruled that the Secret Service violated this act when it acknowledged the plaintiff's status as a publisher but still refused to return the computers. The court also held the Secret Service violated one of the Electronic Communications Privacy Act's precepts barring access of unread, stored messages. As the intended recipient of those messages had not yet read them, the court found for the plaintiff for $303,040 in damages for unauthorized access to stored electronic communications. The court found, however, that the Secret Service did not "intercept" the e-mail as defined by the statute.

Statutory Protections of the Right to Privacy

Numerous federal statutes protect an individual's privacy on the Internet, some of which are discussed here. They currently include, but are not limited to, the Electronic Communications Privacy Act of 1986, the Computer Fraud and Abuse Act of 1994, the Privacy Protection Act of 1980, and the Children's Online Privacy Protection Act of 1998. The Electronic Communications Privacy Act covers electronic-based forms of communications, whereas the older statutes generally protect privacy but without the focus on computers and computer networks that the Electronic Communications Privacy Act has.

The Electronic Communications Privacy Act of 1986 (ECPA) affects all persons and businesses, including the government, and covers all electronic communications, including those using the Internet.[49] Essentially, there may not be unauthorized interception of electronic communications, either in transit or storage, without the consent of one party or a warrant. Electronic communications include e-mail, voice mail, chat, and presumably, *instant messages* between networked users.

Numerous exceptions, however, exist to the ECPA's seemingly sweeping language. Operators of publicly accessible e-mail systems, for example, may not disclose the contents of a message in storage. Those operators who manage "closed" private, internal e-mail systems may disclose such content. The rationale is that because internal e-mail systems are purely internal, employers can ensure that employees are using the e-mail system solely for work purposes, and not, for example, using it to send frivolous jokes or graphics. There may, however, be a separate employer-employee agreement concerning e-mail privacy.

The Computer Fraud and Abuse Act of 1994 (CFAA), among other things, forbids a party from intentionally accessing federal or financial institutions' computers to obtain financial information about an individual.[50] It is illegal, in other words, to intentionally access computers of financial institutions, consumer reporting agencies, or credit card issuers to retrieve personal financial information.[51] The Privacy Protection Act of 1980 states that materials "a person reasonably believe[s] to have a purpose . . . [in publishing] a newspaper, book, broadcast, or similar public communications" may not be subject to search or seizure by the government unless probable cause exists.[52] Under this act, computers are protected if they are used to publish or transmit information to a publisher.

The Children's Online Privacy Protection Act of 1998 (COPPA) applies to "service providers and Web sites directed toward children or to those service providers [who knowingly] collect information from children."[53] Those who fall under COPPA's provisions must, among other things, (1) clearly indicate where and what information it collects, and how that collected information is used; (2) obtain parental consent before collecting, using, or disclosing the children's personal information; (3) provide a reasonable method for parents to review the collected information and allow parents the option to delete and refuse further use of that information; (4) not collect more information than necessary for a child to participate in a game, contest, or other activities; and (5) protect the confidentiality, integrity, and security of the collected information.[54] These rules greatly improve the privacy protections of children who use the Internet.

Employee Privacy

Contrary to popular opinion, an employee does not necessarily have the same expectation of privacy at work that he or she may have at home. Essentially, an employer may monitor an employee's e-mail, telephone calls, or Internet-browsing habits without violating that employee's expectation of privacy.[55] The rationale underlying that position is that the employee works for the employer and it is the employer's right to ensure that relevant work is performed. Overseeing the employee's use of electronic communication is an acceptable method of supervision, despite the employee's lack of consent to be monitored. Employers, therefore, may access their employees' electronic mail without any consent required.

Interception by an employer of an employee's public e-mail is prohibited, but the situation is less clear if the private e-mail system allows public e-mail to pass through. Given that the employer then has the ability to intercept public e-mail, the employer probably would not legally be allowed to intercept an employee's e-mail because e-mail other than the employee's could be intercepted.

It is highly recommended that an employer have a written e-mail policy discussing the employees' use of the e-mail system and detailing the lengths to which the employer may review employees' e-mail. Ensuring that all employees sign an acknowledgment of the policy will help protect against any suits against the employer. The policy should also address e-mail content, because an employer may be held liable for discriminatory jokes forwarded by company employees to other company employees. Forbidding the forwarding of such jokes received via outside e-mail communication to other company employees will preclude any employer liability for discrimination.

Misappropriation and Identity Theft

With the growing availability of online databases and the use of the Internet for fraud, it becomes easier for information to be misappropriated. Typically, a misappropriation statute prevents the use of a person's name and address in a postal mailing list without his or her consent. Although courts have yet to apply such statutes to lists of e-mail addresses, given the rise of unsolicited e-mail advertisements, the time is ripe.

The most common example of misappropriation is *spamming*, where the person's name and e-mail address are included on a list of addresses. That list is then dispersed to advertisers, who then inundate recipients with unsolicited e-mail advertisements, typically pornographic. Statutes preventing unsolicited faxes are in place in most states; similar statutes could be enacted forbidding unsolicited e-mail advertisements. Unfortunately, prosecution remains an issue as unsolicited e-mail may originate from outside the United States or the originator of the e-mail may disguise the actual geographic origin of that e-mail.

Misappropriation also occurs when a person's online identity is taken over for nefarious purposes. For example, one common scam is performed on person-to-person electronic auctions sites. A person places a bid and "wins" an object, typically at far below market value. The offeror, in an apparent good faith effort, obtains the name and address of the person and asks that the recipient wait until the goods arrive before sending the money. The goods arrive, but the scam lies in the fact that the goods usually are charged to the recipient, using the recipient's name and address but with a credit card that the recipient never applied for. The credit card is usable and real but the recipient would be liable for any charges accrued.

Cookies

Those who "surf" the Internet may be unaware that whenever they access a Web page, a tiny file, called a cookie, may be placed by that Web page onto the viewer's computer. This cookie typically enables Web sites and Web site advertisers to keep track of the pages that a viewer accesses. Cookies also enable e-commerce sites to keep track of the items a user intends to order and perhaps even a user's password and credit card number. The Web site, among other things, may know when a user accessed that site, what items interested that person, and how long that person spent on each page.

Advertisers also use cookies to identify which ads interested a user in order to "place" more ads with similar subject matter on other pages and Web sites that user may visit. These types of cookies are typically anonymous in nature, in that they decline to obtain personal information from the computer. The concern is that a viewer's browsing habits, combined with what a Web site can learn about you from your computer, could lead to an unacceptable loss of privacy. Perhaps most invidious are cookies that obtain a user's e-mail address from his or her browser. Once obtained, unsolicited e-mail advertisements may be sent to that address.

In early 2000, there was an uproar when the Internet advertiser DoubleClick announced that it would combine both its online databases, containing the anonymous Web "surfing" habits of millions of people, and its offline databases, allowing the correlation of a heretofore anonymous computer with an actual geographic address. Non-Internet advertisers could then use that database to send mail directed toward a person, based on that person's viewing habits, garnered by DoubleClick's online databases. DoubleClick withdrew its proposed plan in response to the uproar. Some Internet advertisers have allowed users to "opt out" of being included in their databases. In other words, upon signing up, which, ironically, itself requires the placement of a cookie on the user's computer, the advertiser will no longer be able to track that person's viewing habits.

Although industry and banking organizations have published guidelines concerning the protection of information collected, such guidelines are purely voluntary. Given that adherence is voluntary, many organizations are currently lobbying the government to impose legislation or regulations supervising the collection of information about a Web surfer's viewing habits and personal computer.

Anonymous Speech

With the growing ability of Web sites to obtain information about you and your viewing habits, anonymous speech may perhaps be endangered. The Supreme Court has held that anonymous speech "play[s] an important role in the progress of mankind . . . persecuted groups and sects from to time to time throughout history have been able to criticize oppressive practices and laws . . . either anonymously or not at all."[56] Cookies are the first step in ensuring that whatever communication a person has on the Internet is no longer anonymous. Unless that person is technically savvy, for example, using "proxies" to disguise the geographic origin of that person's computer or "anonymous" e-mail servers, speech intended to be anonymous may not be so.

Granting only technically savvy users the ability to surf and communicate anonymously on the Internet, however, is considered unacceptable. The voices of the majority may be left unheard if they do not communicate for fear of being identified. Those who espouse unpopular viewpoints may also decline to take advantage of the Internet's ability of mass communication. Users who need the ability to speak anonymously on the Internet should be granted such without discrimination. The other side of the coin is that some anonymous speech may violate the law but law enforcement would be unable to locate that speaker. Spoken through an anonymous source, the user may speak without any legal repercussion—again, an unpalatable result.

COPYRIGHTS ■

On her personal Web site, a young woman lists her interests and hobbies as a way to keep in touch with family and friends, and perhaps meet new people. She also includes on her Web site some poems she composed, a few pieces of graphic artwork she created, and a photograph she snapped at Yosemite National Park. One day, in checking her e-mail the woman discovers an acquaintance has sent her a message with a poem attached and the note "This is such a lovely poem. Send this to five people you know and brighten their day too." When she opens the attachment, she discovers it is her poem verbatim—sans byline—which has been circulating on the Internet. Two weeks later, when doing research online, the young woman discovers on two separate Web sites her graphic artwork and a picture of Yosemite that looks remarkably similar to hers. The young woman is crestfallen and feels as though her creative works have been stolen. Could other people copy her work outright? Did they at least have to ask for her permission? Should she have tried to protect her work before posting it on her Web site?

These questions become more pressing as the Internet gains popularity as a tool for expression and communication. Its far-ranging capacity and global reach make the Internet a popular medium for writers and artists to express themselves. But with the sharing of creative works comes the risk that others may reproduce or claim that work as their own. Whether in a physical or virtual world, copyright law seeks to protect original authors of a work from infringement.

Background

Copyright protection is drawn from Article I Section 8 Clause 8 of the United States Constitution, which states that Congress may "secure for limited times to authors . . . the exclusive right to their respective writings."[57]

The purpose of such constitutional protection is not only to allow authors to control the use of their work but to encourage the free flow of ideas and information within society. As a result, the Copyright Act of 1909 was created, and subsequently amended in 1976, to grant specific protections to an author's work.[58]

The Copyright Act of 1976 protects original works of authorship that are fixed in any tangible medium of expression.[59] Therefore, it is not enough simply to speak of or describe a work. The statute only protects the work once it is expressed as words, numbers, notes, sounds, pictures, or other symbols.[60] This expression allows the work to be embodied in a written, photographic, recorded, or other permanent form, allowing it to be perceived or otherwise communicated.[61] This fixation requirement causes an author's intangible idea to be translated into a tangible form, thus creating a property interest. Once the work is fixed, copyright protection is automatic. There is no need to apply to the federal government for registration, or to publish the work, to receive protection.[62]

However, copyright law protects only the expression of the work in the form in which it is fixed, not the underlying idea or information.[63] For this reason, it is possible to have several newspaper articles describing the same event. Each article is a distinct expression protected by copyright, but the underlying facts of the story are not. The most common example of the ability to have several expressions of the same idea is exemplified by the creation of a book, movie, and television show based on the same story.

Because the underlying idea in a work is not protected, it is also possible, then, for two separate copyrights for the same work to independently exist. For example, two tourists can photograph the same waterfall at Yosemite National Park from a footbridge as the sun is setting. Each photograph as a fixed expression is entitled to copyright protection, even if taken from the same vantage point under the same lighting conditions. It is not germane that the same subject is fixed in the same medium because each photograph is viewed as an independent original work.

The scope of the Copyright Act is delineated by specific categories. Works of authorship are recognized to fall into one of the following groups: literary, musical, dramatic, pantomime or choreography, pictorial/graphical works, motion pictures/audiovisual, sound recordings, and architectural. Works that are not expressly protected in these categories are not necessarily excluded from copyright protection. New forms of creative expression that may emerge as a result of scientific discoveries or technological developments are considered to fall within the congressional intent of the act and are therefore protected.[64] The expression of works embodied in the Internet, whether fixed as an HTML (Hypertext Markup Language) file, e-mail attachment, or MPEG ("em-peg," discussed later in this chapter) digital recording may be copyrighted.

Copyright protection for a particular work grants the author five exclusive rights. An author may reproduce, distribute copies of, perform, display, or create derivative versions of the copyrighted work.[65] If third parties were to engage in any of these actions without authorization, they would infringe the author's copyright. These rights granted by copyright protection last for the life of the author plus 70 years.[66] After the copyright expires, the work passes to the public domain for all to use.

Misappropriating Content: Linking and Framing

The Internet is a resource used by millions worldwide, whether as a tool for communication or a vehicle for creative expression. The appeal lies in the wealth of content available and the speed at which it may be conveyed. But for every positive aspect the Internet brings, there is an equal risk that someone's words, art, music, or research will be used without that person's authorization. The misappropriation of a person's work can be as simple as an e-mail attachment forwarded without permission or graphic art filched from a Web site. How and when this work is used will determine if the misappropriation amounts to copyright infringement. Any one of a copyright holder's five exclusive rights may be infringed on any aspect of the Internet—be it e-mail, chat room, newsgroup, or Web, although the most visible infringement suits have occurred over the latter.

Linking

Links permit seamless and rapid navigation on the Web by allowing a user to move from one Web page to another within a hierarchy through the use of a *hypertext link*. A hypertext link is composed of two parts: the anchor reference and the object referred to.[67] The anchor may be a word or picture, and the object may be a new Web site or a specific place within the content of a Web page. Some basic problems arise with linking especially where permission to link is not first obtained by the parties.[68] Often Web site administrators are wary when traffic is shunted to or from their site and an undesired source, which may imply an affiliation where there is none. For example, consider the student who places nude pictures of herself on her Web site, and in her biography links to the school she is currently attending. This unwanted affiliation is even clearer where the student links from the school's site to her personal Web page that contains the photographs. Although increased traffic to a Web site is often desirable, traffic flowing from an undesirable link is of legitimate concern to Web site administrators. The simple courtesy of asking for permission to link avoids any misunderstandings and unintended endorsements.

Because links create the ability to jump from one point to any another, oftentimes the object linked to will not be the first page (or homepage) of a Web site. Thus, a user may find himself dropped in the middle of a new site when following a link. This type of link to a Web page below the homepage in the site's hierarchy is referred to as a *deep link*. The initial problem with deep linking is that in bypassing the homepage, the linker may unintentionally (or intentionally) make it appear as if the new content is an extension of his own, rather than that of the linkee. The linker is in effect appropriating the content of another Web site by using a deep link, because he fails to give proper credit to the real source of the material. Legally, such misappropriation may amount to copyright reproduction or display violations.

There is virtually no guidance from courts on the matter of deep linking. The most visible dispute over linking, between TicketMaster and Microsoft, never went to trial, but rather was settled out of court. In this case, a city guide Web site sponsored by Microsoft provided users with a link to the TicketMaster Web site to purchase tickets for local performances. TicketMaster's main objection was that the links were to specific venues and events rather than the company's homepage. To this extent, it claimed that Microsoft was acting as a free-rider by making use of the link and association.[69] After the suit was filed in federal court, the parties settled and the link was taken down.

Because a court was unable to rule on the merits of the case, no precedent has been established and the heart of the matter remains unanswered: Does deep linking without permission amount to appropriation of content? Microsoft might have argued that directing users to the TicketMaster site was free advertising and not appropriation. TicketMaster could counter that its proprietary content was being used to generate advertising revenue for Microsoft's city guide Web site. Without guidance as to whether deep links infringe copyright protection, many Web site administrators are acquiescing to demands not to link in order to avoid potential lawsuits. For example, in August of 1999, Jean-Pierre Bazinet was approached by Universal Pictures to cease linking to the studio's movie trailers. Bazinet's Web site Movie-List is a collection of links to movie trailers, and some clips of the movies themselves. In addition, he also sold CD-ROMs containing these movie trailers. Universal requested that Bazinet cease displaying and selling trailers of Universal Pictures movies on his site and CD-ROMs.[70] He complied and avoided a potential copyright infringement suit.

Should courts decide that deep linking does amount to copyright infringement, a defendant may have a possible fair use defense. If a copyrighted work is used under certain circumstances, such as for criticism, news reporting, research, or educational purposes, there may be no infringement.[71] Courts will generally look to four factors to determine if the use of the work falls under the fair use exception. These factors are (1) the purpose of the use, (2) the nature of the work, (3) the amount and substantiality of the portion used in relation to the whole, and (4) the effect of the use on the value of the work.[72] Based on these factors, if a school library linked to a single Web page discussing a chapter of a book, it might constitute fair use. Compare this hypothetical to the entrepreneur who links multiple pages of sports statistics and athlete biographies from his commercial Web site and charges for access to the information. The former would be more likely to constitute fair use of linking, and not infringe the copyright.

Framing

Just as linking issues have yet to be resolved by courts, an equally controversial copyright issue on the Web is the use of frames. Frames divide a Web page into multiple, independently scrollable regions. For example, an ISP's Web page may have one frame arranged column style containing the business' services. The remainder of the page might be a second frame describing each of those services in turn. This type of formatting is accomplished by building each frame of the Web page as a separate HTML file, all of which are controlled by one master HTML file.[73] Frames may allow for information to be displayed in a more flexible and useful manner, since each frame may be given an individual URL allowing it to load information independent of other frames on the page.[74]

As with linking, similar copyright issues arise with the use of frames. By framing the content from another Web site, the site administrator may be appropriating another person's work. This may lead to copyright infringement of display or derivative work rights since the content is automatically displayed as a *part* of the framed site. Furthermore, the framer's name, advertising, and other information may be constantly visible above or around the framee's content. Even if the framee's work is not seen as displayed on—but rather subsumed by—the new framed site, then it is arguably the creation of a derivative work, which is still considered infringement.

Little in the way of framing has been determined by the courts. The single case to contest the use of frames, *Washington Post Co. v. Total News, Inc.*, was settled out of court. Six media companies and their subsidiaries that operated news Web sites and licensed news and information to other Web sites brought suit when their content was framed. Three companies and three individuals operated the contested Web site, called totalnews.com. The Total News site framed the media companies' news content to create a one-stop news outlet. Total News added little of its own content, and sold advertising space within the frames to turn a profit.

The media companies alleged a combination of copyright, trademark, and unfair competition violations. They claimed that

> defendants were engaged in the Internet equivalent of pirating copyrighted material from a variety of famous newspapers, magazines, or television news programs; packaging those stories to advertisers as part of a competitive publication or program . . . and pocketing the advertising revenue generated by their unauthorized use of that material . . . just as that conduct would not be tolerated in the world of print and broadcasting, it is equally unlawful in the world of "cyberspace."[75]

Although settlement was reached before the defendants filed an answer, they generally contended that it is a user's choice how he or she wishes to view a Web site, and Total News was only facilitating that choice. Proponents of framing are quick to point out that frames increase the traffic to the framed Web sites where a user may "click through" to the framed content. Nevertheless, the defendants agreed to cease framing the media companies' content and not to use the companies' proprietary logos or graphics in any way reasonably likely to (1) imply affiliation; (2) dilute the marks; or (3) cause confusion, mistake, or deception. The defendants also agreed to link to the media companies only by a hyperlink that is plain text, but the media companies retained the right to revoke the permission to be linked in any way.[76]

In a situation where a party is accused of copyright infringement via framing, the party may have a defense where he or she can show a license to use the work existed. A license, whether express or implied, grants the temporary right to one or more of the five exclusive rights of authorship to a third party. Specifically, a nonexclusive license may be expressly given orally, or implied from the author's conduct.[77] Implied licenses, however, occur only if there is a "meeting of the minds" and the work is offered with the intent that others may use it. In the context of the Web, though, it would be difficult to demonstrate that the mere posting of content to a Web page creates an implied license to use the work. Web sites are commonly used for informational purposes or to express ideas—not as a method to trade or swap material. In an e-mail context, however, the request to forward material may arguably imply a license to use the work. A sender intends for the message to be reproduced and distributed when forwarding it to other users.

Since the framing dispute over Total News was settled, little other guidance is available on the use of frames. Based on a theory of misappropriation, whether by framing or linking, there is serious potential for copyright violations on the Web. The few cases that have been brought indicate that first obtaining permission to link or frame is the safest course, or in the alternative immediately taking down a frame or link at the request of the author. It is unclear at this time whether any party has an absolute right to link or frame another's content without infringing the copyright on the work. If linking or framing is determined to infringe the copyright, a party may, however, have a possible defense under the fair use doctrine or if an implied license can be shown.

Music and Video Piracy

As technology becomes more advanced, sound recording and motion picture works are being fixed in an increasing variety of digital formats. The introduction of a digital format has allowed music and video to be compressed and communicated more rapidly than ever before. But no matter what the newest format may be—whether phonograph, magnetic tape, or sound byte—the copyright issues remain the same: Is the reproduction of the work a violation of an author's copyright? This question is being asked most recently over MP3 for musical recordings and DVD for videos.

MP3 Music

MP3 (MPEG-1 Audio Layer-3) is a format for compressing a digital sound sequence without sacrificing the original level of sound quality when played.[78] The digital audio is created by taking 16-bit samples per second of an analog signal.[79] The creators of MP3, the Moving Pictures Experts Group (MPEG), accomplished this by creating a compression algorithm that reduces the amount of data when encoding the audio. The end result is music compressed in an ".mp3" file available for downloading on the Internet.

Although there is nothing inherently illegal about a new audio compression format, the potential for abuse is high. MP3 allows a person to copy and distribute unlicensed music on the Internet, in violation of copyright law. First, the uploading of the music from a compact disc (CD) into an MP3 format on a computer violates an artist's exclusive right to reproduce. "Owning" a CD does not give a person the right to upload digital copies of the music on a computer, regardless of whether the copies are for personal use.[80] Second, making MP3 files available to others violates an artist's exclusive right to distribute. It makes no difference whether a disclaimer is attached to the .mp3 files, the act is still a copyright violation. The copying and distribution of MP3 music are particularly common on the Web, where hundreds of sites make full-length audio recordings available to others.[81]

Proponents of MP3 music claim that artists are actually benefited, not harmed, by the new audio format. According to these groups, an artist can use MP3 to give away one song to promote an album or sell a song individually as a single. Furthermore, using MP3 is a cost-effective and easy way for artists to explore online music. MP3 players are free to download, and software to create MP3 may cost only $20. The key, MP3 proponents claim, is to respect an author's copyright and obtain permission before distributing.[82]

The unresolved issue in the use of the MP3 format is how much damage is being done to the recording industry. It is not uncommon for artists to license their work to recording companies to allow them to distribute the work in exchange for a royalty. The ability for people to pirate music in an

MP3 format has the recording industry nervous about lost revenues. At this time, it is unclear how many users are downloading an artist's music rather than purchasing that artist's CD. But the Recording Industry Association of America (RIAA)[83] is leaving nothing to chance. It has recently filed lawsuits against two companies for copyright infringement.

The first suit was brought against MP3.com, challenging its services that allow subscribers to store, customize, and listen to music from any computer on the Internet. MP3.com purchased thousands of CDs and, without authorization, copied their recordings onto its computer servers so that it could replay the recordings for its subscribers. MP3.com subscribers could access the music in one of two ways. They could use the "Beam-it" service, which required subscribers to prove that they already owned the CD version of the recording by momentarily inserting their copy of the CD into their computer CD-ROM drive. Alternatively, a subscriber could use the "Instant Listening" service, which required a subscriber to first purchase the music from an online retailer. Although MP3.com argued that its service was the functional equivalent of storing its subscriber's CDs on the Internet, the court objected and found that it was merely replaying for subscribers converted versions of the recordings it copied.[84] MP3.com was therefore liable for copyright infringement based on the use of sound recordings that it did not own or license.

The second suit was brought against the Napster Web site, the music-swapping site that has single-handedly increased public awareness of MP3 technology issues. Napster's site uses software of its own creation, which allows users to easily swap MP3 music files on its trading network. The RIAA and individual recording artists objected to this practice, claiming copyright violations in Napster's service because it enabled and facilitated the copying and distribution of protected sound recordings.[85] Napster in its defense has claimed immunity as an ISP, citing that it is merely a conduit for the services and does not itself copy or store the copyright protected materials on its servers. A federal district court did not agree, however, and enjoined Napster from facilitating the swapping of music files. Napster countered with a stay, allowing the site to continue running until trial. Currently, Napster is working to settle the case out of court, and has thus far agreed to form an alliance with multimedia conglomerate Bertelsmann AG to develop a new secure file-sharing music service. Unfortunately, it is unclear when and how the case will ultimately be resolved, and what the future of MP3 will be.

DVD Videos

The newest digital video format, DVD, is rife with copyright issues similar to that of MP3. DVDs, or digital versatile discs, allow a motion picture to be viewed on either a television or personal computer. The data on a DVD are encrypted by the Content Scramble System (CSS) to prevent tampering and unauthorized copying. But the CSS encryption has been circumvented by software called DeCSS. DVDs may now be reproduced at will and traded over the Internet.

The Copyright Act of 1976 was amended by the Digital Millennium Copyright Act in 1998.[86] Among other things, the new act prohibits gaining unauthorized access to a work by circumventing technological protections that control it. It also prohibits the manufacture and distribution of the means of circumventing the technological protection. Based on these portions of the statute, it is a copyright violation to use DeCSS to circumvent CSS protection. Furthermore, the distribution of the DeCSS software will also be deemed a copyright violation.

Based on the potential for copyright infringement of DVDs, several organizations are bringing suit. The Motion Picture Association of America has filed against several Web sites for copyright infringement for making the DeCSS software available. Likewise, the DVD Association had brought a separate action alleging the willful misappropriation of proprietary information by similar Web sites. Recently, judges in both California and New York have ruled that posting of DeCSS violates the Copyright Act.

The battle over DeCSS is not as simple as it may appear. Although the legal issues may be relatively straightforward, there is a more complicated philosophical debate at the core. This is a tension between copyright protection, on one hand, and user access, on the other. Copyright law seeks to protect a work by granting the author exclusive rights. The effect of such a system is the exchange of ideas and information. But proponents of unlimited access claim that copyrights create an untoward proprietary interest. The exchange of ideas and information can be better achieved if software systems are open and available to everyone; an idea referred to as the open source movement. Followers of the open source movement are supportive of open software standards and shareware such as Linux. Such nonproprietary software maximizes the number of people who have access to and may use the applications. Predictably, open source proponents support the use of DeCSS and shun the creation of software copy protection systems because this reinforces proprietary interests. When and if open source movement proponents gain a strong enough voice to generate a change in copyright policy remains to be seen. Until then, the use of DeCSS software will remain a copyright violation.

Copyright protection seeks to promote the exchange of ideas by granting authors the right to reproduce, distribute, perform, display, and create derivative versions of their work. The popularity of the Internet as a tool for self-expression is causing authors to question whether their works are at risk in this new medium. The possibility of misappropriation by linking or framing has forced courts to consider copyright infringement on the World Wide Web. Unfortunately, little guidance is available in these areas, compared to the definite answers that may be forthcoming in music and video piracy.

■ EPILOGUE

This chapter opened with a quotation from Justice Fortas, who bemoaned the fact that applying traditional jurisprudential tools to emerging law was like trying to repair a television set with a mallet. The crux of the matter is that judicial precedent and technology are often at odds, and without some give on both sides, the two cannot coexist.

Recent copyright developments in the Napster MP3 music-swapping case indicate that law and technology are both capable of giving a little, with satisfactory results. The injunction against Napster to halt its file-swapping service was stayed, pending appeal. On February 12, 2001, the Court of Appeals for the Ninth Circuit affirmed the district court's decision that Napster was infringing musical copyright by facilitating others in downloading and transmitting the MP3 files. The court recognized, however, that the injunction was overbroad, and remanded it back to the district court to modify. On March 5, 2001, the district court issued the revised injunction, which prohibited Napster from engaging its service under specific circumstances.

Since then, Napster has resolved to bring its services in line with the court's mandate, and will launch its revamped services in early 2002 using new technology. To comply with the injunction, Napster's music will be licensed for sharing in the Napster community and artists will thereby receive a royalty fee.

With the revised injunction and the relaunch of Napster, traditional law has clashed with new technology and the results are startling; both the courts and technology can give a little to coexist.

■ NOTES

1. *Fortnightly Corp. v. United Artists Television, Inc.*, 88 S. Ct. 2084, 2091 (1968) (dissenting opinion discussing the application of the Copyright Act of 1909 to television).

2. *Blumenthal v. Drudge*, 992 F. Supp. 44, 49 (D.D.C. 1998).

3. Intellectual property is nonphysical property created by thought, and legally protected and recognized by the government. Providing intellectual property rights acts as an incentive to individuals to create new products, processes, or works of art. The end benefit of such legal protection is the delivery of a variety of goods and services to the public. Several different legal fields including copyrights, trademarks, unfair competition, patents, and trade secrets protect intellectual property. With the inception of the Internet, computer-related issues now affect these traditional intellectual property fields in addition to being a field of law unto itself.

4. Edward A. Cavazos, "The Idea Incubator: Why the Internet Poses Unique Problems for the First Amendment," 7 *Seton Hall Constitutional Law Journal* 667 (1998).

5. U.S. Constitution, First Amendment.

6. See, for example, *Urofsky v. Allen*, 995 F. Supp. 634 (E.D. Va. 1998) (striking down state statute banning state employees from downloading sexually explicit speech). The statute, the court concluded, violated the employee's First Amendment rights because the state's interest in the speech restriction did not outweigh the right of the employee to view such materials. See, for example, *Cyber Promotions, Inc. v. America Online, Inc.*, 948 F. Supp. 436 (E.D. Pa. 1996) (holding that AOL (America Online), as a nongovernmental private entity, was allowed to prevent plaintiff from sending unsolicited e-mail to AOL subscribers).

7. See, for example, *Whirlpool v. G. E. Holdings*, 67 F.3d 605 (7th Cir. 1995) (imposing a duty to search the Internet to meet due diligence standard). The problem, naturally, is that one cannot wave a magic wand and have the Internet disgorge the requested information; search engines are simply, at the time of this writing, incapable of searching the entire Internet.

8. George B. Delta and Jeffrey H. Matsuura, *Law of the Internet*, § 8.01[A] (New York: Aspen Law and Business, 2000) (citing, among others, the seminal obscenity possession case *Stanley v. Georgia*, 394 U.S. 557 [1969]).

9. See *Ginsberg v. New York*, 390 U.S. 629 (1968).

10. *Miller v. California*, 413 U.S. 15, 24 (1973).

11. *Roth v. United States*, 354 U.S. 476, 487 (1957).

12. *Id.* at note 20 (citing Model Penal Code § 207.10(2) cmt. at 10 [Tenth Draft No. 6, 1957]).

13. See *Miller*, 413 U.S. at 32 ("It is neither unrealistic nor constitutionally sound to read the First Amendment as requiring that the people of Maine or Mississippi accept public depiction of conduct found tolerable in Las Vegas, or New York City.").

14. See *id.* at 27 ("No one will be subject to prosecution for the sale or exposure of obscene materials unless such materials depict or describe patently offensive 'hard core' sexual conduct specifically defined by the regulating state law.").

15. See Delta and Matsuura, *Law of the Internet*, 8-11 (noting that lawyers refer to this as the "SLAPS test").

16. See *Pope v. Illinois*, 481 U.S. 497 (1987).

17. See *id.* at 501.

18. See 47 U.S.C. § 223 (1996).

19. Delta and Matsuura, *Law of the Internet*, 8-25.

20. See 47 U.S.C. § 231 et seq.

21. See, for example, *ACLU v. Reno*, 217 F.3d 162 (3d Cir. 2000) (affirming lower court's decision to preliminary enjoin COPA).

22. *United States v. Thomas*, Nos. 94-6648, 94-6649, 1996 U.S. App. Lexis 1069, 74 F.3d 701 (6th Cir. 1996).

23. See Alan Freedman, *The Computer Glossary*, 30 (8th ed., New York: American Management Association, 1998). A bulletin board is defined as

a computer system used as an information source and forum for a particular interest group . . . [and] used to distribute shareware and drivers in the U.S. and had their heyday before the World Wide Web took off. A BBS functions somewhat like a stand-alone Web site [but] unlike [a] Web site, each BBS system has its own telephone number to dial into.

24. Delta and Matsuura, *Law of the Internet*, 8-40.1.

25. *Id.*

26. 4 F. Supp. 2d 1029 (1998).

27. *United States v. Kurfrovich*, 997 F. Supp. 246 (1997).

28. For example, e-mail and Web traffic may be routed through multiple computers that employ software to remove any identifying information. Additionally, these computers themselves do not necessarily know the actual point of origin. See http://www.privada.com for additional information.

29. *Stanley v. Georgia*, 304 U.S. 557 (1969).

30. See F. Lawrence Street, *Law of the Internet*, 588-590 (Newark, NJ: LexisNexis, 1998).

31. See *Cyber Promotions, Inc. v. America Online, Inc.*, 948 F. Supp. 436, 462 (E.D. Pa. 1996).

32. See *id.* at 447.

33. Dan Goodin, *Antiabortion Site Owner Sues MindSpring*, C/Net News.Com, June 10, 1999, at http://www.news.com/News/Item/0,4,37665,00.html.

34. See 18 U.S.C. § 2252.

35. See *New York v. Ferber*, 458 U.S. 742 (1982).

36. *FCC v. Pacifica Found., Inc.*, 438 U.S. 726, 731-32 (1978).

37. *ACLU v. Reno*, Civ. No. 96-963, Plaintiffs' Memo. of Law in Support of a Motion for a TRO and Preliminary Injunction (E.D. Pa. February 8, 1996).

38. *ACLU v. Reno*, Civ. No. 96-963, Defendant's Opposition to Plaintiffs' Motion for a TRO (E.D. Pa. February 8, 1996) (quoting excerpts from 47 U.S.C. § 223(a)(1)(B)).

39. For example, minors would be unable to obtain information regarding the sexual proclivities of harvester ants or obtain information about Judy Bloom's banned books, and so on.

40. See, for example, *FCC v. Pacifica Found., Inc.*, 438 U.S. 726 (1978).

41. A recent case challenges the presumption that a state may not employ filters to control access. See *Mainstream Loudon v. Board of Trustees of the Loudoun County Library*, 24 F. Supp. 2d 552, 2 F. Supp. 2d 783 (E.D. Va. 1998). The court found unconstitutional the Loudoun County public library system's decision to use filters on all library computers connected to the Internet.

42. For example, due to Internet traffic or problems, some Web sites may simply be unavailable during the time the user is "surfing" the Internet. A user employing such filtering software may not necessarily know.

43. See S. Warren and L. Brandeis, "The Right to Privacy," 4 *Harvard Law Review* 193 (1890).

44. Restatement (Second) of Torts §§ 652B-652E.

45. See *Stern v. Delphi Internet Serv. Corp.*, 626 N.Y.S.2d 694 (Sup. Ct. 1995).

46. *United States v. Maxwell*, 42 M.J. 568 (A.F.C.C.A. 1995).

47. *Id.* at 576.

48. 816 F. Supp. 432 (W.D. Tex. 1993).

49. See 18 U.S.C. § 2510 to -22, 2701 to -10, 2711 (1996).

50. See 18 U.S.C. § 1030(e) (1994).

51. See 18 U.S.C. § 1030(a).

52. 42 U.S.C. § 2000aa(a).

53. Street, *Law of the Internet*, 152. *Children* includes anyone under the age of 13 according to Section 6510 of Title 15 of the United States Code.

54. See 64 *Fed. Reg.* 59888 (1999). On July 10, 2000, Toysmart.com became the first company charged with violating COPPA's regulations. See *FTC v. Toysmart.com, LLC & Toysmart, Inc.*, No. 00-11341-RGS (D. Mass. filed July 10, 2000).

55. See, for example, *Smyth v. Pillsbury Co.*, 914 F. Supp. 97 (E.D. Pa. 1996); *Shoars v. Epson America, Inc.*, No. SWC II2749 (Cal. App. Dep't. Super. Ct., December 8, 1992).

56. *Talley v. California*, 362 U.S. 60, 64 (1960).

57. U.S. Constitution, Article I, § 8, cl. 8. This clause also protects inventors' discoveries, and is the basis for patent law.

58. Copyright Act of 1976, 17 U.S.C. §§ 101-810; 1001-1010.

59. Copyright Act, 17 U.S.C. § 102.

60. See Melville B. Nimmer, *Nimmer on Copyright*, § 2.03(B)(1) (New York: Matthew Bender, 1999).

61. Copyright Act, 17 U.S.C. § 101.

62. The remedy for copyright infringement does, however, depend on whether the work is federally registered. Authors of nonregistered works are entitled only to obtain an injunction against the infringing party. Authors of registered works are additionally entitled to damages and attorney's fees. Copyright Act, 17 U.S.C. § 412.

63. Copyright Act, 17 U.S.C. § 102(b) ("In no case does copyright protection for an original work of authorship extend to any idea, procedure, process, system, method of operation, concept principle, or discovery, regardless of the form in which it is described, explained illustrated, or embodied in such works.").

64. See Nimmer, *Nimmer on Copyright,* § 2.03(A).

65. Copyright Act, 17 U.S.C. § 106.

66. Copyright Act, 17 U.S.C. § 302(a).

67. *What Is . . . a Link* (visited March 12, 2000), http://www.whatis.com/link.htm.

68. Permission to link to another site is not a legal requirement, but it is considered good "netiquette." Likewise, a specific request to take down a link should be honored.

69. TicketMaster alleged various trademark and unfair competition violations, but did not actually claim copyright infringement even though the complaint made reference to the appropriation of its proprietary content. See *TicketMaster Corp. v. Microsoft Corp.*, No. 97-3055 DDP (C.D. Cal. complaint filed April 28, 1997) ("By accessing TicketMaster's live event information and services without TicketMaster's approval, and by prominently offering it as a service to their users, Microsoft is feathering its own nest at TicketMaster's expense. It is, in effect, committing electronic piracy.").

70. Carl S. Kaplan, *Is Linking Always Legal?* (August 6, 2000), http://www.nytimes.com/library/tech/99/08/cyber/cyberlaw/06law.html.

71. Copyright Act, 17 U.S.C. § 107.

72. Copyright Act, 17 U.S.C. § 107.

73. *What Is . . . Frames* (visited March 12, 2000), http://www.whatis.com/frames.htm.

74. Netscape Assistance, *Frames: An Introduction* (visited March 12, 2000), http://www.netscape.com/assist/net_sites/frames.html.

75. See *Washington Post Co. v. Total News, Inc.*, No. 97 Civ 1190 (PKL) (S.D.N.Y. complaint filed February 20, 1997).

76. See *Washington Post Co. v. Total News, Inc.*, No. 97 Civ 1190 (PKL) (S.D.N.Y. settlement filed June 5, 1997).

77. See Nimmer, *Nimmer on Copyright*, § 10.03(A).

78. *What Is . . . MP3* (visited March 12, 2000), http://www.whatis.com/mp3.htm.

79. Analog sound is a function of amplitude, frequency, and phase of a sine wave. Digital sound is the encoding of sound into a binary form (1s and 0s).

80. Under Section 1008 of the Copyright Act, consumers are immune from copyright infringement actions when they make copies of sound recordings for personal, noncommercial use. This exception allowing consumers to copy sound recordings without penalty was made because the manufacturers of the recording

devices instead pay a statutory royalty on each device sold. But the exception is extended only to digital and analog recording devices that are primarily marketed for sound recording. Therefore, multipurpose media, such as CD-ROMs and computers, are not covered by such an exception. A consumer can make a copy of a CD with his or her stereo system without penalty (because the stereo manufacturer is likely paying a royalty) but cannot copy that CD with a CD-ROM or computer.

81. Recording Industry Association of America, Inc., *Soundbyting: Top 10 Myths* (visited March 26, 2000), http://www.soundbyting.com/html/top_10_myths_index.html.

82. Michael Robertson, *Top 10 Things Everyone Should Know About MP3* (July 23, 1998), http://www.mp3.com/news/070.html.

83. RIAA is a trade group for recorded music. Its members include BMG Entertainment, EMI-Recorded Music, Sony Music Entertainment, Inc., Rhino, and La Face, among others. RIAA, *Frequently Asked Questions* (visited March 26, 2000), http://www.riaa.com/about/ab_faq.htm.

84. *RIAA v. MP3.com*, (visited December 20, 2000), http://www.virtualrecordings.com/riaamp3.htm.

85. RIAA, *FAQ About RIAA's Lawsuit Against Napster* (visited March 26, 2000), http://www.riaa.com/piracy/press/031300.htm.

86. Copyright Act, 17 U.S.C. §§ 1201-1205.

CHAPTER **9**

LAW AND REGULATION, PART II

Business Interests

Janessa Light

Katherine Neikirk

> *Our inquiry cannot be limited to ordinary meaning and legislative history, for this is a statute that was drafted long before the development of the electronic phenomena with which we deal here. In 1909 radio itself was in its infancy, and television had not been invented. We must read the statutory language of 60 years ago in the light of drastic technological change.*
>
> — Justice Stewart[1]

At the dawn of a new millennium, a new technology is sweeping the world: the Internet. Like previous technological developments, the Internet has created a number of new legal issues. It might seem strange that legal principles developed over hundreds of years can apply to something as new as the Internet. Yet this is not the first time that courts have applied traditional legal principles to a new technology. The law has dealt with radio, television, and other modern wonders that our Founding Fathers could not have begun to imagine. And as the above quotation by Justice Stewart demonstrates, the flexibility of our legal system continues to allow the courts to extend the law to cutting edge technologies such as the Internet.

When courts extend existing laws to fit new technology, the result is a ripple-like effect that changes the way people handle that technology. It is therefore important that consumers and companies are aware of the legal issues in transacting business over the Internet. Therefore, the focus of this chapter is to identify and explain the rights and remedies that concern a person's business interests in cyberspace. The next section analyzes some legal ramifications of intellectual property[2] on the Internet; specifically, the use of trademarks in domain names, meta-tags, and ad keying. The section following that addresses the Internet's impact on the field of jurisdiction. Last, we examine defamation law on the Internet with respect to liability and defenses.

■ TRADEMARKS

In June 1996, two college students hatched an ambitious plan late one night over coffee in a crowded café. The quarter was ending, and they needed summer jobs. But rather than pass the time working for minimum wage, they decided to put their computer skills to the test and offer their services as Internet consultants. Once they had decided to form a partnership, and taken care of the requisite licenses and bank accounts, they had only to settle on a name to set the business in motion. But when the college students tried to register their chosen domain name to establish the business Web site, they discovered it was already taken. Furthermore, there were other companies operating under similar business names, and some of those companies were also in the computing field. Could they still use their chosen business name, or would they have to change it? But what about the domain name—if their first choice was taken what recourse did they have?

Unknowingly, the college students stumbled into the morass of conducting business on the Internet. But they are not alone as entrepreneurs, small businesses, and corporations also question how they may conduct their business in cyberspace. The increase in business conducted over the Internet has introduced novel issues as to how a company may protect its products, name, and goodwill in a virtual marketplace.[3] Whether that company maintains a Web site to supplement a brick-and-mortar operation or is conducting a pure e-commerce business, traditional legal protections afforded to a company are in flux in cyberspace.

Background

There are several traditional forms of protection a company can obtain for its products and name in the marketplace. A company may legally protect any word, name, symbol, device (or combination thereof) it uses in commerce to identify its goods, a right recognized as a trademark.[4] For example, "Hershey's Kisses" is a trademark used by said company on its chocolate candies. Companies may also protect the look of the products they sell, in the form of the color scheme, shape, and size of the goods' packaging. This overall look of a product is referred to as the trade dress.[5] Hershey is therefore entitled to protect the conical shape of its chocolate kisses as they are wrapped in foil with their signature plume. And finally, companies may protect the business names they use—their trade names.[6] Hershey's trade name, "Hershey Foods Corporation," as the name the company uses in its business is therefore protected. Trademarks, trade dress, and trade name are used separately or in combination by a company to help protect its goodwill.

Legal protection for these types of marks arose out of unfair competition law, which recognized the interest of the business not to have its goods misappropriated and the interest of the public not to be deceived.[7] The result of such policies is the protection of marks by both statute and at common law.[8] Statutorily, federal protection is given in the Trademark Act of 1946 (the Lanham Act).[9] Protection under the Lanham Act is extended only to federally registered marks, however, and to be registered a mark must meet specific criteria. Marks that are unregistered are still afforded some degree of protection under common law.

The legal protection that a trademark grants to the holder makes it a valuable intellectual property right. Trademarks become a business asset because the holder has exclusive use of that mark in the marketplace. Such value was acknowledged by Justice Frankfurter when he noted:

> The owner of a trademark exploits [the psychological function of symbols] by making every human effort to impregnate the atmosphere of the market with the drawing power of a congenial symbol. Whatever the means employed, the aim is the same—to convey through the mark, in the minds of potential customers, the desirability of the commodity upon which it appears. Once this is attained, the trademark owner has something of value. If another poaches upon the commercial magnetism of the symbol he has created, the owner can obtain legal redress.[10]

Trademark law serves a number of purposes other than to simply protect a company's assets. The most basic function of a trademark is to designate the quality of goods and their source of origin.[11] To this extent, trademarks play a role in consumerism by helping buyers make purchasing decisions.

But trademarks also serve an important public policy function by fixing the responsibility of the goods to the identified manufacturer.[12]

The infringement, or unauthorized use, of a trademark by another party is determined from the point of view of the consumer. The likelihood of confusion by the public is used as the most basic test to determine whether there has been trademark infringement.[13] This is measured in two dimensions, (1) by the type of goods the mark represents[14] and (2) by the geographic location of the trademark's use.[15] Hypothetically, if a furniture store decides it wants to name a new line of baby products "Hershey high chairs" there would be no infringement of any Hershey Foods Corporation trademark. The Hershey Foods Corporation deals mostly in chocolate, and certainly not in furniture. It is therefore possible for two companies to have the same trademark on two different products if they represent different types of goods. It is unlikely that the public would confuse the furniture maker's product with the chocolate maker's product. The same concept is true of the geographic use of a trademark. If the hypothetical furniture company was a small business located only in California, and Hershey operated only in Pennsylvania, there would again be no trademark infringement. The two companies are operating in geographically separate markets and so there is likely to be little confusion among the public as to whose product they are purchasing. The "likelihood of confusion" test prevents consumers from being deceived while discouraging opportunistic parties from passing off their goods as belonging to another company.

But the test for trademark infringement breaks down in the Internet context, throwing the legal protection for trademarks into disarray. Because the Internet is a global network of computer networks, it knows no geographic bounds. How can the geographic marketplace be measured when navigating the World Wide Web can bring a user to a Web site located anywhere in the world? The blurring of geographic boundaries on the Internet is forcing courts and legislatures to rethink the application of trademark law and the protection previously afforded to trademark holders. The testing ground for trademark law in cyberspace has become the World Wide Web because it is the most graphic and image-oriented facet of the Internet. It is on the Web that companies advertise and conduct business, and naturally where trademark issues are arising first. Trademark disputes over their use in location and navigation on the Web are becoming more commonplace.

Using Trademarks for Location: Domain Names

Trademarks, as they are used in domain names, are a valuable tool to direct users to the location of a company's Web site. Whereas a user may rely generally on search engines to find the information he or she is looking for on the Web, a domain name gives the user a quick shortcut to a homepage. It is more efficient to simply type the domain name of a company directly into the uniform resource locator (URL) field of a browser than to search among engine results.

Domain names locate a particular server hosting a Web site on the Internet, much like a street address is used to locate a person's residence. The domain name system (DNS) operates by mapping domain names to Internet protocol (IP) addresses to denote the physical point of a computer on the Internet. For example, Villanova University uses the domain name "villanova.edu," which is mapped to the IP address 199.0.02. Typing "http://www.villanova.edu" directs a Web browser to connect to the server located at 199.0.02. Because IP addresses are cumbersome and impossible to remember, using a simple domain name is the easiest way to locate a Web site. Domain names therefore have an inherent value in locating information.

Because of the desirability of using simple and descriptive domain names to direct consumers to company Web sites, businesses are quick to secure their own. A problem arises, however, in that the universe of domain names is finite. Domain names are broken into levels, the highest of which is the "top level" domain. A top-level domain is a suffix attached to every domain name on the Web. There are six top-level domain suffixes (there are also designations for countries, e.g., .ca for Canada, .th for Thailand), and each represents the purpose of the entity that uses it:

com = commercial

net = network

org = organization

edu = education

mil = military

gov = government[16]

Subsuming this level is the second-level domain, which adds to the suffix the name of the entity. For example, the second-level domain for Hershey Foods Corporation is "hersheys.com." But because there are only six top-level domains, Hershey would be at a loss if this particular .com domain were already registered to another party.[17] The company would be forced to create some variation of its name to still use a ".com" designation, such as "hershey.com," "hershey_foods_corp.com," or "hershey-chocolate.com."

Although finding an alternative second-level domain name seems like a simple solution to top-level scarcity, it in fact raises more questions than answers. The first problem with this approach is that a user would be hard-pressed to formulate all the varieties of the Hershey name before hitting on the correct combination to the company's Web site. The second problem is that whoever holds the registration to the original "hersheys.com" wields tremendous power over the company to divert consumers who are seeking Hershey on the Web. And what of the hypothetical furniture company who is also legitimately using a HERSHEY trademark in conjunction with its baby high chairs? Should that company be entitled to use the "hershey.com" domain name too?

Complicating the scarcity of domain names are the rights of trademark holders. If Hershey Foods Corporation uses the HERSHEY trademark, does it have a superior right to the domain name "hersheys.com"? Arguably, any commercial use of that domain name by a party other than Hershey Foods Corporation would be trademark infringement. What if the domain name were registered to another party but unused? Could the simple denial of use of a particular domain name infringe Hershey's rights? These are domain name registration and *cybersquatting* issues, which intersect with trademark rights. Courts are struggling to resolve these issues, but there are no bright-line rules as of yet.

Registration of Domain Names

The Internet thus far has been a self-regulating medium, and there have been few guidelines to indicate to users how and when they may register domain names. Registration was originally handled by Network Solutions Incorporated (NSI), a private company under contract with the National Science Foundation. In dealing with early disputes, and in an effort to indemnify itself against trademark violation suits, NSI created a domain dispute policy. The policy states that NSI is not an arbiter of disputes, but allows it to revoke a domain name at its discretion under certain circumstances.[18] Although this particular policy set some registration guidelines, it mostly insulated and protected NSI.[19] Nonprofit groups, such as the International Trademark Association (ITA) and the Internet Ad Hoc Committee (IAHC), have proposed additional guidelines, but they have not been universally accepted or adopted.

The most recent registration policy has been proposed by the Internet Corporation for Assigned Names and Numbers (ICANN). ICANN, affiliated and supported by the Internet Society (a nonprofit group that administers the standard protocols of the Internet), created the Uniform Domain Name Dispute Resolution Policy in September 1999. The policy requires registrants to affirmatively state that they are not infringing the rights of a third party in their attempt to register a domain name. Additionally, common law trademark holders can use the policy because it is not restricted to registered trademark holders.[20] Remedies set forth in the policy include cancellation of the domain name or transfer of ownership. The policy is especially innovative because it allows for complaints to be made via e-mail and for decisions to be posted on the Internet. Initially, the future of ICANN's policy was uncertain because NSI refused to recognize ICANN in any form. This was especially damaging because NSI is currently the main organization that registers domain names. But in recent developments, NSI has finally acknowledged ICANN as a fellow Internet-governing body, indicating that the Uniform Domain Name Dispute Resolution Policy will be the latest addition to the few guidelines that currently exist.

NSI's and ICANN's respective domain name policies answer some, but not all, questions about trademarks and domain names. Domain name policies, although helpful, do not supersede or control federal trademark law.[21] The ultimate determination as to the use of trademarks as domain names is still left to the judicial system. Courts are applying traditional trademark law to evaluate the domain name policies and address questions left unanswered by those policies.

Within the past few years, courts have begun to develop a patchwork of domain-related trademark law. Generally, judges have concluded that trademark holders do not have an outright claim to their marks as domain names.[22] This gives the priority to the first party to register for the domain name. Thus, if Hershey Foods Corporation wanted to register "hersheys.com" but it was already taken, the company would have no superior right to claim that domain name even if it is the trademark holder. But the reverse is true as well—acquiring a domain name does not give a party priority in obtaining a trademark on that name.[23] In other words, the registration and use of a domain name does not create trademark protection. By registering "hersheys.com," an opportunistic party would not have a superior right to claim any HERSHEY mark under trademark law. These principles indicate a cautious integration of trademark infringement law and domain name registration.

Trademark dilution claims, however, reflect a more aggressive clash between the rights of a trademark holder and a domain name registrant. Domain name registrants may still run the risk of violating the rights of a trademark holder (depending on how the domain name is used) even where the name was legitimately registered first. Rather than infringement, the domain name registrant may be liable for the dilution of the mark under the Federal Trademark Dilution Act of 1995.[24] Courts, however, have been explicit in that the act alone of registering a domain name that is also a trademark is not dilution.[25]

Trademark dilution claims are distinct from infringement claims. Dilution occurs where the value of a trademark is lessened in some manner when it is used commercially. This may take the form of either blurring or tarnishment. Blurring occurs when the value of a mark is whittled away by its use on a dissimilar product. If the domain name "hersheys.com" were registered to a third party who used it to sell hardware supplies on the Web, Hershey Foods Corporation could argue its HERSHEY mark has been blurred. On the other hand, tarnishment occurs when the value of a mark is diminished by the association with an inferior or unwholesome product or service. Again, if a third party registered "hersheys.com" but this time used it to market an escort service on the Web, Hershey Foods Corporation could claim its HERSHEY mark had been tarnished.[26] In both blurring and tarnishment, the strength of the mark has been diluted by the improper use of a trademark as a domain name.

Courts are beginning to define the rights of trademark holders who register their domain names on the World Wide Web. Although significant inroads are being made in infringement and dilution domain name disputes, there is one facet of registration that is still amorphous: cybersquatting.

Cybersquatting

Because courts have determined that trademark holders do not have priority to register their marks as domain names, opportunists take advantage of the "first come, first served" approach to domain name registration. These opportunists register a spate of domain names that other parties may find valuable, and then sell them for prices higher than the registration fee to turn a profit. These domain names may be a celebrity's name or a company's product. Common English words are also registered, such as "furniture.com" or "drugstore.com," in the hopes it may be valuable now or in the future.[27] This act of registering domain names without the intent to use them, but rather to sell them, is referred to as cybersquatting.[28]

Often a party seeking a domain name that is already registered will prefer to deal with a cybersquatter because it is less expensive than taking legal action. But does that party whose name is registered have any legal remedies against a cybersquatter? Does the simple act of preventing another party from using a domain name violate trademark law? Courts have issued opinions on some, but not all, of these legal questions that cybersquatting raises.

Courts have ruled that where a cybersquatter registers a domain name that is also a trademark, that person has diluted the mark.[29] Normally, the simple act of registering a trademarked domain name is not enough to create a commercial use in violation of the Federal Trademark Dilution Act of 1995. But in the case of cybersquatting, the registration *and subsequent attempt to sell* the trademarked domain is considered a commercial use in violation of the Federal Trademark Dilution Act. Because cybersquatters' business is to sell trademarked domain names, they engage in commercial use of the trademark when offering to sell it. Courts commonly view cybersquatting as extorting money from companies by trading on the value of their trademarks.

Where a registered domain name is not a trademark (e.g., a surname), it is less likely that a court will find the cybersquatting to violate a law. For example, Jerry Sumpton registered more than 12,000 surnames as domain names in 1998. Among his domains were "avery.net" and "dennison.net." The Avery Dennison Corporation brought suit against Sumpton claiming infringement and dilution of its AVERY and DENNISON marks. Whereas the lower court found in Avery Dennison Corporation's favor, on appeal the district court reversed. The district court determined that Sumpton, in using the domain names to license e-mail addresses, was not capitalizing on the value of the trademarks. Rather, he was using words that happened to be trademarks for their nontrademark value.

In part because few cybersquatting cases have been decided by the courts, the legislature created the Anti-cybersquatting Consumer Protection Act in 1999 in an effort to establish a bright-line rule.[30] The act, which amends the Trademark Act of 1946, prohibits the registration, trafficking in, or use of a domain name that is identical or confusingly similar to a trademark or service mark of another where it results in fraud, confusion, or burden to the trademark holder. Furthermore, the cybersquatter must have a bad-faith intent to profit from that domain name as a trademark or service mark. To determine bad faith, a court may consider several factors such as whether the cybersquatter has used the domain name, offers to sell it, or has registered multiple domain names. If bad faith is found, the court can order the cancellation or forfeiture of the domain name, in addition to awarding damages resulting from the cybersquatting.

It should be noted that it is unlikely that cybersquatting on domain names that are common English words or generic terms will be found to violate any law. Trademark dilution on the Internet, as determined under case law and the Anti-cybersquatting Consumer Protection Act, is based on the rationale that one party is profiting from the goodwill of another party's marks. But domain names that are common or generic would not be afforded trademark protection and therefore would have no goodwill to exploit. Trademark law does not usually grant protection to descriptive and generic terms,[31] such as "chocolate" or "candy." This preserves fairness, to allow competitors to use such terms without penalty in describing their own products. It follows then that "chocolate.com" or "candy.com" would not impinge on the goodwill of a mark because it generally would not be protected as a trademark.

Using Trademarks for Navigation: Meta-Tags and Ad Keying

Aside from domain names, trademarks appear in other forms on the World Wide Web. Specifically, trademarks often aid users in navigating their way to a particular Web site. Whereas using a domain name requires the user to affirmatively type the trademark into the URL field or a search engine, using trademarks to navigate the Web is more passive. In this situation, a user may be unknowingly coaxed to a site when the trademark is used as a meta-tag or in ad keying.

Meta-Tags

Hypertext Markup Language, or HTML, is a nonproprietary publishing language for the World Wide Web. HTML is literally a markup language since special tags, denoted in brackets, are used to mark text to be displayed in a particular way on a Web page. For example <STRONG> is an HTML tag that instructs a Web browser to display words with emphasis, usually in boldface type.[32] In addition to regular tags, HTML uses *meta-tags* to convey to the browser information about the HTML page. So if an HTML page contained the meta-tag <META NAME="Keywords" CONTENT="law, trademarks">, the Web server would include in the header information of the document "Keywords: law, trademarks."

When used, meta-tag information is hidden from the user. Meta information, such as keywords describing the content of a Web page, is primarily used by search engines. Although meta-tags are useful in identifying Web page content, trademark violations may arise if that Web page is using another party's trademarks in the meta-tag information.

The benefit to using another party's trademark in a meta-tag is to capitalize on the goodwill of the mark. A search engine will identify the mark from the meta-tag, and return that Web site as a false positive. Meta-tagging therefore allows a party to divert business from the mark's holder to his or her own site. In *Brookfield v. West Coast Entertainment*, the misuse of meta-tags was addressed by a federal court. West Coast Video, a national video rental chain, was using the word "MovieBuff" in a meta-tag. However, MOVIEBUFF is a trademark belonging to Brookfield Communications, Incorporated.[33] The court reasoned that by using the trademark in a meta-tag, West Coast Entertainment was effectively posting a sign that misled consumers to visit its own site rather than Brookfield's. The consumers would not be confused in a narrow sense, because it would be clear that they were indeed at the West Coast site. But such use in meta-tagging amounted to the misappropriation of Brookfield's goodwill in the trademark.[34]

Ad Keying

Trademark abuse again arises in the context of search engines in *ad keying*. Ad keying is the practice of linking Web page banner advertisements to particular search keywords, including trademarked terms. From users' perspectives, advertisements will normally appear that match their query or reflect their interests. But by using ad keying, competitors may divert business from another party's Web site. For example, Playboy Enterprises filed suit against Excite Incorporated and Netscape Communications Corporation for ad keying to Playboy's trademarks. When a user searched Excite using a Playboy trademark like PLAYMATE, Excite's engine would respond with an advertisement for a competitor's adult site. Playboy sought an injunction and damages for trademark infringement and unfair competition. It claimed that the unauthorized use of its marks to sell targeted banner ads created confusion. A court refused to grant the injunction, and Playboy appealed. The case had not been definitively decided.

Objections to ad keying are occurring more frequently. Estée Lauder Companies, Incorporated, also brought suit against Excite for ad keying as trademark infringement. When a user searched for the Estée Lauder name, a banner ad appeared for The Fragrance Counter, Incorporated, an online cosmetic retailer.

Whether or not ad keying is deemed to amount to trademark infringement remains to be seen. Courts will likely look to whether (1) a search engine is earning a profit by selling advertising space tied to another party's trademark and (2) that advertising space is being sold to a competitor of the mark's holder, to determine if infringement has occurred.

Trademarks not only protect consumers but also allow businesses to legally protect their products and name in the marketplace. The movement of commerce to the Internet has raised questions as to how and when trademarks may be used in cyberspace. Trademark law and the World Wide Web have proven an imperfect fit as courts struggle to define trademark holder rights and the rights of domain name registrants. Courts must also address novel issues such as the use of trademarks in meta-tagging and ad keying in navigating the Web. The minimal case law that does currently exist indicates that courts will continue to apply traditional trademark infringement and dilution tests in cyberspace, looking to whether there is a likelihood of confusion or a third party is capitalizing on the value of the mark.

JURISDICTION ■

A Hawaii resident collects Tiffany glass. One day, while searching the Web for information on Tiffany glass exhibits, she finds a seller who specializes in Tiffany glass. This seller lives in Delaware and runs a lamp shop there. The seller's business is located and incorporated in Delaware. The seller also maintains a Web site where she offers lamps for sale. On this Web site, viewers can look at pictures of the lamps and order them online. The Hawaii resident decides to purchase one of the Tiffany lamps displayed on the site for $110,000. The buyer e-mails the seller with some questions, likes the answers she receives, and orders the lamp by filling out an order form on the Web site. The seller then sends the lamp to the buyer. By the time the buyer receives the lamp, it has shattered into many pieces. The buyer attempts to return the broken lamp to the seller and asks for her money back, but the seller refuses to take the lamp back or refund the buyer's money. As a result of the seller's actions, the buyer decides that she wants to sue the seller to recover the money she spent on the broken lamp. Now comes the hard part. Where can the buyer sue the seller? Can the buyer sue the seller in federal or state court? Can the buyer sue the seller in Hawaii? Or will the buyer have to go all the way to Delaware to recover from the seller? This hypothetical illustrates some of the issues surrounding jurisdiction on the Internet.

Types of Jurisdiction

Before a plaintiff may sue a defendant in court, the court must have jurisdiction over the case and the parties. Jurisdiction "is the power of a court to decide a matter in controversy."[35] If a court lacks jurisdiction, then it cannot hear or decide the case. Therefore, it is extremely important for the parties to ascertain whether a particular court can hear their case. There are two different types of jurisdiction that a court must have to hear a case. First, a court must have subject matter jurisdiction, which means that the court may hear the subject matter of the case. Second, a court must have personal jurisdiction, which means that the court has the authority to enter a judgment against the defendant (personal jurisdiction is not an issue for plaintiffs because by suing in a particular court they consent to that court exercising personal jurisdiction over them).

In federal courts, subject matter jurisdiction is defined by Article III, Section 2 of the Constitution. The Constitution allows federal courts to hear lawsuits between citizens of different states (diversity jurisdiction) and lawsuits involving federal questions. For a federal court to have diversity jurisdiction, the plaintiff and defendant must be citizens of different states and the amount in controversy must exceed $75,000. The amount in controversy is how much money the plaintiff is seeking from the defendant. A corporation has dual citizenship; it is a citizen of the state it is incorporated in and the state where its principle place of business is. Federal cases are "all civil actions arising under the Constitution, laws, or treaties of the United States."[36]

In state courts, state statutes establish subject matter jurisdiction. State statutes usually define subject matter jurisdiction based on the subject matter of the claim and the amount in controversy. Often state courts will hear certain types of cases. For example, family courts will decide child custody cases, and small claims courts will hear cases involving amounts in controversy under $1,000.

The Internet also raises many questions of personal jurisdiction. Obviously, if the defendant and plaintiff are residents of the state that the court sits in, then the court may hear the case. Even if the defendant is a nonresident of the forum, personal jurisdiction is proper if the defendant operates an office in the state or has an agent there. A nonresident defendant may also consent to the forum exercising personal jurisdiction. Often the situation is more complicated. In the hypothetical above, for example, the plaintiff is a citizen of Hawaii and wants to sue a company located and incorporated in Delaware. The plaintiff wants to sue in Hawaii because that is most convenient for her. But may a Hawaii court decide a case involving a company located and incorporated in Delaware?

The Due Process Clause of the Constitution limits states' power to enter judgments against nonresidents. Originally, courts based personal jurisdiction on whether the defendant was physically present in the forum state. But over time, it was possible for defendants (especially corporations) to transact business within a state without actually having any offices or employees physically present in that state. As a result of this change, courts adapted their personal jurisdiction analysis to address the fact that corporations could transact business within a state without being physically present in that state. Today, courts must adjust their personal jurisdiction analysis to deal with companies conducting business over the Internet.

Requirements of Personal Jurisdiction

Before deciding the constitutionality of personal jurisdiction, courts look at state law. State long-arm statutes establish when states may exercise personal jurisdiction over nonresident defendants. Often state long-arm statutes extend jurisdiction to the limits of the Constitution, but occasionally states choose not to exercise personal jurisdiction to the limits allowed by the Constitution. Even if personal jurisdiction is proper under the Constitution, a court may not exercise personal jurisdiction if it is not allowed under the state's long-arm statute. Federal courts look to the law of the state where they are located to determine whether they can exercise personal jurisdiction.[37]

Once deciding that a state long-arm statute authorizes personal jurisdiction, a court must determine if this exercise of jurisdiction is constitutional. In *International Shoe Co. v. Washington*,[38] the Supreme Court of the United States laid out the constitutional requirements for personal jurisdiction. This test, with some subsequent modifications, still applies today. In that case, the Supreme Court held that courts may exercise personal jurisdiction over nonresident defendants if those defendants have "certain minimum contacts with [the forum state] such that the maintenance of the suit does not offend 'traditional notions of fair play and substantial justice.'"[39] This statement boils down to a two-part test for personal jurisdiction. First, a court must look at whether a nonresident defendant has sufficient minimum contacts with the state. Second, if there are sufficient minimum contacts, the court must decide whether exercising personal jurisdiction over the nonresident is reasonable. A court will consider several factors in deciding whether the exercise of personal jurisdiction is reasonable. These factors include the burden on the defendant in defending itself in a distant forum, the forum state's interest in the litigation, the plaintiff's interest in obtaining relief, the court system's interest in obtaining efficient resolution of the case, and the state's interest in furthering substantive social policies.

Personal Jurisdiction on the Internet

So what exactly constitutes minimum contacts? That is a difficult question. Courts usually find that minimum contacts are present if a defendant has purposefully availed itself of the benefits of acting in a state or could "reasonably anticipate being haled into court there."[40] Mere foreseeability of injury in the forum, however, does not support personal jurisdiction. Even before the advent of the Internet, courts struggled with the minimum-contacts analysis. With the creation of the Internet, courts have had to apply these already difficult standards to an entity lacking geographic boundaries. In *Zippo Manufacturing Co. v. Zippo Dot Com, Inc.*,[41] the U.S. District Court for the Western District of Pennsylvania laid out the current test for the exercise of personal jurisdiction over nonresident defendants whose contacts with the forum state were conducted over the Internet. Generally, personal jurisdiction is "directly proportionate to the nature and quality of commercial activity that an entity conducts over the Internet."[42] According to this court's analysis, there are three categories of Web site conduct that may or may not support personal jurisdiction.

Level of Web Site Activity That Triggers Personal Jurisdiction

The first category includes Web sites where the defendant is clearly conducting business with the forum state. If the defendant is clearly conducting business over the Internet with the forum state, then a court sitting in that state may exercise personal jurisdiction. The defendant's business contacts with the forum might include sales to forum residents or contracts with forum companies. So an online merchant such as Amazon.com, which conducts business worldwide over the Internet, is probably subject to personal jurisdiction in every state.

The second category includes passive Web sites, which usually do not support personal jurisdiction. If the defendant's only contact with the forum state is through a passive Web site, then personal jurisdiction is probably not proper. A passive Web site is a site that only displays information; the viewer does not interact with the site. In *Bensusan Restaurant Corp. v. King*,[43] for example, the U.S. District Court for the Southern District of New York refused to exercise personal jurisdiction over the defendant based on a Web site that displayed information about the defendant's club. Although the Web site included information on buying tickets to the defendant's club, it was impossible to buy tickets through the site. People actually had to go to Missouri to pick up tickets for the club. However, something as small as a toll-free number might transform a passive Web site into a Web site supporting the exercise of personal jurisdiction. In *Inset Systems, Inc. v. Instruction Set, Inc.*,[44] a Connecticut court held that the nonresident defendant intended to reach customers all over the country including Connecticut because its Web site included a toll-free number. Because the defendant intended to reach Connecticut residents and the site was available to Connecticut residents, the defendant had sufficient minimum contacts with Connecticut for the exercise of personal jurisdiction.

The third category includes interactive Web sites. The exercise of personal jurisdiction over interactive Web sites depends on the site's level of interactivity. If a user interacts with a Web site by submitting his or her e-mail address or ordering something, then that site probably supports personal jurisdiction. In *Maritz v. Cybergold, Inc.*,[45] the U.S. District Court for the Eastern District of Missouri concluded that the nonresident's Web site was interactive enough to support personal jurisdiction because Missouri residents could sign onto a mailing list through the Web page.

Other Approaches to Personal Jurisdiction on the Internet

Courts are not limited to the *Zippo* framework in deciding whether personal jurisdiction is proper. For example, courts may look at the defendants' non-Internet as well as Internet contacts in deciding if personal jurisdiction is proper. A defendant who has contacted the forum by phone or mail, as well as by e-mail, is probably subject to personal jurisdiction. In *Blumenthal v. Drudge*,[46] the U.S. District Court for the District of Columbia used the defendant's non-Internet activities (personal visits, mail, and phone calls to the forum) as well as Internet activities to justify its exercise of personal jurisdiction. This "Internet plus" approach is especially useful in cases where the defendant's contacts with the forum were not over the Web. The *Zippo* analysis was based on Web pages and not all Internet activity takes places on the Web.

The effects test is another possible approach to personal jurisdiction on the Internet. Under the effects test, a nonresident defendant is subject to personal jurisdiction if the forum state was the "focal point" of the plaintiff's injury.[47] The Supreme Court created this test in *Calder v. Jones.*[48] In that case, the Supreme Court found that California could exercise personal jurisdiction over two nonresident defendants. The defendants had written and edited an allegedly libelous article about entertainer Shirley Jones for the *National Enquirer*. Although the defendants were residents of Florida, their actions had the most impact in California where Jones lived and worked. Because the defendants knew their actions hurt the plaintiff in California, the Court found that their "actions were expressly aimed" at the forum.[49] Therefore, California could exercise personal jurisdiction over the defendants.

Courts have used the effects test in Internet cases. In *Panavision International v. Toeppen,*[50] the Ninth Circuit held that California could exercise personal jurisdiction over a nonresident defendant who engaged in cybersquatting against a California corporation. The plaintiff suffered the effects of the defendant's conduct in California (where it was located) and the defendant knew this. Therefore, the defendant was subject to personal jurisdiction in California.

Fair Play and Substantial Justice

Even if a court concludes that a defendant has sufficient minimum contacts with the forum state, it can still refuse to exercise personal jurisdiction if it decides that personal jurisdiction offends "traditional notions of fair play and substantial justice."[51] Courts have rarely found that the exercise of personal jurisdiction would be unfair, and this issue has not arisen often in Internet cases. One exception, however, is *Expert Pages v. Buckalew*. In that case, the California court refused to exercise personal jurisdiction over the defendant (even though he had sufficient minimum contacts with California) because he was unsuccessful, lived in Virginia, and lacked the resources to defend himself in California.[52] The unfairness argument is particularly strong in cases where the defendant is engaged in noncommercial activity on the Internet. As one court noted, exercising "personal jurisdiction over non-commercial on-line speech that does not purposefully target any forum would result in hindering the wide range of discussion permissible on listserves, USENET discussion groups and with Web sites that are informational in nature."[53]

■ DEFAMATION

Imagine accountants subscribing to a mailing list for tax practitioners. They may respond to other members' questions and post questions of their own. One day, a user notices that an anonymous party has posted a message falsely stating that the user has been convicted of tax fraud. This message is forwarded to other accounting groups, and some of the user's clients see this message. As a result of this untrue posting, the user's reputation is tarnished and his or her business begins to suffer.

One day, a person begins receiving many threatening phone calls. It turns out that someone posted a message on an online bulletin board falsely claiming that this person is selling offensive T-shirts mocking the Oklahoma City bombing. This post includes the person's name and phone number. A local radio show reads this online message over the air and encourages listeners to call and express their disgust. In addition to hundreds of irate calls, this person receives death threats.[54]

A corporation does business all over the world. Someone claiming to be a company insider posts a message on a stock market Web site falsely claiming that this corporation is about to file for bankruptcy. As a result of this post, stock values plummet and investors flee the company.

An avid JFK assassination conspiracy buff subscribes to a Usenet group dedicated to discussion of this topic. This person frequently posts derogatory posts about another participant who has published a book on the assassination. The author posts a message to the group falsely claiming that his critic subscribes to child pornography groups. Even though the critic posts a message denying these accusations, a number of participants decry his perverted interests.[55]

Types of Defamation

The examples above illustrate the dangers of online defamation. Defamation is the "intentional false communication, either published or publicly spoken, that injures another's reputation or good name."[56] There are two types of defamation: slander and libel. Slander is oral defamation, and libel is written or printed defamation. To succeed on a defamation claim, the plaintiff must show that the defendant made (1) a false and defamatory statement about the plaintiff, (2) that was published by a third party, (3) by a publisher who was at least negligent in communicating the information, (4) and this statement damaged the plaintiff.[57] Falseness is an important element of defamation. If a defendant publishes a true statement about a plaintiff, then the plaintiff will not succeed in a defamation claim no matter how much harm he or she suffered. Therefore, defendants will often seek to avoid liability for defamation by arguing that their statements about the plaintiff were true.

On the Internet, defamation may occur on Usenet groups, mailing lists, Web pages, and chat rooms. Usually, online defamation will be libel since most Internet communications are written. Even chat room communications are usually considered libel because they appear in print on a computer screen or printout. But as audio use increases on the Internet, slander claims could increase. Most Internet users have encountered or even participated in the "flame wars" that pop up on various Internet discussion groups. In flame wars, users often insult each other. Expressing an insulting opinion, however, does not meet the requirements of defamation. Calling someone a nasty name is unlikely to constitute defamation because it probably qualifies as an opinion. Writing a negative review of a book or actor's performance would also qualify as an opinion rather than defamation. But accusing somebody of frequenting child pornography sites or carrying out fraud is defamation because it hurts that person's reputation and/or business.

Defamation can injure corporations as well as individuals. People have posted defamatory statements online claiming that certain companies are undergoing financial difficulties or breaking the law. As a result of such statements, a company's stock may drop or its reputation can suffer. Defamation can cost a corporation thousands or even millions of dollars if it causes a deal to fall through or stock prices to drop. Furthermore, a corporation will need to spend money to rebut defamatory statements made about it. Recently, corporations have begun bringing libel suits against individuals who allegedly posted libelous statements on the Internet.[58]

Damages for Defamation

In suing for defamation, a plaintiff may recover compensatory and punitive damages. Compensatory damages compensate the plaintiff for the loss he or she suffered as a result of the defendant's conduct. Compensatory damages might include lost profits in the case of a defamed corporation or the damage caused to a defamed individual's reputation. It can be difficult for a court to assign a dollar value to something intangible like a person's good reputation. If a plaintiff did not have an especially good reputation prior to the defendant's defamatory statement, then he or she may be unable to recover much if anything in the way of compensatory damages since the defendant did little damage. Unlike compensatory damages, punitive damages are based on the defendant's actions rather than the plaintiff's injury. Punitive damages punish the defendant for his or her wrongdoing. In addition to punishing the defendant for his or her bad behavior, punitive damages deter other people from acting in a similar manner. So a plaintiff who succeeds on a defamation claim can recover money based on the damage to his or her reputation and money designed to punish the defendant for his or her behavior.

In some states, a plaintiff must demand retraction or correction of a defamatory statement from the defendant before suing for damages. These state statutes may or may not extend to online publications. In *It's In The Cards, Inc. v. Fuschetto*,[59] for example, a Wisconsin court held that an online sports publication was not covered by the state's retraction statute and therefore the plaintiff was not required to demand a retraction from the defendant before suing.

Issues Regarding Defamation on the Internet

One issue is whether making a defamatory statement on the Internet satisfies the publication requirement of a defamation claim. Publication is usually satisfied if the statement was communicated to a third party, but the Internet poses challenges to this formula.[60] Would an e-mail between two parties count as a publication?[61] Or would it qualify as a publication if the recipient of the message forwarded it to other people? It is also important to determine the date of publication because that establishes when the statute of limitations begins to run. Statutes of limitations set the time period during which a plaintiff may file a cause of action against a defendant. If the statute of limitations has expired, then the plaintiff cannot sue the defendant.

Often people communicate over the Internet anonymously, which creates problems for defamation suits resulting from online communications. First, can someone who posted a defamatory statement about a person's pseudonym be liable for defaming the pseudonym? A victim might succeed in a defamation claim if other Internet users associated that pseudonym with the victim and the victim suffered harm as a result.[62] Second, how can victims of online defamation track down anonymous people who defamed them? Anonymous defamers are not necessarily free from liability. Defamation victims have successfully gone after Internet service providers (ISPs) to obtain the identities of subscribers who made defamatory statements under pseudonyms. When served with subpoenas, ISPs have turned over personal information about users accused of posting defamatory statements.

Traditional and Nontraditional Defenses to Defamation

Defamation Standard of Proof for Public Officials and Public Figures

The standard of proof in defamation claims is higher for public officials and public figures than for private citizens. The standard of proof is how much evidence the plaintiff needs to provide in order to win his or her case (in civil cases the plaintiff usually must prove his or her case by a preponderance of the evidence). Public officials include politicians and government figures, and public figures include movie stars and other celebrities. In *New York Times Co. v. Sullivan*,[63] the U.S. Supreme Court held that a defendant who makes a defamatory statement about a public official's official conduct is not liable unless he or she published that statement with actual malice. Actual malice is knowledge that the statement was false or with reckless disregard to whether or not the statement was false. This higher standard of proof was extended to public figures in *Curtis Publishing Co. v. Butts*.[64] The Supreme Court created this requirement because critics of public officials might exercise self-censorship out of fear of defamation liability and refuse to publish true statements. Furthermore, public figures and public officials choose to enter the public arena and have access to the media in order to correct any defamatory statements made about themselves. Because the actual malice standard is difficult to meet, a defendant will try to show that the plaintiff was a public figure or official in order to escape liability for defamation. Unlike public officials and public figures, a private figure needs only to prove that the defendant was negligent in publishing a defamatory statement, and this is much easier to prove than actual malice.[65]

So who are public officials and public figures in the context of the Internet? Could someone who actively participates in an online discussion group or mailing list qualify as a public figure? If so, then that person could succeed in a defamation claim only by showing that the defendant published a false statement with actual malice. Some commentators have argued that anyone who participates online should be considered a public figure.[66] If a defendant makes a defamatory posting about a person with access to the Internet, then that victim can post back with the truth. Other commentators, however, have argued that the public figure exception was not intended to extend so broadly.[67] Even if a defamation victim can use the Internet to deny the charges, viewers of the initial defamatory statement may not ever see the rebuttal.[68] It will also take time to respond, and by then the victim's reputation could already have suffered irreparable injury.

Publisher Versus Distributor Liability for Defamation

In making or defending against a defamation claim, it is important to remember that courts distinguish among publishers, distributors, and common carriers. Publishers are liable for defamation even if they did not know the published statement was false, whereas distributors are liable only if they knew that the material was false. Newspapers are publishers, and institutions such as public libraries and bookstores are distributors. Courts hold publishers liable because they exercise editorial control and have the opportunity to discover whether a statement was defamatory. To escape liability, defendants will prefer to characterize themselves as distributors rather than publishers because they will face liability for defamation only if they knew the statement was false. Common carriers, such as telephone companies, are not liable for defamation at all because they transmit information without exercising any kind of editorial control.

There has been dispute over whether ISPs are publishers or distributors. This classification is important because it is often difficult to track down the originator of a defamatory statement on the Internet. Even if a plaintiff can find the person who made the false statement, he or she is probably not wealthy. A plaintiff would prefer seeking relief from the ISP where the defamatory statement was published because the ISP will have greater resources. In *Cubby v. CompuServe, Inc.*,[69] the U.S. District Court for the Southern District of New York held that CompuServe was a distributor and therefore not liable for the defamatory statements of a contractor. In *Stratton Oakmont, Inc. v. Prodigy Services Co.*,[70] however, the New York Supreme Court held that Prodigy was a publisher because it advertised itself as a family service and exercised editorial control over its services. Prodigy was liable as a publisher for the defamatory statements of a third party that appeared on one of its bulletin boards. This decision encouraged ISPs to avoid exercising any kind of editorial control or parental screening in order to avoid liability as publishers.

Section 230 of the Communications Decency Act (CDA)[71] was enacted to overrule the *Stratton Oakmont* decision. Section 230 of the CDA states that ISPs are not publishers. As a result of the CDA, ISPs were no longer liable for defamation as publishers, but it was unclear whether ISPs could still face liability as distributors. Would an ISP face liability if it had knowledge of defamatory statements appearing on its site?

This question was answered negatively in *Zeran v. America Online, Inc.*[72] In that case, the Fourth Circuit held that America Online (AOL) was not even liable for defamation as a distributor. An unknown party had posted to an AOL bulletin board claiming that the plaintiff was selling tasteless merchandise related to the Oklahoma City bombing. This anonymous third party included the plaintiff's phone number and name in the posting. As a result of this post, the plaintiff received hundreds of irate phone calls. The plaintiff complained to AOL that the statement was false but AOL refused to publish a retraction as a matter of company policy. AOL did remove the post, although Zeran and AOL disagreed over when this removal occurred. Even though AOL seemed to have knowledge of the defamation, the Fourth Circuit held that AOL was not liable under Section 230 as a publisher or distributor.

In *Blumenthal v. Drudge*,[73] the U.S. District Court for the District of Columbia held AOL was not liable for allegedly defamatory statements made by the defendant whose column appeared on AOL. Matt Drudge, who wrote a gossip column about Washington political figures, claimed that Sidney Blumenthal had a history of spousal abuse. Blumenthal sued Drudge for writing these false statements and AOL for carrying them. AOL had a contract with the defendant to publish his gossip column and remove any material that violated its service terms. Under traditional defamation law, the court noted that AOL would have been liable as a publisher or distributor. A newspaper or bookstore acting like AOL would have been liable. But under the

CDA (at least according to the court's interpretation of it), AOL was immune from liability as a publisher or distributor for the defendant's statements. Interestingly, the CDA does not mention ISPs' potential liability as distributors; it only states that ISPs are not publishers. Despite the CDA's silence on whether or not ISPs are distributors, courts have interpreted the CDA as granting ISPs immunity from liability as both publishers and distributors.

The common law may also shield ISPs from liability for online defamation. Courts usually develop the common law, and legislatures create statutory law (the CDA is an example of statutory law). In *Lunney v. Prodigy Services Co.*,[74] for example, New York's highest court relied on common law to hold that Prodigy was not the publisher of allegedly defamatory e-mail messages and electronic bulletin messages. Because Prodigy was not the publisher of these communications, it was not liable for defamation. The plaintiff sued Prodigy (on behalf of his minor son) for defamation after someone had posted and e-mailed several offensive messages using the son's name.

As a result of these decisions, plaintiffs are unlikely to recover from ISPs for defamation. These cases discourage ISPs from attempting to control or stop the rampant defamation of their subscribers. Unlike newspapers, which are required to do some fact checking of articles that appear in their papers, ISPs do not have to do any kind of fact checking. Because ISPs do not face liability for the defamatory statements of their users, they have little incentive to respond to injured plaintiffs.

■ EPILOGUE

In the quotation at beginning of this chapter, Justice Stewart recognizes that laws drafted decades ago must be interpreted to apply to circumstances of today. The difficulty is that legislators cannot possibly imagine the scope of the technology to which their statues will be applied. With broad legal interpretation, and an understanding of the ramifications of emerging technology, yesterday's laws can still be germane today.

In light of how individuals and companies engage in business transactions on the Internet, the necessity to liberally apply seemingly antiquated law to technological advances is best represented by the Microsoft antitrust case. Antitrust laws are enacted by the government to prevent businesses from engaging in unfair competition and practices that hurt consumers. Although antitrust violations were not focused on in this chapter, they still have some application in the context of other subjects discussed here.

Just as companies are restricted in how they use their trademarks to market their products, so are they restricted in the business practices they engage in under antitrust laws. Microsoft, as an international business with multiple product lines to offer, decided to streamline its offerings to the public by packaging several products together. Microsoft chose to bundle its Windows operating systems for personal computers together with its proprietary World Wide Web browser, Internet Explorer. Because Microsoft's Windows is the dominant operating system in the computer market, packaging its Web browser with it was seen as an attempt to monopolize the industry and an alleged violation of Section 4 of the Sherman Act (15 U.S.C. § 4, and 28 U.S.C. §§ 1331, 1337).

Not only did Microsoft face a civil antitrust case in federal courts in 1998, but nine states have recently brought suit against the company in state courts. AOL also jumped into the fray in January of 2002, filing a private antitrust suit against Microsoft. This flurry of antitrust litigation represents the necessity to interpret existing law in the context of new technological innovation. When legislators drafted antitrust laws to deal with business practices, they were liberally applied to companies producing aluminum and steel. No one could have foreseen that the same laws would be interpreted to apply to business practices in the computer industry 50 years in the future. But as the Microsoft suits come closer to a final resolution and settlement, it becomes clear that existing law is as applicable to businesses today as when such laws were first drafted.

NOTES ■

1. *Fortnightly Corp. v. United Artists Television, Inc.*, 88 S. Ct. 2084, 2087 (1968) (discussing the application of the Copyright Act of 1909 to television).

2. Intellectual property is nonphysical property created by thought, and legally protected and recognized by the government. Providing intellectual property rights acts as an incentive to individuals to create new products, processes, or works of art. The end benefit of such legal protection is the delivery of a variety of goods and services to the public. Intellectual property is protected by several different legal fields including copyrights, trademarks, unfair competition, patents, and trade secrets. With the inception of the Internet, computer-related issues now affect these traditional intellectual property fields in addition to being a field of law unto itself.

3. Goodwill is an intangible business asset that is an amalgamation of such things as the production or sale of a reputable brand name product, a good relationship with customers and suppliers, and the standing of the business in its community. Steven H. Gifis, *Law Dictionary*, 221 (4th ed., Hauppauge, NY: Barron's, 1996).

4. Lanham Act § 45, 15 U.S.C. § 1127 (1998). The equivalent protection for a company's services is aptly called a service mark. *Id.*

5. See J. Thomas McCarthy, *McCarthy on Trademarks and Unfair Competition*, § 8:4 (4th ed., San Francisco: Bancroft-Whitney, 1999).

6. Lanham Act § 45, 15 U.S.C. § 1127 (1998).

7. See McCarthy, *McCarthy on Trademarks and Unfair Competition*, § 2:3.

8. Common law is judgemade law created when a court issues an opinion. It is a system of judicial precedent, in contrast to statutory law, which is created by the legislature. Gifis, *Law Dictionary*, 88.

9. Lanham Act §§ 1-46, 15 U.S.C. §§ 1051-1127 (1998).

10. See *Mishawaka Rubber & Woolen Mfg. Co. v. S.S. Kresge Co.*, 316 U.S. 203 (1942), *reb'g denied*, 316 U.S. 712 (1942).

11. See McCarthy, *McCarthy on Trademarks and Unfair Competition*, § 2:3.

12. Ibid.

13. Ibid., § 23:1.

14. Ibid., § 23:78.

15. Ibid., § 26:1.

16. *What Is . . . a Domain Name* (visited March 12, 2000), http://www.whatis.com/domainna.htm. A top-level domain can also be geographic, based on the country the server is located in. This convention, however, is not widely used in the United States. *Id.*

17. Hypothetically, Hershey might be able to secure a ".net" or an ".org" top-level domain. But "netiquette" dictates that these are usually reserved for computer networks and organizations, respectively. The remaining top-level domains (".edu" and ".gov") are issued under more stringent standards.

18. Network Solutions, *Network Solutions' Domain Name Dispute Policy* (effective September 9, 1996), http://www.internic.net/policy/internic/internic-domain.html.

19. See, for example, *Lockheed Martin Corp. v. Network Solutions, Inc.*, 985 F. Supp. 949 (C.D. Cal. 1997) (finding that NSI was not liable for contributory infringement because it had no affirmative duty to police the Internet and furthermore did not know nor did it have reason to know of infringement by other parties in its limited role as a registrar of domain names).

20. Internet Corporation for Assigned Names and Numbers, *Uniform Domain Name Dispute Resolution Policy* (effective September 1999), http://www.icann.org/udrp/udrp-policy-29sept99.html.

21. See *Cardservice International, Inc. v. McGee*, 950 F. Supp. 737 (E.D. Va. 1997).

22. See *Hasbro, Inc. v. Clue Computing, Inc.*, 994 F. Supp. 34 (D. Mass. 1997) ("The kind of confusion that is more likely to result from Clue Computing's use of the 'clue.com' domain name; namely, that consumers will realize that they are at the wrong site and go to an Internet search engine to find the right one is not substantial enough to be legally significant."); see *Interstellar Starship Services, Ltd. v. Epix, Inc.*, 983 F. Supp. 1331 (1997) (finding the public is not likely to be confused or deceived by the use of a domain name that is similar to a registered trademark); cf. *Inset Systems, Inc. v. Instruction Set, Inc.*, 937 F. Supp. 161 (D. Conn. 1996) (finding a likelihood of confusion could result from the use of similar domain names).

23. See *Brookfield Communications, Inc. v. West Coast Entertainment Corp.*, 174 F.3d 1036 (9th Cir. 1999).

24. Pub. L. No. 104-98, 109 Stat. 985. The Federal Trademark Dilution Act amended the Trademark Act of 1946.

25. See *Academy of Motion Picture Arts & Sciences v. Network Solutions, Inc.*, ____ F. Supp. ____, 1997 WL 810472 (C.D. Cal. December 22, 1997) (finding the mere registration of a domain name does not constitute a commercial use); see also *Lockheed Martin Corp. v. Network Solutions, Inc.*, 985 F. Supp. 949 (C.D. Cal. 1997) (NSI's acceptance of a domain name for registration is not a commercial use within the meaning of the Trademark Dilution Act).

26. See, for example, *Hasbro, Inc. v. Internet Entertainment Group, Ltd.*, 1996 WL 84853 (not reported in F. Supp.) (preliminary injunction issued after Hasbro

demonstrated a likelihood of prevailing on its claims that the use of the domain name "candyland.com" by Internet Entertainment Group for an adult entertainment Web site diluted its federally registered trademark CANDYLAND).

27. *What Is . . . Cybersquatting* (visited March 12, 2000), http://www.whatis. com/cybersquatting.htm.

28. The term *cybersquatting* is derived from *squatting*, which is the practice of dwelling or using another's landed property without permission in an attempt to gain title. *What Is . . . Cybersquatting* (visited March 12, 2000), http://www.whatis. com/cybersquatting.htm.

29. See *Panavision Int'l, LP v. Toeppen*, 141 F.3d 1316 (9th Cir. 1998); see also *Intermatic Inc. v. Toeppen*, 947 F. Supp. 1227 (N.D. Ill. 1996).

30. Anti-cybersquatting Consumer Protection Act, S. 1255, Lanham Act § 43(d), 15 U.S.C. § 1125(d) (1999).

31. The party would have to establish "secondary meaning" to gain trademark protection for a descriptive or generic term. Secondary meaning occurs when consumers associate the company or product name with the goods; that is, the term has gained a second meaning in the minds of the public. Lanham Act § 2(f), 15 U.S.C. § 1052(f) (1998).

32. Therefore HTML Example would be displayed on a Web browser as **HTML Example**.

33. Compare "MovieBuff" to "movie buff." Note that West Coast could still use "movie buff" in a generic sense, under a fair use doctrine. Trademark protection cannot prevent a word or name from being used by competitors to describe another's product.

34. Carl S. Kaplan, *Court Lays Down the Law on Labels for Web Sites* (April 30, 1999), http://www.nytimes.com/library/tech/99/04/cyber/cyberlaw/30law.html.

35. *Black's Law Dictionary*, 853 (6th ed., St. Paul, MN: West, 1990).

36. 28 U.S.C. § 1331 (2000).

37. See *Fed. R. Civ. P.* 4(e)(1).

38. 326 U.S. 310 (1945).

39. *International Shoe Co. v. Washington*, 326 U.S. 310, 316 (1945) (quoting *Milliken v. Meyer,* 311 U.S. 457, 463 [1940]).

40. *World-Wide Volkswagen Corp. v. Woodson*, 444 U.S. 286, 297 (1980).

41. 952 F. Supp. 1119 (W.D. Pa. 1997).

42. *Id.* at 1124.

43. 937 F. Supp. 295 (S.D.N.Y. 1996), *aff'd*, 126 F.3d 25 (2d Cir. 1997).

44. 937 F. Supp. 161 (D. Conn. 1996).

45. 947 F. Supp. 1328 (E.D. Mo. 1996).

46. 992 F. Supp. 44 (D.D.C. 1998).

47. See *Calder v. Jones*, 465 U.S. 783, 789 (1984) (holding nonresident defendants subject to personal jurisdiction in California because plaintiff suffered brunt of injury there).

48. 465 U.S. 783 (1984).

49. *Id.* at 789.

50. 141 F.3d 1316 (9th Cir. 1998).

51. *Milliken v. Meyer,* 311 U.S. 457, 463 (1940).

52. See *Expert Pages v. Buckalew*, No. C97-2109-VRW, 1997 WL 488011, *4-*5 (N.D. Cal. August 6, 1997).

53. *Barrett v. Catacombs Press,* 44 F. Supp. 2d 717, 731 (E.D. Pa. 1999).

54. See *Zeran v. America Online, Inc.*, 129 F.3d 327 (4th Cir. 1997) for a further description of the facts of this case.

55. See *Bochan v. La Fontaine*, No. Civ. A. 98-1749-A, 1999 WL 343780, *1 (E.D. Va. May 26, 1999) for a further description of the facts of the case.

56. *Black's Law Dictionary*, 417.

57. F. Lawrence Street, *Law of the Internet* (Newark, NJ: LexisNexis, 1998).

58. See Bruce P. Smith, "Cybersmearing and the Problem of Anonymous Online Speech," 18 *Journal of Media, Information & Communication*, 3, 5 (Fall 2000) (giving examples of corporations suing for online defamation). Smith defines *cybersmearing* as "the use of websites, newsgroups, message boards, and chat rooms to criticize companies and their executives." *Id.* at 3.

59. 535 N.W.2d 11, 14 (Wis. App. 1995).

60. Sheri Hunter, "Defamation and Privacy Laws Face the Internet," 17 *Journal of Media, Information & Communication*, 16 (Fall 1999) ("The point when something is 'published' in cyberspace remains less than clear.").

61. Robert M. O'Neil, "The Drudge Case: A Look at Issues in Cyberspace Defamation," 73 *Washington Law Review*, 623, 629 (1998) (arguing that e-mail is so insecure that "publication should be presumed in an online libel suit").

62. Hunter, "Defamation and Privacy Laws Face the Internet," 17 (questioning whether traditional defamation law would cover this situation).

63. 376 U.S. 254, 279-80 (1964).

64. 388 U.S. 130 (1967).

65. See *Gertz v. Robert Welch, Inc.*, 418 U.S. 323 (1974).

66. See, for example, Terri A. Cutrera, "Computer Networks, Libel and the First Amendment," 11 *Computer/Law Journal*, 555, 570 (1992) (arguing that plaintiff defamed on bulletin board has opportunity to respond and may have waived his or her privacy by becoming involved in discussion); Bruce W. Sanford and Michael J. Lorenger, "Teaching an Old Dog New Tricks: The First Amendment in an Online World," 28 *Connecticut Law Review*, 1137, 1157-1158 (1996) ("Any person who participates in an online debate arguably becomes a 'public figure' with respect to defamatory statements stemming from that debate."); Jeremy Stone Weber, Note, "Defining Cyberlibel: A First Amendment Limit for Libel Suits Against Individuals Arising From Computer Bulletin Board Speech," 46 *Case Western Reserve Law Review*, 235, 236 (1995) (stating that when a "libel plaintiff has been defamed by a message posted on a computer bulletin board, and he or she has access to the bulletin board to post a reply, the First Amendment requires that the plaintiff prove that the defendant acted with 'actual malice' in defaming the plaintiff").

67. See, for example, O'Neil, "The Drudge Case," 623, 632-633 (describing argument that plaintiffs defamed online can use Internet to fight back as "questionable"); Michael Hadley, Note, "The Gertz Doctrine and Internet Defamation," 84 *Virginia Law Review*, 477, 504-506 (1998) (claiming that negligence standard is more appropriate for plaintiffs defamed online because they face so many challenges in obtaining relief).

68. O'Neil, "The Drudge Case," 623, 632-633.

69. 776 F. Supp. 135 (S.D.N.Y. 1991).

70. 1995 WL 323710 (N.Y. Sup. Ct. May 24, 1995).

71. 47 U.S.C. § 230 (1996).

72. 129 F.3d 327 (4th Cir. 1997).

73. 992 F. Supp. 44 (D.D.C. 1998).

74. 723 N.E.2d 539 (N.Y. 1999), *cert denied*, 120 S. Ct. 1832 (2000).

APPENDIX

U.S. Radio Spectrum Allocations and Uses (30 MHz–300 GHz)

30-30.56 MHz	Defense and other federal mobile and fixed radio
30.56-32 MHz	Private Mobile Radio Services[a]
32-33 MHz	Defense and other federal mobile and fixed radio
33-35.19 MHz	Private Mobile Radio Services
35.19-35.69 MHz	Paging and Radiotelephone Service
35.69-36 MHz	Private Mobile Radio Services
36-37 MHz	Defense and other federal mobile and fixed radio
37-38 MHz	Private Mobile Radio Services; radio astronomy
38-38.25 MHz	Radio astronomy
38.25-39 MHz	Defense and other federal mobile and fixed radio
39-40 MHz	Private Mobile Radio Services
40-42 MHz	Defense and other federal mobile and fixed radio; meteor burst communications; Industrial, Scientific and Medical; scientific telemetry
42-43.19 MHz	Private Mobile Radio Services
43.19-43.69 MHz	Private Mobile Radio Services; Paging and Radiotelephone Service
43.69-46.6 MHz	Private Mobile Radio Services; cordless phones
46.6-47 MHz	Defense and other federal mobile and fixed radio; cordless phones
47-49.6 MHz	Private Mobile Radio Services; cordless phones
49.6-50 MHz	Defense and other federal mobile and fixed radio; cordless phones; baby monitors, toys
50-54 MHz	Amateur Radio Service
54-72 MHz	TV channels 2, 3, and 4
72-73 MHz	Private Mobile Radio Services; paging control; auditory assistance; radio-controlled model aircraft
73-74.6 MHz	Radio astronomy
74.6-74.8 MHz	Private Mobile Radio Services; paging control; auditory assistance
74.8-75.2 MHz	Aviation runway marker beacons
75.2-76 MHz	Private Mobile Radio Services; paging control; auditory assistance, radio-controlled model boats and cars
76-88 MHz	TV channels 5 and 6

88-108 MHz	FM radio broadcasting; future digital audio radio services; wireless microphones
108-117.975 MHz	Air navigation aids
117.975-121.9375 MHz	Air traffic control; search and rescue beacons
121.9375-123.0875 MHz	Aviation services communications
123.0875-123.5875 MHz	Aviation services communications
123.5875-128.8125 MHz	Air traffic control
128.8125-132.0125 MHz	Aviation services communications
132.0125-136 MHz	Air traffic control
136-137 MHz	Aviation services communications
137-138 MHz	Non-Voice Non-Geostationary Mobile Satellite Service (Little LEO) for data communications; weather satellites
138-144 MHz	Defense and other federal mobile and fixed radio, 139-140.5 and 141.5-143 MHz to be reallocated to private sector
144-146 MHz	Amateur Radio Service, including satellites and space station operations
146-148 MHz	Amateur Radio Service mobile operations
148-150.05 MHz	Non-Voice Non-Geostationary Mobile Satellite Service (Little LEO), federal fixed, mobile and satellite uses, science telemetry
150.05-150.8 MHz	Defense and other federal mobile and fixed radio
150.8-152 MHz	Private Mobile Radio Services
152-152.255 MHz	Paging and Radiotelephone Service
152.255-152.495 MHz	Private Mobile Radio Services
152.495-152.855 MHz	Paging and Radiotelephone Service
152.855-154 MHz	Private Mobile Radio Services, Broadcast Auxiliary Services
154-156.2475 MHz	Private Mobile Radio Services, maritime radio
156.2475-157.0375 MHz	Maritime radio
157.0375-157.1875 MHz	Federal maritime radio
157.1875-157.45 MHz	Maritime radio
157.45-157.755 MHz	Private Mobile Radio Services
157.755-158.115 MHz	Paging and Radiotelephone Service
158.115-161.575 MHz	Private Mobile Radio Services, maritime radio
161.575-161.625 MHz	Maritime radio
161.625-161.775 MHz	Broadcast Auxiliary Services
161.775-162.0125 MHz	Maritime radio, Private Mobile Radio Services
162.0125-173.2 MHz	Federal mobile and fixed radio; weather broadcasts; Stolen Vehicle Recovery Service; Private Mobile Radio Services; Broadcast Auxiliary Services; wireless microphones
173.2-173.4 MHz	Private Mobile Radio Services
173.4-174 MHz	Federal mobile and fixed radio
174-216 MHz	TV channels 7-13; biomedical telemetry; wireless microphones
216-220 MHz	Defense radar; maritime radio; geophysical telemetry; Interactive Video and Data Service; Amateur Radio; Low-Power Radio Service for

	theft tracking, auditory assistance and health care. To be reallocated to private sector
220-222 MHz	Private Mobile Radio Services
222-225 MHz	Amateur Radio Service
225-328.6 MHz	Defense air, ground and maritime uses (fixed and mobile); search-and-rescue beacons; car alarms; radio astronomy
328.6-335.4 MHz	Defense air, ground and maritime uses (fixed and mobile); search-and-rescue beacons; car alarms; radio astronomy
335.4-399.9 MHz	Defense air, ground and maritime uses (fixed and mobile); search-and-rescue beacons; car alarms; radio astronomy
399.9-400.05 MHz	Non-Voice Non-Geostationary Mobile Satellite Service (Little LEO) for data communications
400.05-400.15 MHz	Standard frequency and time signal satellites (not used)
400.15-401 MHz	Non-Voice Non-Geostationary Mobile Satellite Service (Little LEO) for data communications; meteorological aids and defense weather satellites
401-402 MHz	Meteorological aids; weather balloons; science telemetry
402-406 MHz	Meteorological aids; animal tracking; proposed for medical implants
406-406.1 MHz	Satellite-based search-and-rescue beacons
406.1-410 MHz	Defense and other federal mobile and fixed radio
410-420 MHz	Defense and other federal mobile and fixed radio; Space Research Service; airborne radar
420-450 MHz	Defense and scientific radar and balloons; Amateur Radio Service
450-451 MHz	Broadcast Auxiliary Services
451-454 MHz	Private Mobile Radio Services
454-455 MHz	General Aviation Air-Ground Radiotelephone Service; Paging and Radiotelephone Service
455-456 MHz	Broadcast Auxiliary Services, proposed for Non-Voice Non-Geostationary Mobile Satellite Service (Little LEO)
456-459 MHz	Private Mobile Radio Services
459-460 MHz	General Aviation Air-Ground Radiotelephone Service; Paging and Radiotelephone Service, proposed for Non-Voice Non-Geostationary Mobile Satellite Service (Little LEO)
460-462.5375 MHz	Private Mobile Radio Services
462.5375-462.7375 MHz	General Mobile Radio Service (GMRS) and Family Radio Service (FRS) for personal communications
462.7375-467.5375 MHz	Private Mobile Radio Services, including emergency medical telemetry

467.5375-467.7375 MHz	General Mobile Radio Service (GMRS) and Family Radio Service (FRS) for personal communications
467.7375-470 MHz	Private Mobile Radio Services, including emergency medical telemetry; weather satellites
470-512 MHz	TV channels 14-20; biomedical telemetry
512-608 MHz	TV channels 21-36; biomedical telemetry
608-614 MHz	Radio astronomy; biomedical telemetry; formerly TV channel 37
614-746 MHz	TV channels 38-59
746-764 MHz	TV channels 60-62. Reallocated to special broadcasting, fixed and mobile services
764-776 MHz	TV channels 63, 64. Reallocated to Private Mobile Radio Services for public safety use
776-794 MHz	TV channels 65-67. Reallocated to special broadcasting, fixed and mobile services
794-806 MHz	TV channels 68, 69. Reallocated to Private Mobile Radio Services for public safety use
806-821 MHz	Specialized Mobile Radio Services; Private Mobile Radio Services
821-824 MHz	Private Mobile Radio Services for public safety use
824-849 MHz	Cellular Radiotelephone Service
849-851 MHz	Commercial Aviation Air-Ground Systems
851-866 MHz	Specialized Mobile Radio Services; Private Mobile Radio Services
866-869 MHz	Private Mobile Radio Services for public safety use
869-894 MHz	Cellular Radiotelephone Service
894-896 MHz	Commercial Aviation Air-Ground Systems
896-901 MHz	Specialized Mobile Radio
901-902 MHz	Personal Communications Service (PCS)— Narrowband for advanced paging
902-928 MHz	Defense radar; Location and Monitoring Service; amateur radio; Industrial, Scientific and Medical; unlicensed devices
928-929 MHz	Multiple Address Systems
929-930 MHz	Private Mobile Radio Services, especially paging
930-931 MHz	Personal Communications Service (PCS)— Narrowband for advanced paging
931-932 MHz	Paging and Radiotelephone Service, especially nationwide paging
932-935 MHz	Multiple Address Systems; federal and nonfederal fixed microwave
935-940 MHz	Specialized Mobile Radio
940-941 MHz	Personal Communications Service (PCS)— Narrowband for advanced paging
941-942 MHz	Fixed microwave
942-944 MHz	Fixed microwave
944-960 MHz	Broadcast Auxiliary Services; Multiple Address Systems; fixed microwave
960-1215 MHz	Aerospace radar; defense communications

1215-1240 MHz	Aerospace radar; synthetic aperture radar for earth sensing; global positioning system (GPS) navigation satellites
1240-1300 MHz	Aerospace radar; Amateur Radio Service; thermotherapy
1300-1350 MHz	Aerospace radar
1350-1400 MHz	Aerospace radar; defense communications, remote control and nuclear alerting; earth sensing. 1385-1400 MHz to be reallocated to private sector
1400-1427 MHz	Radio astronomy; satellite earth sensing. No transmissions permitted
1427-1435 MHz	Defense air telemetry and fixed uses. To be reallocated to private sector
1435-1525 MHz	Aerospace test telemetry; satellite audio broadcasting to foreign countries
1525-1544 MHz	Satellite "L-band": Geostationary Mobile Satellite Service
1544-1545 MHz	Safety-related mobile satellite communications
1545-1559 MHz	Geostationary Mobile Satellite Service
1559-1610 MHz	Global positioning system (GPS) satellites, radio altimetry
1610-1610.6 MHz	Non-Geostationary Mobile Satellite Service (Big LEO); radio altimetry
1610.6-1613.8 MHz	Non-Geostationary Mobile Satellite Service (Big LEO); radio astronomy
1613.8-1626.5 MHz	Non-Geostationary Mobile Satellite Service (Big LEO)
1626.5-1645.5 MHz	Geostationary Mobile Satellite Service
1645.5-1646.5 MHz	Safety-related mobile satellite communications
1646.5-1660.5 MHz	Geostationary Mobile Satellite Service; radio astronomy
1660.5-1668.4 MHz	Radio astronomy; no transmissions permitted
1668.4-1670 MHz	Radio astronomy
1670-1690 MHz	Weather satellites and balloons. 1670-1675 to be reallocated to private sector
1690-1700 MHz	Weather satellites
1700-1710 MHz	Weather satellites; fixed microwave
1710-1850 MHz	Defense and other federal satellite, fixed, mobile, and aerospace uses; radio astronomy. 1710-1755 MHz to be reallocated to private sector
1850-1990 MHz	Personal Communications Services (PCS)—Broadband; unlicensed PCS devices; fixed microwave
1990-2025 MHz	Mobile Satellite Services; Broadcast Auxiliary Services; cable TV and local broadcast TV relay
2025-2110 MHz	Broadcast Auxiliary Services; Space Research Service
2110-2150 MHz	Broadcast Auxiliary Services; Space Research Service; fixed microwave; Emerging Technologies

2150-2160 MHz	Multipoint Distribution Service
2160-2165 MHz	Fixed microwave; Emerging Technologies
2165-2200 MHz	Mobile Satellite Services; fixed microwave; Emerging Technologies
2200-2290 MHz	Defense and science satellites and telemetry
2290-2300 MHz	Space Research Service for deep space use
2300-2305 MHz	No primary use. Amateur Radio secondary use
2305-2320 MHz	Wireless Communications Service
2320-2345 MHz	Satellite "S-band": Satellite Digital Audio Radio Service
2345-2360 MHz	Wireless Communications Service
2360-2390 MHz	Aerospace testing; planetary radar. 2385-2390 MHz to be reallocated to private sector
2390-2400 MHz	Amateur Radio Service; unlicensed Data-PCS
2400-2483.5 MHz	Amateur Radio Service; unlicensed devices and Industrial, Medical equipment; fixed microwave. Portions available for other private sector and educational use
2483.5-2500 MHz	Non-Geostationary Mobile Satellite Service (Big LEO)
2500-2690 MHz	Multipoint Distribution Service; Instructional Television Fixed Service; satellite earth sensing
2690-2700 MHz	Radio astronomy; satellite earth sensing. No transmissions permitted
2700-2900 MHz	Defense and civil aerospace and weather radar
2900-3100 MHz	Defense and maritime navigation radar
3.1-3.3 GHz	Defense radar; satellite earth sensing
3.3-3.5 GHz	Defense aerospace; Amateur Radio Service
3.5-3.6 GHz	Defense radar
3.6-3.7 GHz	Defense radar; data communications; Geostationary Fixed Satellite Service. 3.65-3.7 GHz to be reallocated to private sector
3.7-4.2 GHz	Satellite "C-band": Geostationary Fixed Satellite Service; fixed microwave
4.2-4.4 GHz	Radio altimetry
4.4-4.5 GHz	Defense aerospace; mobile and fixed uses; nuclear antiterrorism
4.5-4.66 GHz	Defense, scientific aerospace, naval uses. 4.635-4.66 GHz reallocated to private sector
4.66-4.685 GHz	General Wireless Communications Service
4.685-4.99 GHz	Defense aerospace; mobile and fixed uses
4.99-5 GHz	Radio astronomy. No transmissions permitted
5-5.25 GHz	Aviation landing systems; missiles; weather and ocean radar. Unlicensed National Information Infrastructure
5.25-5.35 GHz	Defense and weather radar; satellite earth sensing. Unlicensed National Information Infrastructure
5.35-5.65 GHz	Defense and weather radar
5.65-5.85 GHz	Defense radar; automatic door openers. Unlicensed National Information Infrastructure

	and other unlicensed devices; Amateur Radio Service
5.85-5.925 GHz	Defense radar; Geostationary Fixed Satellite Service; Amateur Radio Service; unlicensed devices; Dedicated Short Range Communications
5.925-6.425 GHz	Geostationary Fixed Satellite Service; fixed microwave
6.425-6.525 GHz	Broadcast Auxiliary Services; TV relay; satellite feeder links
6.525-6.875 GHz	Fixed microwave; radio astronomy
6.875-7.075 GHz	Broadcast Auxiliary Services; audio satellite feeder links
7.075-7.125 GHz	Broadcast Auxiliary Services
7.125-7.19 GHz	Fixed microwave for aviation facilities
7.19-7.235 GHz	Space Research Service for deep space use
7.235-7.9 GHz	Fixed microwave for aviation facilities; weather satellites
7.9-8.025 GHz	Satellite "X-band": Defense satellites and fixed microwave; control of electrical power distribution
8.025-8.4 GHz	Earth remote sensing satellites
8.4-8.45 GHz	Space Research Service for deep space use
8.45-8.5 GHz	Space Research Service
8.5-9 GHz	Defense and civil radar for navigation, weather and ocean study; weapon location; planetary radar
9-9.2 GHz	Defense aerospace radar
9.2-9.3 GHz	Maritime navigation and safety radar; control of unmanned air vehicles
9.3-9.5 GHz	Maritime navigation and safety radar; weather radar
9.5-10 GHz	Weather radar; control of unmanned air vehicles; satellite earth sensing
10-10.5 GHz	Defense missile radar; weather and ocean radar; Amateur Radio. Proposed educational use
10.5-10.55 GHz	Police speed radar; automatic door openers; alarms
10.55-10.6 GHz	Fixed microwave
10.6-10.68 GHz	Fixed microwave; satellite earth sensing
10.68-10.7 GHz	Radio astronomy; weather study. No transmissions permitted
10.7-11.7 GHz	Fixed microwave; Geostationary Fixed Satellite Service
11.7-12.2 GHz	Satellite "Ku-band": Direct-to-Home Fixed Satellite Service; Broadcast Auxiliary Service
12.2-12.7 GHz	Direct Broadcast Satellite Service
12.7-13.25 GHz	Broadcast Auxiliary Service; Cable Television Antenna Relay Service; fixed microwave
13.25-13.4 GHz	Airborne navigation radar; Space Research Service

13.4-13.75 GHz	Maritime radar; satellite altimetry for ocean study
13.75-14 GHz	Geostationary Fixed Satellite Service; maritime radar, weather, ocean scientific radar; Space Shuttle radar; Space Research Service
14-14.5 GHz	Geostationary Fixed Satellite Service; maritime, air navigation radar; Space Station
14.5-15.35 GHz	Defense radar and microwave links; Space Research Service; aviation facility links
15.35-15.4 GHz	Radio astronomy
15.4-15.7 GHz	Mobile satellite links; aviation landing systems
15.7-17.2 GHz	Aerospace and scientific radar
17.2-17.3 GHz	Radar and satellite earth sensing
17.3-17.7 GHz	Direct Broadcast Satellite Service
17.7-20.2 GHz	Satellite "K-band": Geostationary Fixed Satellite Service; Non-Geostationary Fixed Satellite Service; Mobile Satellite Service; weather satellites; defense signals intelligence satellites; fixed microwave
20.2-21.2 GHz	Defense satellites
21.2-23.6 GHz	Fixed microwave; satellite earth sensing; radio astronomy; intersatellite links
23.6-24 GHz	Radio astronomy; satellite earth sensing. No transmissions permitted
24-24.05 GHz	Amateur Radio Service; unlicensed fixed links; satellite earth sensing; Industrial, Scientific, Medical
24.05-24.25 GHz	Police speed radar; security sensors; unlicensed fixed links
24.25-24.45 GHz	Digital Electronic Message Service
24.45-24.65 GHz	Airport surface detection radar
24.65-24.75 GHz	Intersatellite and radar satellite links
24.75-25.05 GHz	Aerospace radar. Proposed for future Direct Broadcast Satellites
25.05-25.25 GHz	Digital Electronic Message Service. Proposed for future Direct Broadcast Satellites
25.25-27.5 GHz	Space-to-space links for scientific missions; defense broadband on-site networks
27.5-29.5 GHz	Local Multipoint Distribution Service; satellite "Ka-band"; Geostationary and Non-Geostationary Fixed and Mobile Satellite Services
29.5-30 GHz	Geostationary and Non-Geostationary Fixed Satellite Services
30-31 GHz	Defense signals intelligence satellites; radio astronomy
31-31.3 GHz	Local Multipoint Distribution Service; fixed links for traffic control
31.3-31.8 GHz	Satellite earth sensing. No transmissions permitted
31.8-32 GHz	Aerospace navigation; deep space communications

32-33.4 GHz	Intersatellite links; deep space communications
33.4-36 GHz	Weather radar; satellite earth sensing; deep space communications; police radar
36-37 GHz	Satellite earth sensing
37-37.5 GHz	Proposed general commercial wireless services; manned space exploration; satellite earth sensing
37.5-38.6 GHz	Proposed broadband satellite services and general commercial wireless services
38.6-40 GHz	Broadband local exchange services
40-40.5 GHz	Scientific and commercial satellite services; manned space exploration
40.5-41.5 GHz	Proposed broadband satellite services and general commercial wireless services
41.5-42.5 GHz	Proposed Licensed Millimeter Wave Service
42.5-43.5 GHz	Radio astronomy
43.5-45.5 GHz	Defense satellites
45.5-46.9 GHz	Vehicle anticollision radar
46.9-47 GHz	Proposed general commercial wireless services
47-47.2 GHz	Amateur Radio Service
47.2-50.2 GHz	Point-to-multipoint broadband services; stratospheric platforms; Non-Geostationary and Geostationary Fixed Satellite Services; radio astronomy
50.2-50.4 GHz	Satellite earth sensing; no transmissions permitted
50.4-51.4 GHz	Defense satellites
51.4-59 GHz	Satellite earth sensing; proposed for intersatellite links
59-64 GHz	Unlicensed communications; industrial safety and control; satellite earth sensing; proposed for intersatellite links; Industrial, Scientific, Medical
64-66 GHz	Satellite earth sensing
66-71 GHz	Mobile Satellite Services; aerospace radar
71-74 GHz	Proposed Licensed Millimeter Wave Service; unlicensed communications devices
74-75.5 GHz	Fixed, Fixed Satellite and Mobile Services
75.5-76 GHz	Amateur Radio Service
76-77 GHz	Vehicle anticollision radar; Amateur Radio
77-81 GHz	Amateur Radio Service; weather radar; microscopy
81-84 GHz	Fixed and Mobile Satellite Services
84-86 GHz	Proposed Licensed Millimeter Wave Service; satellite earth sensing
86-92 GHz	Radio astronomy; satellite earth sensing; videography
92-95 GHz	Proposed vehicle anticollision radar; synthetic vision systems; radio astronomy
95-100 GHz	Proposed vehicle anticollision radar; weather radar
100-102 GHz	Satellite earth sensing; radio astronomy
102-105 GHz	Proposed Licensed Millimeter Wave Service; unlicensed communications devices

105-116 GHz	Satellite earth sensing; radio astronomy
116-134 GHz	Proposed Licensed Millimeter Wave Service; unlicensed devices; satellite earth sensing
134-142 GHz	Proposed vehicle anticollision radar
142-149 GHz	Amateur Radio Service; satellite earth sensing
149-150 GHz	Fixed, Fixed Satellite and Mobile Satellite Services
150-151 GHz	Satellite earth sensing
151-164 GHz	Proposed Licensed Millimeter Wave Service; unlicensed devices; Big Bang cosmic radiation
164-168 GHz	Satellite earth sensing; radio astronomy. No transmissions permitted
168-170 GHz	Fixed and Mobile Services
170-174.5 GHz	Fixed and Mobile Services; intersatellite links
174.5-176.5 GHz	Satellite earth sensing
176.5-182 GHz	Fixed and Mobile Services; intersatellite links
182-185 GHz	Satellite earth sensing; radio astronomy. No transmissions permitted
185-190 GHz	Fixed and Mobile Services; intersatellite links
190-200 GHz	Mobile, Mobile Satellite, Radionavigation and Radionavigation; Satellite Services
200-202 GHz	Satellite earth sensing
202-217 GHz	Fixed, Fixed Satellite and Mobile Services
217-231 GHz	Satellite earth sensing; radio astronomy. No transmissions permitted
231-235 GHz	Fixed, Fixed Satellite and Mobile Services
235-238 GHz	Satellite earth sensing
238-241 GHz	Fixed, Fixed Satellite and Mobile Services
241-250 GHz	Amateur Radio Service; Industrial, Scientific, Medical; radar
250-252 GHz	Satellite earth sensing
252-265 GHz	Mobile, Mobile Satellite, Radionavigation and Radionavigation; Satellite Services
265-275 GHz	Fixed, Fixed Satellite and Mobile Services; radio astronomy
275-300 GHz	Fixed and Mobile Services

SOURCE: *Manual of Regulations and Procedures for Federal Radio Frequency Management*, September 1995 edition, Washington, DC: U.S. Department of Commerce, National Telecommunications and Information Administration (NTIA); "U.S. Radio Spectrum Allocations and Uses (30 MHz–300 GHz)" [Poster], 1998, *America's Airwaves*, Bennett Z. Kobb.

a. For information on this servisce and others in the appendix, see the Federal Communications Commission's (FCC) Web site (www.fcc.gov). The FCC's Wireless Telecommunications Bureau (http://wireless.fcc.gov/) handles nearly all FCC domestic wireless telecommunications programs and policies. Wireless communications services include Amateur, Cellular, Paging, Broadband PCS, and Public Safety.

GLOSSARY

Ad keying The practice of linking Web page banner advertisements to particular search keywords, including trademarked terms.

AM (amplitude modulation) A process by which an audio signal modulates the amplitude of a carrier. In AM radio, the carrier consists of a sine wave whose amplitude is made to copy the variations of an audio source.

Analog bandwidth The frequency range between the lowest and highest frequencies used to transmit analog radio signals. For example, a standard commercial AM radio channel in the United States uses a bandwidth of 9 kHz, while a standard analog television signal uses 6 MHz. Bandwidth is measured in cycles per second (cps; otherwise known as hertz, Hz).

B2B Business-to-business transactions on the Web.

B2C Business-to-consumer transactions on the Web.

Binary code A communication system using two symbols (e.g., 1s and 0s) to carry information. Binary code can carry any type of information including text, images, and sound.

Bits per second (bps) The fundamental measure of digital bandwidth. *Bit* is short for *binary digit*, the smallest quantity of information that can be carried in digital code. In numerical form, a bit consists of a single digit, either a 1 or a 0; in an electrical circuit, a bit is the state of being either on or off—in other words, the circuit is either closed, allowing electricity to flow, or open, stopping the flow of electricity.

Boolean algebra A method of logical deduction invented by English mathematician George Boole. Boole's system uses three basic constructs to make logical inferences and perform mathematical calculation with symbols and numbers, respectively, called AND, OR, and NOT gates. Boole's gates are binary in nature because they categorize statements as either true or false.

Broadband Information channels that can handle data streams requiring large bandwidth. A single AM radio channel, for example, uses 9 kHz of radio spectrum, whereas a single analog television channel uses 6 MHz. The television channel requires more space because it has to pass more information. Channels are therefore either narrow or broad, depending on how much information they can pass. In general, voice channels require less bandwidth than those carrying sound, pictures, and color information. Internet traffic featuring television-quality streaming video would therefore be considered a broadband service.

Carrier That part of any communication system used for moving intelligence from one point to another (e.g., in a radio signal, the carrier is the high-frequency sine wave on which audio signals are imposed; in a written letter, the carrier is the paper on which a message is written and the ink used to do the writing).

Clipper Chip An integrated circuit designed to allow federal agencies to access computer systems to decrypt what is stored for the sake of security. One justification for the Clipper Chip is to fight terrorism.

Code Prior agreements between senders and receivers about what various signals will mean. All methods of communicating rely on codes. Successful communication relies on both unimpeded reception of a message's physical component and accurate decoding of the pattern of information (or *intelligence*) it contains.

Cookie A tiny file placed on a user's computer whenever a particular Web page is accessed. Cookies typically enable Web sites and Web site advertisers to keep track of the pages that viewers access. To be "cookied" means to be tracked online as a consumer, and perhaps targeted for future marketing campaigns.

Cyberspace An umbrella term referring to the digital telecommunication and broadcast communication infrastructures enabling users to create, store, manipulate, transmit, retrieve, and share information in the form of text, data, images, and sound, including motion visuals.

Cybersquatting The act of registering domain names without the intent to use them, but rather to sell them.

Data mining The act of digging into old databases and extracting the rules of operation as well as data for that business.

Dialogic technologies Technologies that allow for information sharing and interaction between people via the telephone, teleconferences, voice mail, cable and satellite television, point-to-point microwave radio communication, electronic blackboards, computer instruction, and more recently, computer-mediated communication such as e-mail, bulletin boards, and computer instant messaging and conferencing. Dialogic systems may be either *synchronous* (interaction takes place in real time) or *asynchronous* (interaction takes place at different times and at users' convenience).

Digital bandwidth A measure of a digital medium's ability to transmit information from one point to another in a given amount of time, usually expressed in terms of bps (bits per second) transmitted.

Dilution of trademark The act of diminishing the value of a trademark held by another. Trademark dilution claims in court reflect a clash between the rights of a trademark holder and a domain name registrant. Two types of trademark dilution are *blurring*, use of a trademark on a dissimilar product, and *tarnishment*, association of a trademark with an inferior or unwholesome product or service.

Distance learning Conducting education and providing instruction in settings beyond the normal face-to-face classroom through the use of telecommunication technologies and audiovisual media.

Domain names An Internet address that locates a particular server hosting a Web site on the Internet, much like a street address that is used to locate a person's residence. The six "top level" domain suffixes are .com = commercial; .net = network; .org = organization; .edu = education; .mil = military; and .gov = government (there are also designations for countries, e.g., .ca for Canada, .th for Thailand).

Dot.com 1. A suffix used with a URL (universal resource locator) to direct Internet traffic to the intended destination. 2. Any company conducting its business either exclusively or largely through the use of a Web site. Examples in e-commerce include Amazon.com and Travelocity.com.

E-commerce (electronic commerce) The use of electronic communication technologies to conduct business, including business-to-business (B2B) and business-to-consumer (B2C) interactions. The purposes of the interactions may vary from advertising to purchasing to account and inventory management functions.

Encode The act of expressing or inputting information, externalizing it in some form that can be shared by consumers or users. Writing a letter, making a speech, and using a computer keyboard for data entry are all forms of encoding.

Fiber-optic cable A communication transmission technology that uses flexible glass fiber in place of copper or aluminum wire or cable, and light pulses in place of electrical signals, to move digital information from one point to another. Signals through fiber-optic cable may be encoded using either a laser light or light-emitting diode (LED) and are decoded by a photodiode at the receiving end.

Flaming A practice in which persons use aggressive and inflammatory language on the Internet.

FM (frequency modulation) A process by which an audio signal modulates the frequency of a carrier. FM radio is called such because it is the frequency, not the amplitude, of the carrier wave that is changed by an audio source. FM is less subject to noise, static, and interference than AM, making it a desirable alternative for functions requiring greater fidelity and sound quality (i.e., radio broadcasts of symphonic music).

Frames Multiple, independently scrollable regions on a Web page.

Hertz (Hz) A synonym for cycles per second (cps), named for the German scientist Heinrich Hertz, who in 1887 demonstrated that electromagnetic waves could be propagated and detected amid other waves using oscillating circuits.

Hypertext Markup Language (HTML) A nonproprietary publishing language for the World Wide Web. Special tags, denoted in brackets, are used to mark text to be displayed in a particular way on a Web page.

Instructional technologies (IT) All the available means used to create, store, transmit, retrieve, and manipulate information for training and/or educational purposes (these can include computer and telephone networks, video teleconferencing, e-mail, even correspondence courses via the traditional postal service).

Intellectual property Nonphysical material and content created by thought and protected by copyright laws as recognized by the United States and other governments. Providing intellectual property rights acts as an incentive to individuals to create new products, processes, or works of art.

Legacy programs Computer databases and operating systems that have been outmoded by newer versions but that are still in use on mainframe and older computer systems and are in need of upgrading or replacement. *Legacy work* is the upgrading of computer databases or facilities for private corporations that need to make a transition, often from mainframe storage to PC platforms, without losing any data.

Link A highlighted entry (usually a word or phrase) on a Web page that, when clicked, permits seamless and rapid navigation from that Web page to another.

Local area network (LAN) An interconnection of computer and telephone systems linking a number of users in an area, usually within a company, to provide faster exchange of information than would otherwise be possible using the public switched telephone network.

Meta-tag A hidden HTML code that provides information about a Web page, such as which keywords represent the Web page's content and who created the page. Many search engines use this information.

Microwave relay A wireless communication facility that uses radio energy in the GHz range to send messages from point to point. Radio transmission in the form of microwaves is used to carry broadcast signals, telephone traffic, and a myriad of satellite and mobile and fixed radio services in the United States. Microwave radio energy must follow a line-of-sight path; it is blocked by physical obstructions.

Modem The first device built for sending computer data over analog phone lines by converting digital signals into analog sound and vice versa. The term *modem* stands for modulator-demodulator. When placed between a computer terminal and a telephone line, it produces tones from carrier signals modulated by binary code, performing translation functions between them. ·

Modulate To vary some aspect of a communication medium or carrier in order for it to contain a message. Some modulation (variation or change) is required to impose a pattern of intelligence on any medium.

Multimedia communication Content featuring voice, text, data, images, and/or motion visuals.

Multiplexing The use of a single transmission channel to carry multiple signals.

Multiuser domain (MUD) An interactive, multiplayer game played on the Internet.

Multiuser domain, object-oriented (MOO) An object-oriented MUD.

Multiuser shared hallucination (MUSH) A type of MUD in which the players themselves create new objects, construct new rooms, and so on.

Netiquette The rules of etiquette on the Internet, such as guidelines for posting messages to online services.

Packet switching A method of transmitting digital information by sending it out in small bundles or units independent from one another and then reassembling them into their proper order after they are received at their destination.

Personal communication service (PCS) A wireless digital technology service using beepers, cellular phones, and data and paging devices to deliver messages intended for individual users. Most recently, wireless Internet is becoming another PCS The *PCS band* is that portion of the radio spectrum where cellular telephones and other PCS devices operate.

Personal digital assistant (PDA) A device, such as the Palm Pilot, used for information storage and retrieval. As greater convergence of digital devices continues, devices like cell phones and PDAs will become more and more indistinguishable from one another.

Public switched telephone network (PSTN) All the network infrastructure used to provide seamless telephone service to the public, including telephone instruments, wire and cable connections, cellular technology, fiber-optic lines, satellites designated for carrying telephone traffic, exchange offices, and so on.

Radio frequency (RF) carrier Any high-frequency radio transmission suitable for radio transmission. Before sound waves can be transmitted to distant points without wires, they must first be transformed into an electrical signal and then superimposed onto an RF carrier. The RF carrier is created with an oscillator, an electronic circuit that produces a sine wave at a specific frequency. The RF carrier, after being modulated by the audio signal, is then propagated into space at the speed of light. This is the essence of radio and television broadcasting.

Radio technologies Technologies that harness natural qualities of electricity and electromagnetic radiation to transmit sound, voice-modulated audio signals.

Radio waves Electromagnetic radiation that carries radio frequencies—the physical phenomena that make broadcasting possible. At the simplest level, radio waves can be generated by rotating a loop of copper wire in a magnetic field. Such rotation induces an electric current in the wire. As the wire passes through each full rotation, the intensity and direction of the flow of electrons vary in an orderly pattern called a *sine wave*. Sine waves produced by continuous rotation feature several characteristics, including a *frequency*, the number of cycles per second; a *period*, the time it takes for one cycle to occur; an *amplitude*, the magnitude of the voltage in the wire; a *wavelength*, the length of one cycle in meters; and a *phase*, the difference between the same points on different waves. Radio waves travel at the speed of light, about 186,000 miles per second, or 300,000,000 meters per second.

Satellite Wireless communication facilities in *geosynchronous* earth orbit that use radio energy to transfer messages from point to point. Satellite technology enables microwave signals to cross the ocean. By placing satellites 22,300 miles above the equator, they enter a geosynchronous orbit, meaning that they take 24 hours to make one revolution of the earth, thereby staying above the same spot on earth at all times. Radio transmission between a satellite and a ground station is therefore constant and reliable when the satellite maintains the same position relative to the earth.

Search engine A program that searches documents on the Web for specified keywords. *Search engine* is a general class of programs, but the term is often used to describe systems such as Alta Vista and Excite that allow users to search for information and files.

Spammers Entities, colloquially known as "spammers," that e-mail unsolicited advertisements in mass sendings. The manner in which the Internet transmits data precludes easy identification of those spammers, ensuring that the geographic source of those entities may remain hidden or disguised.

Throughput A measure of the amount of bandwidth carrying meaningful data compared to the overall information capacity of a device or transmission line.

Transduction The process of transforming sound waves into electrical audio signals. (The telephone is therefore a transducer. At the receiving end of a telephone, the electrical pattern is transformed back into sound.)

Transmissional technologies Technologies that engage users in noninteractive modalities such as watching television or listening to the radio.

Universal resource locator (URL) The name for Internet Web locations. URLs contain several parts. The first section, the http://, designates which Internet protocol is to be used. The next section, the www, designates what Internet resource is being requested. The last section, the .org or .net and so on, designates the Web server to be reached and locates a specific home page or document on the Internet. URLs can be thought of as addresses.

Virtual reality (VR) Mediated simulation of reality such as role-playing games (RPGs) and 3-D simulation technology. VR technologies create a feeling of immersion: Viewers or players feel as if they are inside the virtual space, as if they are surrounded by it, similar to the way the natural world surrounds us in real life.

Vocoder The device, in a digital cell phone, that takes the audio signal produced by the voice and converts it into a digital bit stream through a process of sampling. It is the synthetic speech signal that is then transmitted over the telephone network.

REFERENCES

Acker, S., & McCain, T. (1993). *The contribution of interactivity and two-way video to successful distance learning applications: A literature review and strategic positioning*. Columbus: Ohio State University, Center for Advanced Study in Telecommunications.

Argyris, C., & Schon, D. (1978). *Organizational learning: A theory of action perspective*. Reading, MA: Addison-Wesley.

Augarten, S. (1984). *Bit by bit: An illustrated history of computers*. New York: Ticknor and Fields.

Austen, I. (2001, January 11). Quantum computers: Using light instead of moving atoms. *New York Times*.

Bain, A. (1996, May). The school design at Brewster Academy: Technology serving teaching and learning. *T.H.E. Journal, 23*(10), 72-79. Retrieved from www.thejournal.com/past/may/65bain.html

Ball-Rokeach, S. J., & Reardon, K. (1988). Monologue, dialogue, and telelogue: Comparing an emergent form of communication with traditional forms. In R. P. Hawkins, J. M. Wiemann, & S. Pingree (Eds.), *Advancing communication science: Merging mass and interpersonal processes* (pp. 135-161). Newbury Park, CA: Sage.

Barlow, J. (1994, March). The economy of ideas: Patents and copyrights in the digital age. *Wired*, pp. 84-90.

Barnett, S., & Silverman, M. (1979). *Ideology and everyday life*. Ann Arbor: University of Michigan Press.

Bass, R. (2000). *Engines of inquiry: A practical guide for using technology to teach American culture*. Washington, DC: Georgetown University, Center for Electronic Projects in American Cultural Studies.

Bell, D. (1979). Communication technology—For better or for worse? *Harvard Business Review, 57*, 20.

Berliner, D. (1992). Redesigning classroom activities for the future. *Educational Technology*, pp. 7-13.

Blanck, G., & Blanck, R. (1979). *Ego psychology II—Psychoanalytic developmental psychology*. New York: Columbia University Press.

Blatner, A. (1985). *Role development—A systematic approach to building basic skills*. San Marcos, TX: Adam Blatner, M.D.

Bork, A. (1999, July/August). The future of learning: An interview with Alfred Bork. *Educom Review, 34*(4), 24-30.

Boyer Commission on Educating Undergraduates. (1998). *Reinventing undergraduate education: A blueprint for America's research universities*. Retrieved from http://notes.cc.sunysb.edu/Pres/boyer.nsf/images/$File/boyer.txt

Brown, R. G. (1993). *Schools of thought: How the politics of literacy shape thinking in the classroom*. San Francisco: Jossey-Bass.

Burgess, P. (2000). Strategy application disorder: The role of the frontal lobes in human multitasking. *Psychological Research, 63*(3-4), 279-288.

Carnie, A. (2001, January 5). How to handle cyber-sloth in academe. *Chronicle Review*. Retrieved from http://chronicle.com

Carr, S. (1999, October). Distance-learning group blends offerings of 2- and 4-year colleges. *Chronicle of Higher Education, 46*(7), A37.

Carr, S. (2000a, January). Distance-education company woos bastions of the liberal arts. *Chronicle of Higher Education, 46*(21), A43.

Carr, S. (2000b, February). Logging in with Ray Steele: A distance-education advocate calls for better financing for such programs. *Chronicle of Higher Education, 46*(22), A50.

Chambers, G. (1999, November). Towards shared control of shared education. *Chronicle of Higher Education, 46*(13), B8.

Chrisman, G., & Holliday, C. (1996, November). An Rx for 20/20 vision: Vision planning and education. *T.H.E. Journal, 24*(4), 106-110. Retrieved from www.thejournal.com/past/nov/1196feat3.html

Connolly, F. (1995, April). Intellectual honesty in the era of computing. *T.H.E. Journal, 22*(10), 86-88. Retrieved from www.thejournal.com/past/april.54con.html

Corrigan, E., & Gordon, P. (1995). *The mind object*. Northvale, NJ: Aronson.

Costello, R. (1997, November). The leadership role in making the technology connection. *T.H.E. Journal, 25*(4), 58-62. Retrieved from www.thejournal.com/past/Nov/1197/feat4.html

Coyle, K. (1996). Copyright in the digital age [Talk given at the San Francisco Public Library]. Retrieved from http://www.kcoyle.net/

Cuban, L. (1986). *Teachers and machines: The classroom use of technology since 1920*. New York: Teachers College Press.

Daggett, W. (1994). Today's students, yesterday's schooling. *The Executive Educator*, pp. 18-21.

Dardig, J. C. (1997, December). Enriching the teaching/learning process with computers: Spreading the word on a college campus. *T.H.E. Journal, 25*(5), 52-54. Retrieved from www.thejournal.com/past/DEC/1297feat2.html

Davies, H., & Wharton, M. (1983). *Inside the chip*. London: Usborne.

Davis, S. M., & Meyer, C. (1999). *Blur: The speed of change in the connected economy*. New York: Time Warner.

DeFleur, M., & Ball-Rokeach, S. (1989). *Theories of mass communication* (5th ed.). New York: Longman.

Dewey, J. (1938). *Experience and education*. New York: Collier.

Dewey, J. (2000). *Democracy and education*. Philadelphia: Pennsylvania State University, Electronic Classics Series. Retrieved from www.hn.psu.edu/faculty/jmanis/johndewey/demded.pdf

Distance-learning forecast calls for megaclasses. (1999, December 10). *Chronicle of Higher Education, 46*, A47.

Dominick, J. R., Sherman, B. L., & Copeland, G. A. (1996). *Broadcasting/cable and beyond: An introduction to modern electronic media* (3rd ed.). New York: McGraw-Hill.

Dominick, J. R., Sherman, B. L., & Messere, F. (2000). *Broadcasting, cable, the Internet, and beyond: An introduction to modern electronic media* (4th ed.). New York: McGraw-Hill.

Dommering, E. (1992). Information law. In W. Altes, E. Dommering, P. Hugenholtz, & J. Kabel (Eds.), *Information law towards the 21st century* (pp. 3-11). Boston: Kluwer Law and Taxation Publishers.

Drucker, P. (1993). *Post-capitalist society*. New York: HarperCollins.

Duderstadt, J. J. (2000, February). A choice of transformations for the 21st-century university. *Chronicle of Higher Education, 46*(22), B6.

Dunn, S. L. (2000, March-April). The virtualizing of education. *The Futurist, 34*(2), 34-38.

Dyson, E. (1998). Release 2.1 A Design for Living in the Digital Age. New York: Broadway Books.

Edwards, H. M. (1999, September). South Africa's GAELIC; The Gauteng and Environs Library Consortium. *Information Technology and Libraries, 18*(3), 123-128.

Ehrmann, S. C. (1991, Fall/Winter). Gauging the educational value of a college's investment technology. *Educom Review, 24*(4), 24-28.

Ehrmann, S. C. (1995, July). New technology, old trap. *Educom Review, 30*(5), 41-43.

Ehrmann, S. C. (1997). Asking the right question: What does research tell us about technology and higher education? *Change Magazine, 27*(2), 20-27.

Eisenberg, A. (2000, November 6). Unlike viruses, bacteria find a welcome in the world of computing. *New York Times.*

Eisenstein, E. (1979). *The printing press as an agent of change.* Cambridge, UK: Cambridge University Press.

Erikson, E. (1950). *Childhood and society.* New York: Norton.

Fischer, C. S. (1992). *America calling: A social history of the telephone to 1940.* Berkeley: University of California Press.

Flynn, L. J. (2000, August 14). *Internet is more than just fun for women New York Times,* Section C, p. 4

Forman, P. P. (2000, January). VAR serves society with education, libraries solutions. *Computer Reseller News, 87*(9), 61-62.

Fraiberg, S. (1959). *The magic years.* New York: Scribner.

Freud, S. (1961). *Civilization and its discontents.* New York: Norton.

Freire, P. (1993). *Pedagogy of the oppressed.* New York: Continuum.

Gabbard, G. (2001). Cyberpassion: E-rotic transference on the Internet. *Psychoanalytic Quarterly, 70*(40), 719-737.

Gallup national survey in conjunction with CNN, USA Today, and the National Science Foundation. (1997). *Teens and technology.* Retrieved from www.nsf.gov/od/lpa/nstw/teenov.htm

Garcia, L. (2000, February). Maximizing the on-line education experience. *Health Management Technology, 21*(2), 67-68.

Gardner, H. (1991). *The unschooled mind: How children think and how schools should teach.* New York: Basic Books.

Gardner, R. (2000, June 12). Is AOL worse than TV? *New York Magazine.*

Gates, B., with Hemingway, C. (1999). *Business @ the speed of thought: Using a digital nervous system.* New York: Warner Books.

Gilbert, S. (1996, March/April). Making the most of a slow revolution. *Change,* p. 1023.

Gilder, G. (1989). *Microcosm: The quantum revolution in economics and technology.* New York: Simon & Schuster.

Ginsburg, J. (1992). Reproduction of protected works for university research or teaching. *Journal of the Copyright Society of the USA, 39,* 181-223.

Gorman, R. (1998). Intellectual property: The rights of faculty as creators and users. *Academe, 84*(3), 14-18.

Greene, B. (1999). *The elegant universe: Super strings, hidden dimensions, and the quest for the ultimate theory.* New York: Norton.

Greenspan, S. (1997). *The growth of the mind.* Reading, MA: Addison-Wesley.

Gruman, G. (2000, February). A governor's tech crusade. *Upside, 12*(2), 124-132.

Grunwald Associates. (2000, June 7). *Children, families and the Internet*. Burlingame, CA: Author. Retrieved from www.grunwald.com/survey/survey_content.html

Hafner, K. (2000, May 25). What do you mean, "It's just like a real dog?" *New York Times*.

Hayles, K. (1999). *How we become post human: Virtual bodes in cybernetics* (Literature and Informatics). Chicago: University of Chicago Press.

Head, S. W., Sterling, C. H., & Schofield, L. B. (1994). *Broadcasting in America* (7th ed.). Boston: Houghton Mifflin.

Healy, J. M. (1998). *Failure to connect*. New York: Simon & Schuster.

Hesse, C. (1996). Books in time. In G. Nunberg & E. Eco (Eds.), *The future of the book* (pp. 21-36). Berkeley: University of California Press.

Hillis, S. (2000, March 21). *Plugged in: Web companies give educator a lesson*. Retrieved from http://news.lycos.com/headlines/Technology/Internet/article.asp

Holmberg, B. (1995). *Theory and practice of distance education*. London: Routledge.

Huizinga, J. (1950). *Homo ludens*. Boston: Beacon.

Hunter, J., & Bowman, C. (1996). *The state of disunion: 1996 survey of American political culture* (postmodernity project). Charlottesville: University of Virginia.

Innis, H. (1951). *The bias of communication*. Toronto: University of Toronto Press.

IT spending boom forecast for colleges. (1999, September). *Business Communications Review, 29*(9), 8.

Jones, B., Valdez, G., Nowakowski, J., & Rasmussen, C. (1995). *Plugging in*. Oakbrook, IL: North Central Regional Educational Laboratory.

Kelleher, K. J., McInery, T. K., Gardner, W. P., Childs, G. E., & Wasserman, R. C. (2000). Increasing identification of psychosocial problems: 1979-1996. *Pediatrics*, pp. 105-106, 1313-1321. Retrieved from http://www.Pediatrics.org

Kember, D. (1995). *Open learning courses for adults*. Englewood Cliffs, NJ: Educational Technology Publications.

Kleiner, C. (2000, September 25). Logging on young, and paying later. *U.S. News & World Report*. Retrieved from http://www.usnews.com/usnews/issue/000925/nycu/computers.b1.htm

Koechlin, E., Basso, G., Pietrini, P., Panzer, S., & Grafman, J. (1999). Exploring the role of the anterior prefrontal cortex in human cognition. *Nature, 399* (6732).

Kraut, R., Lundmark, V., Patterson, M., Kiesler, S., Mukopadhyay, T., & Scherlis, W. (1998). Internet paradox: A social technology that reduces social involvement and psychological well-being? *American Psychologist*, pp. 53-59, 1017–1031. Retrieved from www.apa.org/journals/amp/amp5391017.html

Kurzweil, R. (1999). *The age of spiritual machines: When computers exceed human intelligence*. New York: Viking.

Lehman, B. (1995). What's ahead in patents and trademarks? *Bulletin of the American Society for Information Science, 21*, 26-29.

Lewis, M. (1982). *Clinical aspects of child development*. Philadelphia: Lea & Febiger.

Lifton, R. J. (1993). *The protean self—Human resilience in an age of fragmentation*. New York: Basic Books.

Lu, C. (1998). The race for bandwidth: understanding data transmission. Microsoft Press: Redmond, WA.

Luna, C., & McKenzie, J. (1997, February). Testing multimedia in the community college classroom. *T.H.E. Journal, 24(8)*, 78-81. Retrieved from www.thejournal.com/past/FEB/0297feat1.html

Magdoff, J., & Barnett, S. (Fall, 1986). Beyond narcissism in American culture of the 1980's. *Cultural Anthropology*.

Mahler, M. (1971). *Separation—Individuation; essays in honor of Margaret S. Mahler* (J. B. McDevitt & C. F. Settlage, Eds.). New York: International Universities Press.

Marchese, T. (1998, May). Not-so-distant competitors: How new providers are remaking the postsecondary marketplace. *AAHE Bulletin*. Retrieved from www.aah.org/Bulletn/Not-So-Distant%20Competitors.htm

Marshack, A. (1999). The art and symbols of ice age man. In D. Crowley & P. Heyer (Eds.), *Communication in history: Technology, culture, society* (3rd ed.). New York: Longman.

Marshall, H. (1992). Seeing, redefining, and supporting student learning. In H. Marshall (Ed.), *Redefining student learning* (pp. 1-32). Norwood, NJ: Ablex.

Maxwell, L. (1996). Community leader perspectives on education, assessment, and communication technology (Doctoral dissertation, Ohio State University, 1996). *Dissertation Abstracts International, 57* (07A), AAG96-39302.

Maxwell, L., & McCain, T. (1997). Gateway or gatekeeper: Implications of copyright and digitalization on education. *Communication Education, 46*, 141-157.

McCain, T., Morris, S., Green, C., & al-Najran, T. (1999, November). *To do is to empower: Relationships between experience with networked computing, efficacy, and attitudes toward life online*. Paper presented at the National Communication Association Convention, Chicago.

McDaniel, E. A., & Klonoski, E. (1995-1996). Engaging the faculty in information technologies training. *Journal of Staff, Program & Organizational Development, 13*(2), 61-62, 65.

McLuhan, M. (1964). *Understanding media: The extensions of man*. New York: McGraw-Hill.

McLuhan, M., & Fiore, Q. (1967). *The medium is the massage*. New York: Bantam.

McQuail, D. (1991). *Mass communication theory* (2nd ed.). London: Sage.

Means, B. (1994). Using technology to advance educational goals. In B. Means (Ed.), *Technology and education reform* (pp. 1-22). San Francisco: Jossey-Bass.

Meyrowitz, J. (1985). *No sense of place: The impact of electronic media on social behavior*. New York: Oxford University Press.

Moore, M. (1990). Introduction: Background and overview of contemporary American distance education. In M. Moore (Ed.), *Contemporary issues in American distance education* (pp. xii-xxvi). Oxford, UK: Pergamon.

Mottl, J. N. (2000, January 3). Learn at a distance. *Information Week*, pp. 75-78. Retrieved from www.informationweek.com/767/learn.htm

National Center for Education Statistics. (1997). *Distance education in higher education institutions*. (Document No. NCES 98-062). Washington, DC: U.S. Department of Education.

National Center for Education Statistics. (1998). *Distance education in higher education institutions*. Retrieved from http://nces.ed.gov/pubs98/distance/

National Center for Education Statistics. (1999). *Distance education at postsecondary education institutions: 1997-1998*. (Document No. NCES 2000-013). Washington, DC: U.S. Department of Education.

Nie, N., & Ebring, L. (2000, February). *The Internet Study*. Stanford, CA: Stanford Institute for the Quantitative Study of Society. Available: http://www.stanford.edu/group/siqss/press_Release/Preliminary_Report.pdf

NII Task Force Issues Preliminary Report. (1994). *Bulletin of the American Society for Information Science, 20*, 2-4.

Noll, A. M. (1998). *Introduction to telephones and telephone systems*. Boston: Artech House.

Nonaka, I., & Takeuchi, H. (1995). *The knowledge-creating company*. New York: Oxford University Press.

Nunberg, G., & Eco, U. (Eds.). (1996). *The future of the book*. Berkeley: University of California Press.

Olsen, D. (1974). Introduction. In D. Olsen (Ed.), *Media and symbols: The forms of expression, communication, and education*. Chicago: University of Chicago Press.

Oppenheimer, T. (1997). The computer delusion [Online version]. *Atlantic Monthly*, pp. 45-62. Retrieved from http:// www.theatlantic.com/issues/97jul/computer.htm

Paul, D. (1994). An integration/inservice model that works. *T.H.E. Journal, 21*(9), 60-62.

Peek, R. (2000, February). A distance learning reality check. *Information Today, 17*(2), 30.

Perelman, L. (1992). *School's out*. New York: Avon.

Petzold, C. (1999). *Code: the hidden language of computer hardware and software*. Redmond, WA: Microsoft.

Piaget, J. (1971). *The construction of reality in the child*. New York: Ballantine.

Piaget, J., & Inhelder, B. (1969). *The psychology of the child*. New York: Basic Books.

Pinchot, G., & Pinchot, E. (1994). *The end of bureaucracy and rise of the intelligent organization*. San Francisco: Berrett-Koehler.

Postman, N. (1986). *Amusing ourselves to death: Public discourse in the age of show business*. New York: Penguin.

Postman, N. (1992). *Technopoly*. New York: Knopf.

Rafaeli, S. (1988). Interactivity: From new media to communication. In R. P. Hawkins, J. M. Wiemann, & S. Pingree (Eds.), *Advancing communication science: Merging mass and interpersonal processes* (pp. 110-134). Newbury Park, CA: Sage.

Richter, C., Maxwell, L., & McCain, T. (1995, May). *Distance education as communication process: Transmission vs. dialogue in higher education*. Paper presented at the 45th annual conference of the International Communication Association, Albuquerque, NM.

Rideout, V. J., Foehr, U. G., Roberts, D. F., & Brodie, M. (1999, November). *Kids and media at the new millennium* (Henry J. Kaiser Family Foundation Publications No. kff 1536, No. kff 1537, pp. 1-89). Menlo Park, CA: Henry J. Kaiser Family Foundation. Retrieved from www.kff.org

Rowe, M. (2000, February 17). Study shows Internet use stunts social growth. Stanford study.

Rowland, W. (1997). *Spirit of the Web: The age of information from telegraph to Internet*. Toronto: Somerville House.

Rubin, J. B. (1998). *A psychoanalysis for our time: Exploring the blindness of the seeing I*. New York: New York University Press.

Russell, T. (1999). *The no significant difference phenomenon* (5th ed.). Montgomery, AL: International Distance Education Certification Center.

Salomon, G. (1997, January). Of mind and media: How culture's symbolic forms affect learning and thinking. *Phi Delta Kappan, 79*, 375-380.

Samuelson, P. (1996). The copyright grab. *Wired*, pp. 134-138, 188-191.

Schiller, D. (1994). From culture to information and back again: Commoditization as a route to knowledge. *Critical Studies in Mass Communication, 11*, 93-115.

Schwartau, W. (1996). *Information warfare: Cyberterrorism—Protecting your personal security in the electronic age* (2nd ed.). New York: Thunder's Mouth Press.

Seel, J. (1997). Plugged in, spaced out, and turned on: Electronic entertainment and moral mindfields. *Journal of Education, 179*(3), 17-32.

Shale, D., & Garrison, D. (1990). Education and communication. In D. Garrison & D. Shale (Eds.), *Education at a distance* (pp. 41-52). Malabar, FL: Krieger.

Shannon, C. (1938). A symbolic analysis of relay and switching circuits. In *The transactions of the American Institute of Electrical Engineers* (Vol. 57, Paper No. 38-80). American Institute of Electrical Engineers (AIEE).

Sherry, L. (1997, September). The Boulder Valley Internet Project: Lessons learned. *T.H.E. Journal, 25*(2), 68, 70.

Shyles, L. (1990). *Improving pilot efficiency in the age of the glass cockpit: Designing intelligent software interfaces for the military aviation setting*. Dayton, OH: U.S. Air Force Office of Scientific Research, Wright Patterson Air Force Base.

Shyles, L. (1997). *Video production handbook*. Boston: Houghton Mifflin.

Simon, H. (1997). Designing organizations for an information-rich world. In D. Lamberton (Ed.), *The economics of communication and information*. Cheltenham, UK: Edward Elgar.

Snyder, T., & Wirt, J. (1998). *The condition of education* (Indicator 37: Homework and television viewing. Publication No. 98013). Washington, DC: National Center for Education Statistics. Retrieved from http://nces.ed.gov

Strangelove, M. (1994). The Internet as catalyst for a paradigm shift. *The Internet Business Journal, 2*(4-5), 30-34.

Straus, L. A. (1959). *Mirrors and masks: The search for identity*. Glencoe, IL: Free Press.

Subrahmanyam, K., Kraut, R., Greenfield, P., & Gross, E. (2000). The impact of home computer use on children's activities and development. *The Future of Children—Children and Computer Technology, 10*(2), 123-144.

Tapscott, D. (1996). *The digital economy: Promise and peril in the age of networked intelligence*. New York: McGraw-Hill.

Tapscott, D. (1998). *Growing up digital: The rise of the Net generation*. New York: McGraw-Hill.

T.H.E. Journal. (1998). Volume 25.

Tierney, R. (1992). *Computer acquisition: A longitudinal study of the influence of high computer access on students thinking, learning, and interactions*. Apple Classrooms of Tomorrow. (ERIC Document Reproduction Service No. ED354856)

Tishman, S., Jay, E., & Perkins, D. (1993). Teaching thinking dispositions: From transmission to enculturation. *Theory Into Practice, 32*, 147-153.

Turkle, S. (1995). *Life on the screen: Identity in the age of the Internet*. New York: Simon & Schuster.

U.S. Web-Based Education Commission. (2000). *The power of the Internet for learning: Moving from promise to practice*. Retrieved from http://interact.hpcnet.org/webcommission/index.htm

Wachowski, L., & Wachowski, A. (1996). *The matrix* (script). Retrieved from www.screentalk.org/moviescripts/The%20Matrix.pdf

Wallace, M. P. (1999). *The psychology of the Internet*. New York: Cambridge University Press.

Walters, R. (1993). *Computer telephone integration*. Boston: Artech House.

Walther, J. B. (1992). Interpersonal effects in computer-mediated interaction: A relational perspective. *Communication Research, 19*(1), 52-90.

Wartella, E., & Jennings, N. (2000). Children and computers: New technology—Old concerns. *The Future of Children—Children and Computer Technology, 10*(2), 31-43.

Webb, W. (1998). *Understanding cellular radio*. Boston: Artech House.

Willis, B. (1993). *Distance education: A practical guide*. Englewood Cliffs, NJ: Educational Technology Publications.

Wood, R., & Smellie, D. (1991). Educational technology: Initiative for change. *Educational Media and Technology Yearbook, 17*, 5-17.

Yager, T. (2000, January). Latest tool book disappoints. *InfoWorld, 22*(2), 43.

Yocam, K. (1996, November). Teacher-centered staff development for integrating technology into classrooms. *T.H.E. Journal, 24*(4), 88-91.

Young, J. (1997, October 3). Rethinking the role of the professor in an age of high-tech tools. *Chronicle of Higher Education, 44*, A26-A28.

Zuboff, S. (1984). *In the age of the smart machine: The future of work and power*. New York: Basic Books.

FURTHER READINGS

ARTIFICIAL INTELLIGENCE ■

Can robots rule the world? Not yet. (2000, September 12). *New York Times*.

An electronic circuit that draws its inspiration from life. (2000, June 29). *New York Times*.

Schechter, B. (1999, August 3). A man, a plan, and a robot that makes eye contact. *New York Times*. Retrieved August 3, 1999, from http://www.nytimes.com/library/national/science/080399sci-artficial-intelligence.htm

BROADCASTING AND CYBERMEDIA ■

Brinkley, J. (1998, October 26). The dawn of HDTV, ready or not. *New York Times*. Retrieved October 26, 1998, from http://www.nytimes.com/library/tech/98/10/biztech/articles/26hdtv.html

Brinkley, J. (1998, August 24). FCC wants HDTV glitch solved soon. *New York Times*. Retrieved August 24, 1998, from http://www.nytimes.com/library/tech/98/08/biztech/articles/24fcc.html

Brinkley, J. (1999, October 11). Stations challenge digital-TV standard. *New York Times*. Retrieved October 11, 1999, from http://www.nytimes.com/library/tech/99/10/biztech/articles/11dtv.htm

Carter, B. (1999, May 17). TV networks scramble to deal with era of new media. *New York Times*. Retrieved May 17, 1999, from http://www.nytimes.com/library/tech/99/05/biztech/articles/17tube.html

Gartner, J. (1998, November 18). DVD developers wait for Windows. *New York Times*. Retrieved November 18, 1998, from http://www.nytimes.com/techweb/TW_DVD_Developers_Wait_For_Windows.html

Hansell, S. (1998, June 10). NBC buying a portal to the Internet. *New York Times*. Retrieved June 10, 1998, from http://www.nytimes.com/library/tech/98/06/biztech/articles/10cnet.html

Kaplan, C. S. (2000, May 12). Napster may have weak defense in fight with music industry. *New York Times*. Retrieved May 12, 2000, from http://www.nytimes.com . . . ech/00/05/cyber/cyberlaw/12law.html

Kuczynski, A. (2000, January 6). Radio squeezes empty air space for profit. *New York Times.* Retrieved January 6, 2000, from http://www.nytimes.com/library/financial/columns/010600radio-ads.htm

Labaton, S. (2000, May 31). U.S. seeks to ease some restrictions on broadcasters. *New York Times.* Retrieved May 31, 2000, from http://www.nytimes.com/library/financial/053100fcc-ownership.html

Labaton, Stephen. (1998, November 20). Some digital TV services to be taxed. *New York Times.* Retrieved November 20, 1998, from http://www.nytimes.com/library/tech/98/11/biztech/articles/20digi.html

Lehmann-Haupt, R. (1998, November 5). Web radio expands listening horizons. *New York Times.* Retrieved November 5, 1998, from http://www.nytimes.com/library/tech/98/11/circuits/library/05libe.html

Lewis, P. H. (1999, January 28). Life after the VCR: Choosing DVD or Divx. *New York Times.* Retrieved January 28, 1999, from http://www.nytimes/com/library/tech/99/01/circuits/articles/28pete.html

Meyer, Michael. (1998, September 28). Ready for prime time? *Newsweek,* pp. 83-85.

Mifflin, L. (1998, October 12). 24-Hour news channels force change at big three. *New York Times.* Retrieved October 12, 1998, from http://www.nytimes.com/yr/mo/day/news/financial/tv-news-media.html

Mifflin, L. (1999, February 1). Watch the tube or watch the computer? *New York Times.* Retrieved February 1, 1999, from http://www.nytimes.com/library/tech/99/02/biztech/articles/01tube.html

Mirapaul, M. (1999, January 21). Making movies, the do-it-yourself way, on the Web. *New York Times.* Retrieved January 21, 1999, from http://www.nytimes.com/library/tech/99/01/cyber/artsatlarge.html

Reuters (2000). Soft rock or software—"Tech" radio is coming. *New York Times.* Retrieved January 4, 2000, from http://www.nytimes.com/reuters/technology/tech-media-techradio.htm

Roberts, Johnnie L. (1998, October 19). TV turns vertical. *Newsweek,* pp. 52-56.

Schiesel, S. (1998, December 7). PC makers and bells in joint petition to U.S. on networks. *New York Times.* Retrieved December 7, 1998, from http://www.nytimes.com/library/tech/98/12/biztech/articles/07phone-data.html

Schiesel, S. (1998, March 9). Another setback in quest to marry TV and phones. *New York Times.* Retrieved March 9, 1998, from http://www.nytimes.com/library/tech/98/03/biztech/articles/09phone.html

Schiesel, S. (1999, March 23). Cable TV and the Internet, too: Battling the bells, but with some high-speed whistles. *New York Times.* Retrieved March 23, 1999, from http://www.nytimes.com/library/tech/99/03/biztech/articles/23comcast.html

Weinraub, B. (1999, December 20). Technology could soon hand TV control to the viewer. *New York Times.* Retrieved December 20, 1999, from http://www.nytimes.com/library/tech/yr/mo/biztech/articles/122099outlook-tele.htm

West, Don. (2000, January 3). The millennavision. *Broadcasting & Cable,* pp. 38-62.

COPYRIGHT ■

Clausing, J. (1998, October 28). Clinton signs digital copyright act. *New York Times*. Retrieved October 29, 1998, from http://www.nytimes.com/library/tech/98/10/cyber/articles/29wipo.html

Clausing, J. (1998, October 9). House and Senate agree on complex copyright bill. *New York Times*. Retrieved October 9, 1998, from http://www.nytimes.com/library/tech/98/10/cyber/articles/09wipo.html

Clausing, J. (2000, January 17). Wrestling group wins back use of its name on Internet. *New York Times*. Retrieved January 17, 2000, from http://www.nytimes.com/library/tech/00/01/biztech/articles/17name.htm

Digital copyright agreement for video. (1999, February 17). *New York Times*. Retrieved February 17, 1999, from http://www.nytimes/com/library/tech/99/02/biztech/articles/17blue.html

Kaplan, C. S. (1998, September 25). Can a Web link break copyright laws? *New York Times*. Retrieved September 25, 1998, from http://www.nytimes.com/library/tech/98/09/cyber/cyberlaw/25law.html

Kaplan, C. S. (1998, October 30). Free book sites hurt by copyright law. *New York Times*. Retrieved October 30, 1998, from http://www.nytimes.com/library/tech/98/10/cyber/cyberlaw/30law.html

Long, Doris, Risher, Carol, & Shapiro, Gary F. (1997). *Questions and answers on copyright for the campus community*. Oberlin: National Association of College Stores.

Markoff, J. (1998, December 7). Microsoft's Cleartype sets off debate on originality. *New York Times*. Retrieved December 7, 1998, from http://www.nytimes.com/library/tech/98/12/biztech/articles/07microsoft-flat.html

Markoff, J. (1999, February 25). Sony to propose a method for protecting digital music. *New York Times*. Retrieved February 25, 1999, from http://www.nytimes.com/library/tech/99/02/biztech/articles/25sony.html

Markoff, J. (2000, May 10). The concept of copyright fights for Internet survival. *New York Times*. Retrieved May 10, 2000, from http://www.nytimes.com . . . /05/biztech/articles/10digital.html

Mirapaul, M. (1998, December 17). Composers of game soundtracks seek Grammy recognition. *New York Times*. Retrieved December 17, 1998, from http://www.nytimes.com/library/tech/98/12/cyber/artsatlarge/17artsatlarge.html

Pareles, J. (1999, February 1). Trying to get in tune with the digital age. *New York Times*. Retrieved February 1, 1999, from http://www.nytimes.com/library/tech/99/02/biztech/articles/01tune.html

Richtel, M. (1999, July 14). Standards are set for thwarting music pirates. *New York Times*. Retrieved July 14, 1999, from http://www.nytimes.com/library/tech/99/07/biztech/articles/14standard.htm

Riordan, T. (1999, December 20). Parents considered vital to thrive on the Internet. *New York Times*. Retrieved December 20, 1999, from http://www.nytimes.com/library/tech/yr/mo/biztech/articles/122099outlook-pate.htm

Robinson, Sara. (2000, January 24). 3 copyright lawsuits test limits of new digital media. *New York Times*. Retrieved January 24, 2000, from http://www.nytimes.com/library/tech/00/01/biztech/articles/24onli.htm

Strauss, N. (1999, April 15). Technology you can dance to. *New York Times.* Retrieved April 15, 1999, from http://www.nytimes.com/library/tech/99/04/biztech/articles/15popx.html

■ CYBERLAW

ACLU in the Courts. (1997, June 20). *ALA v. Pataki Decision.* ACLU. Retrieved February 2, 1999, from http://www.aclu.org/court/nycdadec.html

ACLU in the Courts. (1999). *Kathleen R. v. City of Livermore.* ACLU. Retrieved February 11, 1999, from http://www.aclu.org/court/kathleenrvlivermorepubliclibrary.html

ACLU in the Courts. (1998, October 21). *Kathleen R. vs. City of Livermore.* ACLU. Retrieved February 18, 1999, from http://www.aclu.org/court/kathleenrvslivermore.html

ACLU vs. Reno Decision—Dalzell Decision. (1999). Retrieved September 8, 1999, from http://www.pas.rochester.edu/~mbanks/CDA/decision/dalzell.htm

ACLU vs. Reno Decision—Introduction. (1999). Retrieved September 8, 1999, from http://www.pas.rochester.edu/~mbanks/CDA/decision/intro.htm

ACLU vs. Reno Decision—Sloviter Decision. (1999). Retrieved September 8, 1999, from http://www.pas.rochester.edu/~mbanks/CDA/decision/sloviter.htm

ACM, Inc. (1999). *PICS: Internet access controls without censorship.* Retrieved February 9, 1999, from http://www.w3.org/PICS/iacwcv2.htm

American Civil Liberties Union (ACLU). (1999, January 14). *Court upholds Livermore Library's uncensored Internet access policy.* ACLU. Retrieved February 11, 1999, from http://www.aclu.org/news/n011499a.html

American Civil Liberties Union (ACLU). (1999). *Supreme Court of the United States: Reno v. American Civil Liberties Union.* ACLU. Retrieved February 2, 1999, from http://www.aclu.org/court/renovacludec.html

American Civil Liberties Union (ACLU). (1999). *White Paper: Censorship in a box.* ACLU. Retrieved February 18, 1999, from http://www.aclu.org/issues/cyber.box.html

Associated Press. (1999, March 12). FCC: No Internet regulation plans. *New York Times.* Retrieved March 12, 1999, from http://www.nytimes.com/library/tech/99/03/biztech/articles/12fcc-net.html

Associated Press. (1999, March 18). FCC wants phone rates on Internet. *New York Times.* Retrieved March 18, 1999, from http://www.nytimes.com/aponline/w/AP-FCC-Phone-Matters.html

Associated Press. (1999, February 25). Virginia passes law against unsolicited e-mail. *New York Times.* Retrieved February 25, 1999, from wysiwyg://24/http://www.nytimes.com/library/tech/99/02/biztech/articles/25spam.html

Auletta, Ken. (1999, August 16). Annals of communications: Hard core: Why does Bill Gates think that the Microsoft antitrust trial has been such a disaster for him and for the company? *The New Yorker,* pp. 42-69.

Availability of bombmaking information. (1997, June 20). Retrieved March 18, 1999, from http://jya.com/abi.htm

Beeson, Ann, Hansen, Chris, & Steinhardt, Barry. (1999). ACLU White Paper: Fahrenheit 451.2: Is cyberspace burning? ACLU. Retrieved September 8, 1999, from http://www.aclu.org/issues/cyber/burning.htm

Biemiller, Lawrence, & Blumenstyk, Goldie. (1997, July 3). Supreme Court strikes down law on Internet indecency. *Chronicle of Higher Education*.

Brinkema, Leonie M. (1998, February 26). ACLU in the Courts: *Urofsky v. Allen, E.D.* Virginia Decision. ACLU. Retrieved February 16, 1999, from http://www.aclu.org/court/urofskyvallendec.html

Brinkema, Leonie M. (1998, November 23). *Mainstream Loudoun v. Board of Trustees of the Loudoun County Library*. Retrieved February 11, 1999, from http://censorware.org/legal/loudoun/981123_memopin_jb.htm

Brinkley, J. (1998, June 23). Appeals court overturns ruling on Windows 95. *New York Times*. Retrieved June 23, 1998 from http://www.nytimes.com/library/tech/98/06/biztech/articles/24microsoft.html

Brinkley, J. (1998, October 20). As Microsoft trial gets started, Gates's credibility is questioned. *New York Times*. Retrieved October 20, 1998, from http://www.nytimes.com/library/tech/98/10/biztech/articles/20microsoft.html

Brinkley, J. (2000, April 4). U.S. judge says Microsoft violated antitrust laws with predatory behavior. *New York Times*. Retrieved April 4, 2000, from http://www.nytimes.com/library/tech/yr/mo/biztech/articles/04soft.html

Brinkley, J. (2000, June 1). Microsoft files its final arguments against breakup. *New York Times*. Retrieved June 1, 2000, from http://www.nytimes.com/library/tech/00/06/biztech/articles/01soft.html

The Brown Daily Herald, Inc. (1999). Retrieved February 22, 1999, from http://www.netspace.org/herald/issues/111795/cornell.f.html

Carroll, Michael W. (1996). Garbage in: Emerging media and regulation of unsolicited commercial solicitations. *Berkeley Technology Law Journal*, *11*(2). Retrieved April 5, 1999, from http://www.law.berkeley.edu/journals/btlj/articles/11-2/carroll.html

Clausing, J. (1998, September 28). House backs away from regulating spam. *New York Times*. Retrieved September 28 1998, from http://www.nytimes.com/library/tech/98/09/cyber/articles/28spam.html

Clausing, J. (1998). Marketers and Net activists reach agreement on spam. *New York Times*. Retrieved December 8, 1998, from http://www.nytimes.com/library/tech/98/12/cyber/articles/08spam.html

Clausing, J. (1998, October 12). Technology bills languish as Congress races for exit. *New York Times*. Retrieved October 12, 1998, from http://www.nytimes.com/library/tech/98/10/biztech/articles/12technology-legislation.html

Clausing, J. (1999, February 11). More states consider laws restricting junk e-mail. *New York Times*. Retrieved February 11, 1999, from http://www.nytimes.com/library/tech/99/02/cyber/articles/11spam.html.

Clausing, J. (1999, January 24). State lawmakers ready scores of Internet bills. *New York Times*. Retrieved January 25, 1999, from http://www.nytimes.com/library/tech/99/01/, cyber/articles/24states.html

Clausing, J. (1999, January 27). U.S. argues case on online smut law. *New York Times*. Retrieved January 27,1999, from http://www.nytimes.com/library/tech/99/01/cyber/articles/27copa.html

Compuserve, Inc. v. Cyber Promotions, Inc. (1997, February 3). Retrieved April 5, 1999, from http://www.leepfrog.com/ELaw/Cases/CompuServe_v_Cyber_Promo.html

Cyber Promotions, Inc. v. America Online, Inc. (1996, November 4). Retrieved April 5, 1999, from: http://www.leepfrog.com/E-Law/Cases/Cyber_Promo_v_AOL.html

Electronic Commerce & Law Report. (1999). *ACLU v. Janet Reno*: June 11, 1996. Retrieved February 2, 1999, from http://www.bna.com/e-law/cases/aclureno.html

Electronic Commerce & Law Report. (1999). *The Washington Post v. Total News Inc.* (Settlement). Retrieved September 23, 1999, from: http://zeus.bna.com/e-law/cases/totalset.htm

Electronic Privacy Information Center. (1999). Child Online Protection Act. EPIC. Retrieved February 2, 1999, from http://www.epic.org/free_speech/censorship/copa.html

Excerpts from government's suit against Microsoft. (1998). *New York Times*. Retrieved May 19, 1998, from http://www.nytimes.com/library/tech/yr/mo/biztech/articles/19microsoft-text.html

Fairley Raney, R. (1999, January 29). Charges filed in U.S. hate e-mail case. *New York Times*. Retrieved March 25, 1999, from http://www.nytimes.com/library/tech/99/01/cyber/articles/29mail.html

Fairley Raney, R. (1999, April 29). Internet stalking case ends in plea. *New York Times*. Retrieved April 29, 1999, from http://www.nytimes.com/library/tech/99/04/cyber/articles/29stalk.html

Fairley Raney, R. (1999, February 3). Plea entered in Internet stalking case. *New York Times*. Retrieved March 25, 1999, from http://www.nytimes.com/library/tech/99/02/cyber/articles/03stalk.html

FindLaw. (1969, June 9). United States Case Law: Supreme Court: *Brandenburg v. Ohio*. Retrieved March 16, 1999, from http://caselaw.findlaw/com/cgi-bin/getcase.pl?navby =case&court=US&vol=395&page=447

FindLaw. (1986, February 25). United States Case Law: U.S. Supreme Court: *Renton v. Playtime Theatres, Inc.* Retrieved February 17, 1999, from http://caselaw.findlaw.com/scripts/getcas . . . %GRAPHURL%>&court=US&case=/us/475/41.html

FindLaw. (1997, December 4). United States Case Law: 4th Circuit Court of Appeals: *Rice v. Paladin Enterprises*. FindLaw. Retrieved March 16, 1999, from http://caselaw.findlaw.com/cgi-bin/getcas . . . court=4th&navby=case&no=962412Pv2&exact=1

FindLaw. (1999). United States Case Law: 2nd Circuit Court. *Bensusan Restaurant Corporation v. Richard B. King*. Retrieved October 7, 1999, from wysiwyg://177/http://caselaw.findlaw.com/ . . . avby=search&case=/uscircs/2nd/969344.htm

FindLaw. (1999). United States Case Law: 6th Circuit Court: *United States of America v. Abraham Jacob Alkhabaz*. Retrieved March 23, 1999, from http://caselaw.findlaw.com/cgi-bin/getcase.pl?court=6th&navby=docket&no=970036p

FindLaw. (1999, February 10). United States Case Law: 4th Circuit Court of Appeals: *Urofsky v. Gilmore*. Retrieved February 16, 1999, from http://caselaw.findlaw.com/cgi-bin/getcase.pl?court=4th&navby=docket&no=981481P.

FindLaw. (1999). U.S. 2nd Circuit Court of Appeals: *Hickerson v. City of New York*. Retrieved March 10, 1999, from http://caselaw.findlaw.com/scripts/ getcas . . . avby=search&case=/uscircs/2nd/987269.html

FindLaw. (1999). U.S. Supreme Court: *Perry Education Association v. Perry Local Educators' Association*. Retrieved March 10, 1999, from http://caselaw.findlaw.com/cgi-bin/getcase.pl?court=US&vol=460& invol=37

FindLaw. (1999). U.S. Supreme Court: *Renton v. Playtime Theatres, Inc*. Retrieved March 10, 1999, from http://caselaw.findlaw.com/scripts/getcas . . . %GRAPHURL%>&court=US&case=/us/475/41.html

Hafner, K. (1998, October 15). Library grapples with protecting Internet freedom. *New York Times*. Retrieved October 15, 1998, from http://www.nytimes.com/library/tech/98/10/circuits/articles/15filt.html

Howe Verhovek, S. (1999, February 3). Creators of anti-abortion Web site told to pay millions. *New York Times*. Retrieved February 3, 1999, from http://www.nytimes.com/library/tech/99/02/biztech/articles/03abortion.html

Interest of the Amici. Retrieved February 9, 1999, from http://www.cilp.org/firstam/copaamici.html

Internet Society (ISOC). (1998, February 20). All about the Internet: A brief history of the Internet (last revision). Retrieved February 2, 1999, from http://www.isoc.org/internet-history/brief.html

Janofsky, M. (1999, March 9). Journalist sentenced in Internet pornography case. *New York Times*. Retrieved March 9, 1999, from http://www.nytimes.com/library/tech/99/03/biztech/articles/09porn.html

Kaplan, C. S. (1998, November 20). Anti-porn law enters Court; delay soon follows. *New York Times*. Retrieved November 20, 1998, from http://www.nytimes.com/library/tech/98/11/cyber/cyberlaw/20law.html

Kaplan, C. S. (1998, October 2). In library filtering case, an unusual ally. *New York Times*. Retrieved October 2, 1998, from http://www.nytimes.com/library/tech/98/10/cyber/cyberlaw/02law.html

Kaplan, C. S. (1998, October 9). Strict European privacy law puts pressure on U.S. *New York Times*. Retrieved October 9, 1998, from http://www.nytimes.com/library/tech/98/10/cyber/cyberlaw/09law.html

Kaplan, C. S. (1998, January 1). The year saw many milestones in cyberlaw. *New York Times*. Retrieved June 11, 1998, from http://www.nytimes.com/library/cyber/law/01019law.html

Kaplan, C. S. (1999, March 12). Companies fight anonymous critics with lawsuits. *New York Times*. Retrieved March 12, 1999, from http://www.nytimes.com/library/tech/99/03/cyber/cyberlaw/12law.html

Kaplan, C. S. (1999, April 30). Court lays down the law on labels for Web sites. *New York Times*. Retrieved April 30, 1999, from wysiwyg://10/http://www.nytimes.com/library/tech/99/04/cyber/cyberlaw/30law.html

Kaplan, C. S. (1999). Junk e-mail filters spawn a suit against Microsoft. *New York Times*. Retrieved February 19, 1999, from http://www.nytimes.com/library/tech/99/02/cyber/cyberlaw/19law.html

Kaplan, C. S. (1999, April 9). Ruling against domain name speculator could set precedent. *New York Times*. Retrieved April 9, 1999, from http://www.nytimes.com/library/tech/99/04/cyber/cyberlaw/09law.html

Kaplan, C. S. (2000, February 4). Another legal defeat for victim of online hoax. *New York Times*. Retrieved February 4, 2000, from http://www.nytimes.com/library/tech/00/02/cyber/cyberlaw/04law.htm

Kaplan, C. S. (2000). DVD lawsuit questions legality of linking. *New York Times*. Retrieved January 7, 2000, from wysiwyg://9/http://www.nytimes.com/library/tech/yr/mo/cyber/cyberlaw/07law.htm

Kaplan, C. S. (2000). When the Internet moves faster than the courts. *New York Times*. Retrieved February 25, 2000, from http://www.nytimes.com/library/tech/00/02/cyber/cyberlaw/25law.htm

Kozlowski, M. J. (1998, October 22). Site shutdown after PA AG files suit. *Law Journal Extra*. Retrieved March 25, 1999, from http://www.ljx.com/LJXfiles/paag.html

Labaton, S. (2000, April 4). Judge builds legal argument aimed at surviving an appeal. *New York Times*. Retrieved April 4, 2000, from http://www.nytimes.com/library/tech/00/04/biztech/articles/04legal.html

Law Journal Extra. (1999). *Commonwealth of Pennsylvania v. Alpha HQ*. LJX. Retrieved March 25, 1999, from http://www.ljx.com/LJXfiles/harassment/paaghate.html

Lessig, Lawrence. (1998, Summer). What things regulate speech: CDA 2.0 vs. filtering. *Jurimetrics*, pp. 629-670.

Like the live view? Here's how we did it. (1999). Cornell University Home Page. Retrieved October 13, 1999, from http://www.info.cornell.edu/CUHomePage/liveview.htm

Lohr, S. (1998, December 14). If Microsoft loses case, remedies are thorny. *New York Times*. Retrieved December 14, 1998, from http://www.nytimes.com/library/tech/98/12/biztech/articles/14soft.html

Lohr, S. (1998). An Intel executive testifies of a "credible and fairly terrifying" threat by Microsoft. *New York Times*. Retrieved November 10, 1998, from http://www.nytimes.com/library/tech/98/11/biztech/articles/10soft.html

Lohr, S. (1998, November 18). Microsoft told to stop shipments that violate contract with rival. *New York Times*. Retrieved November 18, 1998, from http://www.nytimes.com/library/tech/98/11/biztech/articles/18sun.html

Lohr, S. (1998, October 19). Sherman's 1890 nod to populism has been broadly interpreted. *New York Times*. Retrieved October 19, 1998, from http://www.nytimes.com/library/tech/98/10/biztech/articles/19law.html

Lohr, S. (1998). U.S. vs. Microsoft: Government sets the stage. *New York Times*. Retrieved May 19, 1998, from http://www.nytimes.com/library/tech/yr/mo/biztech/articles/19microsoft-justice.html

Loving v. Boren. (1997, January 28). Retrieved February 16, 1999, from http://www.gse.ucla/edu/iclp/loving.html

Macavinta, C. (1998, February 11). Conviction in online threat case. CNET News. Retrieved March 25, 1999, from http://www.news.com/News/Item/0,4,19046,00.html

Macavinta, C. (1998, May 4). Prison time for email threats. CNET News. Retrieved March 25, 1999, from http://www.news.com/News/Item/0,4,21766,0.html

Mainstream Loudoun v. Loudoun County Libraries. (1999). *Tech Law Journal*. Retrieved February 9, 1999, from http://www.techlawjournal.com/courts/loudon/80407mem.htm

Major, April M. (1997). Internet red light district: A domain name proposal for regulatory zoning of obscene content. *John Marshall Journal of Computer and Information Law, 16*, 21-33.

Major, April M. (1998). Copyright law tackles yet another challenge: The electronic frontier of the World Wide Web. *Rutgers Computer & Technology Law Journal, 8*. Retrieved March 15, 1999. LexisNexis

Markoff, J. (1998, May 18). Defiant Gates defends his business practices. *New York Times.* Retrieved May 19, 1998, from http://www.nytimes. com/library/tech/yr/mo/biztech/articles/19microsoft-gates.html

Mendels, P. (1998). Court tackles new angle on library Internet filtering. *New York Times.* Retrieved December 4, 1998, from http://www.nytimes. com/library/tech/98/12/cyber/cyberlaw/04law.html

Mendels, P. (1999, February 1). Decision expected Monday on Web anti-pornography law. *New York Times.* Retrieved February 1, 1999, from http://www.nytimes.com/library/tech/99/02/biztech/articles/01kids. html

Mendels, P. (1999, January 28). Hearings end in online pornography case. *New York Times.* Retrieved January 28, 1999, from http://www.nytimes. com/library/tech/99/01/cyber/articles/28copa.html

Mendels, P. (1999, April 28). Intel e-mail ruling raises free speech questions. *New York Times.* Retrieved April 29, 1999, from http://www.nytimes. com/library/tech/99/04/cyber/articles/29intel.html

Mendels, P. (1999, January 21). Internet smut law enters Court, with a snag. *New York Times.* Retrieved January 21, 1999, from http://www.nytimes. com/library/tech/99/01/cyber/articles/21copa.html

Mendels, P. (1999, February 1). Judge delays online pornography law. *New York Times.* Retrieved February 2, 1999, from http://www.nytimes. com/library/tech/99/02/cyber/articles/02copa.html

Mendels, P. (1999, June 24). Michigan faces challenge on online porn law. *New York Times.* Retrieved June 24, 1999, fromwysiwyg://13/http:// www.nytimes.com/library/tech/99/06/cyber/articles/24michigan.html

Mueller, Christopher B., & Kirkpatrick, Laird C. (1996). Relevance. In *Evidence under the rules: Text, cases, and problems* (3rd ed., pp. 59-114). Boston: Little, Brown.

Olson, E. G. (1997, November 24). Nations struggle with how to control hate on the Web. *New York Times.* Retrieved March 25, 1999, from http://www.nytimes.com/library/cyber/week/112497racism.html.

Patrizio, A. (1999, February 16). Pentium III chips could hit 1 GHz this year. *New York Times.* Retrieved February 17, 1999, from http://www. nytimes. com/techweb/TW_Pentium_III_Chips_Could_Hit_1_GHz_This_Year. html

Perritt, Henry H., Jr. (1995, September 11). Villanova Center for Information Law and Policy: What is the Internet? Retrieved February 2, 1999, from http://www.law.vill.edu/vcilp/technotes/whatis5.htm

Post, David G. (1998, Fall). *Law of Cyberspace Seminar syllabus.* Philadelphia: Temple University Law School.

Pregerson, Dean D. (1997, November 17). EPLR: *Lockheed Martin Corp. v. Network Solutions Inc.* Retrieved September 18, 1999, from http://zeus. bna.com/e-law/cases/locknsi.htm

Raney, R. F. (1998, October 1). More trouble for man in hate mail case. *New York Times.* Retrieved March 25, 1999, from http://www.nytimes. com/library/tech/98/10/cyber/articles/01email.html

Reuters. (1999, September 28). Analysts fear heavy Microsoft regulation most. *New York Times.* Retrieved September 28, 1999, from http://www. nytimes.com/reuters/technology/tech-microsoft-remedi.htm

Rosenbaum, D. E. (1999, June 30). Vexing party, Clinton backs Year 2000 law. *New York Times.* Retrieved June 30, 1999, from http://www.nytimes. com/library/tech/99/06/biztech/articles/30year.html

Supreme Court—State of New York. *Stratton Oakmont, Inc. and Daniel Porush vs. Prodigy Services Company*. (1999). Retrieved April 5, 1999, from http://www.epic.org/free_speech/stratton_v_prodigy_1995.txt

Tech Law Journal. (1998, April 7). Brinkema Opinion: *Mainstream Loudoun v. Loudoun County Libraries*. Retrieved February 19, 1999, from http://www.techlawjournal.com/courts/loudon/80407mem.htm

Text of the latest CDA (21/21/95). (1999). Retrieved February 2, 1999, from http://www.cdt.org/policy/freespeech/12_21.cda.html

Tysver, Daniel A. (1999). BitLaw Source Cases: *Cubby, Inc. v. Compuserve, Inc.* BitLaw. Retrieved April 5, 1999, from http://www.bitlaw.com/source/cases/copyright/cubby.html

United States Court of Appeals for the Fourth Circuit. *Zeran v. America Online, Inc.* (1999). Retrieved April 5, 1999, from http://www.law.emory.edu/4circuit/nov97/971523.p.html

Wallace, D. J. (1999, March 11). Internet crimes attracting attention of states. *New York Times*. Retrieved March 11, 1999, from http://www.nytimes.com/library/tech/99/03/cyber/articles/11crime.html

Weinstein, M. M. (1998, June 9). Intel case gives antitrust law a new twist. *New York Times*. Retrieved June 8, 1998, from http://www.nytimes.com/library/tech/98/06/biztech/articles/09intel-analysis.html

Weinstein, M. M. (1998, October 19). Previous antitrust cases leave room for both sides to cite them now. *New York Times*. Retrieved October 19, 1998, from http://www.nytimes.com/library/tech/98/10/biztech/articles/19case.html

Zimmerman, C. (1999, May 4). Judge puts lock on look-alike Web names. *New York Times*. Retrieved May 5, 1999, from http://www.nytimes.com/techweb/TW_Judge_Puts_Lock_On_Look_Alike_Web_Names.html

■ DISTANCE EDUCATION/DISTANCE LEARNING

The Annenberg/CPB Project; The PBS Adult Learning Service. (1994). *Going the distance: A handbook for developing distance degree programs using television courses and telecommunications technologies*. Bethesda, MD: Toby Levine Communications.

Arenson, K. W. (1998, November 2). More colleges plunging into uncharted waters of online courses. *New York Times*. Retrieved November 2, 1998, from http://www.nytimes.com/library/tech/98/11/biztech/articles/02online-education.html

Banks, Ingrid. (1998, October 16). Reliance on technology threatens the essence of teaching. *Chronicle of Higher Education*, pp. B5-B6.

Biemiller, Lawrence. (1998, October 9). U. of Utah president issues a pointed warning about virtual universities. *Chronicle of Higher Education*, p. A32.

Bronner, E. (1998, December 1). Textbooks shifting from printed page to screen. *New York Times*. Retrieved December 1, 1998, from http://www.nytimes.com/library/tech/98/12/biztech/articles/01school-etex.html

David, J. (1994). Realizing the promise of technology: A policy perspective. In B. Means (Ed.), *Technology and education reform* (pp. 169-190). San Francisco: Jossey-Bass.

Ehrmann, S. C. (1995, July). *Moving beyond campus-bound education*. Retrieved from http://www.learner.org/edtech/distlearn/chronicle.html

Goldin, N. (1999, October 13). Online presentations boom as colleges compete for the brightest students. *New York Times*. Retrieved October 13, 1999, from http://www.nytimes.com/library/national/101399 web-tours-edu.htm

Guernsey, Lisa. (1998, March 27). Distance education for the not-so-distant. *Chronicle of Higher Education*, pp. A29-A30.

Guernsey, Lisa. (1998, October 9). Some colleges try attracting students with their own on-line innovations. *Chronicle of Higher Education*, pp. A31-A32.

Honan, W. H. (1999, January 25). College freshmen's Internet use a way of life, but disparities emerge. *New York Times*. Retrieved January 25, 1999, from http://www.nytimes.com/library/tech/99/01/biztech/articles/25frosh.html

Honan, W. H. (1999, January 27). High tech comes to the classroom: Machines that grade essays. *New York Times*. Retrieved January 27, 1999, from http://www.nytimes.com/library/tech/99/01/biztech/articles/27grade.html

Labriola, Don. (1997, October 7). Desktop video-conferencing. *PC Magazine*, pp. 219-231.

Macavinta, C. (1999, September 27). Teachers see major obstacles to wiring schools. *New York Times*. Retrieved September 27, 1999, from http://www.nytimes.com/cnet/CNET_0_4_201238_00.htm

McCain, Thomas A. (1994). *A perspective on communication technology policy for higher education instruction in the state of Ohio*. Columbus, OH: Center for the Advanced Study in Telecommunications (CAST).

McGrath, B. (1998, April). Partners in learning: Twelve ways technology changes the teacher-student relationship. *T.H.E. Journal*, *25*(9), 58-61. Retrieved from bmgrath@stevens-tech.edu

Means, B., & Olson, K. (1994). Tomorrow's schools: Technology and reform in partnership. In B. Means (Ed.), *Technology and education reform* (pp. 191-222). San Francisco: Jossey-Bass.

Mendels, P. (1998, November 18). Lawsuit challenges Internet subsidy for parochial schools. *New York Times*. Retrieved November 18, 1998, from http://www.nytimes.com/library/tech/98/11/cyber/education/18education.html

Mendels, P. (1998, November 25). School laptop program raises concerns about equal access. *New York Times*. Retrieved November 25, 1998, from http://www.nytimes.com/library/tech/98/11/cyber/education/25education.html

Mendels, P. (1998, October 14). Schools get Internet access, but how do teachers use it? *New York TimesOnline*. Retrieved October 15, 1998, from http://www.nytimes.com/library/tech/98/10/cyber/education/14education.html

Mendels, P. (1998, November 4). Survey shows a sharp rise in Net-savvy academics. *New York TimesOnline*. Retrieved November 4, 1998, from http://www.nytimes.com/library/tech/98/11/cyber/education/04education.html

Mendels, P. (1998, September 23). Test preparation company offers virtual law degree. *New York TimesOnline*. Retrieved September 23, 1998, from http://www.nytimes.com/library/tech/98/09/cyber/education/23education.html

Mendels, P. (1999, July 14). Focus shifts to effectiveness of education technology. *New York TimesOnline*. Retrieved July 14, 1999, from http://www.nytimes.com/library/tech/99/07/cyber/education/14education.htm

Mendels, P. (1999, October 13). Kentucky reaches for high school students with Internet courses. *New York Times*. Retrieved October 13, 1999, from http://www.nytimes.com/library/tech/99/10/cyber/education/13education.htm

Mendels, P. (1999, February 24). Report calls for teacher training in technology. *New York TimesOnline*. Retrieved February 24, 1999, from http://www.nytimes.com/library/tech/99/02/cyber/education/24education.html

Mendels, P. (1999, September 22). Study finds problems with Web class. *New York Times*. Retrieved September 22, 1999, from http://www.nytimes. com/libra . . . ch/99/09/cyber/education/22education.htm

Mendels, P. (1999, March 31). Universities grapple with computer use policies. *New York Times*. Retrieved March 31, 1999, from http://www.nytimes.com/library/tech/99/03/cyber/education/03education.html

Mendels, P. (1999, October 20). University with long history in correspondence ventures onto Net. *New York Times*. Retrieved October 20, 1999, from http://www.nytimes.com/library/tech/99/10/cyber/education/20education.htm

Mendels, P. (1999, February 17). Virginia law could hamper educators at state schools. *New York TimesOnline*. Retrieved February 17, 1999, from http://www.nytimes.com/library/tech/99/02/cyber/education/17education.html

National Education Commission on Time and Learning. (1994). *Prisoners of time*. Washington, DC: Government Printing Office. (ERIC Document Reproduction Service No. ED366115)

Negroponte, N. (1995). *Being digital*. New York: Knopf.

Stuart, Anne. (1998, September 1). Beyond the campus. *CIO WebBusiness Magazine, 11*(22), 30-40.

Watkins, Beverly T. (1991, September 4). The electronic classroom: Vanderbilt courses mix film, video, graphics, sound, and text; use of the facility spreads. *Chronicle of Higher Education*, pp. A26-A30.

Young, Jeffrey R., Guernsey, Lisa, Kiernan, Vincent, & Blumenstyk, Goldie. (1998, April 24). Microsoft's reach in higher education. *Chronicle of Higher Education*, pp. A25-A34.

■ E-COMMERCE

Associated Press. (1998, June 24). AT&T agrees to buy TCI in $48 billion deal. *New York Times*. Retrieved June 23, 1998, from http://www.nytimes.com/yr/mo/day/late/#business

Associated Press. (1999, December 28). Web shoppers report satisfaction. *New York Times*. Retrieved December 28, 1999, from http://www.nytimes.com/library/tech/99/12/biztech/articles/28web-shopping.htm

Barboza, D. (1999, February 8). Cisco and Motorola to develop wireless Internet system. *New York Times*. Retrieved February 8, 1999, from http://www.nytimes.com/library/tech/99/02/biztech/articles/08wire.html

Bloomberg News. (2000, January 5). Chip sales climb 25%. *New York Times*. Retrieved January 5, 2000, from http://www.nytimes.com/library/tech/00/01/biztech/articles/05chip.htm

Branscum, D., & Napoli, L. (1999, February 8). Taking a Web meeting. *New York Times*. Retrieved February 8, 1999, from http://www.nytimes.com/library/tech/99/02/biztech/articles/08data.html

Brinkley, J. (1998, November 18). Microsoft hampered OS/2, IBM official tells court. *New York Times*. Retrieved November 18, 1998, from http://www.nytimes.com/library/tech/98/11/biztech/articles/18soft.html

Caruso, D. (1999, July 19). A new model for the Internet: Fees for services. *New York Times*. Retrieved July 19, 1999, from http://www.nytimes.com/library/tech/99/07/biztech/articles/19digi.htm

Chartrand, S. (1998, October 5). Patents: Software that tracks Web usage. *New York Times*. Retrieved October 5, 1998, from http://www.nytimes.com/library/tech/98/10/biztech/articles/05patents.html

Clausing, J. (1998, November 30). White House unveils e-commerce plans. *New York Times*. Retrieved December 1, 1998, from http://www.nytimes.com/library/tech/98/12/cyber/articles/01magaziner.html

Clausing, J. (1999, June 8). FTC holds meeting on international e-commerce. *New York Times*. Retrieved June 8, 1999, from http://www.nytimes.com/library/tech/99/06/cyber/capital/08capital.html

Clausing, J. (2000, February 15). Government fights spread of online auction fraud. *New York Times*. Retrieved February 15, 2000, from http://www.nytimes.com/library/tech/00/02/cyber/capital/15capital.htm

Cohen, N. S. (1999, August 23). Corporations try to bar use of e-mail by unions. *New York Times*. Retrieved August 23, 1999, from http://www.nytimes.com/library/tech/99/08/biztech/articles/23unio.htm

Dobrzynski, J. H. (2000, June 2). In online auctions, rings of bidders. *New York Times*. Retrieved June 2, 2000, from http://www.nytimes.com/library/tech/00/06/biztech/articles/02ebay.html

Elliott, S. (2000, February 1). Shocking defeats and other Super Bowl XXXIV marketing memories. *New York Times*. Retrieved February 1, 2000, from http://www.nytimes.com/libr . . . ancial/columns/020100super bowl-adcol.htm

Freierman, S. (1998, December 2). Microsoft bets on barter advertising network. *New York Times*. Retrieved December 2, 1998, from http://www.nytimes.com/library/tech/98/12/biztech/articles/02microsoft-link.html

Hansell, S. (1998, November 17). Amazon stretching beyond its roots in books. *New York Times*. Retrieved November 17, 1998, from http://www.nytimes.com/library/tech/98/12/biztech/articles/02microsoft-link.html

Hansell, S. (1998, November 25). America Online sets its sights on e-commerce. *New York Times*. Retrieved November 25, 1998, from http://www.nytimes.com/library/tech/98/11/biztech/articles/25commerce.html

Hansell, S. (1998, August 24). Marketers ponder how to sell soap without the operas. *New York Times.* Retrieved August 24, 1998, from http://www.nytimes.com/library/tech/98/08/biztech/articles/24advertising.html

Harmon, A. (1998, November 11). E-mail takes the stand and companies take a stand on e-mail. *New York Times.* Retrieved November 11, 1998, from http://www.nytimes.com/library/tech/98/11/biztech/articles/11email.html

Harmon, A. (1998, December 14). Witness in Microsoft case keeps the list of all lists. *New York Times.* Retrieved December 14, 1998, from http://www.nytimes.com/library/tech/98/12/biztech/articles/14farb.html

Johnston, D. (2000, February 17). U.S. officials lay out plan to fight computer attacks. *New York Times.* Retrieved February 17, 2000, from http://www.nytimes.com/library/tech/yr/mo/biztech/articles/17net.htm

Karpinski, R. (1998, October 20). New spec breaks the e-commerce ICE. *New York Times.* Retrieved October 20, 1998, from http://www.nytimes.com/techweb/TW_New_Spec_Breaks_The_E_Commerce_ICE.html

Krochmal, M. (1998, November 24). Nader's group to contest AOL-Netscape merger. *New York Times.* Retrieved November 25, 1998, from http://www.nytimes.com/techweb/TW_Nader_s_Group_to_Contest_AOL_Netscape_Merger.html

Labaton, S. (1998, December 15). Three proposed telecommunications mergers draw challenges at an F.C.C. hearing. *New York Times.* Retrieved December 15, 1998, from http://www.nytimes.com/library/tech/98/12/biztech/articles/15bell.html

Levy, Steven, & Stone, Brad. (2000, February 21). Hunting the hackers. *Newsweek*, pp. 38-44.

Lohr, S. (1998, October 1). White House to increase efforts to help fight software piracy. *New York Times.* Retrieved October 1, 1998, from http://www.nytimes.com/library/tech/98/10/biztech/articles/01software-piracy.html

Lohr, S. (2000, January 11). A mass medium for Main Street. *New York Times.* Retrieved January 11, 2000, from http://www.nytimes.com/library/financial/011100time-online.htm

Lohr, S. (2000, January 12). Merger may produce rival Microsoft has dreaded. *New York Times.* Retrieved January 12, 2000, from http://www.nytimes.com/library/financial/011200time-soft.htm

Lohr, S. (2000, April 25). U.S. hoping 2 Microsoft monopolies are gentler than one. *New York Times.* Retrieved April 25, 2000, from http://www.nytimes.co . . . 00/04/biztech/articles/25split.html

Markoff, J. (1998, July 1). In AT&T-TCI deal, cost and logistical problems. *New York Times.* Retrieved July 2, 1998, from http://www.nytimes.com/library/tech/98/07/biztech/articles/02phone. html

Markoff, J. (1998, October 12). Microsoft memo offers a glimpse of Gates 2.0. *New York Times.* Retrieved October 12, 1998, from http://www.nytimes.com/library/tech/98/10/biztech/articles/12microsoft-gates.html

Markoff, J., & Robinson, S. (2000, February 15). Chat systems yield clues in Web attacks by hackers. *New York Times.* Retrieved February 15, 2000, from http://www.nytimes.com/library/tech/00/02/biztech/articles/15net.htm

Marriott, M. (1998, December 17). Luck, be a microchip tonight. *New York Times.* Retrieved December 17, 1998, from http://www.nytimes.com/library/tech/98/12/circuits/articles/17gamb.html

Mendels, P. (1999, December 8). Major players going online with SAT prep courses. *New York Times*. Retrieved December 8, 1999, from http://www.nytimes.com/library/tech/99/12/cyber/education/08education.htm

Napoli, L. (1998, August 26). You say "page view," I say "visit": How to count Web traffic. *New York Times*. Retrieved August 27, 1998, from http://www.nytimes.com/library/tech/98/08/cyber/articles/26traffic.html

Napoli, L. (1999, March 2). EBay says it is under investigation by U.S. *New York Times*. Retrieved March 2, 1999, from http://www.nytimes.com/library/tech/99/03/cyber/articles/02ebay.html

Napoli, L., & Schiesel, S. (1998, December 7). "Literate smut" site tries electronic commerce. *New York Times*. Retrieved December 7, 1998, from http://www.nytimes.com/library/tech/98/12/biztech/articles/07comp.html

Non, S. G. (1998, November 18). Microsoft will dump RealNetworks. *New York Times*. Retrieved November 19, 1998, from http://www.nytimes.com/techweb/TW_Microsoft_Will_Dump_RealNetworks.html

Pareles, J. (1999, February 9). Leading recording companies to test online digital sales. *New York Times*. Retrieved February 9, 1999, from http://www.nytimes.com/library/tech/99/02/biztech/articles/09blue.html

Richtel, M. (1998, November 4). In search of a free ISP. *New York Times*. Retrieved November 4, 1998, from http://www.nytimes.com/library/tech/98/11/cyber/articles/04isp.html

Richtel, M. (1999, June 21). As e-commerce surges, so do technical problems. *New York Times*. Retrieved June 21, 1999, from http://www.nytimes.com/library/tech/yr/mo/biztech/articles/21tuff.html

Richtel, M. (1999, December 19). The next waves of electronic commerce. *New York Times*. Retrieved December 20, 1999, from http://www.nytimes.com/librar . . . /biztech/articles/122099outlook-nett.htm

Richtel, M. (1999, February 8). Plan for free PCs has a few attachments. *New York Times*. Retrieved February 8, 1999, from http://www.nytimes.com/library/tech/99/02/biztech/articles/08free.html

Richtel, M. (2000, February 8). Yahoo attributes a lengthy service failure to an attack. *New York Times*. Retrieved February 8, 2000, from http://www.nytimes.com/library/tech/00/02/biztech/articles/08yahoo.htm

Rosenthal, E. (2000, January 27). China issues rules to limit e-mail and Web content. *New York Times*. Retrieved January 27, 2000, from http://www.nytimes.com/library/tech/00/01/biztech/articles/27china.htm

Tedeschi, B. (1998, November 24). Holiday shopping season puts e-commerce to the test. *New York Times*. Retrieved November 24, 1998, from http://www.nytimes.com/library/tech/98/11/cyber/commerce/24commerce.html

Tedeschi, B. (1999, August 23). Online sales can be messy, especially those pesky returns. *New York Times*. Retrieved August 23, 1999, from http://www.nytimes.com/library/tech/99/08/cyber/commerce/23commerce.htm

Thompson, C. (1998, December 1). Catalogue companies slow to set up shop online. *New York Times*. Retrieved December 1, 1998, from http://www.nytimes.com/library/tech/98/12/cyber/commerce/01commerce.html

Wald, M. L. (1998, October 9). Senate spares Internet from taxes. *New York Times*. Retrieved October 9, 1998, from http://www.nytimes.com/library/tech/98/10/biztech/articles/09net.html

■ ENCRYPTION/SECURITY

Associated Press. (2000, February 3). Experts warn of Web surfing risk. *New York Times*. Retrieved February 3, 2000, from http://www.nytimes.com/library/tech/00/02/biztech/articles/03internet-warning.htm

Bloomberg News. (1998, October 13). Congress passes anti-piracy bill. *New York Times*. Retrieved October 13, 1998, from http://www.nytimes.com/library/tech/98/10/biztech/articles/13software-piracy.html

Bloomberg News. (2000, May 1). Polaroid fingerprint reader for computer security gains use. *New York Times*. Retrieved May 2, 2000, from wysiwyg://69/http://www.nytimes.com/library/tech/articles/02polaroid-prints.html

Clausing, J. (1998, July 7). Administration to allow limited data-scrambling exports. *New York Times*. Retrieved July 8, 1998, from http://www.nytimes.com/library/tech/98/07/biztech/articles/08encrypt.html

Clausing, J. (1998, March 4). Gore letter seems to soften stance on encryption. *New York Times*. Retrieved March 5, 1998, from http://www.nytimes.com/library/tech/yr/mo/cyber/articles/05encrypt.html#1

Clausing, J. (1998, June 9). U.S. and industry discuss data encryption. *New York Times*. Retrieved June 10, 1998, from http://www.nytimes.com/library/tech/98/06/biztech/articles/10encrypt.html

Clausing, J. (1999, March 12). Panel passes bill to halt limits on encryption. *New York Times*. Retrieved March 12, 1999, from http://www.nytimes.com/library/tech/99/03/cyber/articles/12encrypt.html

Clausing, J. (2000, January 18). New encryption rules leave civil libertarians unhappy. *New York Times*. Retrieved January 18, 2000, from wysiwyg://5/http://www.nytimes.com/library/tech/00/01/cyber/capital/18capital.htm

Common questions about encryption and computer privacy. (1998). Americans for Computer Privacy (ACP). Retrieved March 4, 1998, from http://www.computerprivacy.org/questions/

Dalton, Gregory. (1998, August 31). Acceptable risks. *Information Week*, pp. 36-48.

Encryption glossary. (1998). Americans for Computer Privacy (ACP). Retrieved March 4, 1998, from http://www.computerprivacy.org/glossary/

Hafner, K. (2000, February 4). PC's vulnerable to security breaches, experts say. *New York Times*. Retrieved February 4, 2000, from http://www.nytimes.com/library/tech/00/02/biztech/articles/04compute.htm

Kimber, L. (1999, February 24). How Nokia guards against crackers. *New York Times*. Retrieved February 24, 1999, from http://www.nytimes.com/techweb/TW_How_Nokia_Guards_Against_Crackers.html

Markoff, J. (1998, February 27). Encryption issue threatens Silicon Valley rapport with Clinton. *New York Times*. Retrieved February 27, 1998, from http://www.nytimes.com/library/tech/yr/mo/biztech/articles/27industry.html

Markoff, J. (1998, December 4). International group reaches agreement on data-scrambling software. *New York Times*. Retrieved December 4, 1998, from http://www.nytimes.com/library/tech/98/12/biztech/articles/04 encrypt.html

Markoff, J. (1998, September 28). Potentially big security flaw found in Netscape software. *New York Times*. Retrieved September 28, 1998, from http://www.nytimes.com/library/tech/98/09/biztech/articles/28java.html

Markoff, J. (2000, January 11). Internet extortionist and thief challenges computer experts. *New York Times*. Retrieved January 11, 2000, from http://www.nytimes.com/library/tech/00/01/biztech/articles/11cyber.htm

Mosquera, M. (1999, January 22). Clinton seeks more funds for cyberterrorism. *New York Times*. Retrieved January 25, 1999, http://www.nytimes.com/techweb/TW_Clinton_Seeks_More_Funds_For_Cyberterrorism.html

Mosquera, M. (1999, July 13). Encryption bill gaining momentum in House. *New York Times*. Retrieved July 14, 1999, from http://www.nytimes.com/techweb/TW_Encryption_Bill_Gaining_Momentum_In_House.htm

Mondex Security Strategy. (1998). Mondex International. Retrieved June 14, 1998, from http://www.mondex.com/mxi/cgibin/printpa . . . l?english+global&technology_security.html

Rosen, James. (2000, June 25). Reno: Government alone can't stop online crimes. *Panorama Daily Local News*.

Solomon, D., & Johnson, K. (2000, February 10). FBI launches cyberhunt. *USA Today*, *18*(105).

Varian, H. R. (2000, June 1). Managing online security risks. *New York Times*. Retrieved June 1, 2000, from http://www.nytimes.com/library/financial/columns/060100econ-scene.html

Wayner, P. (1998, June 10). Cryptographers discuss finding of security flaw in "smart cards." *New York Times*. Retrieved June 14, 1998, from http://www.nytimes.com/library/tech/98/06/cyber/articles/10smartcard.html

Wayner, P. (1998, August 25). IBM says encryption system prevents hacker attack. *New York Times*. Retrieved August 25, 1998, from http://www.nytimes.com/library/tech/98/08/cyber/articles/25encrypt.html

Wayner, P. (2000, January 5). Attacks on encryption code raise questions about computer vulnerability. *New York Times*. Retrieved January 5, 2000, from http://www.nytimes.com/library/tech/00/01/biztech/articles/05 secu.htm

FILTERING TECHNOLOGY ■

Clausing, J. (1999, January 27). Filtering bill comes to life again in Senate. *New York Times*. Retrieved January 27, 1999, from http://www.nytimes.com/library/tech/99/01/cyber/education/27education.html

Mendels, P. (1998, November 23). Judge rules against filters at library. *New York Times*. Retrieved November 24, 1998, from http://www.nytimes.com/library/tech/98/11/cyber/articles/24library.html

Mendels, P. (1999, March 10). Schools split on using Internet filters. *New York Times*. Retrieved March 10, 1999, from http://www.nytimes.com/library/tech/99/03/cyber/education/10education.html

LONGEVITY OF DIGITAL INFORMATION ■

Gajilan, Arlyn Tobias. (1999, July 12). History: We're losing it. *Newsweek*.

Hafner, K. (1999, April 8). Books to bytes: the electronic archive. *New York Times*. Retrieved April 8, 1999, from http://www.nytimes.com/library/tech/99/04/circuits/articles/08arch.html

Nicholson, Leslie J. (1999, September 30). The post-Y2K bug: Technical obsolescence. *Philadelphia Inquirer.*

Pollack, A. (1998, March 16). Digital film restoration raises questions. *New York Times.* Retrieved March 15, 1998, from http://www.nytimes.com/library/tech/98/03/biztech/articles/16restore.html

Rothenberg, Jeff. (1995, January). Ensuring the longevity of digital documents. *Scientific American*, pp. 42-47.

■ NEW FRONTIERS OF TECHNOLOGY

Associated Press. (1998, October 22). Implant transmits brain signals directly to computer. *New York Times.* Retrieved October 22, 1998, from http://www.nytimes.com/library/tech/98/10/circuits/articles/22brai.html

Associated Press. (1999, September 1). Intel introduces new Internet chip. *New York Times.* Retrieved September 1, 1999, from http://www.nytimes.com/aponline/f/AP-Intel-Internet-Chip.htm

Brain, Marshall. (2000). How a cell phone works (How Stuff Works). Retrieved January 24, 2000, from http://www.howstuffworks.com/cell-phone.htm

Calem, Robert E. (1992, December 6). The network of all networks. *New York Times.*

Communications, computers, and networks. (1991, September). *Scientific American* [Special issue].

How a Web page works (How Stuff Works). (2000). Retrieved January 25, 2000, from http://www.howstuffworks.com/web-page.htm

How Web servers and the Internet work (How Stuff Works). (2000). Retrieved January 25, 2000, from http://www.howstuffworks.com/web-server1.htm

Felton, Carole. (2000, January 25). Why is everyone jumping on the bandwidth? *Jewish Exponent.*

Fischer, Claude. (1992). Technology and modern life. In *America calling* (pp. 1-32). Berkeley: University of California Press.

Fowler, John Henry. (2000, May). Music software on the PC. *Blueprints* [Villanova University publication].

Hertzberg, Robert. (1931). Is television coming around that corner at last? *Radio Design, 4*(1), 28-34.

Coming to your desktop: The digital darkroom. (1998, June 10). *New York Times.* Retrieved June 11, 1998, from http://www.nytimes.com/library/tech/98/06/circuits/articles/11foto-side.html

On this day (1915): Phone to Pacific from the Atlantic. (1999, January 25). *New York Times.* Retrieved January 25, 1999, from http://www.nytimes.com/learning/general/onthisday/990125onthisday_big.html

Alexander, H. (1998, October 1). Behind the lowly mouse: Clever technology close at hand. *New York Times.* Retrieved October 1, 1998, from http://www.nytimes.com/library/tech/98/10/circuits/howitworks/01how.html

Austen, I. (2000, February 3). The case of the flickering pixels. *New York Times.* Retrieved February 3, 2000, from http://www.nytimes.com/library/tech/00/02/circuits/articles/03read.htm

Barringer, F. (2000, May 15). Newspapers bring threat of Web into perspective. *New York Times*. Retrieved May 15, 2000, from http://www.nytimes. com/library/tech/00/05/biztech/articles/15medi.html

Biersdorfer, J. D. (1999, October 7). Trapped in the Web without an exit. *New York Times*. Retrieved October 7, 1999, from http://www.nytimes. com/library/tech/99/10/circuits/articles/07tric.htm

Bloomberg News. (1998, November 17). Cable and wireless to build new network. *New York Times*. Retrieved November 17, 1998, from http://www.nytimes.com/library/tech/98/11/biztech/articles/17cable.html

Brinkley, J. (1999, July 12). Broadcaster seeks change in digital TV format. *New York Times*. Retrieved July 12, 1999, from http://www.nytimes. com/library/tech/99/07/biztech/articles/12hdtv.htm .

Carrier, J. (1998, September 28). Satellites guiding industries on the move. *New York Times*. Retrieved September 28, 1998, from http://www. nytimes.com/library/tech/98/09/biztech/articles/28find.html

Editorial. (1998, March 4). Mr. Gates takes the stand. *New York Times*. Retrieved March 3, 1998, from http://www.nytimes.com/yr/mo/day/ editorial/04wed1.html

Fisher, L. M. (1999, December 19). Software evolving into a service rented off the Net. *New York Times*. Retrieved December 20, 1999, from wysiwyg://11/http://www.nytimes.com/libra . . . /biztech/articles/122099 outlook-soft.htm.

Fisher, L. M. (2000, February 7). New era approaches: Gigahertz chips. *New York Times*. Retrieved February 7, 2000, from http://www.nytimes. com/library/tch/00/02/biztech/articles/07chip.htm

Friedlin, J. (2000, February 28). AOL, Microsoft, BellSouth announce wireless deals. *New York Times*. Retrieved February 29, 2000, from wysiwyg:// 70/http://www.nytimes.com/libra . . . 0/02/biztech/articles/ 29tsc-wireless.htm

Goldberg, C. (1998, March 11). Where do computers go when they die? *New York Times*. Retrieved March 12, 1998, from http://www.nytimes. com/library/tech/yr/mo/circuits/articles/12die.html

Greenman, C. (1998, August 20). There's more than one way to scan a bar code. *New York Times*. Retrieved August 20, 1998, from http://www. nytimes.com/library/tech/98/08/circuits/howitworks/20how.html

Guernsey, L. (2000, April 13). A chip in every pot. *New York Times*. Retrieved April 13, 2000, from wysiwyg://121/http://www.nytimes.co . . . 00/04/ circuits/articles/13need.html

Hafner, K. (1999, February 4). Talk is cheap, if you're careful. *New York Times*. Retrieved February 4, 1999, from http://www.nytimes.com/library/ tech/99/02/circuits/articles/04cell.html

Hafner, K. (1999, April 15). Web phones: the next big thing? *New York Times*. Retrieved April 15, 1999, from http://www.nytimes.com/library/ tech/99/04/circuits/articles/15mobi.html

Hansell, S. (1998, November 4). Got a dime? Citibank and Chase end test of electronic cash. *New York Times*. Retrieved November 4, 1998, from http://www.nytimes.com/library/tech/98/11/biztech/articles/04card.html

Hara, Y. (1998, November 16). U.S., Japan to set common digital interface. *New York Times*. Retrieved November 17, 1998, from http://www.nytimes. com/techweb/TW_U_S_Japan_To_Set_Common_Digital_Interface.html

Hewlett Packard Labs. (1999, July 15). *HP labs scientists are building computer chips in a whole new way*. Hewlett Packard. Retrieved July 19, 1999, from http://www.hpl.hp.com/news/molecules_that_compute.htm

Johnson, G. (1999, March 23). Mindless creatures acting "mindfully." *New York Times*. Retrieved March 23, 1999, from http://www.nytimes.com/library/national/science/032399sci-cellular-automata.html

Johnson, R. C. (1998, December 2). Themescape creates information map. *New York Times*. Retrieved December 2, 1998, from http://www.nytimes.com/techweb/TW_Themescape_Creates_Information_Map.html

Johnson, R. C. (1999, February 24). Nuance expands speech-recognition technology. *New York Times*. Retrieved February 25, 1999, from http://www.nytimes.com/techweb/TW_Nuance_Expands_Speech_Recognition_Tecnology.html

Kaplan, C. S. (2000, May 5). Governments learn how to censor the Internet, report says. *New York Times*. Retrieved May 5, 2000, from wysiwyg://87/http://www.nytimes.com . . . ech/00/05/cyber/cyberlaw/05law.html

Katz, M. (1998, November 16). Wireless portable e-mail devices grow up. *New York Times*. Retrieved November 16, 1998, from http://www.nytimes.com/library/tech/98/11/cyber/articles/16portable.html

Kennedy, R. (2000, January 24). Subways trade No. 2 pencils for 21st-century technology. *New York Times*. Retrieved January 24, 2000, from http://www.nytimes.com/yr/mo/day/news/national/regional/ny-subway-trains.htm

Krochmal, M. (1999, January 25). High definition comes into focus. *New York Times*. Retrieved January 25, 1999, from http://www.nytimes.com/techweb/TW_High_Definition_Comes_Into_Focus.html

LaPedus, M. (1999, April 14). Samsung to develop line of wireless chips. *New York Times*. Retrieved April 14, 1999, from http://www.nytimes.com/techweb/TW_Samsung_To_Develop_Line_Of_Wireless_Chips_.html

Larsen, Judith K. (1990). Silicon Valley: A scenario for the information society of tomorrow. In *Mediation, information, and communication* (Vol. 3, pp. 193-200). New Brunswick, NJ: Transaction.

Lewis, P. H. (1998, June 17). Bigger, faster, more 3-D: The anatomy of the coming PC's. *New York Times*. Retrieved June 18, 1998, from http://www.nytimes.com/library/tech/yr/mo/circuits/articles/18anat.html

Lewis, P. H. (1998, September 10). How fast is your system? Whose test are you using? *New York Times*. Retrieved September 10, 1998, from http://www.nytimes.com/library/tech/98/09/circuits/articles/10benc.html

Lewis, P. H. (1998, December 3). How to kick the tires when buying a computer. *New York Times*. Retrieved December 3, 1998, from http://www.nytimes.com/library/tech/98/12/circuits/articles/03pete.html

Lewis, P. H. (1998, June 10). Shoot first, e-mail photos to Grandma later. *New York Times*. Retrieved June 11, 1998, from http://www.nytimes.com/library/tech/yr/mo/circuits/articles/11foto.html

Licalzi O'Connell, P. (1999, September 30). Beyond geography: Mapping unknowns of cyberspace. *New York Times*.

Lievrouw, Leah A. (2000, January). Nonobvious things about new media: "Dead media" and the loss of electronic cultural heritage. *International Communication Association Newsletter, 28*(1).

Lievrouw, Leah A. (2000, March). Nonobvious things about new media: How fast is fast? *International Communication Association Newsletter*.

Lohr, S. (2000, April 18). Microsoft will challenge Palm's hand-held computer dominance. *New York Times*. Retrieved April 18, 2000, from wysiwyg://36/http://www.nytimes.com . . . /00/04/biztech/articles/18soft.html

Markoff, J. (1998, November 17). Microsoft develops software to improve appearance of screen text. *New York Times*. Retrieved November 17, 1998, from http://www.nytimes.com/library/tech/98/11/biztech/articles/17font.html

Markoff, J. (1998, September 23). New venture to map Internet 3D. *New York Times*. Retrieved September 23, 1998, from http://www.nytimes.com/library/tech/98/09/biztech/articles/23internet-map.html

Markoff, J. (1998, April 13). Researchers crack code in cell phones. *New York Times*. Retrieved April 14, 1998, from http://www.nytimes.com/library/tech/yr/mo/biztech/articles/14phone.html

Markoff, J. (1999, July 19). Chip designers search for life after Silicon. *New York Times*. Retrieved July 19, 1999, from http://www.nytimes.com/library/tech/99/07/biztech/articles/19chip.htm

Markoff, J. (1999, February 8). One man's dream to spin a faster Web. *New York Times*. Retrieved February 8, 1999, from http://www.nytimes.com/library/tech/99/02/biztech/articles/08band.html

Markoff, J. (2000, January 24). Chip innovator bets on brainpower, not battery power. *New York Times*. Retrieved January 24, 2000, from wysiwyg://36/http://www.nytimes.com/library/tech/00/01/biztech/articles/24meta.htm

Markoff, J. (2000, January 3). Internet pioneer to be named top F.C.C. technologist. *New York Times*. Retrieved January 3, 2000, from http://www.nytimes.com/library/tech/00/01/biztech/articles/03farb.htm

Marriott, M. (1998, November 19). As the battery goes, so goes the . . . *New York Times*. Retrieved November 19, 1998, from http://www.nytimes.com/library/tech/98/11/circuits/articles/19batt.html

Marvin, Carolyn. (1988). *When old technologies were new: Thinking electric communication in the late 19th century*. New York: Oxford University Press.

Murphy, J. (1998, July 5). It's not the size that counts, but how you measure it. *New York Times*. Retrieved July 7, 1998, from http://www.nytimes.com/library/tech/98/07/cyber/articles/05big.html

Ozer, Jan. (1997, October 7). The complete video desktop. *PC Magazine*.

Pareles, J., Strauss, N., Ratliff, B., & Powers, A. (2000, January 3). Albums as mileposts in a musical century. *New York Times*. Retrieved January 3, 2000, from http://www.nytimes.com/yr/mo/day/news/arts/albums-century.htm

Parker, Edwin B. (1973). Implications of new information technology. *Public Opinion Quarterly,* pp. 590-600.

Poole, Lon. (1992, October). Your computer revealed: Inside the processor. *Macworld*.

Richtel, M. (1998, October 27). Judge clears way for digital player. *New York Times*. Retrieved October 27, 1998, from http://www.nytimes.com/library/tech/98/10/cyber/articles/27rio.html

Riordan, T. (1999, February 22). Microsoft move sparks controversy over standards. *New York Times*. Retrieved February 22, 1999, from http://www.nytimes.com/library/tech/99/02/biztech/articles/22pate.html

Robinson, S. (1999, August 23). Multimedia transmissions drive Net toward gridlock. *New York Times*. Retrieved August 23, 1999, from http://www.nytimes.com/library/tech/99/08/biztech/articles/23tcp.htm

Rogers, E. M., & Shoemaker, F. (1971). Elements of diffusion: An overview. In *Communication of innovations* (2nd ed., pp. 1-40). New York: Free Press.

Rogers, Everett M. (1990). Introduction: The emergence of information societies. In *Mediation, information, and communication* (Vol. 3, pp. 185-192). New Brunswick, NJ: Transaction.

Salvaggio, Jerry L., & Nelson, Richard A. (1990). Marketplace vs. public utility models for developing telecommunications and information industries. In *Mediation, information, and communication* (Vol. 3, pp. 253-266). New Brunswick, NJ: Transaction.

Sawhney, Harmeet. (1992, September/October). The public telephone network: Stages in infrastructure development. *Telecommunications Policy,* pp. 538-552.

Schement, Jorge Reina, & Stout, Daniel A., Jr. (1990). A time-line of information technology. In *Mediation, information, and communication* (Vol. 3, pp. 395-424). New Brunswick, NJ: Transaction.

Schiesel, S. (1998, November 16). Meteor storm poses threat to satellites. *New York Times.* Retrieved November 16, 1998, from http://www.nytimes.com/library/tech/98/11/biztech/articles/16mete.html

Schiesel, S. (2000, January 17). Broadband Internet: How broadly? How soon? *New York Times.* Retrieved January 17, 2000, from http://www.nytimes.com/library/tech/00/01/biztech/articles/17band.htm

Semiconductor Business News. (1998, November 4). Growth of new wafer technology boosts Ibis. *New York Times.* Retrieved November 5, 1998, from http://www.nytimes.com/techweb/TW_Growth_Of_New_Wafer_Technology_Boosts_Ibis.html

Shields, Peter, & Samarajiva, Rohan. (1993). Competing frameworks for research on information-communication technologies and society: Toward a synthesis. In *Communication yearbook 16* (pp. 349-380). Newbury Park, CA: Sage.

Sterngold, J. (1999, February 22). Coming attractions: Digital projectors could change film industry. *New York Times.* Retrieved February 22, 1999, from wysiwyg://12/http://www.nytimes.com/library/tech/99/02/biztech/articls/22film.html

Stites, J. (1999, February 8). A computer program that thinks like a human (almost). *New York Times.* Retrieved February 8, 1999, from http://www.nytimes.com/library/tech/99/02/biztech/articles/08pros.html

Streeter, Thomas. (1987). The cable fable revisited: Discourse, policy, and the making of cable television. *Critical Studies in Mass Communication, 4,* 174-200.

Taub, E. A. (1998, December 3). Elevator technology: Inspiring many everyday leaps of faith. *New York Times.* Retrieved December 3, 1998, from http://www.nytimes.com/library/tech/98/12/circuits/articles/03howw.html

TechWeb. (1998, November 15). Intel to put big money into research. *New York Times.* Retrieved November 16, 1998, from http://www.nytimes.com/techweb/TW_Intel_To_Put_Big_Money_Into_Research.html

Tedeschi, B. (1999, June 14). Seeking ways to cut the Web-page wait. *New York Times.* Retrieved June 14, 1999, from wysiwyg://20/http://www.nytimes.com/library/tech/99/06/cyber/commerce/14commerce

Totally typed out. (2000, June 5). *Newsweek,* p. 8.

Wade Rose, B. (1998, October 22). Trailing strings of battery packs, a marriage of cyborgs is made. *New York Times.* Retrieved October 22, 1998, from http://www.nytimes.com/library/tech/98/10/circuits/articles/22mann.html

PRIVACY ■

Andrews, E. L. (1998, October 26). European law aims to protect privacy of personal data. *New York Times*. Retrieved October 26, 1998, from http://www.nytimes.com/library/tech/98/10/biztech/articles/26privacy.html

Associated Press. (2000, January 18). Internet privacy safeguards sought. *New York Times*. Retrieved January 18, 2000, from http://www.nytimes.com/library/tech/00/01/biztech/articles/18internet-safeguards.htm

Bannan, K. J. (2000, May 12). Parents remain unclear on online privacy law. *New York Times*. Retrieved May 12, 2000, from http://www.nytimes.com/library/tech/00/05/cyber/articles/12coppa.html

Bernstein, N. (1997, September 15). High-tech sleuths find private facts online. *New York Times*. Retrieved March 18, 1998, from http://www.nytimes.com/library/cyber/week/091597privacy.html

Branscum, Deborah. (1998, April 27). bigbrother@the.office.com. *Newsweek*.

Branscum, Deborah. (2000, June 5). Guarding online privacy. *Newsweek*.

Clausing, J. (1998, June 23). On eve of privacy conference, trade groups jockey for position. *New York Times*. Retrieved June 22, 1998, from http://www/nytimes.com/library/tech/98/06/cyber/articles/23privacy.html

Clausing, J. (1998, August 22). Want more online privacy? Join the crowd. *New York Times*. Retrieved August 24, 1998, from http://www.nytimes.com/library/tech/98/08/cyber/articles/22privacy.html

Clausing, J. (1999, April 8). Lawmaker plans bill to protect consumer privacy online. *New York Times*. Retrieved April 8, 1999, from http://www.nytimes.com/library/tech/99/04/cyber/articles/08privacy.html

Cohen, J. (2000, February 17). Love, honor, cherish. But reveal my password? *New York Times*.

Dyson, Esther. (1998, September). Privacy matters. *Brill's Content*.

Labaton, S. (1999, April 21). U.S. urges new rules to guard privacy of children on Internet. *New York Times*. Retrieved April 21, 1999, from http://www.nytimes.com/library/tech/99/04/biztech/articles/21privacy.html

Lewis, P. H. (1999, April 15). Peekaboo! Anonymity is not always secure. *New York Times*. Retrieved April 15, 1999, from http://www.nytimes.com/library/tech/99/04/circuits/articles/15pete.html

Markoff, J. (1999, March 3). A growing compatibility issue in the digital age: Computers and their users' privacy. *New York Times*. Retrieved March 3, 1999, from http://www.nytimes.com/library/tech/99/03/biztech/articles/03privacy.html

Markoff, J. (1999, April 29). Intel goes to battle as its embedded serial number is unmasked. *New York Times*. Retrieved April 29, 1999, from http://www.nytimes.com/library/tech/99/04/biztech/articles/29chip.html

Marriott, M. (2000, January 27). It's not Big Brother, it's customer service. *New York Times*. Retrieved January 27, 2000, from http://www.nytimes.com/library/tech/00/01/circuits/articles/27serv.htm

Mendels, P. (1999, July 21). The two faces of online anonymity. *New York Times*. Retrieved July 21, 1999, from http://www.nytimes.com/library/tech/99/07/cyber/articles/21anonymity.htm

Napoli, L. (1998, September 29). Judge throws out request to view cookie files. *New York Times*. Retrieved September 29, 1998, from http://www.nytimes.com/library/tech/98/09/cyber/articles/29putnam.html

Privacy online: A report to Congress. (1998). Federal Trade Commission (FTC). Retrieved August 31, 1998, from http://www.ftc.gov/reports/privacy3/toc.htm

Purdy, Jedediah. (2000, June 30-July 2). An intimate invasion. *USA Weekend*.

Quittner, Joshua. (1997, August 25). Invasion of privacy. *Time*.

Richtel, M. (1998, December 14). Crusader thwarts invaders of the e-mailbox. *New York Times*. Retrieved December 14, 1998, from http://www.nytimes.com/library/tech/98/12/biztech/articles/14spam.html

Safire, William. (1999, September 23). Nosy Parker lives. *New York Times*. Retrieved September 23, 1999, from http://www.nytimes. com/library/opinion/safire/092399safi.htm

Sussman, Vic. (1995, January 23). Policing cyberspace. *U.S. News & World Report*.

Tedeschi, B. (2000, February 7). Critics press legal assault on tracking of Web users. *New York Times*. Retrieved February 7, 2000, from http://www.nytimes.com/library/tech/00/02/cyber/commerce/07commerce.htm

Wayner, P. (1998, June 22). Code breaker cracks smart cards' digital safe. *New York Times*. Retrieved June 21, 1998, from http://www.nytimes.com/library/tech/98/06/biztech/articles/22card.html

Whiting, Rick. (2000, March 6). Mind your business. *Informationweek*.

■ SOCIAL IMPACT

Annenberg Public Policy Center of the University of Pennsylvania. (1999, May 4). National survey shows parents deeply fearful about the Internet's influence on their children [Press release]. Washington, DC: Author.

Biernatzki, William E. (1997). Globalization of communication. In *Communication research trends* (Vol. 17). Saint Louis University, Centre for the Study of Communication and Culture.

Bradsher, K. (2000, February 4). Ford offers workers PC's and Internet service for $5 a month. *New York Times*. Retrieved February 4, 2000, from http://www.nytimes.com/library/tech/00/02/biztech/articles/04ford.htm

Brody, J. (2000, May 16). Cybersex gives birth to a psychological disorder. *New York Times*.

Clausing, J. (1998, October 5). Planning the Internet's final privatization. *New York Times*. Retrieved October 5, 1998, from http://www.nytimes.com/library/tech/98/10/biztech/articles/05domain.html

Clausing, J. (1999, September 27). Internet governing body needs limits, consumer advocate says. *New York Times*. Retrieved September 27, 1999, from wysiwyg://124/http://www.nytimes.com/library/tech/99/09/cyber/articles.27icann.htm

Deutsch, C.H. (1999, September 2). The digital brain drain: So many computers, so little interest in hard science. *New York Times*. Retrieved September 2, 1999, from wysiwyg://30/http://www.nytimes.com/library/tech/99/09/biztech/articles/02chem.htm

Egan, J. (2000, December 10). Lonely gay teen seeking same. *New York Times Magazine*.

Eisenstock, Bobbie. (1999, July). *A parent's guide to the TV ratings and V-chip*. Washington, DC: Center for Media Education.

Fairley, R. (2000, May 11). Study finds Internet of social benefit to users. *New York Times*.

Fairley Raney, R. (1999, September 8). Regulators ready to set some rules on Internet campaigning. *New York Times*. Retrieved September 8, 1999, from http://www.nytimes.com/library/tech/99/09/cyber/articles/08campaign.htm

Greenman, Catherine. (1998, November 5). From yakety-yak to clackety-clack: What do teen-agers do online? What do they do everywhere else: Talk, talk, talk. *New York Times*. Retrieved November 5, 1998, from http://www.nytimes.com/library/tech/98/11/circuits.articles/05teen.html

Hafner, K. (1998, December 10). Tracking the evolution of e-mail etiquette. *New York Times*. Retrieved December 10, 1998, from http://www.nytimes.com/library/tech/98/12/circuits/articles/10mail.html

Jehl, D. (1999, March 18). The Internet's "open sesame" is answered warily. *New York Times*. Retrieved March 18, 1999, from http://www.nytimes.com/library/tech/99/03/biztech/articles/18riyadh.html

Kalb, C. (2001, January 22). Seeing a virtual shrink. *Newsweek*.

Kunkel, Dale. (1998, September). Deciphering the new V-chip policy. *International Communication Association Newsletter, 26*(5).

Leyner, M. (2000, September). The doctor is on. *Elle*.

Lievrouw, Leah A. (2000, May). Babel and beyond: Languages on the Internet. *ICA News*.

Lohr, Steve. (2000, January 9). Welcome to the Internet, the first global colony. *New York Times, Week in Review*.

Mendels, P. (1999, May 12). Survey indicates increased use of filters. *New York Times*. Retrieved May 12, 1999, from http://www.nytimes.com/library/tech/99/05/cyber/education/12education.html

More blacks are using Internet, survey finds. (2000, October 23). *New York Times*.

Reuters. (1999, September 18). Another report on "digital divide." *New York Times*. Retrieved September 18, 1999, from wysiwyg://137/http://www.nytimes.com/library/tech/99/09/biztech/articles/18digital-divide.htm.

Sanger, D. E. (1999, July 9). Report shows increase in "digital divide." *New York Times*. Retrieved July 9, 1999, from http://www.nytimes.com/library/tech/99/07/biztech/articles/09internet.htm

Smith, M. (2000, February 18). Online but not antisocial. *New York Times*.

Stites, J. (1999, February 22). Black entrepreneurs spread the word about "digital freedom." *New York Times*. Retrieved February 22, 1999, from http://www.nytimes.com/library/tech/99/02/biztech/articles/22pros.html

Turow, Joseph. (1999, May). *The Internet and the family: The view from parents, the view from the press* (Report Series No. 27). Philadelphia: Annenberg Public Policy Center of the University of Pennsylvania.

Wayner, P. (1998, October 15). It may be snail mail, but technology gets it where it's going. *New York Times*. Retrieved October 22, 1998, from http://www.nytimes.com/library/tech/98/10/circuits/howitworks/22howw.html

Zack, I. (1999, September 1). To professors' dismay, ratings by students go online. *New York Times*. Retrieved September 1, 1999, from wysiwyg://5/http://www.nytimes.com/library/tech/99/09/biztech/articles/01eval.htm

■ TELECOMMUNICATION

Furchgott, R. (1998, September 17). Cutting the phone cord to stick with cellular. *New York Times*. Retrieved September 17, 1998, from http://www.nytimes.com/library/tech/98/09/circuits/articles/17cell.html

Hafner, K. (1999, January 28). Everything but a dial: Phone choices. *New York Times*. Retrieved January 28, 1999, from http://www.nytimes.com/library/tech/99/01/circuits/articles/28phon.html

Hafner, K. (2000, January 17). AOL deal puts pressure on competition. *New York Times*. Retrieved January 17, 2000, from http://www.nytimes.com/library/tech/00/01/biztech/articles/17onli.htm

Robinson, S. (1999, December 7). Researchers crack code in cell phones. *New York Times*. Retrieved December 7, 1999, from http://www.nytimes.com/library/tech/99/12/biztech/articles/07code.htm

Schiesel, S. (1999, December 20). Wireless industry looks beyond phone. *New York Times*. Retrieved December 20, 1999, from http://www.nytimes.com/library/biztech/articles/122099outlook-wire.htm

INDEX

ABOUT THE CONTRIBUTORS

Josepha Silman Banschick is a journalist who writes on family issues and child psychology. She has collaborated with Mark R. Banschick on a number of projects, including several textbook chapters, child development spirituality, and the Divorce Course, a course on parenting for divorcing parents.

Mark R. Banschick, M.D., is a child and adolescent psychiatrist in full-time private practice. He is a lecturer and contributing author in the areas of child development and the psychology of moral/spiritual behavior. He is Adjunct Professor at Hebrew Union College, New York, where he teaches in the Doctor of Ministry program, and the cofounder of the Integrated Medicine Study Group in Katonah, New York.

Keith Lee is a second-year law student at Villanova University School of Law in Villanova, Pennsylvania. He is a member of the *Villanova Sports and Entertainment Law Journal*, the Intellectual Property Society, and the Digital Law Forum. His casenote, "Resolving the Dissonant Constitutional Chords Inherent in the Federal Anti-Bootlegging Statute in *United States v. Moghadam*," will appear in an upcoming issue of the *Villanova Sports and Entertainment Law Journal*. In 1997, he graduated from the University of Maryland with a B.A. degree in government and politics and a B.A. degree in criminology and criminal justice.

Janessa Light graduated from Villanova University School of Law in Villanova, Pennsylvania, in 2000. At Villanova, she served as President of the Villanova Intellectual Property Society for two years and contributed as a student representative on both the Villanova E-mail Policy Task Force and the Villanova Web Publishing Task Force. She received her dual undergraduate degree in rhetoric and communication and sociology from the University of California at Davis, where she graduated magna cum laude.

JoAnn Magdoff received her master's degree in social work from Fordham University and a Ph.D. in anthropology from Princeton University. She pursued postdoctoral training at the Psychoanalytic Center for Training and Research at Columbia University and served as a supervisor in the Doctoral Program in Clinical Psychology at the City University of New York. She was founder and first president of the New York chapter of the American Association of Marriage and Family Therapists. She has also been a private consultant; her clients include international advertising agencies, financial institutions, and utility companies, among others. She is a frequent lecturer and writer on psychology and American culture and is a psychotherapist in private practice in New York City.

Leigh Maxwell (Ph.D., telecommunications, Ohio State University, 1996) publishes research examining the impact of digital technologies on teaching, learning, and intellectual property. She resides in Madison, Wisconsin, where she works as a writer and consultant in private practice.

Thomas A. McCain received his Ph.D. in communication from the University of Wisconsin. He has been on the faculty of the Ohio State University since 1973 and was Director of the Center for Advanced Study of Telecommunications (CAST) from 1990 to 1997. His research examines the relationship between communication technology and society. He is a former editor of the *Journal of Broadcasting and Electronic Media* and has authored more than 175 scholarly papers, book chapters, and articles, including *The 1000 Hour War: Communication in the Gulf* (1994). McCain has served as consultant to numerous communication companies, government agencies, and universities in the United States and abroad, including the Ohio Board of Regents and Department of Education.

Katherine Neikirk is a second-year law student at Villanova University School of Law in Villanova, Pennsylvania. She is a member of the *Villanova Law Review*, the Intellectual Property Society, and the Digital Law Forum. Her casenote, "Squeezing Cyberspace Into International Shoes: When Should Courts Exercise Personal Jurisdiction Over Non-Commercial Online Speech?" will appear in an upcoming issue of the *Villanova Law Review*. In 1996, she graduated from Oberlin College in Oberlin, Ohio, with a B.A. degree in English.

Judy C. Pearson received her B.A. degree from St. Cloud University and her M.A. and Ph.D. degrees from Indiana University. She has taught in K-12 and at the college level. Her university positions were at Indiana, Bradley, Purdue, Iowa State, Michigan State, and Ohio. She has been both a faculty member and administrator. She is currently a full professor of human development and communication at Virginia Tech. In addition to several books, Pearson has published articles in numerous journals including the *Journal of*

Communication, Communication Monographs, Communication Education, and *Adolescence*. She has served on the National Communication Association task force on technology and communication with Vinton Cerf, father of the Internet, and U.S. Representative Rick Baucher, originator of the Tele-communications Act of 1996. Pearson is currently Director of the Northern Virginia Center and Associate Dean of the Graduate School of Virginia Polytechnic Institute (VPI) and State University, where she administers the adoption of instructional technology.

Jeffrey B. Rubin practices psychoanalysis and psychoanalytical psychotherapy in New York City and Bedford Hills, New York. He has taught at various psychoanalytic institutes including the Postgraduate Center for Mental Health, the Object Relations Institute, and the C. G. Jung Foundation of New York. He currently teaches at the Harlem Family Institute and the Union Theological Seminary. Rubin is author of *Psychotherapy and Buddhism: Toward an Integration* and *A Psychoanalysis for Our Time: Exploring the Blindness of the Seeing I*. He is also author of two forthcoming books, *The Art of Living* and a new book integrating psychology and spirituality.

Leonard Shyles (Ph.D., communication, Ohio State University) is Associate Professor of Communication at Villanova University in Villanova, Pennsylvania. His publications include journal articles and book chapters analyzing the content and impact of political media in presidential elections and other settings. He is coeditor and coauthor of *The 1000 Hour War: Communication in the Gulf* (1994), dealing with the use of telecommunication technologies to conduct the war in the Persian Gulf and to provide journalistic coverage of the conflict. Most recently, Shyles has published a comprehensive television production textbook, *Video Production Handbook* (1997). His current research focuses on understanding digital technology in the contexts of markets and policy.